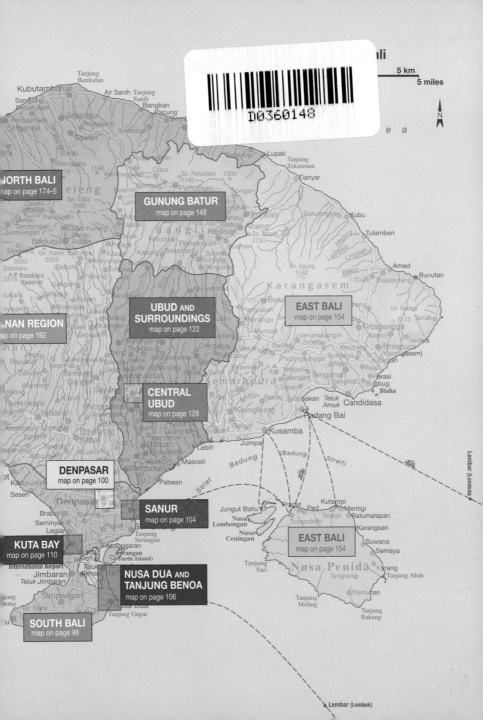

Map Legend

════╪════	Motorway with Junction
‒ ‒ ‒ ‒	Motorway (under construction)
════════	Dual Carriageway
──────	Main Road
──────	Secondary Road
══════	Minor road
──────	Track
▬▬ ▪ ▪	International Boundary
‒ ‒ ‒ ‒	Province Boundary
‒ • ‒ ‒	National Park/Reserve
‒ ‒ ‒ ‒	Ferry Route
✈ ✈	Airport
† ⛪	Church (ruins)
†	Monastery
▟ ▞	Castle (ruins)
⁂	Archaeological Site
∩	Cave
★	Place of Interest
⌂	Mansion/Stately Home
※	Viewpoint
⚑	Beach
════════	Motorway
════════	Dual Carriageway
════════	Main Roads
════════	Minor Roads
════════	Footpath
▬▬▬▬	Railway
▭	Pedestrian Area
▬	Important Building
▭	Park
❶	Numbered Sight
🚌	Bus Station
❶	Tourist Information
✉	Post Office
✚	Cathedral/Church
☪	Mosque
✡	Synagogue
⚨	Statue/Monument
▯	Tower
⌖	Lighthouse

INSIGHT GUIDES

BALI
& LOMBOK

✴ INSIGHT GUIDE

BALI
& LOMBOK

Commissioning Editor
Sarah Clark
Series Editor
Carine Tracanelli

Distribution

UK & Ireland
Dorling Kindersley Ltd,
a Penguin Group company
80 Strand, London WC2R 0RL, UK
sales@uk.dk.com

United States
Ingram Publisher Services
One Ingram Blvd
PO Box 3006
La Vergne, TN 37086-1986
ips@ingramcontent.com

Australia and New Zealand
Woodslane
10 Apollo St
Warriewood
NSW 2102
Australia
info@woodslane.com.au

Worldwide
Apa Publications GmbH & Co.
Verlag KG (Singapore branch)
7030 Ang Mo Kio Ave 5
08-65 Northstar@AMK
Singapore 569880
apasin@singnet.com.sg

Printing

CTPS – China

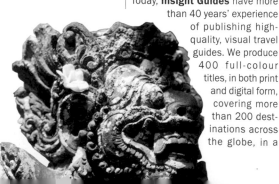

ABOUT THIS BOOK

The first Insight Guide – which happened to be about Bali – pioneered the use of creative full-colour photography in travel guides in 1970. Since then, we have expanded our range to cater for our readers' need not only for reliable information about their chosen destination but also for a real understanding of that destination. Today, **Insight Guides** have more than 40 years' experience of publishing high-quality, visual travel guides. We produce 400 full-colour titles, in both print and digital form, covering more than 200 destinations across the globe, in a variety of formats to meet your different needs.

Insight Guides are written by local authors who use their on-the-ground experience to provide the very latest information; their local expertise is evident in the extensive historical and cultural background features. All the reviews in Insight Guides are independent; we strive to maintain an impartial view. Our reviews are carefully selected to guide you to the best places to stay and eat, so you can be confident that when we say a restaurant or hotel is special, we mean it.

How to use this book

Insight Guide: Bali & Lombok is carefully structured to convey an understanding of the islands' culture and to guide you through their sights.

◆ The Travel Tips section includes all the practical information you'll need, divided into four key sections: transport, accommodation, activities and an A–Z listing of practical tips. A handy phrasebook with Bahasa Indonesia words and expressions, plus Further Reading recommendations, are also included.

The contributors

This new edition of *Insight Guide: Bali & Lombok* was commissioned by Commissioning Editor **Catherine Dreghorn** and managed by Senior Commissioning Editor **Sarah Clark**. It was copyedited by **Paula Soper**.

The book was thoroughly updated by **Rachel Lovelock**. Born and raised in England, Rachel's childhood dream was to become a writer and live on a tropical island, but she followed the advice of her careers teacher and worked for a UK-based corporate company instead. She finally realised her dream when she moved to Bali on a whim in 1998. She fell in love with the island and has been living there ever since, writing prolifically for magazines, guidebooks and websites. You can read about her travels on her blog: www.indiestravelwriter.com

This guide has at its foundation the very first edition, published in 1970, which became the ground-breaking prototype that led to the creation of the Insight Guides series.

It also builds on later editions by then-Insight Guides' Singapore-based managing editor **Francis Dorai**.

CONTACTING THE EDITORS

We would appreciate it if readers would alert us to errors or outdated information by writing to:

Insight Guides, P.O. Box 7910, London SE1 1WE, England.
email: insight@apaguide.co.uk

◆ The Best of Bali and Lombok section at the front of the book gives you a snapshot of the islands' most beguiling sights and experiences, to help you prioritse your time.

◆ The next section covers Bali's history and culture in lively, authoritative essays written by specialist writers who live on the islands.

◆ The main Places section provides a full run-down of all the attractions worth seeing. The main places of interest are coordinated by number with full-colour maps.

◆ Photo features illustrate various facets of Bali, from festivals and temple offerings to beach activities and royal water parks.

◆ Photographs throughout the book are chosen not only to illustrate geography and culture but also to convey the pulse of their people.

Contents

LEFT: rice terraces at Belimbing village, Tabanan region, Bali.

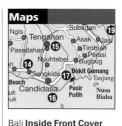

Maps

THE BEST OF BALI AND LOMBOK: TOP SIGHTS

Discover incense-filled temples and the splendour and spiritual richness of their associated festivals; trek through landscapes of rice terraces, waterfalls and mountains; or explore the treasures of the marine world.

▽ **Elephant Safari Park**. Children will have the opportunity to hand-feed these native pachyderms, and the elephant safari ride through the jungle is fun too. *See page 141*

◁ Witness an ***odalan*** (temple anniversary festival), which take place somewhere on Bali almost every day. They provide an ideal opportunity to see the island decked out in ceremonial splendour. *See pages 47 and 52–3*

▽ Just off the northwest coast of Lombok, the island escape of **Gili Trawangan** has stunning beaches of powdery white sand besides the partying reputation held by its bars and restaurants. *See page 214*

△ **Jatiluwih** presents a landscape of endless sculpted rice terraces against a mountain backdrop. *See page 197*

▽ One of Bali's most dramatic all-male dances is **kecak**. *See pages 64 and 250*

▽ **Trekking**. In Lombok, don't miss the waterfalls and ancient forests in **Rinjani National Park**. *See page 219*

▷ **Diving**. Aficionados head for Tulamben in the east or Pulau Menjangan in the northwest. Or try the Gili Islands for their rich aquatic life – good for snorkelling too. *See pages 77, 167, 185, 213 and 267*

△ **Gunung Kawi**. This ancient temple comprises an amazing complex of facades and monks' niches hewn from solid rock, all set on the banks of a river valley. *See page 143*

△ At **Penelokan** there are dramatic views to be had of the active volcano, Gunung Batur, and its crater lake. *See page 148*

▷ **Pottery**. Lombok pottery is best seen at Banyumelek and Penujak villages. *See pages 208, 224 and 266.*

THE BEST OF BALI AND LOMBOK: EDITOR'S CHOICE

Setting priorities, saving money, unique attractions... here, at a glance, are our recommendations, plus some tips and tricks that even locals won't always know.

BALI FOR FAMILIES

ABOVE: get all wet at the Waterbom Park.

● **Taman Burung Bali Bird Park**. See exotic birds from all over Indonesia, including the giant cassowary, hornbills, kingfishers and more than 250 bird species in a lush garden setting. A special highlight is the enclosure containing the endangered Bali starling. *See page 123.*

● **Taman Tirtagangga**. Spring-fed pools, water spouts and fountains set in gardens. Kids will have a splashing good time at this royal water park (head for the larger and cleaner pool in the middle). *See pages 166 and 170–1.*

● **Waterbom Park**. Located in the heart of Kuta, the artificial pools and rivers with slides, tubes and ramps make for wet and wild fun rides (under the watchful eye of lifeguards). *See page 112.*

● **Bali Botanical Gardens**. Located in the cooler northern highlands, there are walking trails that meander through high-altitude pine forests. *See page 180.*

● **Reef Seen Aquatics**. See baby turtles being reared until they are old enough to be released into the ocean. You can even sponsor the release of a turtle. *See page 185.*

ONLY IN BALI

● **Petulu**. At sunset, thousands of white herons return to roost daily in the trees at Petulu. Said to be a manifestation of human souls, the birds blanket the trees like snow. *See page 141.*

● **Nyepi**. On the first day of the Hindu New Year, no one is allowed outside (not even tourists) and all lights are put out. *See page 53.*

● **Cremations**. These are boisterous and colourful public ceremonies sometimes involving the entire village. *See page 51.*

● **Muncan**. On the eve of the Hindu New Year, a pair of large male and female figures undergo the simulation of a public mating as part of a traditional fertility rite. *See page 155.*

● **Trunyan**. The pre-Hindu Balinese people here do not cremate the dead (unlike Hindu Balinese) but instead leave them exposed to the elements. *See page 150.*

● **Makare**. Using thorny leaves, macho males at Tenganan in east Bali draw each other's blood in this vicious ritual as offerings to demons. *See page 164.*

ABOVE: taking offerings to an *odalan* (temple festival) at Pura Silayakti in Padangbai.
LEFT: high priest at a temple ceremony.

BEST VIEWS

- **Antosari to Pupuan.** North of Antosari, passing Belimbing and Sanda all the way to Pupuan takes you past incredible rice terraces. *See page 193.*
- **Pura Pasar Agung.** Stunning setting for a remote temple on the slopes of Gunung Agung. *See page 156.*
- **Ujung to Amed.** Breathtaking ocean views and black sand beaches filled with hundreds of outrigger canoes. *See page 166.*
- **Pura Luhur Uluwatu.** Spectacular ocean views from a cliff-top temple. *See page 107.*

- **Lombok Strait.** Magnificent sunsets across the Lombok Strait to Bali, viewed from along the west coast. *See page 206.*
- **Kuta to Selong Blanak, Lombok.** Breathtaking views of the southern coast from its wind- and surf-lashed cliffs. *See pages 225–6.*
- **Gunung Rinjani, Lombok.** On one side you'll be treated to views of the crater lake; on the other, stunning vistas across to the coast. *See page 220.*

ABOVE: dramatic coastline at Pura Luhur Uluwatu.

BEST BEACHES

- **Jimbaran.** Greyish white sands and clean waters in a picturesque bay south of Kuta but minus the persistent beach vendors. *See pages 109 and 232.*
- **Nusa Dua.** Gentle waves caressing white sands lined with luxury hotels, ideal for families with young children. *See pages 106 and 232.*
- **Seminyak.** Large expanse of grey sands with thundering waves, perfect for boogie boarding and surfing. *See pages 112 and 232.*
- **Kuta Bay, Bali.** Crowded with surfers, half-naked bodies basking in the sun and persistent vendors, Kuta draws people for its

stunning sunsets. The firm grey sands are also great for walking. *See page 109.*
- **Pemuteran.** Idyllic stretch of beach, sandy in parts, rocky in others, with a clutch of boutique hotels and nearby snorkelling and diving at Pulau Menjangan. *See pages 185 and 232.*
- **Nipah, Lombok.** Lovely beach with great snorkelling offshore. *See page 210.*
- **Selong Blanak, Lombok.** Blessed with powdery white sands and aquamarine waters. *See page 226.*
- **Kuta, Lombok.** Great beach on the south coast. *See page 225.*

BEST ACTIVITIES

- **Golfing.** Enthusiasts have four choices. Particularly stunning are **Pan Pacific Nirwana Bali Resort**, or **Handara Kosaido** club in the highlands. *See pages 79, 113, 179 and 255.*
- **Whitewater rafting.** This is best done during the rainy season at **Ayung River.** *See pages 81, 133 and 255.*
- **Trekking and mountain biking.** Either

plump for more languid walks and rides around the countryside of Ubud or head to the mountains, Gunung Batur or Gunung Agung. In Lombok, getting to the top of Gunung Rinjani takes three days. *See pages 79, 220 and 256.*
- **Surfing and boogie boarding.** Kuta beach is one of the best places to learn either. *See pages 78, 110, 256.*

LEFT: working on a rice terrace. **BELOW:** diver and a school of Jack fish near where the *Liberty* wreck lies in Tulamben.

Best Temples and Ancient Sites

● **Pura Puncak Penulisan**. Atmospheric terraced temple perched on the crater rim of Gunung Batur with swirling mists and ancient statues. *See page 150.*

● **Pura Luhur Batukau**. Ancient forests surround this remote temple at the foot of Gunung Batukau. *See page 196.*
● **Yeh Pulu**. Scenes of an unknown ancient era are carved in stone amidst scenic rice fields. *See page 140.*
● **Pura Rambut Siwi**. Serene temple built on a cliff overlooking the quiet southwest coast. *See page 188.*
● **Pura Tanah Lot**. Much-visited temple on an islet just off the coast. Sunsets here are glorious but it gets very crowded. *See page 113.*
● **Brahma Arama Vihara**. Colourful Thai-style Theravada Buddhist temple built on a hill with scenic views. *See page 178.*

● **Pura Beji**. Pink sandstone towers with intricate carvings. *See page 176.*
● **Goa Gajah**. Enter the gaping jaws of an ancient man-made cave. *See page 137.*
● **Pura Taman Ayun**. Pretty temple with a series of soaring *meru* (pagoda), protected by a moat. *See page 194.*
● **Pura Ulun Danu Bratan**. Supremely photogenic lakeside temple. *See page 179.*
● **Pura Tirtha Empul**. Busy temple with a holy spring. *See page 142.*
● **Pura Lingsar, Lombok**. Both Hindu and Muslims come to pray here. *See page 208–9.*
● **Pura Suranadi, Lombok**. Among the holiest and oldest temples in Lombok. *See page 209.*
● **Pura Batu Bolong, Lombok**. Dramatic temple perched on the edge of a cliff. *See page 210.*
● **Taman Narmada, Lombok**. A complex of temples, pools, a lake and lush gardens. *See page 208.*

Above: *legong* dance performance in Ubud's municipal hall.
Left: holy spring at Pura Tirtha Empul, north of Ubud.
Below: moss-covered statue at Pura Luhur Batukau.

Best Performing Arts

● **Gambuh**. Elegant court dance dramas performed at temples. *See page 64.*
● **Barong and Rangda**. Exciting ritual performances with trance and self-stabbing with daggers. *See pages 62 and 249.*
● **Legong**. A popular narrative court dance with young girls as the performers. *See pages 63 and 250.*
● **Wayang Kulit**. Puppets create flickering shadows on stage. *See pages 65 and 250.*

● **Senggigi Festival, Lombok**. Held in July every year, it showcases the best traditional performances from all around the island. *See page 265.*
● **Taman Budaya, Lombok**. This is Lombok's only permanent venue to regularly host traditional music and dance. *See page 265.*
● **Peresean fighting, Lombok**. Men fight each other using rattan sticks and shields made of cowhide (ask at your hotel for venue details).

Best Museums and Galleries

● **Neka Art Museum**. One of the finest collections of Balinese and Indonesian paintings. *See page 131.*
● **Taman Werdi Budaya Art Centre**. Good displays of all the different Balinese visual arts. *See page 102.*
● **Seniwati Gallery of Art**. Small gallery with a focus on paintings by women from all over Indonesia. *See page 123.*
● **Museum Puri Lukisan**. A well-respected museum with a large collection of traditional and contemporary Balinese art. *See page 129.*
● **Agung Rai Museum of Art**. Run by a local art dealer, it has a fine collection of both Balinese and Indonesian art. *See page 135.*

ONLY IN LOMBOK

● **Gendang Belek**. Traditional music featuring the big drums for which Lombok is famous (ask at your hotel for performance venues).

● **Bau Nyale Festival**. Takes place every year in February at Mandalika beach, near Kuta. *See page 225.*

● **Ayam Pelecing**. Fried chicken doused with a fiery chilli sauce – a Lombok speciality!

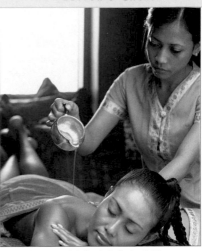

Left: the big drums typical of Lombok's Gendang Belek.
Above: deep relaxation at Prana Spa.

BEST CLUBS AND BARS

● **Townhouse**. Super sleek entertainment venue with lounge and nightclub on the third and fourth floors. *See page 251.*

● **Ku De Ta**. Chic dining and drinks spot that draws a beautiful crowd. *See page 251.*

● **Jazz Café**. Where serious jazz fans hang out. Great cocktails. *See page 251.*

● **The Office Bar & Restaurant**. A friendly bar right on Senggigi beach. A great location for viewing Lombok's fantastic sunsets. *See page 265.*

● **Marina**. This is the most popular nightclub in Senggigi with live bands. *See page 265.*

● **Pyramid**. Pharaoh-themed nightclub located between Kuta and Seminyak. *See page 250.*

● **Square Restaurant & Lounge, Lombok**. Stylish, sophisticated and contemporary. *See page 265.*

● **Horizontal**. Chic, fun spot on Gili Trawangan. Listen to great music while sipping margaritas on the beach. *See page 266.*

BEST SPAS

● **COMO Shambhala Spa**. Much-lauded spa retreat in a stunning setting above Ayung River in Ubud. *See page 258.*

● **Jari Menari**. Yoga inspired massage is the speciality here. *See page 258.*

● **Prana Spa**. A Moghul-inspired spa with a full range of massage and therapies. *See page 258.*

● **Thermes Marins Bali.** Treatments here use mineral-rich sea water. *See page 258.*

● **Spa at Maya Ubud**. Award-winning spa perched on the banks of the Petanu River. *See page 258.*

● **Spa at Four Seasons Jimbaran**. Discover the benefits of Balinese ayurvedic healing. *See page 258*

MONEY-SAVING TIPS

Cheap Food & Drink. Night markets open before sunset in most urban and tourist centres, but could pose a health risk to those with sensitive stomachs.

Happy Hours. As in most of Asia, alcohol attracts high import duties, so save money during happy hours.

Free Entertainment. Most temple festivals have free performances of music and dance at night. Check with Bali's tourism offices *(see page 277)*. Also, check with the local hotels to see which offer special buffet evenings with free traditional dancing and music.

These set-price dinners are good value for money.

Chartering vehicles. The price for hiring a car or a boat in Lombok is often the same regardless of whether it's for two people or six. Get a group together (try posting a note on the hotel notice board) when organising trips.

Use Public Transport. Public *bemo* (mini-vans) operate daily from 6am–6pm between major towns and villages *(see page 233)*. In Lombok, most of the restaurants in the Senggigi area offer free transfers between their eateries and your hotel.

Inexpensive Lodgings. Many families rent out basic rooms in their household compounds, allowing guests to experience a little bit of Balinese communal life.

Bargaining. When shopping, never pay the first price you're quoted even if to you it sounds ridiculously low *(see Bargaining Tips on page 253)*.

Discount Coupons. Look out for free magazines aimed at tourists (like *What's Up? Bali*). Some have discount coupons that you can cut out and use.

BALI

Synonymous with paradise, if not blissful exile, Bali attracts visitors with its relative remoteness and unique culture. Tourism has had its impact, but it's still possible to get off the beaten track.

Apowerful priest wanted to keep his misbehaving son in permanent exile and so prevented him from returning home to Java by drawing his cane across the narrowest point of land to create a watery divide. Thus Bali became separated from Java. This mythological tale has some truth to it as geologically the two islands were connected during the last Ice Age.

The source of all life for the Balinese lies in the mountains, for they are believed to be the abode of deities. Over the years, lava from repeated volcanic eruptions has created fertile soils watered by rivers flowing from crater lakes. The rugged range of mountains running from east to west has created distinct regions. To the north of this divide lies a coastal strip with fertile foothills while to the south are expansive beaches, the rice-growing centres and the nucleus of Bali's tourism infrastructure. The cooler central highlands are dotted with small farms hugging steep slopes, the sparsely populated west is largely dominated by a national park, and the eastern shore is lined with fishing and salt-producing villages, and some rice terraces.

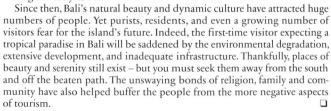

The Austronesian Balinese are ethnically and linguistically related to Malays and Polynesians, with additional infusions of Indian, Chinese and Arab blood, from the merchants who either traded or settled on the island long ago. The Indians also brought Buddhist and Hindu religions that merged with local animistic beliefs and ancestral worship. Centuries of aristocratic Balinese rule influenced by Javanese courts dating from the 10th century ended violently with the Dutch conquest of the island during the early 1900s.

Since then, Bali's natural beauty and dynamic culture have attracted huge numbers of people. Yet purists, residents, and even a growing number of visitors fear for the island's future. Indeed, the first-time visitor expecting a tropical paradise in Bali will be saddened by the environmental degradation, extensive development, and inadequate infrastructure. Thankfully, places of beauty and serenity still exist – but you must seek them away from the south and off the beaten path. The unswaying bonds of religion, family and community have also helped buffer the people from the more negative aspects of tourism. ❑

PRECEDING PAGES: dressed up for Kuta beach festival; Tegallalang rice terraces. **LEFT:** seaweed cultivation at Toyopakeh harbour, Nusa Penida. **ABOVE:** door carving at Neka Art Museum.

PEOPLE

Community participation in time-honoured rituals that celebrate the cycles of life give the Balinese a strong sense of purpose. Village life survives, even though many young people are attracted to work in the richer tourist centres.

The Hindu god of creation Brahma and god of reincarnation Siwa (Shiva) fashioned human figures from dough. The first batch they baked was pale; the second was burnt and black. The last, however, golden brown and deemed perfect, were brought to life by the gods as the first Balinese.

During the 8th century, a legendary Javanese holy man led many of his followers to Bali, a wild and unpopulated place at the time. When a great number of them died there, he and the survivors went back home. After requesting divine blessings, the holy man returned with a smaller group and succeeded in establishing permanent settlements. These first people on the island are the ancestors of today's Bali Aga, aboriginal Balinese *(see text box page 20)*.

Ethnicity and language

Myth and legend aside, the Balinese are one of the many diverse but related Austronesian ethno-linguistic groups inhabiting an immense area stretching from Taiwan to New Zealand, and from Easter Island to Madagascar. Most of these people live in Indonesia, Philippines, Malaysia and the Polynesian islands.

Although linguistically the Balinese language is closer to those spoken on the islands to its east, it has been heavily influenced by the Javanese language. This has led to a rich and complex language spoken by almost 4 million Balinese people in a nation of just over 250 million. As an ethnic and religious minority in Indonesia, the

Balinese are proud of their language and use it most of the time outside of government offices and schools.

Spoken Balinese has several levels, and the one used depends upon the caste, status, age and social relationship between speakers. Friends and equals speak what is known as Low Balinese. A commoner will speak High Balinese to a superior or elder, who then replies in Low or Middle Balinese, depending on familiarity and degree of distance in status. Middle Balinese is polite and is used in most situations. An honorific vocabulary is used when speaking and referring to important persons such as a high priest.

An ancient language called Kawi or Old Java-

LEFT: musicians at Odilan temple festival.
RIGHT: locals in Seseh, Tabanan.

nese, introduced in the 10th century, is mainly used for poetry and drama. In theatre, people who play the roles of deities and royalty speak Kawi. As few people understand Kawi, it is translated into Balinese by servant-advisers.

Balinese is written in an alphabet derived from an ancient south Indian script, but very few young people are proficient in reading and writing it. It is mostly used in ancient texts and in the modern world for street signs and sign boards of schools and government offices.

Younger people mix Balinese with Bahasa Indonesia, the national language, and some English. Complicated grammar is being replaced by the simpler Indonesian one. While purists worry the Balinese language is being lost, the more practical know that language and everything else changes according to the Balinese concept of *desa-kala-patra* (place-time-mode).

Hierachical society

The concept of caste was introduced by the Javanese Majapahit kingdom in the 14th century, but the Dutch colonials altered the system during the 20th century. The highest is the *brahmana* or priestly caste with males named Ida Bagus and females Ida Ayu. Next are *satria*, upper nobility with names like Cokorda, Dewa or Ngakan for males, and Cokorda Istri, Dewa Ayu or Desak for females. *Wesia* are lesser gen-

BALI AGA

In Trunyan *(see page 150)* and Tenganan *(see page 163)* are villages of the Bali Aga, people who have retained old Balinese traditions from pre-Majapahit times, before Javanese and Hindu influences took root. The Bali Aga exist outside of the caste system. Their religion is ancestor focused, therefore exclusive of the Hindu Balinese and centred instead on the primacy of village origin and internal social hierarchy. It is their rituals which, more than anything else, give the Bali Aga their autonomy from the rest of Balinese society.

try, with males called Anak Agung or Gusti Ngurah, and females, Anak Agung Istri or Gusti Ayu. These *triwangsa* (three upper castes) comprise only 3 percent of the population.

Most Balinese are commoner *sudra* or *jaba* (outsiders). Commoner children are named by birth order with the prefix I for males and Ni for females. The oldest is always called Wayan, Putu or Gede; the second Made or Nengah; the third Nyoman or Komang; and the fourth Ketut, all of which invariably leaves foreigners confused. Birth order names are repeated for subsequent children, with Cenik or Alit (little), Balik (return) or Tagel (multiple) tagged on after their first names. The system is also used

What's in a name? Names for Balinese are very important because it is believed that naming a child can affect his or her life. Several factors have to be taken into consideration, therefore at least four names are given.

for children of higher castes with commoner mothers, such as Ida Bagus Made or Gusti Putu. A specific proper name always follows the birth order name and caste title. But nearly every Balinese has a nickname and prefers to be called by this. Even family relationship names, such as

ever, feel that a shopkeeper from the priestly caste need not be shown deference. Instead, such a person should show respect to a commoner medical doctor or lower caste community leader.

Family and sexuality

Many Balinese households are crowded with up to four generations. Mothers and their daughters-in-law have private cooking spaces, which helps to maintain harmony. Infants are carried everywhere by their mother or older sibling. As the child grows up and begins to walk, he or she is free to wander about the village with other children, but an adult is usually nearby watching over them. Balinese children

Nini (grandmother) or Beli (older brother) are more commonly used than actual names.

Balinese identify more with their lineage groups than their caste. There are dozens of commoner clans, such as *pande* (metalsmiths) and *pasek* (ancestral groups). The upper castes have lineages descended from dynasties and priestly families. Many have rewritten their genealogies by finding and even creating connections with the 14th-century Javanese Majapahit kingdom in order to assert their status. Commoners, how-

Left: on the school run. **Above:** villager with roosters for cock fighting, Seseh. **Right:** mother and child from the market town Candi Kuning, north Bali.

are rarely, if ever, spanked, which the Balinese believe would damage their tender souls. Children learn through guidance and example, and it is this raising of children with independence and respect that accounts for their maturity.

Young unmarried Balinese adults mix freely in public and frequently fall in and out of love. Amulets and love spells are sometimes used to enhance one's attractiveness to the opposite sex. Close physical contact between members of the same sex is common as a sign of friendship. This usually does not indicate homosexuality, which is tolerated as long as there are no open displays of affection, a rule that also applies to heterosexual relationships.

Sexual relations between Balinese teenagers are left to proceed in a natural way without interference from the parents, at least in the *Sudra* caste that makes up the vast majority of the population. In the commonest form of marriage, the ceremony does not take place until several days after announcement of consummation or conception. And even in upper-caste 'arranged' marriages, the couple may sleep together for an agreed period before the wedding. To keep the population in check, the government encourages couples to have only two children. The Balinese have generally complied, and Bali's birth rate is among the lowest in Indonesia.

Abortion is not allowed by the Balinese reli-

Community relations

The Balinese are a very sociable people. During the day they are mostly outdoors, where children play in the streets. In the evening, they socialise at gathering spots or watch television together. Villagers even bathe naked together, males upstream from females but in view of each other. Oddly, most Balinese eat their daily meals alone. Even at receptions for ceremonies, they eat quickly and in silence.

The village *(desa)* is headed by an elected person called a *bendesa adap* who is responsible for traditional affairs. There is also an appointed *kepala desa* (village head) responsible to the government. The village is divided into several

gion as it interferes with the reincarnation of an ancestral soul. The legendary underworld punishment for this transgression is for the mother and the abortionist to walk a rickety bridge as the aborted foetus shakes them off into the hell fires below. However, this has not deterred some unwed young women.

Traditional beliefs dictate that children are reincarnated souls from the husband's side. In the case of divorce, the husband usually receives custody of the children, while the wife has to hope that her family accepts her return. Some divorced or widowed Balinese are known to remarry and have more children. A husband can take another wife if his first wife consents.

banjar, a smaller unit of households, with an elected leader, the *klian banjar*. Members assist at communal festivals, each other's family ceremonies and during crises. *Banjar* membership is compulsory for married men.

Villagers are bound by the *awig-awig*, a set of oral and written rules of moral conduct and behaviour. Religion also guides every aspect of life, with some choosing to do additional devotional duties, like sweeping temple grounds. This brings them closer to the deities and increases their respect among villagers. The worst possible punishment for a Balinese is to be banished from the *banjar* for breaking moral codes. Help is not given, property can be confiscated, praying at temples is forbidden, exile from the village can occur, and at death the person can be denied cremation.

Trouble in paradise

Paedophilia in Bali is a growing concern, mostly perpetrated by foreigners who prey on children in impoverished areas. Bali also has a high HIV-AIDS rate due to exposure to tourism and intravenous drug use, which is another problem. The large number of unemployed young Balinese has caused a rise in crime along with drug and alcohol abuse, and while jobs are available in heavy labour and street-food vending, such work is viewed as undesirable and usually done by migrant workers from Java. There have also been a few incidents where unhappy villagers have blocked roads leading to hotels and created other disturbances when their demands at work were not met. Many people feel they are being grossly underpaid compared to the huge amounts of money tourists spend on accommodation and food.

As many young people work in the tourism centres and return home only for religious events, villages today are mostly occupied by children and older people. Few Balinese hold high positions in tourism businesses because of the time off they need to attend ceremonies. This has caused them to resent migrant Indonesians and foreigners who have better jobs and salaries, and are not encumbered by religious commitments. A growing number of these outsiders are settling permanently on the overcrowded island, a situation made worse by migrants from other parts of Indonesia to what is perceived as more prosperous Bali. All this has put additional strains on Bali's already limited resources. Today, Bali has a population of just over 4 million people, of whom about 90 percent are ethnic Balinese. The remaining are Javanese, Madurese, Sasak (Lombok), and other ethnicities. Lombok has a population of over 3 million with the indigenous Sasak making up 90 percent of the population. Small numbers of Balinese, Javanese and Buginese make up the rest.

Gambling at *tajen* (cockfights) has led to domestic problems since husbands and fathers spend a lot of time and money preparing their roosters, with fortunes made or lost during the fights. Traditional belief dictates that the spilling of blood for ceremonies is needed to appease demons. The fight is officially limited to three rounds but that does not stop cockfights from continuing for hours at a time, despite government attempts to ban them.

Balinese women

Women are major players in the world of small business. Local women have long managed *warung* (road-side food stalls) or engaged in home industries like weaving, all this on top of their household chores. These days women also

run clothing boutiques, jewellery shops and restaurants. Women are also making their presence known in the arts, an area once dominated by men. Female painters are growing in number, and while women's *gamelan* music and dance groups have been around for years, today they are the norm. That they find time to practise while managing households is a tribute to their abilities and dedication. In another reversal of traditional gender roles, men are becoming experts at making certain offerings, especially the spectacular *sarad*, in which hundreds of colourful rice-dough sculptures are arranged against a framework of bamboo and cloth for temple ceremonies and weddings. ❑

LEFT: preparing for a festival at Pura Samuan Tiga.
RIGHT: temple festival in Besakih village, East Bali.

GEOGRAPHY

Volcanoes punctuate this enchanting island of rainforests, rice fields and monkeys. But the ingenuity and sheer determination of the Balinese has helped carve out a fruitful terrain from this wild and surf-lashed island.

Bali, one of 18,307 islands that make up the vast Indonesian archipelago, is located about 8 degrees south of the equator and 115 degrees east longitude. The island is separated from Java to its west by the Bali Strait, less than 3km (2 miles) wide and no more than 50 metres (160ft) deep. To the east, the Lombok Strait, an ocean trench that plunges down steeply to a depth of 1,300 metres (4,200ft) – the deepest waters of the archipelago – separates Bali from the neighbouring island of Lombok.

Lying east to west across the island are six volcanic peaks over 2,000 metres (6,500ft) high. The highest is Gunung Agung at 3,014 metres (9,796ft), considered the abode of the deities who cause eruptions to punish the Balinese for wrongdoings or for not showing respect.

By the same token, the rich, fertile mineral soil – a result of those eruptions – is regarded as a gift from the gods as it enables farmers to harvest up to three crops of rice a year.

Climate

Bali's tropical climate is tempered by cool ocean breezes. The northwest monsoon causes the greatest humidity during the rainy season from November to April. The dry season from May to October is far more pleasant. The average temperature at sea level is 26°C (79°F), with an average maximum of 32°C (90°F) in March and 29°C (84°F) in July. In the mountains, the temperature is always a few degrees cooler and the air less humid.

The mountains attract rain-laden clouds and ensure plentiful rainfall, averaging 2,150mm (85ins) yearly. Most of the island's rivers and streams run from mountain lakes, cutting deep ravines through soft volcanic rock.

Plant life

Originally, much of the island was covered by deciduous forests interspersed with grasslands. Vast areas of Bali have since been altered by agriculture, but it is still possible to see what the natural state of the island once was – even if today, original forests are only found in Taman Nasional Bali Barat (West Bali National Park). One such outpost is the vast Bali Botanical Gardens, or Kebun Raya Eka Karya Bali, near the shores of Danau Bratan, which plays home to more than 650 species of trees and more than 450 species of wild and propagated orchids.

The extreme west of Bali, Jembrana, is mainly forested, but because of its arid nature few people live there. At the southern end of the island lies Bukit Badung, a jagged plateau joined to Bali by a narrow isthmus. This dry and barren limestone tableland stands out in sharp contrast to Bali's lush, alluvial plains.

The wide variety of vegetation ranges from many species of palm and bamboo through to flowering plants like frangipani, bougainvillea and orchids. Many Balinese villages have huge, centuries-old, sacred banyan trees. Pandanus and cacti grow in dry lowlands while tall pines

Taman Nasional Bali Barat with its monsoon forests, coastal swamps and pristine seas, all once common throughout the island, provides glimpses of a unique environment. The park, established in 1984 and Bali's largest natural reserve, is home to the endangered white Bali starling and rare Java buffalo as well as several kinds of mammals, including mouse deer and barking deer. Several species of monkeys and carnivores, such as leopard and civet cat, also live in this dense forest. Unfortunately, the magnificent Bali tiger is most probably extinct: the last sighting dates back to 1937 when one was shot dead by a Dutch hunter.

Of the domesticated animals, the most impor-

and cypress trees thrive in the cool and moist mountains. Lofty tree ferns, elephant grass and wild flowers often cling to cliffs.

Animal life

Many kinds of wildlife exist on the island: large insect-eating geckos are found everywhere and reptiles such as lizards and snakes are also common. Monkeys, especially macaques, are to be seen all over Bali. Of the large mammal species, only the wild boar and deer remain.

Left: orchid at the Bali Botanical Gardens.
Above: harvesting rice in the Gianyar region, Bali, where verdant rice fields dot the landscape.

tant are sway-back pigs and Bali cattle, but chickens and ducks are also commonly reared. Mangy street dogs can be found wandering all over the island. The long-haired Kintamani mountain dog, however, is prized as a pet and is believed to be descended from Chinese chows (*see page 41*).

Rice and agriculture

The rice cycle relies as much on religious management as it does on nature and secular concerns. Rice determines the daily rhythm of life as well as many facets of social and religious organisation in most villages. Rice is personified by the goddess Dewi Sri, and offerings must be made to her in order for the harvest

When Hanoman, the monkey general of the Ramayana epic, threw a mountain at the evil king Rawana, some of his monkey army fell to earth on Sangeh. Today their descendants are found here.

to be bountiful. When the grain appears on the stalks, she is said to be pregnant. Before harvesting traditional rice, a small and symbolic mock wedding ceremony is held. When farmers enter drained fields, they conceal the small knives that they carry to cut the grain so as not to frighten

serts and offerings. During the 1970s, Indonesia participated in the infamous Green Revolution by introducing a new, high-yield variety of rice developed by the International Rice Research Institute in the Philippines. Although the intention was to make the country more self-sufficient in rice production, the grain had very little flavour and was unpopular with the Balinese.

The hybrid also rapidly depleted the soil so that large quantities of chemical fertilisers had to be used. The use of limited varieties of rice narrowed the genetic base, which ultimately led to crops becoming more vulnerable to pests. This was detrimental not only to human health, but also killed off much of the animal life in the

the soul of Dewi Sri dwelling in the rice.

Wet-rice cultivation is a complete ecosystem. Flooding the fields brings nutrients to the soil, which supports not only the growing rice, but also a complex food chain. One of Bali's most endearing sights is that of a small boy or old man herding a noisy flock of waddling ducks to feed on the insects, grubs and plants, while also naturally fertilising the fields.

The Balinese mostly grow *baas putih* (white rice) for daily consumption. They also cultivate *padi bali* (indigenous Balinese rice), *gaga* (non-irrigated rice), *baas barak* (red rice), *ketan* (glutinous white rice) and *injin* (glutinous black or purple rice). The last two are mainly used for des-

fields and tainted the water supply. Given the extra expense that farmers had to bear in buying fertilisers and pesticides, it is hardly surprising that they are returning to the indigenous rice varieties and organic farming practices.

Although rice is the most important crop, farmers usually rotate it with corn, peanuts, chilli peppers, onions, soya beans and other vegetables during the dry season. Some crops are exported to other parts of Indonesia and abroad, but farmers have also found lucrative outlets in hotels and restaurants.

The temperate upland areas now produce an astonishing array of fruits, vegetables and flowers. In north Bali where there is less water and therefore only one rice crop a year, farmers cultivate non-irrigated rice as well as fruits, vegetables, peanuts, cocoa, coffee, and spices such as cloves, cinnamon and vanilla.

Irrigation systems

In order to grow rice, the Balinese have to divert water from the rivers to the paddy fields. Because the steep and narrow valleys preclude damming, the farmers have devised an elaborate irrigation system of tunnels, channels and bamboo aqueducts, known as *subak,* to carry the water. This is a centuries-old system, and an inscription on one tunnel dates the construction to AD 944.

Terraces that utilise the land to its maximum efficiency have been carved into the slopes, producing the verdant, classic Balinese landscape so beloved by artists and tourists. Water is brought up to the highest terraces by these channels and from there it uses gravity to flow downhill through the *sawah* (paddy fields). The system cannot work unless water is shared so all farmers belong to an irrigation society. Members of these societies are responsible for repairing dykes and dams, and keeping tunnels and channels flowing freely.

Heading the island's irrigation system are lake temples dedicated to the goddess of the water, Dewi Danu. The Balinese believe that water is a divine gift. The important temples of Pura Ulun Danu Bratan and Pura Ulun Danu Batur are dedicated to the goddesses of these lakes. Temple priests set the schedule of planting and harvesting, and on a daily basis each farmer knows when he will receive water and when he must release it to the next *sawah.* Smaller temples and shrines where offerings are made are found along the system.

However the divine nature attributed to water has not prevented rapid and unrestrained tourist development and its massive impact on the natural environment from causing a deterioration in water quality, the decline of water resources and the escalation of pollution. Hotels have been erected without regard to water supply and waste disposal capacity. With virtually no enforceable environmental protection laws, the island is coming under increasing stress.

FAR LEFT: fishermen at Legian Beach, south Bali.
LEFT: rice terraces at Belimbing, east Bali. **ABOVE RIGHT:** seaweed farming at Toyopakeh harbour, Nusa Penida.

The sea

Strangely, for an island people, the Balinese have mostly avoided the surrounding ocean and its bounty, regarding it as a place of demonic forces. Poorer Balinese who cannot afford to buy or lease irrigated land tend to make their living from the sea. Most of the catch is destined for restaurants catering to tourists rather than as a primary food source for the island's people. Prawn cultivation is also important. Most of it is exported to Japan with less than 1 percent sold to the local tourism sector. Another important resource in recent years is farmed seaweed, which is mainly used for thickening food and cosmetics.   ❑

LIFE ON THE LINE

Sir Alfred Russel Wallace (1822–1913), a British naturalist and contemporary of Charles Darwin, noted that there were marked differences in flora and fauna between Bali and Lombok. The large mammals of Bali and Java, elephants, tigers and rhinoceros, gave way in Lombok to marsupials and birds common to Australia. He concluded that Lombok Strait defined an ecological separation (later known as the Wallace Line) between the Asian and Australian continents. Although he wasn't wrong, modern scientists have since revised his findings. Bali and Lombok are now considered to be in a species transition zone called Wallacea.

DECISIVE DATES

Prehistoric years

2500–1500 BC
Migrants from southern China and mainland Southeast Asia reach the archipelago and mix with aboriginal peoples.

500 BC–AD 300
Bronze-age culture in Bali.

Indianised kingdoms

AD 78
Indian influences sweep the Indonesian archipelago.

AD 400
Hindu kingdoms emerge in west Java and east Kalimantan (Borneo).

AD 670
Chinese pilgrim records visit to the Buddhist island of Bali.

AD 882–914
Buddhist dynasty issues bronze inscriptions in Old Balinese.

AD 910
Political centre moves to central Java; rise of Buddhist kingdoms in Bali.

Javanese influences

AD 989
Marriage of Buddhist Balinese king with Hindu Javanese princess leads to union.

1011
Airlangga succeeds to the throne in Java; his brother Anak Wungsu rules Bali.

1049
Civil war breaks out in Java; Bali becomes autonomous.

13th–15th centuries
Islamic sultanates in Sumatra and Malaysia control trade.

1284
Singasari kingdom retakes Bali.

1292
Singasari attacked by Kublai Khan; Bali becomes independent.

1293
Birth of Majapahit kingdom.

1343
Majapahit invasion of Bali.

1383
Gelgel kingdom founded.

Early 16th century
Islam spreads to Java; Hindu-Javanese priests, aristocracy and artisans move to Gelgel, leading to Golden Age in Bali.

1515–28
Majapahit kingdom collapses; Bali becomes independent.

Colonial era

1596
Dutch ships arrive in Java.

1597
Dutch ships arrive in Bali.

1602
Dutch East Indies Company (VOC) founded.

1641
VOC takes over trade in the region.

1651
Civil war in Bali ends Gelgel rule.

1700
Bali breaks up into rival kingdoms that extend power to east Java and Lombok.

1799
VOC bankrupted due to fighting wars against Javanese sultanates; Dutch government rules archipelago as a colony.

1811–16
English rule the archipelago under Stamford Raffles. Colony returned to Holland after peace treaty signed.

1839
Danish trader Mads Lange opens trading port at Kuta.

1849
North Bali conquered through Dutch military force.

1894–96
Karangasem dynasty in Lombok and East Bali submits to the Dutch.

1898
Dutch crush threats to Gianyar from other kingdoms and take control.

1906–8
Dutch defeat royal families of Badung, Tabanan and Klungkung.

1917
Huge earthquake hits Bali.

1920s–30s
New artistic developments.

World War II and independence

1942–5
Japanese Occupation during World War II; declaration of Republic of Indonesia on 17 August 1945.

1945–9
Dutch create State of Eastern Indonesia; after war of independence, the UN recognises Indonesia, and Bali becomes a province.

1963
Gunung Agung erupts, killing thousands.

1965
After failed alleged Communist coup against Sukarno, 500,000 people are massacred, over 100,000 on Bali.

1966
General Suharto formally replaces Sukarno as president. Modern period.

1970–1
Bali receives 15,000 visitors. Mass-tourism programme launched.

1976
Nearly 500,000 tourists visit Bali.

1986
Nusa Dua luxury resorts open.

1997
Indonesia severely affected by Asian economic crisis.

1998
Riots in Jakarta leave over 500 dead; President Suharto resigns.

1999
Rioting when Megawati Sukarnoputri, favoured candidate for president, is not selected. Many visitors and residents of other islands seek refuge on Bali as regional conflicts erupt.

2001
Megawati replaces President Abdurrahman Wahid, who resigns over corruption charges.

2002
Terrorist bombs in Kuta kill more than 200 people.

2004
President Megawati loses re-election bid to Susilo Bambang Yudhoyono after heavily contested polls run twice.

2005
On 1 October, three terrorist suicide bombs explode, one in Kuta Square and two on Jimbaran beach. Twenty die.

2012
A record year for tourism, with 2,888,864 foreign visitors to Bali.

2013
Bali's new panoramic toll road opens, which, together with the completion of the Simpang Siur underpass, is expected to reduce the heavy traffic congestion. Ngurah Rai International Airport undergoes a major upgrade.

LEFT: a young Balinese woman, c. 1940.
RIGHT: recent petrol hikes have added to Balinese woes.

AN ISLAND WHERE CULTURES MEET

Despite years of influence from Indian, Javanese and colonial Dutch forces, Bali has emerged as an island with a strong sense of self-worth and individuality. Periods of calamity and war have shaped a unique land that brims with hope for the future.

Fossil remains indicate that the ancestors of the modern Balinese were Austronesian hunter-gatherers who migrated to the archipelago some 3,000 years ago from Taiwan and the Philippines. These people had contacts through trade with other islands in Southeast Asia, and by the 3rd century BC, the early Balinese had learned bronze casting and were making beautiful bronze kettle drums. Trade links were established 2,000 years ago with India and 1,500 years ago with China.

Unfortunately, a precise history of the social system of these prehistoric Balinese is not known. They practised various kinds of burial – jar burials, burials without coffins and sarcophagi burials – and this suggests some social stratification. Additionally, some of these sarcophagi, probably for those of the highest social status, are carved with masks and anthropomorphic figures.

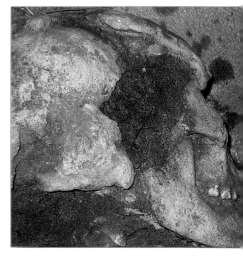

Many of the burials of the prehistoric Balinese included grave goods – jewellery, tools and pottery – indicating a belief in providing for the afterlife.

The only other trace of these prehistoric people on the island are the megalithic structures that remain standing today: terraced structures, stone seats and *menhir* (monuments). Many of these structures are still used today for the veneration of deities as well as ancestors. The religious and social practices of the Bali Aga people, or aboriginal Balinese (*see pages 20, 150 and 163*), who, until recently, were isolated communities, may represent vestiges of the prehistoric Balinese social system.

LEFT: Balinese warriors, c. 1880. **RIGHT:** prehistoric remains from Museum Situs Purbakala *(see page 186).*

Indian influences

Early Balinese rulers adopted certain imported religious and administrative practices from India that enhanced their status and power. An important belief was in the god-king, a divine incarnation on earth who exercised spiritual and political power through a hierarchy of priests. The realm and its people would prosper only as long as the king conducted himself in accordance with divine law. Although India provided social, theological and political models, the Balinese modified these to suit their own needs while retaining many indigenous practices. Indian deities, for instance, existed alongside the ancestral spirits.

Balinese contacts with India and with other Indian-influenced kingdoms in Southeast Asia were established by the 1st century, and a Buddhist dynasty was ruling Bali by the 7th century. Archaeological remains from this era include inscriptions in Old Balinese script on stone and copper, which reveal that shrines or temples were erected for various rulers. Statues may have

been carved and bronzes cast to portray royalty or other important people. Ornamented caves, bathing places and rock-hewn temples were constructed near rivers, springs, ravines and mountain tops, strongly indicating that these places were connected with ancient religious beliefs.

Javanese influences

In AD 989, the Buddhist Balinese king Udayana married the Hindu Javanese princess Mahendradatta *(see box below)* creating a geographic, political and religious union. A Hindu-Buddhist fusion that incorporated the ancient cult of ancestral worship was adopted as the state religion. During this time, Kawi or Old Javanese, replaced Old Balinese as the language of inscriptions and court edicts, indicating a Javanisation of Balinese royalty.

The couple's son, Airlangga, born in AD 991, married a princess from the Javanese kingdom of Sanjaya. When his father-in-law was murdered, Airlangga waged years of warfare to defeat his rivals and enemies on Java. He finally gained control and ruled the island for the next three decades, while his younger brother, Anak Wungsu, was installed as regent of Bali. Airlangga divided his realm in Java among his two sons and retired to become an ascetic, but after his death in 1049, the brothers fought a long civil war against each other to gain supremacy on the island. As Bali was not involved in the struggle, it became an independent kingdom for the next 235 years until the short-lived east Javanese kingdom of Singasari invaded in 1284 to retake the island. However, in 1292 Kublai Khan attacked Singasari for refusing to pay tribute to China and insulting his envoy; thus Bali became independent once again.

The recently founded east Javanese kingdom of Majapahit sent its general Gajah Mada to Bali in 1343. The general was sent to quell the cruel king Bedulu, who was noted for his supernatural powers (he was said to be able to decapitate himself then restore his head, hence his name – meaning "different head"). Acccording to legend, one day the god Siwa (the Balinese name for the Hindu god Shiva) was so offended by the king's audacity, that he caused the king's severed head to fall into a stream and be washed away. The king's minister replaced the king's head with that of a pig he killed. The tale follows that King Bedulu decreed that no one should ever look at his face again. When general Gajah Mada, who was staying at

WIDOW WITCH

The sacred Barong and Rangda dance *(see page 62)* of Bali is based on the semi-historical *Calonarang* tale. The story goes that the Javanese Hindu queen Mahendradatta used sorcery to kill her husband, the Balinese king Udayana, for breaking his promise not to take another wife. Their son Airlangga banished her, accompanied by her unwed daughter, to the forest. Nobody wanted to marry the daughter because of her mother's reputation. Transformed into the furious Rangda (widow), the queen used sorcery to cause more deaths in the kingdom. A priest (Barong) sent his son to steal the widow's book of sorcery, which the priest then used to vanquish her.

the royal court, looked up from his meal to gaze at the king's head, Bedulu became so angry that he was consumed by the fires of his own rage.

In reality, the Majapahit kingdom defeated the Balinese forces and proceeded to govern through a series of puppet rulers. A Javanese-style court along with its culture were introduced to Bali. Life changed when Majapahit broke up the old village structures. The Hindu caste system was introduced; at the apex were *brahmana* high priests, followed by royal *satria*, and *wesia* or merchants. Most of the population was commoner *sudra* or *jaba* (outsiders). Although the royalty ruled, the high priests held the real power because of their knowledge of ancient texts. An

own needs, reinventing the Balinese culture. Much of today's language, music, arts and literature are derived from this time.

The 16th century was Bali's Golden Age under Waturenggong, the king who welded the island into a strongly centralised kingdom based at Gelgel. He conquered Balmbangan in east Java and colonised the neighbouring Lombok. Waturenggong also came to epitomise the concept of a just ruler. One of his biggest supporters, an arrival from Java, was a Brahmin high priest named Danghyang Nirartha or Pedanda Sakti Waurauh (Powerful Newcomer Priest), who is the ancestor of most Balinese high priests. He introduced rituals that were considered to

evil or corrupt king could be replaced by a better one through the intercession of priests.

Rise and fall of classical Bali

The Hindu Majapahit kingdom began to crumble in 1515 with the rise of the Islamic sultanates in Java. Reluctant to succumb, the priests, nobles and artisans of the Majapahit empire chose instead to move to Bali, strengthening the Hindu culture that had taken root there. The Balinese in turn moulded the Majapahit influences to their

be more powerful than those previously performed, particularly the making of holy water, the key rite of the Brahmin priest.

Bali's first encounter with Europe also occurred during this time. The contest by European powers to claim the fabled Spice Islands in the Maluku area further east had begun. Although several European sea captains, including England's Sir Francis Drake, had sighted Bali, the first substantial body of information came from a Dutch expedition led by Cornelis de Houtman in 1597. He observed the height of the Balinese Golden Age, but soon after his visit the court of Gelgel began to decline rapidly. The Dutch failed to strike trade agreements with the

FAR LEFT: temple bas relief depicting hell.
ABOVE: 17th-century map of Bali. **RIGHT:** 17th-century European illustration of a Balinese *raja*.

> *During the 17th century in Dutch-controlled Batavia (Jakarta), out of 18,000 slaves, 9,000 were Balinese. Women were valued as wives and servants, men as labourers and colonial army soldiers.*

Balinese in 1601, and for the next two centuries, encroaching Europeans largely ignored Bali.

Internal problems

A long period during which kingdoms rose and fell in succession began in Bali during the 17th

the tiny southeastern kingdom of Klungkung, founded in 1665, took over the throne of Gelgel. By the late 1700s, nine royal courts had emerged from the chaos, with Klungkung the strongest.

One of the more negative practices to emerge from Bali was slavery. It was a demand for slaves on the part of the Dutch and the ability of the Balinese to supply them that enabled petty kings to seize their moments of power with the common people as the victims. As wars were fought between rival kingdoms, villagers were forced to fight alongside their lords, and they had a vested interest in ensuring their lords won: defeat meant capture and being sold into slavery.

Opium was another commodity that the

century. The prime minister of Gelgel seized control in 1651 because the king's two sons were fighting for succession. The floodgates were opened when other lords saw their chance to become kings of their own domains. The concept of a single ruler was replaced by that of many, inspired by epic narratives such as the *Panji* or *Malat* romances that lent strength to the idea that a brave warrior could emerge from nowhere and take a kingdom for himself. In the north emerged Buleleng, in the west Jembrana, and in the east, Karangasem took over Lombok. In the south a number of kingdoms appeared: Bangli, Tabanan, Badung, Gianyar and Mengwi; the latter expanded into east Java. In the same period,

Balinese rulers exploited to enrich themselves. The Dutch held a monopoly in the region, but Balinese rulers who did not come under Dutch rule decided that they had a right to deal in the drug. The Balinese were also consuming 200 chests of opium a year, in addition to 20 to 30 chests being used by each of the courts.

By the beginning of the 19th century, in order to raise their status, the kings began rewriting genealogies that linked them to the ancient Javanese kingdoms. At the same time, many commoner families were increasing their power. Ultimately, it was the inability of the Balinese to present a united front against the Dutch that led to their downfall.

From 1811–16, Sir Thomas Stamford Raffles administered the Netherlands Indies for the Dutch government, which was exiled in London during the Napoleonic wars. He visited Bali and viewed the people as "noble savages" preserving ancient Javanese civilisation, but failed to recognise their ability to adapt and transform these ideas to meet the future.

In 1815, Gunung Tambora volcano on the island of Sumbawa erupted violently. Bali was covered by volcanic ash that destroyed its rice harvests, and thousands starved to death. At least 25,000 people perished as a result of the eruption and its aftermath. A mudslide in Buleleng that same year killed 10,000 people. This was followed by outbreaks of cholera, dysentery, smallpox and rat plagues that devastated meagre food supplies, causing further famine and disease.

Dutch intrusions

At the beginning of the 19th century, the Dutch were looking for ways to gain a foothold on Bali. Ash deposits from Tambora's eruption created a soil so fertile that the Balinese were able to export food to Singapore. But the Dutch were suspicious of Balinese dealings with the newly established British colony of Singapore. By the end of the 1830s, the Dutch were openly discussing trade, politics, plundering and slavery with the kings – veiled by deceitful treaties of friendship and commerce that would ultimately lead to Dutch sovereignty on the island.

The Dutch wanted to end the practice of plundering shipwrecks, which the Balinese regarded as gifts from the deity of the sea. The ship, cargo and everyone on board automatically became the property of the king who ruled the territory where the incident occurred. Thus, when a Dutch frigate went aground off Kuta in 1841, the Balinese naturally plundered it. The Dutch tried to get the Balinese to sign a treaty putting a stop to this but were rebuffed.

In 1846, the Dutch launched a punitive expedition against Buleleng in the north, but the Balinese put up a strong resistance. A second expedition was sent in 1848, and the Balinese again fought off the Dutch attack. During the third expedition in 1849, backed by heavily armed soldiers, the Dutch attacked the fortifications at Jagaraja. Backed into a corner, the Balinese decided the only honourable course of action was to end it all in self-sacrifice. This was when the Dutch first witnessed a *puputan*, a ritual suicide that traditionally signalled the end of a kingdom (literally meaning "ending" or "finish"). Led by the king of Buleleng, nobles marched into gunfire, and others committed suicide with daggers or poison. Thousands of Balinese men and women died.

Although the Dutch now regarded themselves as holding sovereignty, they did not interfere in the internal affairs of the kingdoms of south and east Bali. However, when Buleleng tried to rebel in 1853, the Dutch took more direct control.

Left: Buleleng's court, c.1880.
Right: a Dutch East Indies Company vessel.

End of an era

Between 1850 and 1888, Bali was hit by seven epidemics of smallpox and five of cholera, four rat plagues, and widespread dysentery outbreaks. In 1891, rival Balinese kings from Badung and Tabanan defeated neighbouring Mengwi and divided up the territory among themselves.

Meanwhile, the Balinese kingdom of Mataram on Lombok enjoyed considerable influence and power, and had been overlords of Karangasem in east Bali since 1849. Most of the people living in Lombok were indigenous Muslim Sasak who rebelled when Mataram ordered them to fight in Bali. This gave the Dutch an excuse to invade Lombok and take over the British trade post.

DAGGERS OF DESTINY

Heirloom *keris*, daggers with straight or wavy blades, have been vital in the mythology connected to the rise of Balinese kingdoms. A *keris* unsheathed by a Majapahit invader conjured up demonic troops that made the Balinese flee. The king of north Bali pointed his dagger at ships to free stranded ones or cause them to become wrecked on reefs. A *keris* found in a piece of wood in a river helped found the Gianyar kingdom. In Klungkung, a *keris* kept away spirits of pestilence and epidemics. A lord of north Bali stabbed his dagger into a mountain side, causing fresh water to gush out for irrigation and thus producing a bumper rice crop.

In 1894, Dutch troops invaded Lombok and quickly conquered Mataram. At nearby Cakranegara, they were attacked by Balinese warriors. The Dutch sent reinforcements and the king eventually surrendered, along with his son and grandson. However, his nephew, Anak Agung Nengah, refused to surrender and chose the rite of *puputan*. Nengah led men, women and children who died either by the *keris* blades (*see box below*) or rushed forward into the fire of the Dutch troops to be killed.

Worse was yet to come. In 1904, a Chinese-owned vessel registered by the Dutch colonial government struck a reef off Sanur in Bali and was plundered. Its owner greatly exaggerated the losses, and the king of Badung refused to pay compensation. He was supported by the king of Tabanan. In retaliation, the Dutch blockaded the Badung and Tabanan coasts and assembled a large military expedition.

In September 1906, the Dutch launched perhaps one of the most shameful episodes in colonial history. Dutch troops marched into Denpasar, and as they approached the palace its gates opened and the royal court dressed in white and ornamented with their finest jewellery filed out and stopped before them. A priest plunged a golden *keris* into the king's chest, while others turned their weapons upon themselves. Some, armed only with spears or bows and arrows, charged at the Dutch. The Dutch fired at them, then looted jewellery from the corpses and sacked the palace ruins.

That afternoon a similar scene was repeated at the smaller court of Pemecutan in Denpasar. News of the *puputan* in Badung turned Dutch public opinion against their government's policy in the East Indies. Karangasem, Bangli and Gianyar reluctantly accepted Dutch authority.

If the Dutch had hoped that events would end there, they were mistaken. The final act of Bali's tragedy took place in 1908 when the king of Klungkung objected to the Dutch imposition of an opium monopoly in his kingdom. In opposition, Balinese burned down a Dutch opium shop in Klungkung and killed a dealer. The Dutch retaliated by attacking Klungkung in April 1908. In response to the attack, the king, carrying his ancestral dagger, solemnly emerged from the palace. His court and more than 200 people accompanied him to face the Dutch. The king knelt down and thrust the blade into the ground because a prophecy had foretold that this magical weapon would open up a chasm in the earth and swallow the enemy. Unfortunately, the prophecy proved to be false, and a Dutch bullet killed the king. His wives knelt around his corpse and drove *keris* blades into their hearts while the others began the rite of *puputan*. Klungkung palace was razed.

After nearly 600 years, the Balinese courts that had descended from the Majapahit empire of Java were gone. Bali was now completely under the control of the Dutch colonialists.

Paradise: colonial style

International protests condemned the Dutch, forcing guilty officials to make amends by intro-

Balinese from exploitation rampant elsewhere in the colony. Christian missionaries were prohibited from converting the Balinese.

Bali came to be regarded as a "living museum" of ancient Hindu-Javanese culture, partly as a way of establishing the island's identity. Sadly, it was an unrealistic view that ignored independent developments on the island. During this time, many Dutch scholars came to study Balinese history, art, culture and religion, but they focused on the esoteric Brahmin high priests, and ignored the ordinary lives of the people. With the aid of Brahmin priests, the Dutch restructured the caste system, understanding little of the system's inherent mobility and flexibility. This rationalisation

ducing reforms. This coincided with what has come to be known as "Balinisation", controlling by indirect rule while attempting to maintain local traditions. Ironically, the Dutch thought that if Balinese culture was to be saved, then the Balinese had to be taught how to become more "authentically" Balinese. The reform policy known as "Balinisation" did go some way towards protecting the Balinese culture.

Foreigners were excluded from owning land. The opening up of tea, rubber, sugar and tobacco plantations were opposed in order to protect the

Left: Dutch artillery against the Balinese.
Above: body of Badung's king after the 1906 *puputan*.

by the Dutch – not only of the caste system, but also of the political units, labour and rice farming – threw the traditional Balinese system into chaos. The restructuring was only advantageous to the upper-caste members who became strong supporters of the Dutch.

From the 1920s onwards, increasing numbers of visitors, including artists, sociologists, economists, dancers and musicians, were captivated by the exotic charm of Bali. Their tales of travel to the island only served to promote the image of Bali as an island paradise. A few influential foreign artists and anthropologists were keen to promote the island, but their works were skewed interpretations of the real Bali. Most of their writings implicitly supported colonialism and implied that the Balinese had little to do with the development and direction of their own culture and history.

Crises and conflict

While resident foreigners created an image of paradise, the Balinese lived with reality. In 1917, a devastating earthquake struck the island, flattening villages and destroying some of the most important temples. More than 1,000 people were killed. This was followed by a rat plague that destroyed crops, then by the worldwide Spanish-flu epidemic that claimed thousands of Balinese lives. The Great Depression in the 1930s hit Bali

The alliance between upper castes and the colonial government was increasingly challenged by educated commoners, especially in 1938 when the Dutch reinstated descendants of the royal families as figurative heads of power in their former kingdoms.

In February 1942, with the spread of World War II, Japanese forces landed at Sanur, marched unopposed into Denpasar and took control of Bali. The military secret police arrested Balinese who associated with the Dutch. As elsewhere in Asia, the Japanese occupiers were brutal, proclaiming themselves anti-colonial, when they were harsher than the Dutch. They ostensibly promoted Balinese culture and fostered nation-

In the Margarana Incident of November 1946, Balinese nationalist I Gusti Ngurah Rai and his forces were surrounded by the Dutch at Marga, Tabanan. Rather than surrender, they resorted to puputan (suicide).

hard, quartering the price of pig and copra (dried coconut flesh) exports and halving the value of the local currency. Poor peasants sold their lands to members of higher castes, while others became tenant farmers to pay off debts to the aristocrats who took their land as collateral.

alism, hoping to garner support from the locals against the Dutch.

When the Japanese surrendered in August 1945, Indonesian leaders Sukarno and Mohammad Hatta declared Indonesia as independent republic. Bali had no strong centre of power, so an interim administration struggled to keep order and gain recognition, while the old kingdoms tried to reassert themselves. Some were pro-Dutch, like the king of Klungkung, while others, like I Gusti Ngurah Rai (*see box above*) were nationalists who supported an independent Indonesia.

The Dutch returned in December to reclaim their former colony and established the State of

Eastern Indonesia. They imprisoned members of the anti-colonial administration, and the struggle for independence went underground. Four years of bitter fighting left more than 2,000 Balinese dead. When the United Nations officially recognised Indonesia as a republic in 1949, the Dutch had to withdraw. Bali became a province of the new nation. Today the island is divided into eight *kabupaten* (counties or regencies) and the municipality of Denpasar. There is further division into *kecamatan* (sub-districts) and *desa dinas* (administrative villages). More numerous and important to the Balinese are *desa adat* (traditional villages), which are subdivided into *banjar* (hamlets or wards), a system unique to Bali.

Problems in paradise

From 1946 to 1949, the split between the pro-Dutch and nationalist factions was pronounced, with many nationalists jailed, tortured or killed by other Balinese. These divisions were compounded by the split between feudal and modern forces, and tensions continued even after the Dutch departure in 1949. Members of the aristocratic castes moved increasingly into business. Political affiliation was similarly divided between the nationalists and socialists, a situation that was to change dramatically in the late 1950s.

Sukarno, then president of Indonesia, claimed empathy with the Balinese because of his background (his mother was Balinese) but did little to enhance the spiritual and material welfare of the people; rampant inflation and corruption under his administration did not help. Nation wide attempts at land reform went some way in loosening the grip that the aristocratic landowners held over their tenants.

When Sukarno banned the Socialist Party, many of its members joined the Communist Party, which was especially strong in Bali. The island was a place of tension and continual political rallies during the early 1960s. Many Balinese feared that supernatural powers were being provoked. In 1963, the eruption of Gunung Agung during the Eka Dasa Rudra ceremony, staged once a century, reinforced this belief. Villages were destroyed and thousands died in the disaster and ensuing famine.

During the early 1960s, many Balinese supported the PKI (Indonesian Communist Party). They urged people to claim back farmland that was owned by a minority. Support came from thousands of Balinese who were badly affected by the 1964 famine after Gunung Agung's eruption. A split developed between supporters of PÑI (Nationalist Party of Indonesia) and PKI, largely seen as a challenge to the old feudal and caste systems. Rallies advocated the overthrow of the caste system. The arts were entwined with propaganda as the Communist organisation LEKRA (Institute for People's Culture) encouraged and sponsored musicians, dancers, puppeteers, writers and artists to spread their proletarian message.

When an abortive coup took place in Jakarta on 30 September 1965, the floodgates were opened. The Communists supposedly murdered some high-ranking military officers, but within a few hours the military, led by General Suharto, put a quick end to the attempt to take over the government. The speed of the countermeasures strongly indicated prior knowledge of the incident, which was played out in order to remove President Sukarno because he was gravitating towards the Soviet Union and its allies.

The Cold War became feverish in Bali, where PNI and other anti-Communists obliterated PKI in a bloodbath that claimed more than 100,000 lives. Old scores were settled between

LEFT: Ida Bagus Nyoman Rai's impression of the 1963 eruption of Gunung Agung. **RIGHT:** a young Sukarno.

villagers, castes and family members, the massacre ultimately having little to do with politics. The surprise is that from this tragedy, Bali has emerged as a tourist paradise.

Focus on tourism

Suharto's government, which came to power in 1966, identified Bali as the best site for mass tourism. This was supported by the World Bank, which drew up a tourism development plan that proposed a huge tourist resort at Nusa Dua that would make profitable use of the dry and infertile land. Because most hotels in Nusa Dua tended to be owned by foreign and Jakarta-based companies, the overall benefits for the Balinese

were initially questionable. But local entrepreneurs began to further develop other tourism centres in Kuta, Sanur and Ubud where Balinese involvement and employment were greater.

Despite the negative aspects of tourism – like kitschy mass-produced souvenirs and blatant sales of land to developers – there is no doubt it has helped to revitalise the island's arts and crafts industry, and performing arts, as well as fund extensive temple renovations. Today, Balinese music and dance schools are packed with students. In fact many villages have their own

ABOVE: artist at work in Ubud.
RIGHT: memorial to the 2002 bomb victims in Kuta.

performing arts groups and stage full-length performances for religious ceremonies, although most visitors only see condensed renditions of dances and shadow plays.

A vulnerable industry

In the late 1990s, Bali remained an outpost of stability while most of Indonesia was torn by conflicts sparked by the Asian economic crisis and a succession of presidents. However crises in the early 20th century exposed the weakness of an economy so dependent on tourism.

Visitor numbers fell after the 9/11 terrorist attacks in the US, but more devastating was the Kuta nightclub bombings by Javanese Muslim

radicals on 12 October 2002 that killed 202 people and injured 240 more. The terrorists were caught and brought to trial a year later, but just when visitor arrivals were showing signs of improvement bombs exploded again in Jimbaran and Kuta on 1 October 2005. This time 20 people were killed. The threats posed by Muslim extremists in the world's largest Islamic nation (even though Bali is predominantly Hindu) combined with the unpredictability of natural disasters like volcanic eruptions and earthquakes, all negatively affected tourism. Yet, despite this, Bali's tourism industry has continued to grow, with foreign visitor arrivals in 2012 and 2013 breaking all previous records. ❏

Chinese Influences on Bali

A 6th-century Chinese trade journal refers to an island called P'o-li (or Poleng), a description which seems to have been of a larger place possibly including east Java.

Although Chinese impact on Bali is not well documented in historical annals and is not obvious to the first-time visitor, Bali has had a distinct Chinese connection from as far back as AD 670, when a Chinese pilgrim-scholar on his way to India wrote about visiting a Buddhist country called Bali.

During the 11th century, a Balinese king married a Chinese princess of the Kang clan and converted her to Buddhism. The couple named their kingdom Bali Kang or Balingkang. The Hindu gods supposedly made her childless, so she died of sorrow and became Batari Mandul, the Barren Goddess, whose stone image is enshrined at the temple of Pura Puncak Penulisan *(see page 150)*. The long-haired Kintamani mountain dogs from here are said to be descended from her pet Chinese chows. Princess Kang is worshipped by Balinese and Chinese as Ida Ratu Ayu Subandar, the Divine Harbour Queen, deity of trade and patron goddess of merchants. Pura Besakih and Pura Ulun Danu Batur temples both have large shrines in her honour.

Dance and design

Barong, of which there are various kinds, is a Balinese dance form usually performed by two men. The female figure in the pair of *barong landung* (tall protective spirits) wears a white mask with Chinese-like facial features – an image identified by many as Princess Kang. These masked mythological creatures animated by two dancers are also found in China and many other parts of Asia. In Bali, moreover, the Chinese-style lion called *barong sae* is just like the traditional Chinese lion dancers in that it dances to the sounds of gongs, drums and cymbals during certain auspicious times of the year in front of houses, businesses and temples.

Balinese architecture also points to distinct Chinese styles. Both Balinese and Chinese homes and temples are surrounded by walls, which are sometimes inlaid with Chinese porcelain plates or ceramic lattice tiles. Just inside the gate, an *aling-aling* (privacy wall) is constructed to prevent demons and malign influences, which can only move straight, from entering. In both

China and Bali, separate buildings with upward curving roof corners are arranged around an open central courtyard. A few Balinese textile patterns and woodcarving motifs are shared with the Chinese, such as *karang cina* (Chinese foliage).

Beyond the Chinese Buddhist temples in every major town, one need not look far to find other vestiges of Chinese influence. Chinese copper-alloy coins with centre holes are used in offerings and strung together to create ritual objects. They are also used as sacred images of the Hindu deities of prosperity and fertility as well as for shrine hangings and effigies. ❑

Right: dragon image at Ling Gwan Kiong Chinese Buddhist Temple in Singaraja.

RELIGION AND RITUALS

The combination of Hindu traditions from Java and Bali's own animist beliefs has imbued the island with a spiritual richness and depth. Everyday life revolves around these beliefs, and temple ceremonies govern the calendar.

Religion in Bali is inseparable from everyday life. Instead of taking their holidays away from home, the Balinese will use their holiday entitlement to attend ceremonies. Every time a small *canang* offering, filled with flower petals and incense, is laid upon the ground; every time an artisan carves out the features of a mythological creature; every time a young baby touches the ground for the first time, or ashes are cast into the sea, substantiation of Bali's living culture is being manifested, acting as a constant reminder of the Balinese-Hindu passion for an authentic existence. The important thing for visitors to understand is that cremations and other ceremonies are not tourist attractions but genuine religious events. The fact that the Balinese allow outsiders to take part in them does not detract from their religious significance.

The Balinese religion is called Agama Hindu Dharma or Agama Tirtha, the religion of holy water, because of its important use in worship and ritual. Bali is the only island in Indonesia – the world's largest Islamic country – where Hinduism is the predominant religion.

The Balinese have long regarded the universe as a structured entity in which everything has its place. They also recognise the duality of nature: male and female, good and evil, day and night, life and death. Order and harmony are personified by deities who live on mountain tops and bestow their blessings on humans.

Demons symbolise disorder and dwell beneath the sea, seeking chaos and destruction. Offerings must be made regularly to acknowledge the life-sustaining forces and prevent disasters such as earthquakes and epidemics.

Fusion of faiths

Buddhism was the state religion of Bali's early kingdoms since the 7th century. In the 10th century, Bali's King Udayana married a Hindu Javanese princess and the two religions fused. During the 16th century, high priests moved from Java to escape the encroachment of Islam. They introduced the caste system to Bali and placed themselves at the top of the hierarchy.

PRECEDING PAGES: festival procession in Tabanan.
LEFT: temple festival offerings at Pura Gunung Lebah.
RIGHT: Sanghyang Widi Wasa, the Supreme Being.

The higher gods of Bali are Hindu and Buddhist, all manifestations of Sanghyang Widi Wasa, the Supreme Singular Deity of Universal Order. Siwa (Shiva), the destroyer and reincarnator, is the main focus of Balinese worship. Two other gods, Brahma the creator and Wisnu (Vishnu) the preserver, are also worshipped. In some temples there is a three-seat shrine for these gods. During ceremonies, the shrine is decked out with coloured banners: red for Brahma, white for Siwa, and black for Wisnu. The Balinese also worship a number of deified ancestors and spirits of mountains, lakes, rivers and trees. Other Indian aspects are the belief in the soul and the idea that every action has a reaction. Reincarnation is due to suf-

> *For Balinese, filing the six upper teeth into an even line diminishes the six negative aspects of human behaviour. These are passion, greed, anger, intoxication, ignorance and jealousy.*

enth month to make sure that the baby develops safely. During the pregnancy, neither parents may cut their hair or help to bathe corpses for funerals. At birth the amniotic fluid, blood, fat covering the skin, and placenta are regarded as *catur sanak* or the "four siblings", guardian spir-

fering caused by inappropriate behaviour. The goal is to escape from the cycle of rebirth and become one with the divine Supreme Being.

Rituals of birth and childhood

Every event from birth to death must be divinely acknowledged to make it legitimate. A series of rites of passage marks these changes from one stage in the life cycle to another. There are five categories of *yadnya* (rituals): *manusa yadnya* for the living, *pitra yadnya* for the dead and ancestors, *buta yadnya* for demons, *dewa yadnya* for deities and *resi yadnya* for priests.

For instance, an expectant mother will undergo a ceremony between her fifth to sev-

its of the baby. The placenta is buried at home outside the north pavilion staircase; right side for a boy, left side for a girl.

When the baby is 12 days old, a spirit medium, in a trance, will reveal which ancestor has been reincarnated. In the first major ceremony at the age of 42 days, the baby receives its name and demonic forces are sent away. The ritual obligation for the parents ends, and they can pray at temples again. The child, however, cannot touch the earth until it is 105 days old when the *telung bulan* or *tigang sasih* (three Balinese months of 35 days each) ceremony is held. From a bowl of water, the baby chooses an object that symbolises its future: a coin means business while an inscribed palm-leaf signifies scholarship. After this ceremony the baby can be taken to temple.

During the baby's first *otonan* (210-day birthday), it is welcomed into the community and its head is shaved clean. By the third birthday, the child is counted as a member of society.

Advancing to adulthood

Puberty is marked for an adolescent girl by her first menstruation and for a boy by the deepening of his voice. Celebrating these changes today is rare except in some high-caste families. A *mapandes* or *potong gigi* (tooth-filing) ceremony marks the passage into adulthood *(see box opposite)*. Uneven teeth and pointed canines are too much like those of demons and animals. Because of the expense of a tooth-filing ceremony, however, it is common to hold it with a wedding. In addition, a corpse or its drawn effigy often has its teeth filed before being cremated, as it is feared that the soul cannot enter heaven if it looks like a fanged demon or animal.

Every Balinese is expected to *nganten* (get married). The most common way is by *mapedik* (request), in which the family and friends of the boy visit the family of the girl, presenting them with offerings and gifts. *Ngorod*, or elopement, is more economical (some say romantic) and just as common, with the boy abducting his girlfriend by car. Her family may feign outrage when they find her gone, even though they may have known of the plan.

In either case, the couple goes through a ceremony that seals the marriage. A formal wedding is held later at the groom's home when a priest sanctifies the union, and prayers are made to the ancestral deities. The aim of marriage is ultimately to have children, and the wedding ceremony is full of symbolism suggesting this. Bride and groom take turns sitting on a coconut to represent fertility. The groom uses a *keris* (dagger) to stab three times through a small mat held by the bride – the sexual symbolism is obvious.

Death and cremation ceremonies *(see page 51)* are even more elaborate and can go on for days.

Temple festivals

Balinese usually visit a temple on holy days and during its *odalan* (anniversary celebration) held every 210 days of the Wuku calendar or 355 days by the lunar-solar Saka year *(see pages 52–3)*. The event may last a single night, for three days, or for 11 days or more during large festivals.

When preparations for an anniversary celebration begin, the temple comes to life. Villagers clean courtyards, unfurl banners and flags, and dress shrines and statues with cloth and ornaments. Men erect altars and structures from wood, bamboo and thatching, while the women prepare offerings *(see pages 74–5)* from flowers and leaves. The men do most of the temple cooking (a task they rarely attend to at home) to feed those who *ngayah* (participate in preparations). *Tajen* (cockfights) are staged to

FAR LEFT: lace worker in Seminyak. **LEFT:** participant in a purification ceremony. **RIGHT:** prayers at a temple.

appease the demons that require blood sacrifice, but the associated gambling activities are strictly entertainment for mortals.

Sacred images are taken out of storage and adorned by priests with flowers, ornaments and textiles. These images and statues are presented with offerings, worshipped, and are even entertained with music, sacred songs, poetry, puppetry and dances. Everyone takes pains to dress in their best clothes for a temple's anniversary celebration. At the closing of the festivities, priests politely request the spirits of visiting deities to depart. Images are undressed and stored away, cloths removed from shrines and parasols closed.

Priests and healers

Through ritual knowledge, the *pedanda* (*brahmana* high priest) and *empu* (clan high priest) transmit divine power to preside over important ceremonies and create extremely potent holy water. The *pemangku* (local temple priests), who mostly come from the lower castes, create less powerful kinds of holy water, in addition to taking on very active roles in temple rituals and in presenting offerings. The Balinese require various types of *tirta* (holy water) in their spiritual life, each with a specific use. These cover all situations including removing spiritual impurities, eliminating crop pests, cleansing the dead, restoring fertility, bestowing knowledge,

TRADITIONAL HEALING METHODS

Herbal recipes for curing physical ailments are recorded in traditional manuscripts. Even with prescription drugs available, many Balinese still go to healers for these remedies. To counteract attacks of witchcraft, a *balian* (spiritual healer) recites incantations and burns incense while subjecting the victim to a painful massage in order to force out the offending spell. Mystical syllables are invisibly written over the body for protection, and sometimes magical charms are given to be worn or even imbibed by the sufferer. Making vows to the deities can also cure mysterious illnesses, as does the drinking of *tirta* (holy water) from certain temples.

receiving divine blessings or curing illnesses.

Even with today's modern medicine, when a Balinese is struck by a mysterious illness the cause is often ascribed to the work of demons, black magic or the violation of a religious law or custom. They are likely to visit a *balian* (spiritual healer), who uses traditional remedies, massage, amulets or talismans to cure them. Some healers even use esoteric knowledge to help locate a lost object or determine auspicious days.

ABOVE: a Balinese man is treated for his ailment using traditional medicine. **RIGHT:** a priest sprinkling holy water at a ceremony.

A *balian* is said to have the power to contact the spirit world in order to help or harm people. A healer always has a spirit guide; the relationship is potentially dangerous and has to be treated with great care and respect, and nourished with constant prayers and offerings. It is believed that certain kinds of sickness are caused by spirits and that the only cure is to learn to communicate with a particular spirit, who will not only neutralise the illness but will also work with that person on future occasions to help others. There are various ways in which Balinese become healers. Many are people who once suffered from serious illness and went to a *balian* for help. They either acquired healing powers through contact with spirits during their treatment or by studying with the *balian* they consulted.

Different healers are known for different sets of skills, some of which fall more into the sphere of traditional, rather than spiritual, medicine. A *balian tulang* specialises in setting broken bones, while a *balian manak* is a midwife. Others such as the *balian tenung* specialise in divining and prophesying. A *balian usada* heals people with the help of *lontar* (palm-leaf manuscripts) that contain magical knowledge about medicine and healing. Although many *balian usada* are highly literate scholars who are consulted because of their ability to interpret these manuscripts, it is the *lontar* itself

TRANCE AND SPIRIT POSSESSION

A boy prances barefooted on hot coals while riding a hobby horse. A weeping old woman screams in an ancient language she never learned. A man rushes at a masked witch figure to stab her with his dagger, but instead turns the blade into his bare chest and bends it without piercing his skin. A young dancer stands on the shoulders of a man and does backbends with her eyes shut. These and many other incidents are quite common in Balinese rituals.

Known generally as *kerauhan* (arrival) or *kesurupan* (descent), trance and possession are how supernatural powers make their presence and power felt, enabling holy people, prepubescent children, and other selected individuals to perform unusual feats. Deities and spirits show their pleasure or displeasure in these physical acts. Anything said by someone in a state of possession is carefully listened to and heeded. A missing offering, an improper action, an unholy presence, or any number of things is enough for this to happen. People are brought back to consciousness with splashes and gulps of holy water *(tirta)*. And it's all quite normal for the Balinese.

that is believed to contain the magical energy.

The most common type of healer is the *balian taksu* who is consulted on matters relating to illness due to a curse – perhaps caused by a deceased person who is not happy for some reason and haunts the living. The *balian taksu* will begin the session by making offerings and falling into trance. The guiding spirit will be summoned and will speak through the healer, questioning the client to find out what the problem is before revealing the cause and cure.

The dark side

Many Balinese will tell you stories of strange creatures they have encountered at night: mon-

erally "left-handed" or black magic. The human form of *leyak* will often remain asleep in bed while the spirit roams outdoors, so it is difficult to know who the *leyak* really are.

It is rare for a Balinese to speak openly about *leyak* for fear that such a practitioner will overhear and harm the speaker. Victims are more than likely to be members of a sorcerer's immediate family, the motives being revenge for simple affronts, jealousy or greed. Babies are most susceptible before their first 210-day birthday ceremony, often crying or suffering mishaps for no apparent reason.

Not all *leyak* are harmful, however, as some practitioners seem to just enjoy the thrill of

Night-time contests between practitioners of black magic happen in "hotspots", especially coastal areas facing the island of Nusa Penida, home of the lord of black magic, Ratu Gede Mas Mecaling.

keys with golden teeth, bald-headed giants, or even a strange ball of light hovering in the sky. These strange manifestations are known as *leyak*, living humans who can change their spirits into another form, such as a strange animal or a headless body. These *leyak* practice *desti*, lit-

supernatural transformation without harming others. Moreover, Balinese believe that both constructive and destructive forces are necessarily present in the world. They believe the important thing is that neither good nor evil gets the upper hand. Learning to become a *leyak* involves many years of dedicated study in secret and considerable self-sacrifice. The Balinese accept the fact that there are individuals who seek to study the black arts for evil purposes, but they are also deeply aware that a person who uses supernatural forces to harm others exposes himself to danger. ❏

ABOVE: Pura Luhur Batakau, one of Bali's holiest temples.

The Cremation Ceremony

A soul merely borrows a physical human body, which upon death is returned to the five elements – wind, earth, fire, water and ether.

The Balinese believe that upon death, the physical body is returned to the five elements so as to release the soul and enable it to reincarnate on earth or unite with the divine Supreme Being. Friends, family and neighbours gather to share memories and provide comfort when someone dies. No weeping or grief is openly displayed, for this makes the soul unwilling to leave. The corpse should be cremated upon death, but this is so costly that a family often waits years to share expenses in a joint ceremony. In the meantime, the body is purified and buried in the village cemetery. A priest, however, cannot be buried and will be cremated as soon as possible.

Once a *ngaben* or *pelebon* (cremation) date is set, ritual specialists, priests, knowledgeable people, friends and neighbours help mobilise the communal spirit. If a body has been buried, the soul is brought home first in an effigy. The corpse is washed, but if there is no body, the action is simulated on a drawing of a human figure. A priest will give advice to the soul for its upcoming journey, guided by a lamp hanging outside the gate.

When the sun is overhead, village men bring down the effigy or corpse and place it inside a colourful *wadah* or *bade* (cremation tower) of wood and bamboo sparkling with gold paper, mirrors and other ornaments. Odd numbers of tiered roofs crown the tower depending on the caste of the deceased: Brahmins have 11, a noble has nine, and commoners have up to seven. A priest's tower has no roofs, but rather is an open throne decorated in white, yellow and gold, the colours of purity. Dozens of men carry the tower in a noisy procession, spinning it at crossroads to confuse the soul so

RIGHT: a bull-shaped cremation sarcophagus.

that it cannot find its way home to disturb the living. A stuffed bird-of-paradise shows the route to heaven.

At the cemetery, the body or effigy is taken down and a pair of young chickens set free, symbolising the soul's release. The body and effigy are placed in a *patulangan* (sarcophagus) of wood, bamboo, cloth and paper. A priest or noble uses a bull, but others have fanciful animals like a winged lion or elephant-fish.

Inside the sarcophagus, the shroud is opened and holy water is poured over the remains. Letters of introduction to the deities are placed inside along with money to

pay the underworld demons. The sarcophagus is then closed and set ablaze.

Deified soul

After the corpse is reduced to ashes, the family gathers and pulverises the charred bone fragments, then puts them in a yellow coconut that they cast into the sea. After at least 12 days, the soul is deified in a *nyekah* or *mukur* ceremony. It is said to enter an effigy of sandalwood, bamboo, flowers, leaves and spices to be worshipped, fed and burned; the ashes are dispersed as before. The deified ancestor is then received in the family temple. ❑

FESTIVALS OF FAITH

Incense, offerings, food, music, dance – festivals are feasts for deities and demons as well as a wonderful spectacle.

Temple festivals are great opportunities to see Bali in all its ceremonial splendour – replete with women balancing offerings of food, flowers and fruit on their heads, music, sacred dances and temple rituals, even an illegal cockfight or two, amid much noise and activity.

The Balinese follow two calendar systems. The Saka solar-lunar calendar year begins in AD 78 and has 354 days with a 13th month added once every three years. The Pawukon (or Wuku) calendar is set by a cycle of 210 days with concurrently running 1- to 10-day periods, the conjunctions of which determine the *odalan* (temple festivals). Together these two calendar systems determine the incredibly complex schedule of holy days and anniversaries celebrated throughout Bali.

The most important Pawukon festival is **Galungan**, an island wide five-day festival when ancestral souls visit their descendants. Pigs are slaughtered for offerings, temples are festooned with decorations and ritual feasting takes place. Ten days later, during **Kuningan**, the spirits take their leave.

RIGHT: the drummer sets the tempo and dynamics for the *gamelan* music that accompanies ceremonies, processions and dance performances during festivals.

NYEPI: DAY OF SILENCE

Nyepi marks the Balinese Saka New Year and occurs in March or April on the day that follows the dark moon of the spring equinox. This is when all of the island retreats into silence for 24 hours. On this day, dedicated to meditation and prayer, there are no flights into or out of Bali, nobody works, cooks or travels, shops remain closed, all streets are deserted and no lights are switched on, even after sunset. The general explanation is that the quietude will trick the *bhutas* and *kalas* (demons) into believing that the island has been abandoned so that they, too, will leave.

Nyepi is perhaps the most important of the Island's religious days and the prohibitions are taken seriously. Hotels are exempt from Nyepi's rigorous practices but the streets are closed to both pedestrians and vehicles (except for emergency vehicles). *Pecalang* (village wardens) are posted to keep people off the streets and the beach.

The night before Nyepi, however, is filled with activity. Exciting street processions take place as the evil spirits are driven away with gongs, drums, cymbals, exploding firecrackers, bamboo cannons and huge, scary, highly creative papier-mâché monster effigies known as *ogoh-ogoh*, some of which are later burnt amid much revelry.

ABOVE: village girls dressed in traditional costume to celebrate their local *odalan*, or temple festival, in Seseh, Tabanan.

FAR LEFT: women carrying sacred offerings. At the start of a temple ceremony, the invisible spirits are invited by priests to occupy physical objects that worshippers then focus upon.

LEFT: sacred verses are chanted by the *pedanda* (Brahmana high priest) while ringing a bronze bell, burning a sacred fire and sprinkling *tirta* (holy water).

TOP: men performing the Melasti Ritual before Nyepi.

LEFT: this lion-like *barong*, danced by two men, roams the streets during Galungan to protect households from evil. During temple festivals it battles against Rangda, the queen of the witches.

CUISINE

Bali's fertile volcanic soils and surrounding seas provide an abundance of tempting fish, fruit, meat and vegetables. International cuisine is so widely available that it can be hard to find authentic local flavours.

It's surprisingly difficult for the visitor to find genuine Balinese cuisine in Bali. This is because the local restaurants, street vendors and *warung* (road-side food stalls) generally offer Indonesian or Indonesian-Chinese food. The numerous restaurants in the main tourism areas, on the other hand, serve an astonishing array of international cuisines, from Italian, French and East-West fusion to Indian and Japanese *(see page 59)*. But if you search hard enough, you can track down genuine Balinese dishes at some market stalls (especially on the main market days), at some *warung* and at an increasing number of restaurants that have begun to realise that visitors actually want to try authentic Balinese cuisine.

The balmy tropical climate and volcanic soil have blessed Bali with a superb range of fruits and vegetables, not to mention several varie-

A favourite delicacy is pepes ikan, *made with minced, spiced fish. The juices are enclosed within a banana leaf parcel and the experience is an explosion of moist, fragrant, smoky flavour.*

ties of rice. And it's not just tropical produce. Up in the cool hills, temperate-climate vegetables such as carrots, cabbages and broccoli are grown. In fact, everything from coffee to cloves,

LEFT: *nasi tumpeng* is served on important occasions.
RIGHT: a market vendor and her wares in Denpasar.

cardamom to corn, and grapes to guavas can be found in this fertile island, while fiery hot chillies and fragrant herbs are frequently planted between the paddy fields.

As with the rest of Indonesia, Balinese food has been influenced by centuries of foreign trade and by Dutch colonialism. Many spices and seasonings used to flavour Balinese cuisine were introduced, including the ever-present chilli (brought to Asia by the Portuguese and Spanish in the 16th century). The Chinese, who traded and eventually settled in Bali, as elsewhere in Indonesia, have also influenced the food, with noodles, soy sauce, bean sprouts and beancurd being the main contributions.

Spice and seasonings

Spices, herbs and a range of other seasonings lend excitingly different flavours to Balinese meat, poultry, fish and vegetable dishes. A heady citrus fragrance is provided by fresh lime juice (from the distinctive *limo Bali*), kaffir lime leaf and lemongrass. Ginger and its relatives – the bright yellow turmeric, *galangal* root and the camphor-scented *kencur* – go hand in hand with shallots and garlic, pounded to a paste with chillies that range from the plump little fiery *tabia* to long, slender ones. A distinctive salty tang is provided by *sera* (fermented shrimp paste), while the sweetness of palm sugar is often offset by the sour *asem* (tamarind).

BABI GULING

The best-known Balinese dish is spit-roasted pig, known as *guling celeng*, or by its Indonesian name, *babi guling*. The inside is stuffed with a mixture of chopped herbs and spices, and the skin is basted with turmeric juice before the pig is spit-roasted over glowing charcoal. A full meal will include tender flesh and portions of crisp skin; a few slices of spicy sausage made from the intestines stuffed with blood and seasoned meat; and *lawar*, an intricate mixture of pounded pork, a touch of pig's blood, steamed vegetables and seasonings. All this is eaten with steamed rice and a vegetable dish of young jackfruit *(nangka)*.

Herbs include basil, *pandan wangi* (fragrant screwpine) and *daun salam*, which looks like bay leaf but has a different taste. When it comes to dried spices, the Balinese have a limited range compared to the West Sumatrans, who are famous for their fiery *padang* dishes. Along with black peppercorns, the Balinese cook makes use of coriander, cinnamon stick or grated nutmeg. Candlenuts *(kemiri)* are often ground to give a rich flavour and texture to the main spice paste or *basa gede*, the basis of many Balinese dishes.

Although almost all these seasonings are found elsewhere in Indonesia, the way the Balinese combine them makes a distinctive difference. Like other Indonesian cooks, the Balinese use coconut milk squeezed from the grated flesh of a ripe coconut to provide the liquid in many dishes. However, by first roasting the coconut chunks directly on hot coals before grating it, the Balinese add a wonderful, faintly smoky tang to their food.

A typical Balinese meal

Balinese meals are always centred on rice, except for breakfast, which is generally a very simple affair. The housewife may come back from the market with sticky sweet cakes, which will probably be eaten with fresh fruit and washed down with coffee or tea. Before the midday meal is enjoyed, offerings of a few grains of cooked rice, incense and flowers must be made to all the resident gods and spirits in the family compound. Once they have been fed, it's time for mortals to tuck in.

The rice will be accompanied by a range of vegetable dishes, with protein in the form of meat (pork is more popular than beef), fish or poultry. *Tempe*, a nutty slab made from fermented soy beans, is a delicious and inexpensive source of protein. As the poultry – especially ducks, which are marched off to the paddy fields each day to fertilise the growing rice – is not usually tender, it is often finely chopped with a cleaver before cooking, as are fish and prawns. One very popular way of cooking is to wrap minced and highly seasoned meat, fish or poultry in banana leaf parcels and steam them, or set the parcels directly onto hot coals to roast. Known as *tum*, these banana leaf packets are served in most Balinese homes. Although these dishes will be seasoned, additional spicing is available with an accompanying chilli-based *sambal*.

There may also be slices of crunchy cucumber to provide a refreshing contrast, as well as something crisp, like deep-fried *krupuk* (wafers made from tapioca flour flavoured with fish, prawns or *melinjo* nuts) or *peyek* (deep-fried rice flour fritters seasoned with tiny anchovies or peanuts). One dish will probably be flavoured with the thick, sweet soy sauce found everywhere in Indonesia, so that taken overall, the meal will have a wide range of flavours (sweet, sour, hot, spicy, fragrant) and textures.

Evening meals usually comprise whatever was left over from midday, served with rice and another dish or two – perhaps an omelette or fried noodles. Dishes that Westerners regard

Once the duck is tender, the package is cooked over charcoal to impart a faint smoked flavour

Saté elsewhere in Indonesia consists of morsels of meat or poultry threaded on skewers and cooked over charcoal, served with a sweet soy sauce gravy enlivened with sliced chilli. The Balinese version, *saté lilit*, is infinitely more delicious, consisting of finely minced fish mixed with pounded herbs, spices and grated coconut. In some tourist restaurants, this pounded mixture is wrapped around sticks of fresh lemongrass rather than wooden skewers; the result is positively ambrosial.

The Balinese, like the Chinese, will eat anything, including eels, snails and frogs from the

as dessert, such as black rice pudding and rice flour dumplings filled with palm sugar, are eaten as a between-meal snack by the Balinese.

Balinese staples

Probably the best-known Balinese dish is *babi guling*, or spit-roasted pig *(see box opposite)*. Also very popular with visitors but generally prepared for special festivals is *bebek* (duck) or *ayam* (chicken) *betutu* marinaded with fragrant herbs, spices and chillies then wrapped in banana leaf and steamed.

LEFT: *bakso* (noodle soup) cart at a Gianyar street-food market in Bali. **ABOVE:** *nasi campur* (mixed rice) for sale at a food market.

paddy fields, along with dragonflies and other exotica. Too sensible to waste anything that nature provides, the Balinese use the tender heart of the banana stem as a vegetable, generally cooking it in a spicy chicken stock to make *ares*. Unripe papaya is also used to make a spicy soup, although in Bali soup is not drunk as a separate course but enjoyed with rice and other dishes.

One of the most common fish found in Balinese waters is tuna, which is often transformed into a spicy salad. Steaks of tuna are slathered with a paste of chilli, garlic, shallots, turmeric and ginger and then fried. The fish is then flaked and mixed with a fresh *sambal*, fragrant with lemon-grass and kaffir lime leaves. The result, *sambal be tongkol*, will put you off tinned tuna for good. Even simple grilled fish takes on a new flavour, with whole fish being seasoned with lime juice, salt and a fiery *sambal* before being roasted over charcoal and served with fresh tomato sauce.

The most interesting vegetable dishes include young fern tips *(pakis)* with a dressing of garlic and *kencur*; young jackfruit simmered in spicy coconut milk, palm heart curries or salads, and the tender leaves of the star fruit tree blanched and mixed with spiced coconut milk. All types of leaves, from star fruit to tapioca to spinach, can be used for *jukut urab*. The leaves are blanched and mixed with bean sprouts before

being combined with grated coconut, chilli, garlic and a touch of dried shrimp paste.

One of Bali's most refreshing dishes is eaten as a snack, and favoured by pregnant women. Simple *warung* indicate that *rujak* is on the menu by a stone mortar and pestle, and a basket of green mangoes, papaya, pineapple and cucumber (you'll also find it served out of boxes balanced on bicycles and prepared at the road side). Place an order and the vendor will start slicing the basic ingredients: bird's-eye chillies, a chunk of palm sugar and some roasted shrimp paste are thrown into the mortar and ground to a paste, with a little sour tamarind and salt added. If you don't want it too hot, ask to go easy on the chilli *(tidak pedas)*.

The result is mouth-puckeringly sour and sweet at the same time, as well as salty and spicy.

Sweet and sticky desserts

The Balinese have a sweet tooth and love to snack on little cakes and dumplings. Many visitors have discovered the delights of the seemingly bizzare black rice pudding or *bubur injin*, in which purplish-black glutinous rice is simmered with fragrant screwpine leaves until it reaches the consistency of a porridge. It is then sweetened with palm sugar and served with thick coconut milk to make what is arguably the archipelago's most delicious breakfast or snack or dessert.

Since bananas are so abundant, it's not surprising to find them either dipped in batter and deep fried, boiled and rolled in grated coconut or simmered in coconut cream sweetened with palm sugar. Little dumplings of glutinous rice flour combined with tapioca flour are cooked in coconut milk to make *jaja batun bedil*. Yet another variation on the glutinous rice theme is *wajik*, made by cooking glutinous rice with water and fragrant screwpine before steaming it with palm sugar and coconut milk. The resulting sticky mixture is spread on a tray and cooled before being cut into chunks.

Drinks hot and cold

Skip the usual fizzy drinks in favour of local favourites like young coconut water *(kopyor)*, served with slivers of the tender coconut flesh. Another excellent option is *air jeruk*, which is juice squeezed from the local green-skinned oranges – completely different in flavour to navel oranges. If you see a blender outside a stall, you'll know they're serving fresh fruit drinks, spiked with sugar syrup, ice and evaporated milk; try soursop *(sirsak)*, avocado *(apokat)*, mango *(mangga)*, pineapple *(nanas)* and banana *(pisang)*.

Tap water is not safe to drink so opt for sealed bottles. Tea and coffee are normally served without milk but laden with sugar unless you specify that you want it *pahit*. Drinking the local coffee or *kopi tubruk*, made by stirring the grounds, sugar and boiling water in a tall glass, is an acquired taste but worth it for the richly roasted flavour.

Should you want to relax over an alcoholic drink at the end of the day, check out the Indonesian Bintang beer, best served icy cold. ❑

Left: a selection of Balinese sticky cakes.

Melting Pot Cuisine

Since the mid-1990s hundreds of restaurants have opened in Bali, serving a variety of cuisines from all corners of the globe.

Bali's dining options are quite incredible, and at prices that constantly amaze tourists when they convert the cost back to their own currency. Most of the best international restaurants are located around Seminyak, Petitenget and Kerobokan, site of the trailblazing eatery La Lucciola, with Seminyak's Jalan Laksmana/Kayu Aya earning itself the name Eat Street. Since then the trend has spread throughout the island's southern tourist areas, with Ubud also offering some of Bali's most exciting dining options. Even more remote areas, such as Lovina (north coast) and the Amed district (east coast) can lay claim to some great-value (albeit more simple) international dining.

Variety is the spice

Eateries in Bali cover the gamut from simple roadside *warung* to chic fine-dining restaurants. Some are beach side, others river side and some even high up in magnificient mountain locations.

Once the food was solely local or Indonesian, but now more than a dozen world cuisines are represented. Pure Balinese restaurants are difficult to come by and Bumbu Bali (in Nusa Dua), Merah Putih and Sate Bali (both in Seminyak) are rare finds, but superb. The contrasts are many; a small bustling Greek taverna (Mykonos, Seminyak), the flavours of Moroccan tagines (Khaima, Seminyak), fresh home-made pasta (Massimo, Sanur), or the elegance of fine dining (Mozaic and CasCades, Ubud). The settings are just as varied: majestic views from above the Ayung River (Kudus House, Ubud), beach side with stunning sunset views (La Lucciola and Ku de Ta, Seminyak; Ma Joly, Tuban) and romantic

garden settings (Sarong, Petitenget, and Slippery Stone, Batubelig). Watch the dolphins while you breakfast (Villa Agung and Kubu Lalang, Lovina) or eat among the fishing boats (Café Indah, Amed).

Fusion fare

International chefs who have made Bali their new home have also created some brilliant fusion fare. Whether you call it Pacific Rim, Modern Australian or Modern French, Californian or New Asian – or whatever fancy name bandied by the international cooking gurus – the hallmark of this trend is the clever combination of Asian flavours with Western meth-

ods of preparation (or is it the other way round?). In expert hands the right balance can produce sensational results.

At Blue Fin (in Tuban), one of its best dishes combines baked scallops, octopus, squid and shrimps with a chilli mayonnaise and fish roe sauce. Mama San (in Seminyak) serves pungent Asian comfort food in fine-dining style with dishes such as roast Peking duck with hoisin sauce, Thai fish cakes with sweet chilli sauce, and black sticky rice with mango and coconut cream.

People used to come to Bali only to surf and shop. Now many come just to eat. ❑

RIGHT: sushi and oysters – grazing food at Ku De Ta.

PERFORMING ARTS

Balinese dance and drama are staged purely for entertainment, or more soberly for temple ceremonies. Performed for deities, demons and mere mortals, frenzied spirit possession and trance are key features of some sacred dances.

Dance, drama, puppetry and music often take place during religious ceremonies to entertain both divine and human audiences. Performers are often possessed by spirits and go into a state of trance in order to dispel evil forces. In the last century, many newer forms of dance and drama have emerged. Many of these are derived from sacred forms but have been adapted for secular situations, like performances staged for tourists.

The dances are often typified by subtle, controlled gestures and a fixed mask-like face with unfocused eyes and closed lips. The dancer's limbs form precise angles and the head sinks down so far that the neck disappears. At other times, gestures replicate nature, hands

Serving as an exorcism of black magic, the Balinese hold the Barong and Rangda dance sacred to their religion; powerful forces are at work and elaborate preparations are made to ensure a balance between good and evil.

flutter like a bird in flight, and limbs follow sudden changes of direction as the performers move in slow horizontal zigzagging circles. The eyes become expressive and beguiling as they flicker and dance, movements become jerky, sometimes provocative and occasionally erotic.

LEFT: a Balinese dancer in full regalia.
RIGHT: dance practice in progress.

Sanghyang

Perhaps the most riveting of the dances is *sanghyang* (divine), which refers to a particular spirit that possesses a dancer. *Sanghyang dedari* is performed by two prepubescent girls to ward off an epidemic or some disaster. Through special songs and incense, *dedari* (celestial maidens) are invited to enter their bodies. The girls then perform simple dances and versions of the *legong* (see page 63).

In *sanghyang deling*, two girls hold sticks connected with a string from which hang two dolls. To the sound of sacred songs, divine spirits make the dolls vibrate and twirl. The spirits then enter the girls, who dance with their eyes shut. But don't expect the soaring steps of Western dance; the dancers stand on the shoulders of two men who hold only their ankles, and from this perch they gracefully sway and bend their bodies while warding off evil spirits. Back on the ground they stomp on glowing embers and are eventually brought out of the trance by a temple priest with holy water and prayers. In *sanghyang jaran*, the spirits of horses possess men dancing on hobbyhorses. They run through the temple grounds and prance barefooted on burning coals.

Women's devotional dances

Sacred dances like *gabor* and *pendet* are usually performed by women to present offerings to

the visiting deities of a temple during a temple ceremony. They carry ritual objects and offerings while improvising dances before the shrines. *Panyembrama* is a secularised version in which the dancers toss flower petals.

Rejang and *sutri* are slow dances regarded as offerings to the deities. Young girls, unwed maidens, and/or post-menopausal women move slowly in long lines towards shrines or in a circle around them, holding their waist sashes and gracefully fluttering fans.

Baris: men's ceremonial dance

Baris gede (rows of great warriors) are named after the weapons that are carried by four to

16 dancers. *Baris tumbak* uses long lances, *baris panah* has bows and arrows, while *baris bedil* bears wooden rifles. In *baris tamiang* they hold small round shields, and in *baris dadap* they carry narrow wooden shields. The lines of dancers often divide into two groups to engage in a mock battle that may lead to trance.

Barong and Rangda

One of Bali's most popular dances, *barong* is a protective spirit in mask and costume danced by two men, especially around a village between the holidays of Galungan and Kuningan. There are many types of *barong* costumes, the most common being *barong keket* or *barong ket*, a mythological red-faced creature with bulging eyes, huge teeth, deer antlers and a golden headdress full of mirrors.

The mask of Rangda, the widow-witch who rules the demons of illness and haunts graveyards, represents negative cosmic forces. She is both feared and respected because she can protect people from harm. Rangda is the Hindu goddess Durga in her malevolent manifestation as the consort of Siwa (Shiva).

The Barong and Rangda confrontation is more than just a struggle between good and evil. The Balinese believe that one cannot exist without the other, that they are essentially two sides of the same coin. So ultimately the battle ends in a state of balance with neither side really winning or losing. When the Barong appears, he snaps his toothy jaws, shakes his shaggy body made of hair or feathers, and swishes his mirrored tail. He protects everyone from harm. Rangda is even more frightening to behold. With pendulous breasts, tresses of goat hair, terrible fangs protruding from her mouth, long finger nails, wide eyes, a lolling tongue and fake human entrails wrapped around her neck, she embodies every imaginable destructive force. She growls and speaks in ancient Kawi (Old Javanese) during the performance.

Men, and sometimes women and children, sit nearby with drawn *keris* (daggers). In a state of trance, they get up to attack Rangda who uses her magical white cloth to cast a spell so that instead of stabbing her they turn their blades on themselves. However, the power of the Barong prevents them from harm (an injury is said to be a sign of divine displeasure). A temple priest will revive those who are possessed by sprinkling them with holy water.

Topeng and wayang wong

Topeng (mask dance) is performed at temple ceremonies, tooth-filings, weddings and cremations. A solo dancer changes wooden masks to assume the roles in the entire story. Some performances have up to five dancers known as *topeng panca* (five masks), which allow for more drama and humour since several figures appear at once to interact with each other. Episodes are drawn from the *Babad*, histories of the Balinese kingdoms based on legendary events and characters.

Wayang wong uses fantastic, sacred wooden masks of humans, monkeys and ogres. Most dramatic dance performances show an episode from the *Ramayana*. Adviser-servants provide humour and translate poetic Kawi (Old Javanese) dialogues into common Balinese for the audience. The play finishes in a great battle with the monkeys defeating the ogres.

Arja

Arja is a folk opera that developed during the 19th century. The dancers must be trained in singing *tembang* (Balinese poetry). In order to

FAR LEFT: Rangda the widow-witch is one scary character. LEFT: *baris* is a ceremonial dance for men. RIGHT: an example of a type of *barong* mask.

hear the voices, musical accompaniment is light, using small drums and gongs, flutes, cymbals, and a bamboo instrument called *guntang*.

Themes are mostly from Javanese-Balinese romances. Packed with sentimentality and melodrama, *arja* was originally performed only by men, but during the 1920s women began to replace them in many roles. All-male *arja muani* or *arja cowok* groups are making a comeback today and are popular because of their risqué humour and hilarious routines.

Prembon and sendratari

Prembon (merger) blends together elements of *topeng* (mask dance) and *arja*. After some intro-

ductory mask dances, a story from the Javanese-Balinese romances begins, but the story is of minimal importance; the Balinese dialogue features lots of humour.

Sendratari, from the words *seni* (art), *drama* and *tari* (dance), was specially created for a festival in the 1960s by teachers at the government performing arts high school in Denpasar. Dancers mime the words spoken by a narrator from stories drawn from Indian epics and Javanese-Balinese semi-historical legends.

Legong

The graceful *legong* dance developed during the 18th century following a king's divine vision.

The original temple version, *sanghyang legong* or *topeng dedari*, is a non-narrative sacred dance with several *topeng* (masks) worn by two performers portraying celestial maidens. Today, it is a dance by three prepubescent girls who tell a story through mime. The costumes are stunning, with the dancers dressed in gold brocade and wearing flower-bedecked headdresses. The stories are mostly drawn from Indian epic literature and Javanese-Balinese romances.

Gambuh

Gambuh first was performed in the 18th-century Balinese courts, but today it is mostly done for temple ceremonies. Males formerly danced all

has been added to and adapted, incorporating scenes mostly from the *Ramayana* epic or other Hindu legends.

Kecak is an amazing cacophony of interlocking sounds and movements. Dozens of bare-chested men, wearing lengths of black and white *poleng* cloth around their waists and a single red hibiscus flower behind the ear, sit in concentric circles and chant in various rhythms without any musical accompaniment, their arms reaching up and fingers outstretched. The "chak-a-chak-a-chak" sounds and vigorous hand gestures are aesthetic elements for narrating the story, such as a dense forest or battling enemies. The players move

the parts, but now women play the female roles and the refined princes. Stories are from Javanese-Balinese romances, but the elegance and proper presentation of the dance and music are more important. Wearing colourful costumes and elaborate make-up, dancers are accompanied by very long bamboo flutes, bowed lute and drums. Stylised dialogues in courtly Kawi are translated into Balinese by attendants for the audience.

Kecak

The popular *kecak* dance was developed during the early 1930s in Bona village in Gianyar. Derived from the *sanghyang dedari* dance, it

in unison, hands stretched out, pulled in, or resting on the shoulder of the next person, waists rotating left and right, while creating at least four different rhythmic patterns. Other dancers then enter the arena to present a core episode of the Hindu epic, the *Ramayana*. The kecak is probably the best known of the many Balinese dances and is sometimes called the monkey dance because at the end of the story, the players of the voice orchestra gyrate like monkeys as Prince Sita is finally rescued by the monkey army.

ABOVE: *kecak* is performed by an all-male ensemble.
RIGHT: *wayang kulit* performer.

Kebyar and janger

Kebyar (flash of lightning) began during the early 20th century in north Bali performed by two young women dressed as men. It was further developed in south Bali by the dancer I Ketut Marya, better known as Mario. This genre is also called *bebancihan* (cross-dressing); however, either sex can dance it. The genius lies in the arm and finger gestures, torso movements and facial expressions. In *kebyar duduk* and *kebyar trompong*, the dancer actually sits most of the time and even plays the *trompong* (gong chimes).

Janger was also choreographed in the early 20th century. Twelve girls in traditional costumes with fan-shaped headdresses sing folk songs while fluttering fans and performing repetitious dance movements. Twelve boys, their youthful faces painted with moustaches and sporting gilded head-cloths and beaded bibs, do frenzied movements partly based on martial arts, accompanied by rhythmic shouts.

The art of wayang kulit

Wayang kulit (shadow play) probably originated in ritual performances to bring ancestors into contact with mortals. The shadows on the screen are the spirits, the screen represents the world, the lamp symbolises the sun, and the *dalang* (puppeteer) embodies the supreme deity, the greatest puppeteer.

Most of the storylines of Balinese *wayang kulit* are taken from the great Indian epics of *Ramayana* and *Mahabhrata (see below)* which relate the exploits of heroes and maidens. These stories have been performed to enraptured audiences for centuries. While Balinese

wayang kulit is probably derived from ancient Javanese sources from the 10th century, it has been adapted and modified over time into a very different modern form.

Wayang ramayana for instance uses episodes from the *Ramayana* and *wayang parwa* from the *Mahabharata*. *Wayang gambuh* and *wayang arja* take stories from the Javanese-Balinese romances. *Wayang babad* tells the legendary histories of Balinese kingdoms. *Wayang cupak* concerns the adventures of the glutton Cupak and his heroic brother Grantang. *Wayang Calonarang* is potentially dangerous because it tells the story of an 11th-century Javanese queen who was banished from the palace for

HINDU EPICS: THE BASIS FOR BALINESE PERFORMING ARTS

Here are capsule accounts of the epic Hindu tales of *Ramayana* and *Mahabharata*, which are key to a greater appreciation of Balinese dance and drama.

Ramayana: Rama is prevented from succeeding his father as king because another queen gets her son the throne. Rama, his wife Sita, and his younger brother Laksmana are exiled into the forest. One day Laksmana cuts off the nose of an ogress that tries to seduce him. Ogre king Rawana seeks revenge, and an ogre disguised as a golden deer tempts Sita. Rama pursues and kills it, but with its dying cries, it imitates Rama calling for help. Sita then orders Laksmana to go and help him. Disguised as a holy man,

Rawana deceives and abducts Sita. Meanwhile, Rama kills one of the twin monkey brothers fighting over their throne. The monkey king sends his general Hanoman to find Sita. After many battles, resulting in the deaths of most of the ogres, Rama finally kills Rawana. In a trial by fire, Sita proves that Rawana never violated her during captivity.

Mahabharata: The five noble Pandawa brothers are tricked out of the right to their own kingdom by their 100 devious Korawa cousins. Forced into exile, the Pandawas begin preparations for battle. During the great Bharatayuddha war, most of the Korawas and their allies are killed. The Pandawas reign for a long time before going to heaven.

practising black magic. A powerful puppeteer can summon and challenge *leyak* (people with dark supernatural powers), but if a performance is not properly done it can bring disaster.

The puppets used in all types of *wayang* are made from cattle parchment pierced with filigree designs, painted and gold-leafed. They are manipulated by rods attached to the body and arms, which are joined at the shoulders and elbows. A comic character will have a moveable lower jaw.

While *wayang kulit* is entertainment, the Balinese are also very much aware that within the stories are important moral lessons. Most performances are regarded as sacred because they occur only during religious occasions like tem-

ple festivals. A *dalang* can be hired to perform as a fulfilment of a religious vow.

The shadow puppets in the episode being performed are introduced to the audience one by one. Good and noble characters such as gods, kings, princes and their attendants are on the right, while evil characters like ogres, demons and witches are on the left.

Puppet shadows are cast by a coconut oil lamp that is suspended above the centre of a vertical screen of tightly stretched white cotton cloth. Warm, flickering flames create a muted and ethereal effect upon the screen, which brings the shadows to life. The *dalang* sits on the side of the lamp to manipulate the puppets. On

each side of the puppeteer sits an assistant who keeps the puppets in order, and behind him are the musicians. The audience mostly prefers to watch the magical shadows, but a small group of men and boys usually sit on the *dalang*'s side to watch him at work.

The accompanying music, using two or four metallophones or a small *gamelan* (*see page 67*) orchestra supports the drama. Musical signals from the *dalang* are conveyed by means of large wooden knobs that he holds in his left hand and between the big and second toes of his right foot to rap the side of the *gedog* (puppet box). Verbal cues are concealed in the narrative.

Master storyteller

The *dalang* is a remarkable person with extraordinary stamina to remain seated during a performance that can last up to four hours without a break. His skills and knowledge are equally impressive, for he has mastered the characters, dialogues and plots for dozens of stories, which he tells without using any script. The puppeteer's knowledge includes details of Balinese religious practice and philosophy, familiarity with folk tales and proverbial knowledge, plus being in tune with current events and local gossip, and adept at comedy.

Because of the wide variety of characters, the *dalang* must have knowledge of Kawi (Old Javanese) and of High, Middle and Low Balinese languages to bring the puppets to life. Royalty is addressed in High Balinese, while common characters are addressed in Low Balinese. The comic *panasar* (servant-advisers) are there to provide humour, pungent critique, slapstick comedy and translate Kawi and High Balinese into everyday language for the audience. Each character has a particular way of speaking, and the puppeteer in one fell swoop must switch from the low pitch of a hero to the sweet high tones of a princess and then to the rough and gruff growls of a giant.

It takes years to master all of this knowledge and skill; a young boy will often follow his puppeteer father to performances and act as his assistant. Others may follow a calling and study from a proficient *dalang*, while some take up the art after a profound mystical experience. ❑
• *See pages 249–50 and page 265 of Travel Tips for details of dance and drama performances.*

LEFT: *wayang kulit* or shadow puppetry.

Gamelan Music

Gamelan accompanies every theatrical, religious and social event, its music serving as entertainment for both deities and humans.

Any given *banjar* (neighbourhood) usually owns a *gamelan* (*gambelan* or *gong* in Balinese) set, and anyone may join a *sekaha gong* (music club) – there are children's *gamelan* clubs where boys and girls as young as nine years old play. Almost two dozen kinds of traditional ensembles exist, ranging from a small *gender wayang* duet or quartet of bronze metallophones to accompany *wayang kulit* (shadow puppet) plays, to a huge *gong gede* temple ensemble with up to 40 players. Ancient *gamelan selonding* have few instruments with iron keys, while *gamelan sarongambang* uses only a handful of instruments with wooden or bronze keys. *Gong balaganjur* and *gong batel* are ceremonial processional groups using a full set.

Some ensembles are named after the dance form that they accompany, such as *gamelan joged*, which uses *grantang*, *rindik* or *tingklik* (small bamboo xylophones) and some bronze instruments for *joged* (social dancing). *Gamelan jegog* only has bamboo instruments, and the deep tones produced by striking the bigger xylophones with padded large mallets resonate through the body so that the listener can feel the vibrations. *Gamelan tektekan* uses single-tuned bamboo tubes and wooden cowbells rhythmically played by dozens of dancing men.

Gongs and keys

A *gamelan* mostly consists of different sizes of *gangsa* (metallophones with bronze keys suspended over bamboo resonators) and *reyong* or *trompong* (racks of small knobbed gongs). They are set in carved and gilded wooden frames. *Gangsa* of various size have different functions; high-pitched

kantilan plays rapid interlocking elaborations, while the very low *jublag* plays the basic melody. All *gangsa* are paired and tuned slightly out of pitch with each other to create pulses of sound that make Balinese music shimmer and vibrate. At the heart of the ensemble are two *kendang* (drums). These control the tempo, with the drummers using their hands and knobbed sticks. Small *ceng-ceng* or *rincik* (cymbals) accent the music, while a small, single *kempli* gong keeps the beat. Large hanging gongs and small *kempur* are struck at important points. The singers are a recent addition to the *gamelan*.

Gongs and keys are forged by hand in the same methods used for centuries. Tuning to the five- or seven-note scale is done by painstakingly filing and hammering away at each piece. The small *gamelan angklung* in south Bali uses a four-note scale, but in north Bali they use a five-note scale. A standard scale does not exist, so each ensemble has its own unique sound.

For the Balinese, *gamelan* instruments have spiritual power. No one steps over an instrument, as this would offend the ensemble's spirits. Respect is shown by presenting them with offerings on particular holy days and before performances. ❑

ABOVE: a *gamelan* orchestra.

ARTS AND CRAFTS

Originally, art on Bali was an obligation to the deities. It still is today, but tourism has changed much of Bali's aesthetic purpose. The beauty of the handiwork is still apparent in stone and wood carvings, textiles, metalwork and painting.

Balinese art has its primary expression in religion, not as a conscious production for its own sake. Bronzes and stone carvings of deities survive from the early centuries AD but the tropical climate is unkind to all but the hardiest of materials: soft volcanic stone quickly erodes, cloth paintings decay in the humidity, and woodcarvings are eaten by termites. Over the years, earthquakes and volcanoes have destroyed numerous works of art. Replacements thus had to be made every few generations.

Art is expressed through music, dance, carving, painting, and especially in offerings for religious ceremonies (*see pages 74–5*). Not all Balinese have the sense of originality that distinguishes artists, but many of them are great craftspeople. Crafts range from woodcarving to weaving, from metalwork to painting. Particular villages are famous for their families of skilled craftsmen.

Balinese silverwork is enhanced by a technique called granulation, where small pellets and tiny coiled silver wires are heated until soft enough to adhere to the piece, in order to form a pattern or decorative feature.

Wood and stone carving

Carving goes back many centuries to when temples and courts needed symbolic decorations and embellishments. Hard tropical woods and

LEFT: making intricate carvings on coconut shells.
RIGHT: a *paras* stone carving at Batubulan.

soft *paras* (sandstone) are used for gates, beams and pillars in many buildings. Sacred wooden images, architectural carvings, and cases for *gamelan* musical instruments are often painted and gold-leafed. During the 1930s, carvers began moving away from stylised religious figures and created new forms from mythology and everyday life. Some highly imaginative and beautiful sculptures became elongated and distorted. The natural shapes of branches and roots also suggested the finished woodcarved forms to many artists. Most carvings in these new styles were unpainted to show the natural beauty of the grain.

Today, most carvings are made in the regency of Gianyar. Wood is used in Mas, Peliatan,

Selakarang and Kemenuh; stone is favoured in Batubulan and Singapadu, while coconut shells and cattle bones are used in Tampaksiring.

Masks

When someone from the West puts on a mask, they're usually pretending to be someone else; but in Bali when someone dons a mask, especially a sacred mask, they become someone else. Sacred masks, most famously used in the *topeng* and the *barong* dances, have a power called *tenget*, which enters the body of the performer who wears one. These very powerful masks are brought to life through a ceremony conducted by a *pedanda*, a Brahman high priest. They are

> *Cheap factory printed batik pieces look good on one side only, while expensive handmade ones feature distinct and intricate patterns and vivid colours on both sides.*

the temple must be members of the Brahman caste since only they know the required rituals involved in making a sacred mask.

With the birth of tourism, visitors started to show an interest in masks as wall decorations, thus initiating a new line of business for the

kept in special shrines and receive offerings every full and new moon, and whenever they are used. They also get special offerings on the day known as Tumpek Wayang.

Masks may represent gods, animals, demons, or humans. They can be half masks, three-quarter face (extending to the upper lip), or full face; some even have a movable jaw.

Masks are carved using more than 30 different tools. After endless sanding at least 40 coats of paint are applied to achieve a strikingly glossy surface. The mask carver, known as the *Undagi Tapel*, is likely to come from a family of carvers, and most come from the villages of Mas or Singapadu. Those who make masks for

carvers. Today, thousands of people worldwide collect these colourful and compelling objects.

Balinese textiles

Bali's claim to fabric fame is a weft *ikat* cloth called *endek*. Plastic raffia is firmly tied around the weft or horizontal threads of a cloth before it is woven and then dyed so that the wrapped areas resist the colour. This is repeated in other parts with different dyes, while previously tied areas are untied to receive new colours. Finally, all the threads are untied and woven, and the intricate patterns emerge. Some *endek* is made from silk, but cheaper cotton and rayon are more widely used. Semi-mechanised looms produce great quantities in Denpasar and Gianyar but some of the finest *endek* comes from Sidemen in Karangasem and Gelgel in Klungkung.

A masterpiece of Balinese craftsmanship, double-*ikat* cloths called *geringsing* are woven only in the small village of Tenganan in Karangasem (east Bali); Japan and India are the only other places where double *ikat* is made. Both the handspun cotton warp and weft threads are tied and dyed with the same patterns before the cloth is woven, which requires special skills and a great attention to detail. Cloths are hand-woven in a back-tension loom, and the dyed threads must be properly aligned so that the unique patterns emerge.

The rich colours of these cloths, with groups of geometrical or floral patterns, are produced by dyeing them with indigo and morinda, a shrub whose roots produce a reddish-brown colour. *Geringsing* is considered sacred, and its name can mean "illness free". It can also mean "speckled", a fitting description of the shimmering colourful patterns. Since it is widely believed that the cloths protect the wearer from earthly and supernatural enemies, they are used in religious ceremonies.

Songket is a brocade cloth with gold, silver or coloured weft threads forming intricate designs on the surface of the cloth. They tend to be heavy and dense, due to the weaving technique that is done from the back of the cloth. In the old days, *songket* could only be worn by aristocrats, but today these expensive fabrics are available to anyone who can afford them. The main centres of *songket* weaving are Gelgel in Klungkung, Sidemen in Karangasem, Singaraja in Buleleng, and Negara in Jembrana.

Kain prada textiles are decorated with gold designs of flowers or birds. The patterns are outlined on plain coloured cloth, and the area spread with glue for adhering gold leaf. Today, cheaper gold paint is used, and more often than not glue is silkscreened onto the fabric and artificial gold leaf applied. These cloths are mostly worn by dancers and participants in religious ceremonies but are also used for making ceremonial parasols and dance fans, and for decorating shrines. Today, most *kain prada* is silkscreened on polyester in Sukawati in Gianyar and Satria in Klungkung.

In batik, wax designs are carefully applied on to plain white cloth which is then immersed in dye. This is repeated for other parts of the design with different dyes, the waxed parts resisting the colours. Finally, the cloth is boiled to remove the wax, revealing the multi coloured patterns beneath. Balinese-style batik pieces are very colourful with waxed outlines and hand-painted dyes that feature big designs and even cartoon characters. A major centre of production is at Tampaksiring in Gianyar. The more traditional batik on sale is produced in Java.

Metalwork

Works in silver and gold were once associated with royalty, whose family members wore heavy

LEFT: crafting a mask for *topeng* dancers, Batuan village.
RIGHT: shadow puppets for sale in Sukawati village.

gold and silver headdresses, belts, bracelets, earrings, anklets and necklaces as symbols of their high status. Even the handles of some *keris* (daggers) were and still are made of gold in the shape of mythological figures and studded with gems. Kamasan in Klungkung is the production centre for traditional jewellery, *keris* handles, ritual vessels and offering bowls.

Numerous workshops in Celuk in Gianyar, produce huge quantities of gold and silver jewellery in traditional and new designs. The Balinese are very quick to pick up on introduced ideas and copy what they know will sell, with some smiths collaborating with foreign jewellery designers living in Bali.

Keris and *gamelan* making are highly technical, demanding skills handed down in families. Forging a *keris* involves repeated folding and fusing of different metals to produce a blade that can wield supernatural force if ritually empowered. The only *keris* foundry is at Kusamba in Klungkung.

Many workers are needed to produce the bronze keys and gongs of a *gamelan* musical ensemble. The coordinated hammering requires quick action by an experienced team. Foundries operate in Tihingan in Klungkung, Blahbatuh in Gianyar, and Sawan in Buleleng.

Painting

The oldest known Balinese paintings, kept at Pura Besakih today, are of a lotus flower and of the Hindu elephant-headed deity Ganesha on two wooden boards dating from the 15th century. Paintings from the 19th century show episodes from Indian epics and other literary sources along with astrological signs. They were commissioned by palaces and temples as decorations and painted with natural pigments on cotton cloth primed with rice starch. Often the paintings were unsigned, for the painter was a craftsman working for the glory of the gods and not for himself.

The traditional painting style is derived from the two-dimensional *wayang kulit* (leather puppets) with strict iconography in facial details, dress and skin colours. Today, works are still made in Kamasan in Klungkung, where the descendants of artists who worked for the nearby Gelgel court use traditional materials and techniques. Other similar styles using manufactured paints are done in Kerambitan in Tabanan, Bedulu and Pengosekan in Gianyar, and Tejakula in Buleleng.

New patronage and styles

When the Dutch dismantled the old system of royal patronage in the early 20th century, there was a real danger that the arts would also decline. Ironically, tourists played a large part in preventing this by becoming new patrons. Balinese artists drew upon traditional forms and techniques, elaborating on them and experimenting with new ideas and expressions. As there was no local market for their creations, they were essentially producing exotic colonial images of Bali for the newly emerging tourist market.

Since Balinese artists created new works to

replace deteriorating ones, a great degree of repetition existed. However, Balinese art was not at all static: paintings from Sanur and Singaraja created during the late 1800s show some perspective and more naturalistic figures and scenery. The artists were also beginning to paint single scenes from everyday life, a concept they borrowed from traditional astrological and agricultural charts.

While some Western artists had a hand in steering the Balinese in a different aesthetic direction, some claims have been overstated. During the 1920s and 1930s, Westerners like Walter Spies from Germany and Rudolf Bonnet from Holland settled in Ubud and promoted the village as the cultural centre of Bali. Spies and Bonnet are

Seniwati Gallery of Art (see page 123) *in Batubulan promotes works by female artists and allows them to develop skills and make contacts.*

with ink on paper to show marine subjects from their area. At a third centre in Batuan south of Ubud, the painting was characterised by half-puppet, half-naturalistic figures in ink and pastel colours depicting daily scenes and supernatural confrontations. And in 1936, the Pitamaha school of art emerged *(see box opposite)*.

Yet another style developed in the early

often credited with setting the tone for modern Balinese art. However, experimentation with new and different media and styles had been going on among Balinese artists since the 19th century, and claims that the Europeans influenced the content of Balinese art are debatable.

Over the years, several styles of painting emerged. Ubud-style painting was characterised by naturalistic polychrome figures in landscapes and everyday scenes such as harvesting and presenting offerings. Another centre of painting developed at Sanur, where artists tended to work

1960s in Penestanan near Ubud. Under the guidance of Dutch-born artist Arie Smit, who had become an Indonesian citizen, a group of young Balinese created a distinctive and naive painting genre known as the Young Artists style, which showed daily and ritual life in strong oil colours with dark outlines. In the 1970s, paintings of flora and fauna were produced in Pengosekan, while miniatures developed in Keliki to the north.

Places to see quality art in the Ubud area are Neka Art Museum, Museum Puri Lukisan and Agung Rai Museum of Art. Taman Werdi Budaya Art Centre in Denpasar also has a good collection of artworks. ❑

LEFT: painting by Rudolf Bonnet (1895–1978).
ABOVE: ceiling paintings at Bale Kerta Gosa, Taman Gili.

GIFTS TO DEITIES AND DEMONS

On pavements, under trees, inside cars and at shrines, these exquisitely crafted offerings are ephemeral works of art.

Banten (offerings) are gifts to deities to ask for blessings and to give thanks, or as payoffs to demons to keep them appeased and away. Flowers, palm leaves, fruits, rice and meat are all assembled into ephemeral works of art, and nearly every village has its own unique style.

Offerings are very visible, like the graceful *penjor* bamboo poles, or personal, like the daily *jotan* of a few grains of cooked rice sprinkled with salt on small squares of banana leaves. For special ceremonies, a towering *sarad* has hundreds of colourful rice-dough figures representing the cosmos, while *sate tungguh* is its counterpart, made from the meat, innards and heads of pigs.

Presenting an offering requires incense, holy water and prayers. The physical parts of the offerings are eaten, regarded as *lungsuran* (left overs) from the deities; those made to demons are discarded. Offerings are used only once and must be newly created each time.

ABOVE LEFT: a roast pig lies among offerings for a temple festival. Pork or chicken along with rice, fruits and other sweets complement each other by symbolising male and female aspects of life. After the invisible essence of the food is offered to the deities, humans eat the physical remains.

TOP: making morning offerings to the sea at Padangbai. Balinese believe that demons symbolising disorder dwell beneath the sea, and offerings must be made to prevent disasters such as earthquakes.

RIGHT: household *canang* offering. This is the most commonly used daily offering. A circular tray fashioned from young coconut leaves holds flowers and fragrant shredded leaves, beneath which lie a few symbolically important betel nuts.

LEFT: a decorative bowl contains an artistic arrangement of fruits, hard-boiled eggs, sweets and rice cakes, while a "crown" with streamers formed from young coconut leaves holds flowers and other essential ingredients.

THE OFFERINGS INDUSTRY

An average household spends at least half of its income on offerings. However, much of the offering eventually becomes part of the household's meals. Creating offerings is an act of devotion, but if there is no time to make them or if more elaborate forms for special ceremonies are needed, they can be purchased in the market or ordered in advance from a *tukang banten* (offerings expert). They are usually members of a priest's household who have gained the skills and knowledge from their families. Another path to becoming a *tukang banten* is to learn the art during preparations for religious events.

One can easily purchase the simple *canang* (coconut leaf tray) that is used in everyday offerings or more complicated *jejaitan* (stitchery), which are created from trimmed palm leaves held together with bamboo pins. Truckloads of young coconut leaves from east Java arrive daily in Balinese markets for this specific use. Today, metal staples and plastic string replace bamboo pins and thread, and coloured paper is used instead of dyed leaves. Purists disapprove, but perhaps it is better for offerings to go in this direction than to disappear completely.

RIGHT: young coconut leaves are cut and pinned together to form all kinds of receptacles for holding various food and flowers as offerings.

OUTDOOR ACTIVITIES

Bali isn't all about temples and culture. Those looking for thrills and spills will find opportunities to dive, snorkel and surf in sparkling seas, paraglide over hills, climb volcanoes, bike through the countryside, or tee off at golf courses.

Blessed with wide open spaces, sparkling seas and an equable climate, Bali is the perfect place to take part in your favourite outdoor sport. The range on offer is astounding and covers both land and sea sports, with a number of specialist adventure tour companies offering exciting excursions such as river rafting, mountain cycling, jungle trekking and four-wheel-drive expeditions. Most companies provide a door-to-door pick-up and drop-off service, and most activities are child-friendly.

Diving and snorkelling

Bali is the ideal location for diving among some of the world's finest tropical reefs. The water is warm and the marine life is abundant. Reputable dive schools, dive resorts and operators offer facilities, equipment and tuition for every PADI course from beginners' discovery

An exhilarating rafting excursion on the Telaga Waja River will please those who want more of a rush from their white-water ride. Rated Class IV, this journey covers 14km (9 miles) and takes about three hours.

dives to the highest recreational level. With a great choice of both easy and challenging world-class sites, speciality courses include drift

LEFT: scuba diving the wreck of the Liberty, near Tulamben. **RIGHT:** surfing at Kuta, a good place for beginners.

dive, night dive, deep dive and underwater photography. Programmes for children are available too; the PADI Bubblemakers offers underwater adventure combined with lots of fun and games for children aged 8–12.

Bali's premier dive site is around the wreck of the *Liberty*, at Tulamben on the east coast. Located 40–50 metres /50yds from the beach, the wreck is 30 metres (100ft) below the surface at the deepest point, with 50 percent of the structure relatively undamaged.

It is the habitat of numerous underwater species, including the rare pigmy seahorse and ghost pipefish. Black tip reef sharks, dolphins and whales bask in nearby waters and the stark volcanic coastline borders a majestic coral garden with a 70-metre (230ft) drop-off.

The reefs around Pulau Menjangan on the northwest corner of Bali have drop-offs ranging from 60–80 metres (200–250ft). The sea here is incredibly calm, protected from winds and strong currents by the Gunung Prapat Agung peninsula. This is where 10-metre (30ft) long toothless whale sharks have been sighted, and where whales and dolphins migrate via the Bali Strait between Java and Bali.

Other popular sites include the Amed area on the east coast, and Nusa Penida island on the southeast where the visibility is superb; this is also the seasonal habitat of the *Mola mola*

and the breaks found at Padang Padang, Balangan and Uluwatu, with its famous entry cave, are world-class barrels.

For novices and surfers of intermediate ability, there are plenty of mellow beachbreaks. With a little bit of local knowledge, it's still possible to find great surf locations without huge crowds. There is a good choice of well-managed surf schools, offering adults and children the opportunity to experience the thrill of the waves, while learning board handling, surf etiquette and safety tips. Surf camps and "surfaris" are available for those who wish to discover secret surf spots with local professionals. Bali is also the starting point for nearly all Indonesian surf trips with charter

(also known as the giant Ocean Sunfish), which is the world's largest bony fish. In addition to day trips, live-aboard trips take divers further afield to explore the waters around neighbouring islands.

Surfing

Bali is renowned as one of the great surfing meccas of the world, offering more than 20 top-quality breaks. The peak surf season is April to October when the southeast trade winds blow offshore and the full force of the southern ocean swells hit the reefs around Kuta, Nusa Dua and the Bukit Badung peninsula. These are great draws for veteran surfers,

boats departing for G-Land (in East Java), Lombok, Sumbawa, and more distant areas like East Nusa Tenggara and North Sumatra.

Dolphin-watching

If you prefer to stay dry, dolphins can also be viewed at Lovina, on Bali's north coast. Every morning at sunrise, the dolphins gather and play in large schools just beyond the coral reefs off the scenic black sand bay. For a nominal fee, dolphin-watchers can go out with the fishermen in tiny, traditional *jukung* fishing boats and be treated to the breathtaking spectacle of these graceful mammals vaulting out of the water in a remarkable aerial display.

Paragliding

A number of paragliding clubs operate from the Bukit Badung peninsula, taking off from the cliff top 80 metres (250ft) above Timbis beach on the southernmost tip of the island. Harnessed to these amazing non-motorised inflatable wings and using only the wind as a source of power, it is possible to soar like an albatross over remote beaches, coral reefs, turquoise waters, luxury hotels and Hindu temples; the views of the ridge-line are spectacular. Experience is not necessary as tandem flights can be arranged with professional instructors and the latest equipment. Full certification courses can also be organised for those aiming for pilot rating. The trade winds blow consistently from the southeast from June to September, making this ridge flyable on most days.

Golf

Bali's four spectacular golf courses are all open to non-members. Pan Pacific Nirwana Bali Golf Club near Tanah Lot is one of the best golf courses in Asia. Designed by Greg Norman, it is bordered by ocean and rice fields, and features dramatic white-sand bunkers, freshwater creeks and mature trees.

The Bali Handara Kosaido Golf and Country Club in Bedugul is located in the caldera of an ancient volcano and is considered to be one of the most beautiful golf courses in the world. This 18-hole, par 72 playground was created by Peter Thompson against a dramatic backdrop of towering mountains, pristine forest and the peaceful Danau Buyan. The refreshing temperature at this high altitude averages 10 degrees below Bali's coastal regions and is the perfect climate for golfing. Other options are the New Kuta Golf Course at Pecatu, which commands splendid ocean views from its signature hole, no. 15; and the Bali Beach Golf Course at Sanur, a 9-hole course.

Horse riding

There are several stables and equestrian resorts on the island offering riding adventures through rice fields, villages, forests and along the beach. All treks are accompanied by personal guides; lessons can be arranged and instruction is of a high standard. Most stables provide a good selection of well-trained horses with varying temperaments and sizes to suit all ages and levels of experience.

Trekking and mountain climbing

The island's geographical diversity allows visitors the opportunity for everything from gentle hikes through rice fields, jungle, rainforests and national parkland, to challenging mountain treks in the dry season.

Recommended is the two-hour sunrise trek to Gunung Batur, which has erupted more than 20 times during the last two centuries. The 1,717-metre (5,632ft) high volcano comprises a

set of cones resting in the centre of a gigantic caldera with an adjacent crescent-shaped lake. The trek begins around 4am, offering a clear view of Danau Batur Lake, the peaks of Gunung Abang and Gunung Agung, the distant sea and even Gunung Rinjani on neighbouring Lombok. The strange landscape is punctuated by bizarre hillocks and a series of craters with jets of white steam puffing out of small holes. At the summit, trekkers will be served a breakfast of baked bananas and hard-boiled eggs cooked in the natural heat belching from the belly of the volcano.

After the descent, the hot springs on the lakeshore at Toya Bungkah are a welcome treat and

LEFT: try jet-boating at Nusa Dua, Bali, for a high-speed adrenaline rush. **RIGHT:** jungle treks are an excellent way to experience another side of Bali and Lombok.

perfect for easing aching limbs. Climbers are advised to take a guide; a local cartel actively discourages independent trekkers by not allowing people to hike alone. "Official" fees for guides are exorbitant, starting around Rp 600,000 per person. However, much cheaper deals can be negotiated at some of the homestays and restaurants beside the lake.

At 3,014 metres (9,796ft), Gunung Agung in east Bali is Bali's tallest and holiest mountain with its resplendent summit dominating much of the island. There are two routes up the volcano, generally undertaken at night so that trekkers can reach the top in time to experience the sunrise. A guide is essential.

From Besakih, the ascent to the summit takes around five–six hours and does not require any technical climbing skills or special equipment apart from a good pair of boots and a torch. The shorter route takes about three hours and begins at the large market temple of Pura Pasar Agung near Selat. This route leads to the rim of the crater and offers a clear view of towering Gunung Rinjani on neighbouring Lombok. A permit is not required, but climbing the mountain is forbidden when major religious events are being held at Pura Besakih, generally in April.

Taman Nasional Bali Barat (West Bali National Park) offers exceptional trekking with the bonus of magnificent panoramas in this region watered

by clear streams and traversed by trails. More like a forest than a jungle, a typical walk takes about five hours. The routes are often steep but relatively easy, although some areas are cross-country with no clear paths and, at times, it is necessary to crawl through undergrowth and use paths frequented by wild ox and deer.

Visitors to the national park must apply for a permit and be accompanied by a guide. Arrangements for one-day permits and guides can be made at the park headquarters in Cekik (tel: 0365-61060; 7.30am–3.30pm), the ranger station at Labuhan Lalang or the Department of Forestry (PPHA) office in Denpasar.

Nature enthusiasts will also enjoy trekking

through the tropical, almost primeval, rainforest that borders Danau Buyan and Danau Tamblingan, close to Bedugul. The pathways through the forest are narrow and the undergrowth is around 2 metres (7ft) high, but in the dry season it's not difficult to negotiate the route. Hidden temples lie in sunlit clearings within the trees, and trekkers may see deer, black monkeys and squirrels. From the lakeside, it is possible to arrange to be rowed across the tranquil waters by one of the local villagers in a *pedau akit,* a traditional double canoe.

Birdwatching

Taman Nasional Bali Barat (West Bali National Park) is home to over 250 different species of bird-life and is the only place where the Bali Starling can be found in the wild. Extremely rare, this is the only surviving bird endemic to Bali, and is one of the world's most endangered species.

Within the boundaries of the reserve in the bay near Gilimanuk are several island sanctuaries for sea birds. Two species of tern nest in large numbers on the sandbanks at the entrance of Teluk Lumpur (Mud Bay) while brown boobies and lesser frigate birds roost on Pulau Burung further to the east.

The inland forests around Bedugul and Gunung Batukau are also abundant with bird-life, and magnificent kingfishers are a common sight along the island's many river banks.

Mountain biking

Specialist adventure tour companies offer exciting mountain biking tours. Starting at around 1,100 metres (3,600ft) above sea level, each tour is an exhilarating descent through farms, hamlets and lush valleys, past ancient temples and beautiful rice fields. The bike tours include a number of stops, allowing participants to sample some of the indigenous fruits and spices, and absorb the beauty of the terrain. Knowledgeable guides will point out places of interest and the variety of crops cultivated in these mountainous areas, while explaining the history of the land, the culture and its people. Some tours incorporate a visit to a typical Balinese compound home before concluding with an Indonesian buffet lunch.

Left: cycling through paddy fields, Tegalalang.
Right: whitewater rafting.

White water rafting

White water rafting is an action-packed journey through class II and III rapids, against an awesome backdrop of pristine rainforest, towering gorges, emerald rice terraces and dramatic waterfalls on the Ayung, Telaga Waja (Karangasem) and Unda rivers. There are quite a number of operators, and the more reputable ones have good safety standards with professional and experienced guides piloting the rafts. Welcome hot showers at the end are followed by a gourmet buffet feast.

Cruising

Bali offers numerous ocean cruise options on luxury catamarans and yachts, including day trips

around the islands of Nusa Lembongan, Nusa Ceningan and Nusa Penida, with plenty to see, not least the giant fruit bats at Bat Rock. These trips include lunch, snorkelling at Crystal Bay, a visit to a seaweed farming village on Nusa Ceningan, and activities such as snorkelling, sea kayaking and banana boat rides at Nusa Lembongan.

Other activities

Other outdoor activities include windsurfing, water skiing, fishing, ecotours, four-wheel drive and bike tours, bungy-jumping and more, all of which can easily be arranged in Bali. ❑
• *Details of activity operators are listed on pages 256–7 and page 267 of the Travel Tips section.*

ARCHITECTURE

The order of the cosmos defines how a traditional building is laid out and constructed in Bali. Some of these ideas have inspired contemporary styles that borrow from European design, often embellished with lush, spectacular gardens.

For centuries, all Balinese buildings have been laid out according to the principles of sacred space. Even in prehistoric times some kind of orientation was used. Ancient megalithic stones, for example, are oriented towards one of the island's main volcanoes. An important concept is the *kaja* (upstream) axis, the high direction where deities and ancestors reside, and the low *kelod* (downstream) direction of demonic forces. In south Bali, *kaja-kelod* is a north–south orientation, but on the northern side of the island, it refers to south–north instead. Another axis is *kangin-kauh* (east–west) based on the rising and setting sun, associated with life and death. At the centre of these four cosmic directions lies the human realm.

The Balinese traditional reverence for mountains was further developed by Indian influences during the 11th century. In Hindu-Buddhist cosmology, the sacred mountain Meru is at the centre of the universe and is the abode of the deities. This idea was embraced by the Balinese, who used the island's highest volcano Gunung Agung as their Mount Meru.

The Hindu-Buddhist concepts also give everything its allotted place in the universe, implying that any transgression of this natural order will lead to disharmony or disaster. The Hindu-Buddhist cosmos is divided into upper, middle and nether worlds. Architectural structures and their layouts follow this orientation

with the roof as heaven, the middle section the earth, and the foundation the underworld.

The household compound

Traditional Balinese houses, from village to court, are built within a walled courtyard or series of courtyards with mostly uncovered earth. Most Balinese feel more at home when surrounded by walls made of mud, brick or stone. Entry is through a small, covered gate with a niche in each side for offerings. Just inside the gate is an *aling-aling* (privacy wall) that obscures the interior from outside view. More importantly, it prevents evil spirits from entering since they cannot turn corners.

LEFT: part of the interior of Bale Kerta Gosa, whose ceiling displays puppet-figure style paintings.
RIGHT: the pink sandstone temple, Pura Beji, in Sangsit.

Within the enclosed compound are several *bale*, open-sided or walled pavilions found throughout most of Southeast Asia. Instead of being raised off the ground on posts, in Bali they are built on platforms of mud, brick or stone. The wooden pillars of a traditional pavilion must be erected in the same way as the tree grew so that it stands "upright". To determine which end is which, a rope is tied around the middle point of the lumber; when raised, the denser root end is heavier.

Pavilions have specific uses and are laid out according to the Hindu-Buddhist idea that the household compound is like a human body. The *sanggah* or *merajan* (family temple) is at

the most sacred *kaja-kangin* (mountain-east) corner, the highest ground and equivalent to the head. The ritual *bale dangin* (eastern pavilion) is where birth ceremonies, tooth-filings and weddings occur. The body is placed here before a cremation or burial. This pavilion and the central courtyard are the torso and navel.

The arms are the *bale daja* (north pavilion) which is reserved for the elders or married couples and where the family heirlooms are stored, and the *bale dauh* (west pavilion) where unwed members stay. The *paon* (kitchen) is the stomach, while the *lumbung* (granary) and *bale delod* (pavilion towards the sea) for sleeping are the legs. The *lawang* (gate) represents the genitals,

> *Measurements for a compound are taken from the owner. The layout is based on the length of the owner's foot and outstretched arms, thereby creating a home in harmony with him.*

the garbage pit the anus. There may also be an area outside of the compound allocated to pig pens, coconut and fruit trees, and enjoyed by free-ranging ducks and chickens. This section of land, where in addition you might find the *semer* (well), is separated by a low wall, marking the border between the human quarters and the animal quarters. The layout of the compound is the same for a poor or wealthy family; only the materials used would differ.

Traditional carpentry joints are fitted together without nails, but wooden wedges are pounded in to hold them snugly. This gives buildings flexibility during earthquakes, allowing them to sway instead of collapsing. Interiors can be rather dark due to tiny windows or absence of them, and the only furnishings might be a simple bed, cabinet or table. Traditional thatched roofs used to be composed of dried grass panels, but clay tiles and metal shingles are commonly used today.

Temple architecture

Since they are the residences of deities, temples follow stricter principles of spatial organisation compared to a household. The mountain and eastern sides are deemed most sacred. The stepped terraces of ancient sacred sites can still be seen in such temples as Pura Besakih on Gunung Agung, Pura Samuan Tiga in Bedulu (Gianyar), Pura Luhur Batukau in Tabanan, and Pura Kehen in Bangli.

A public temple, one not within a family compound, is called a *pura*, a Sanskrit word meaning "fortress or walled enclosure". In Bali there are tens of thousands of temples for clans, holy springs, irrigation, villages, regions, and the entire island. Within a village there usually are *kahyangan tiga* (three sacred spaces): *pura puseh* (temple of origin) dedicated to Brahma, god of creation; *pura desa-bale agung* (temple of the village and great pavilion) for Wisnu (Vishnu), god of life; and *pura dalem* (temple of the dead) near a cemetery, dedicated to Durga and her consort Siwa (Shiva), deities of death and reincarnation.

A temple's *jaba* (outer courtyard) is a public area outside the entrance and is often not walled. Performances occur in a large open-sided *wantilan*. In one corner of the outer walls surrounding a temple's other courtyards may be a *bale kulkul*. The hollow wooden logs hanging in this tower-like structure are struck to signal the arrival and departure of deities.

Entry into a temple is through a *candi bentar* (split gate) in one of the walls, which looks like a slender triangle vertically cut in half with the parts separated. They may be related to memorials for ancient ancestral worship. The *candi*

opening, the terrifying face and long-nailed hands of Boma frightens away evil forces. He is the son of Wisnu and Ibu Pertiwi (Mother Earth), and symbolises uncultivated fertility. Stone demons guard both sides of the gate for the same purpose, and *apit lawang* (gate-flanking shrines) are used for offerings. Just as in domestic structures, an *aling-aling* (privacy wall) prevents evil spirits from entering.

Inner sanctum

Even if the temple is built on level ground, the *jeroan* (inner courtyard) is usually set slightly higher. Rows of shrines or *pelinggih* (sitting places) line the east sides, with pavilions else-

bentar may also symbolise the splitting of the material world, allowing entrance to the spiritual realm. The walled *jaba tengah* (middle courtyard) has more pavilions, such as a *bale gong* for the *gamelan* music ensemble, and other structures where offerings may be prepared or where puppet performances may be presented.

The entrance to a temple's inner courtyard is often through a covered gate known as *candi kurung, kori gelung* or *kori agung*. It usually has steps on both sides of the doorway. Above the

where. Most shrines are made of square brick and stone pillars topped by a small wooden enclosure with a thatched roof made from *alang-alang* (jungle grass) or black *ijuk* (sugar palm fibre). If present, the most outstanding feature is the towering *meru*, a pagoda-like shrine symbolising the Hindu-Buddhist cosmic mountain after which it is named. The more important the deity the more tiers or roofs on the *meru*, but always in odd numbers from 3 to 11.

Another important shrine introduced during the 19th century is the *padmasana* (lotus throne) for Sanghyang Widi Wasa, the Supreme Deity of Universal Order. Located in the most sacred *kaja-kangin* corner, this tall stone seat

LEFT: Bale Kambang, the "floating pavilion", at Taman Gili. **ABOVE:** Pura Besakih, Bali's most important place of worship, also known as the "Mother Temple".

represents the cosmos. The base is carved with the foundation of the universe: the tortoise Bedawang Nala entwined by the two serpents Basuki and Anantaboga.

Receding levels represent the different layers of heaven, and are topped by an open throne. During temple ceremonies, the deities descend to occupy objects that are placed in their shrines. Sacred relics, normally safely stored away, are also brought out for this purpose.

Most prayers are not directed towards this Supreme Being but rather to his manifestations as the temple's deities. Unlike Indian and ancient Javanese Hindu-Buddhist temples, Balinese places of worship do not have enclosed

During the 1920s, German artist Walter Spies built himself a Balinese-style bungalow with bamboo walls and thatched roof in Ubud. Soon after, Belgian artist Adrien-Jean Le Mayeur de Merpres made his studio home on Sanur beach in a walled compound with pavilions set amidst gardens. But until more visitors began staying longer, most were content to live in traditional compounds. Gradually some of them built their own homes, combining the best of local architecture with their own sense of whimsical design.

Today, many expatriate homes and holiday rental villas have imaginative fusions of styles and materials while still retaining the funda-

buildings for people to pray. Instead, praying is done seated on the ground in front of shrines, rain or shine, day or night.

Contemporary homes and hotels

The Balinese are known for borrowing ideas from other cultures, both East and West, and blending them together in unique ways. Chinese influences (see page 41) are visible in some temple structures and in the concept of household pavilions facing a central courtyard. Some palaces blend European and East Asian elements, as in the Dutch-style Bale Maskerdam and Chinese-style Bale Pemandesan at the Puri Agung Karangasem palace in Amlapura.

mentals of traditional Balinese form and function (although by the same token there are quite a few ill-considered architectural hybrids).

Thatched bamboo bungalows have attracted visitors ever since the first hotel in this style opened on Kuta beach in the 1930s. Colonial authorities, who built more European-style accommodation unsuitable for the tropics, dismissed them as unsanitary "native huts".

During the 1980s, the trend was towards the florid, with grand lobbies, soaring roofs and ornamented surfaces. Since the 1990s, the design has become more sparse, with luxurious suites using textured stone walls, marble floors and natural materials for furnishings. Foreign architects like Australians Peter Muller (Oberoi in Seminyak and Amandari in Ubud) and Kerry Hill (Amannusa in Nusa Dua) and Malaysian Cheong Yew Kuan (Como Shambhala Estate near Ubud), have championed the use of natural materials like rough stone and unfinished wood. Retaining the Balinese architectural aesthetic, they have enclosed the traditional pavilions with big picture windows. In smaller places the interior is left whole but verandahs are added, hidden from view by surrounding walls like a traditional compound. Some of the best Bali-style hotels – such as Amandari in Kedewatan, and Alila Ubud and Hanging Gardens in Payangan, all north of Ubud, and Amankila in Manggis near Candidasa – are situated in spectacular natural settings that show off the architecture.

Gardens and landscaping

The average Balinese traditionally did not have need for a home garden as plants could thrive anywhere in the vicinity; and the open central courtyard of a home was usually kept free of plants, since the area was used for ceremonies. Surrounding walls deliberately kept the civilised compound safe and separate from the natural and wild world outside. Although a few wealthy Balinese or royalty built pleasure pavilions in artificial ponds, such as Taman Tirtagangga and Taman Ujung in east Bali, they were mostly influenced by European ideas. A few older temples, such as the beautiful moat-surrounded Pura Taman Ayun in Mengwi, are unusual.

The expatriate community probably introduced landscaping as an integral part of embellishing hotels and homes, but things really began to change during the 1990s when local authorities began road side tree plantings to spruce up villages for competitions. More Balinese who worked in hotels with landscaped gardens also brought the idea home. This created a minor industry in ornamental plants, with rice fields near Sanur and Mas growing all sorts of flowering trees, decorative shrubs and potted plants.

Many domestic compounds now have attractive gardens with grassy areas, flower shrubs, bonsai plants and paved walkways. Private homes allow for more integrated contact with

nature in smaller spaces. Even temples have received the same attention, although some over-zealous devotees have unfortunately covered many dirt courtyards with concrete to keep worshippers dry during rain – but roasting them on a sunny day.

Today, any hotel that lays claim to Balinese architecture must have lots of grassy lawns, flowering plants and shrubs along meandering paths, fishponds with fountains, tropical trees shading intimate pavilions, and even bathrooms open to the sky, complete with interior mini-gardens. Some have gone for a more natural look by keeping as many original trees as possible and building around them.   ❑

LEFT: Balinese villa at the Alila Ubud, with breathtaking views of the Payangan valley. **RIGHT:** lush gardens at the Watergarden Hotel Candidasa.

BALI

A detailed guide to the island, with the principal sites clearly cross-referenced by number to the maps.

Some of the most overused clichés in travel writing have been used to describe Bali: exotic, seductive, enchanting, magical. Although these adjectives succinctly convey the charms of this island and less florid praise would seem inadequate, after a while they lose their power to convince – leaving the writer with a real dilemma.

For a tiny island in the world's largest archipelago, Bali has an astonishing diversity. The southern region of Badung, the urban and commercial centre of Bali, is where most visitors play and party, mainly in the beach towns of Kuta, Legian and Seminyak. Yet south Bali is not without redemption, for behind the blatant commercialism lie some of the island's most traditional aspects. In the regions of Gianyar and Bangli, the contours become softer, the villages smaller and the culture more unfettered. Bali's earliest kingdoms carved out realms in these fertile lands and left behind a legacy of ancient temples. Ubud especially is a magnet for culture, with many of its surrounding villages specialising in some form of the arts.

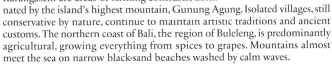

Eastwards in the regions of Klungkung and Karangasem are areas of striking contrasts, dominated by the island's highest mountain, Gunung Agung. Isolated villages, still conservative by nature, continue to maintain artistic traditions and ancient customs. The northern coast of Bali, the region of Buleleng, is predominantly agricultural, growing everything from spices to grapes. Mountains almost meet the sea on narrow black-sand beaches washed by calm waves.

Western Bali, the region of Jembrana and part of Buleleng, is sparsely populated yet culturally diverse; at times dry, at times lush and ignored by most travellers. A national park with rare wildlife anchors this part of the island. Finally, once home to royal dynasties, the southwest Tabanan region is Bali's rice basket, its sloping plains watered by crater lakes nestled under hulking volcanoes.

Take time to explore the many contrasts of this beautiful island; as well as a stunning landscape you will find an intense spirituality, and a warm, gentle, friendly people who refer to tourists as *tamu* – 'guests'. ❑

PRECEDING PAGES: the sacred site Pura Ulun Danu Bratan, north Bali; on the beach, Gili Twanangan, Gili Islands. **LEFT:** at Taman Ujung. **ABOVE:** tending to the grounds at Bali Botanical Gardens in the north.

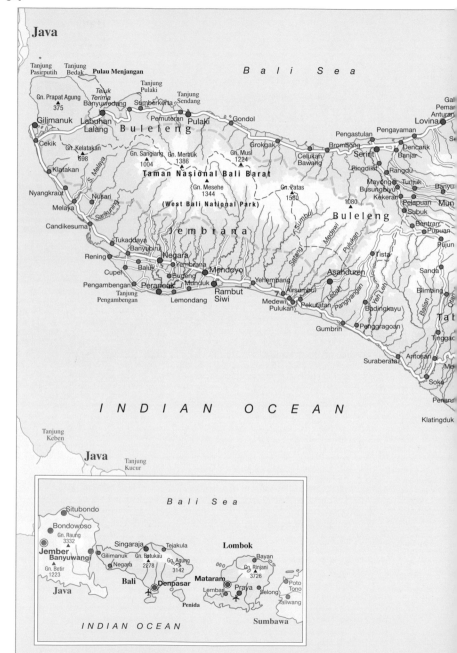

Java

Tanjung Pasirputih   *Tanjung Bedak*   **Pulau Menjangan**   *B a l i   S e a*

Tanjung Pulaki

Gn. Prapat Agung
375

Teluk Terima   Banyuwedang   Sumberkema   *Tanjung Sendang*

Gilimanuk   Labuhan Lalang   B u l e l e n g   Pemuteran   Pulaki   Gondol   Gal Pemar Anturan

Cekik   Gn. Kelatakan 698   Pengastulan   Pengayaman   Lovina   Se

Klatakan   Gn. Sangiang 1004   Gn. Merbuk 1386   Gn. Musi 1224   Grokgak   Celukan Bawang   Brombong   Seririt   Dencarik   Banjar

Nyangkraut   Taman Nasional Bali Barat   Ringdikit   Rangdu   Mayong   Tunjuk   Banyu

Nusari   Gn. Mesehe 1344   Gn. Patas 1560   Busungbiyu   Kekeran   Pelapuan   Mun

Melaya   (West Bali National Park)   1080   B u l e l e n g   Subuk

Candikesuma   J e m b r a n a   Bantiran   Pupuan

Tukaddaya   Pujun

Rening   Banyubiru   Negara   Tista

Cupel   Baluk   Yembrana   Asahduren   Sanda

Pengambengan   Budeng   Munduk   Mendoyo   Yehembang   Blimbing

Tanjung Pengambengan   Perancak   Lemondang   Rambut Siwi   Airsumbul   Pangiyangan   Badingkayu   Tat

Medewi Pulukan   Pekutatan   Tinggac

Gumbrih   Penggragoan   Me

Suraberata   Antosari   Soka

I N D I A N   O C E A N   Penaru

Klatingduk

Tanjung Keben

Java   *Tanjung Kucur*

B a l i   S e a

Situbondo

Bondowoso

Gn. Raung 3332

Jember   Banyuwangi   Singaraja   Tejakula   **Lombok**

Gilimanuk   Gn. Batukau   Bayan   Gn. Betir 1223   Negara   2278   Gn. Agung 3142   Gn. Rinjani 3726

Java   **Bali**   **Denpasar**   **Mataram**   Poto Tono   Lembar   Praya   Selong

Penida   Taliwang   **Sumbawa**

I N D I A N   O C E A N

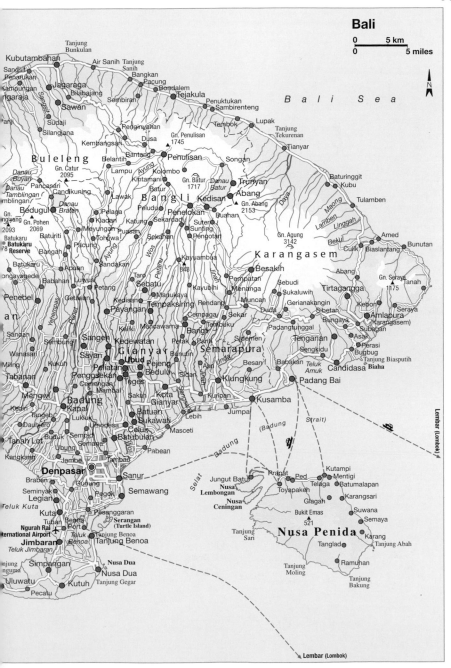

Bali

0 — 5 km
0 — 5 miles

N

Bali Sea

SOUTH BALI

Balinese cosmology considers the sea to be inauspicious. Yet it is on the sandy beaches of South Bali that most travellers end up, and where the widest choice of hotels, restaurants, bars and shops are. Culture hounds who search hard enough will find a sprinkling of temples, markets and museums.

Southern Bali is the first stop for most visitors when they arrive on the island. And it's not surprising. The best beaches are to be found here, anchored by a tourism infrastructure that caters to every creature comfort, from luxury beachfront resorts and fine restaurants to trendy bars and pampering spas. While the area's bustling beaches by day and non-stop bar-hopping and dancing after hours can prove all too frenetic for a restful holiday, this part of Bali is without doubt one of the island's great draws.

The **Badung** district is the location of Ngurah Rai International Airport and the capital Denpasar, a typically busy Indonesian city. South of the city are Bali's beach side tourist enclaves of Kuta, Legian, Seminyak and Jimbaran along the southwestern coast, and Sanur, Nusa Dua and Tanjung Benoa on the southeast stretch. South Bali covers just one-tenth of the island but is Bali's most heavily populated area.

DENPASAR

A growing metropolis of more than 700,000 people, **Denpasar ❶** (meaning "North of the Market", which indicates how much the city has grown) is a perennially busy city of winding

alleys, illogical one-way streets, pungent smells and home to more cars per capita than Jakarta, Indonesia's capital. If your mind has been unwinding on the beach, it may well be jerked back into reality in Denpasar. There are more than a few jewels to be found in Bali's capital city, most of them within a short hop of each other.

Taman Puputan

At the corner of Jalan Udayana and Jalan Surapati is **Taman Puputan ❹** (Puputan Square), a large grassy

Main attractions
MUSEUM BALI
DENPASAR'S MARKETS
MUSEUM LE MAYEUR
PURA LUHUR ULUWATU
JIMBARAN BEACH
WATERBOM PARK
SEMINYAK'S RESTAURANTS
PURA TANAH LOT

LEFT: Kendongan fish market.
RIGHT: surfer on Kuta Beach.

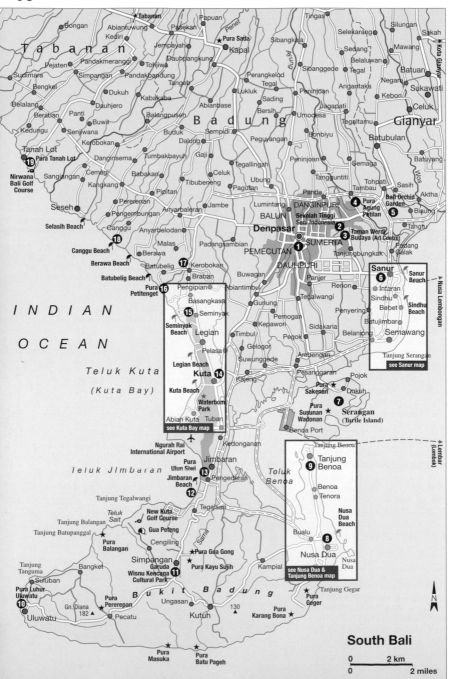

South Bali

0   2 km

0   2 miles

open space commemorating the last battle between the king of Badung and the Dutch militia in 1906. Thousands of Balinese warriors armed only with *keris* (daggers) and spears charged against the line of Dutch soldiers in a tragically heroic sacrifice. They died either by their own hands or by Dutch bullets in a Balinese ritual known as *puputan*. Today, the slaughter of the estimated 600 to 2,000 Balinese is commemorated with the large bronze statue of an adult and two children going to battle armed with bamboo staves, spears and daggers. A solemn ceremony is held here every 20 September to commemorate the tragic event. The space gets busy around sunset and on weekends when people gather to relax and socialise.

At the northwest corner of the square, at the main intersection of Jalan Veteran and Jalan Surapati, is **Catur Mukha**, a great statue with four faces and eight arms. Erected in 1972, it represents Hindu gods of the four main directions: Iswara or Ishvara (east), Brahma (south), Mahadewa (west), and Wisnu or Vishnu (north).

Museum Negeri Propinsi Bali

On the east side of the field is **Museum Negeri Propinsi Bali** **B** (State Museum of Bali Province), more simply known as **Museum Bali** (Sat–Thu 8am–4pm, Fri 8.30am–1pm; charge; tel: 0361-222680). Established in 1932 by the Dutch government, the displays present a comprehensive history of Bali's social and cultural development from prehistoric times to the early 20th century. Items are presented without specific dates of origin, but fortunately English-speaking guides are on hand.

The museum is notable for its fine architecture. The *candi bentar* (split gate) entrance, courtyards and *bale kulkul* (warning drum tower) are reminiscent of a temple, while displays are housed in palace-style buildings echoing architecture from different parts of Bali. Unfortunately, part of the collection is wasting away in storage due to lack of exhibition space and proper care.

The main **Gedung Karangasem** at the back resembles the palaces of east

Statue in Puputan Square.

BELOW: exterior of Museum Negeri Propinsi Bali.

Temple deity at Pura Jagatnatha.

Bali. Inside are prehistoric Neolithic stone implements and sarcophagi, and Buddhist and Hindu bronzes, along with implements for hunting, gathering and farming. Look for the ornate carrying cases for fighting-cock spurs. There are also wonderfully carved antique doors and animals that were used as supports for posts in pavilions.

Gedung Buleleng to its right belongs to the northern palace style and has impressive displays of beautiful wedding costumes, dance masks and ritual items such as tooth-filing implements and human effigies made from silver pieces, and Chinese coins used in death rites. The windowless **Gedung Tabanan** to the right, in the palace style of southwest Bali, displays mainly traditional textiles inside.

Pura Jagatnatha

Adjacent to the museum is **Pura Jagatnatha C** (daily daylight hours; donation). Built in 1953, the tem-

ple is dedicated to Sanghyang Widi Wasa, the Supreme Deity of Universal Order, who is manifested as Bali's many Hindu gods and goddesses, local spirits and divine ancestors. Have a look at this deity in a gilded relief at the very top of the only shrine inside, a towering white *padmasana* (lotus throne) that symbolises the Hindu-Buddhist universe. Supported by a tortoise entwined by two serpents, the receding platforms represent the levels of heaven on the cosmic Mount Meru.

Temple festivals held here on every full and new moon days have the atmosphere of a holiday celebration. Check exact dates with the Denpasar Tourist Office *(see margin tip opposite)*.

Denpasar's markets

Pasar Badung D (daily 6am–3pm) Bali's largest traditional produce market, is found west along Jalan Gajah Mada opposite the Badung River. Inside this four-storey building

Denpasar

are countless stalls selling fruits, vegetables, meat, seafood, spices, cooking utensils, ritual paraphernalia, clothing and much of everything else. For a negotiable fee, some women (at the front) will offer tours through the market's seemingly endless maze, stopping at stalls where they earn commissions on purchases made by their clients.

Across the rather polluted Badung River is **Pasar Kumbasari** Ⓔ (daily 8am–5pm), recently badly damaged by fire, but expected to be operational again soon. This is another sprawling market jammed with stalls mainly selling clothes and handicrafts, as well as small eateries hawking mostly local food. You can spend hours wandering around the market's dark and stifling interior, but keep a close eye on your belongings.

Nightlife in Denpasar revolves around the three huge *pasar malam* (local night markets) that operate at Pasar Kumbasari, **Pasar Kereneng**, near the bus station off Jalan Kamboja, and the **Pekambingan** (Goat Pens) area just off Jalan Diponegoro. Here, an array of temporary stalls offer all kinds of cooked food while hawkers push more unusual items like snake oil and charms as well as the ubiquitous T-shirts and sandals. More hygienic fare and surroundings are found nearby at the **Tiara Dewata Shopping Centre** along Jalan Udayana.

Pura Maospait

Although a bit out of the way but still within walking distance, **Pura Maospait** Ⓕ (daily daylight hours; donation) on Jalan Sutomo is the oldest temple in the city. It dates from the 14th century when invaders arrived from the East Javanese Majapahit (also called Maospait) kingdom to conquer Bali. Extensively damaged in 1917 by an earthquake, most of this brick temple has been rebuilt, although the section at the back still has some of the original architecture. A shrine with real deer antlers is dedicated to the deity of Majapahit. The entrance to the temple is flanked by large brick bas-relief figures of the mythological Garuda bird and the giant warrior hero Bima from the Hindu *Mahabharata* epic.

TIP

Across Jalan Surapati from Pura Jagatnatha is the Denpasar Government Tourist Office (Mon–Thu 8am–2pm; Fri 8am–noon; tel: 0361-234569). While the staff may not be very helpful, they do have a useful schedule of events happening in the city and other places in Bali.

BELOW: selling flowers in Pasar Badung to be used as offerings.

Close-up of a legong dancer – one of the many dances taught at Denpasar's Sekolah Tinggi Seni Indonesia.

Pasar Burung

Head north on Jalan Veteran and continue past the historic **Inna Bali Hotel**, which was built by the Dutch in 1927 and still retains its colonial atmosphere in spite of traffic zooming by outside. Further north at the entrance at Puri Satria is the **Pasar Burung ●** (Bird Market; daily 8am–3pm), a section of the larger **Pasar Satria**, which sells birds of all kinds along with puppies and other small mammals, tropical fish, reptiles, and even fighting crickets. Animal lovers are advised to avoid this place; the creatures are kept in cramped cages and tiny aquariums.

STSI

About 2km (1 mile) east of downtown Denpasar on Jalan Nusa Indah is the **Sekolah Tinggi Seni Indonesia ❷** (STSI) or Indonesia Institute of the Arts (Mon–Fri 8am–2pm; tel: 0361-227316). Started in 1967, the school has gone through several name changes over time. College-level students here study traditional dance, music, puppetry and visual arts, as well as the choreography of new classical styles and contemporary interpretations of traditional art forms.

The campus' **Lata Mahosadhi Museum** exhibits every sort of *gamelan* ensemble known. Another building features new works by students and faculty members in the visual arts programme. Visitors to the institute may watch the classes in progress and see the museum and gallery displays. Seek permission from the institute's secretary at the main office.

Taman Werdi Budaya

Just south of the arts institute is the **Taman Werdi Budaya ❸** (Cultural Development Park), more simply known as the **Art Centre** (Tue–Sun 8am–5pm; charge; tel: 0361-222776). Set among lush gardens and lotus ponds, Bali's main visual arts are represented in this large complex, including painting, woodcarving, shadow puppetry, silverwork, weaving, dance costumes and even some remarkable ivory carving. This is also where the annual Bali Arts Festival takes place (*see box below*).

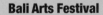

Bali Arts Festival

The Taman Werdi Budaya *(see above)* was built in 1973 to showcase Balinese art and culture, but little goes on here to indicate that. It really only comes alive during the Bali Arts Festival (www.baliartsfestival.com), which opens with a huge parade and runs for a month between June and July every year. Don't expect too much despite the hype surrounding this well-intentioned event. Most performances of traditional and contemporary music, dance and drama occur only at night, with many of the arts and crafts booths closing around lunchtime and re-opening in the evening. The food and merchandise stalls are the only places operating continuously.

Puri Kesiman and Pura Agung Petilan

On the main road from Denpasar to Gianyar stands **Puri Kesiman** (no entry), the residence of one of three royal families that once ruled the Badung kingdom. The towering gates and high brick walls are typical of the southern architectural style. Peer through the gates for interesting glimpses of royal life.

Just east of the palace and on the same side of the main road is **Pura Agung Petilan** ❹ (daily daylight hours; donation), an important temple for many Balinese. The slender red-brick gate is beautifully proportioned while inside the bare court-yard are several meeting pavilions for the deities, one of them with a cave-like opening in the base housing stone figures of the underworld – the tortoise and serpents that support the cosmos. During ceremonies here, villagers bring their sacred images, along with Barong and Rangda masks, in colourful, noisy processions. After praying, scores of men, women and even children become violently possessed, circling the cockfighting pavilion outside while stabbing themselves with sharp daggers.

Bali Orchid Garden

Heading east, the main road from Tohpati to Sanur is lined with many shops growing and selling all kinds of ornamental plants and flowers that have become popular among the Balinese for their homes. The **Bali Orchid Garden** ❺ (daily 8am–6pm; charge; tel: 0361-466010; www. baliorchidgardens.com) offers a more organised experience for orchid lovers. The garden is located at the junction of the bypass road and the coastal road at Padanggalak. A huge variety of orchids that bloom throughout the year are on display, and many of them are for sale. Organised tours are available but call ahead to ask first.

SANUR AREA

During the 1930s, **Sanur** ❻ was little more than a tucked-away beach with barely a hotel to its name. Its guileless charm attracted modest interest from a handful of foreign artists who settled here. By the 1950s, the first cluster of bungalows in Sanur had been built, attracting international travellers.

A Sukarno-era project and something of an eyesore, the 10-storey **Inna Grand Bali Beach Hotel** at the northern end of Sanur beach was built with Japanese reparation money given to Indonesia for hardships suffered during World War II. When the hotel first opened in 1966, it was a source of wonder to the Balinese, with its running water, electricity and lifts. It was Bali's only high-rise structure at the time. Gutted by a fire in 1992, it was refurbished and re-opened two years later.

Meanwhile, other hotels have followed in its wake, and the beach front is lined by establishments with access roads crowded with kiosks selling tourist souvenirs. A wise government regulation forbidding build-

BELOW: fishing boat on Sanur beach.

A charcoal drawing of the Balinese legong *dancer Ni Polok by Belgian artist Jean Le Mayeur de Merpres.*

ings taller than a coconut palm (or 15 metres/50ft) has allowed Sanur to retain its modest character. But while the rule remains in the books, new construction seems to have found creative ways around the law.

Still, the area has managed to retain its heritage as a community headed by *brahmana* (caste of high priests) and as a centre of black magic. Offshore looms the island of **Nusa Penida** *(see page 160)*, home of Ratu Gede Mas Mecaling, the great fanged lord of supernatural forces. Violent trance performances still occur during festivals at temples beside Sanur's luxury hotels.

Sanur's golden-sand beach is calm and shallow, leaving great swathes of sandy mud and coral stretching for hundreds of metres at low tide, when the water can recede to your waist (and sometimes knees). When the tide is high, however, Sanur offers windsurfing and sailing, along with the numbing drone of jet skis.

Museum Le Mayeur

There are few historical sights in Sanur. The only surviving place from the romantic, artistic years of the 1930s is that of the Belgian painter Jean Le Mayeur de Merpres (1880–1958), who moved to Bali in 1932 and lived here until his death. **Museum Le Mayeur** (Tue–Sun 8am–2pm; charge; tel: 0361-286164) is found just on the beach north of the Inna Grand Bali Beach Hotel. Inside its walls are tropical gardens full of statues, luxuriant gold and crimson carvings, and Le Mayeur's paintings, mostly of his wife, Ni Polok, a renowned *legong* dancer whom Le Mayeur married when she was only 15 years old. Ni Polok bequeathed the property to the government after she died in 1985. The paintings are not in mint condition, due to the salty air, but the atmosphere of the Balinese-style home-studio is like a time capsule of tropical tranquillity.

Pura Segara

Just south of the Inna Grand Bali Beach Hotel is **Pura Segara ❶** (daily daylight hours; donation), an unusual temple made entirely of coral that is dedicated to the god of the sea. Some of the statues and shrines are painted in bright (and rather tacky) colours. Profits from the restaurant at the front, which serves tasty seafood in an idyllic setting, are ploughed into supporting the temple and its surrounding community.

Pura Belanjong

At the southern end of Sanur is **Pura Belanjong ❶** (daily daylight hours; donation). This temple houses the island's oldest example of writing, known as Prasasti Belanjong, set on an inscribed 177cm (70ins) tall stone pillar. Dating from AD 913 but found only in the early 1930s, the pillar is not much to look at but is significant because of the two forms of writing it contains, in Old Balinese and in Sanskrit, which indicate the presence of Hindu influence three centuries before the arrival of Java's Hindu Majapahit court.

Pulau Serangan

Once reached only by boat during high tide or by wading across the strait during low tide, the tiny island of **Pulau Serangan ❼**, south of Sanur, is now accessible by a causeway. Turtles once came to lay their eggs here, earning it the nickname Turtle Island. But the beaches were filled in as a result of a grandiose project to turn the island into a tourist resort that ultimately failed. In fact, most of the natural terrain was flattened, and the Bugis fishing community from Sulawesi, which had lived here for generations, was forced to leave; they are returning, however, and there is quite a big harbour here. There is not much to see except environmental destruction in the name of "progress".

On the northwest end of this island is **Pura Sakenan** (daily daylight hours; donation), a small but very important temple for Balinese people. Although not much to look at in terms of architecture, the ceremony here on the Sunday after Kuningan attracts worshippers from all over south Bali. Sacred Barong

Pura Sakenan on the small island of Pulau Serangan.

BELOW: tree on the beach at Sanur.

and Rangda masks are brought, and many people become possessed by spirits.

BUKIT BADUNG

Connected to the mainland by a low, narrow isthmus, the craggy limestone peninsula of **Bukit Badung** (Badung Hill) rises almost 200 metres (660ft) above sea level. Cacti thrive on this arid land, with some areas used for grazing cattle. Good surfaced roads meander across the peninsula bringing development to the area, and scenic vantage points afford breathtaking vistas of Bali with the peaks of distant volcanoes poking above clouds, turbulent waves churning below coastal cliffs and dramatic sunsets over the ocean.

This is also where you will find the up-market beach resort areas of Nusa Dua and Tanjong Benoa on the east coast, and Jimbaran on the west coast, each studded with luxury hotels and accommodation. South of

Jimbaran are the beaches that draw surfers from the world over with their renowned barrels and surf breaks.

Nusa Dua

Strung out on the eastern coast of Bukit Badung, **Nusa Dua** ❽ (Two Islands) is a slightly clinical paradise in a ribbon-wrapped package. A purpose-built luxury hotel enclave sprawling in the middle of a coconut grove and alongside a white sand beach, it caters mainly to the up-market traveller, especially those seeking refuge from the pushy hawkers found elsewhere – they are banned from Nusa Dua, although they continue to flock to its edges. Thin on local ambience, it was built during the 1980s on land that was deemed unsuitable for agriculture by the local government, which was intent on separating tourists from locals.

Today, five-star luxury hotels complete with in-house dining, entertainment and sports facilities line the

BELOW: banana boat ride at Nusa Dua, just one of the many water sports on offer.

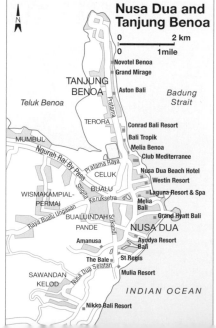

lovely white-sand beach; one stretch of it, separated by a tiny spit of land, is even prettier and less crowded than the other *(see margin tip)*.

There are a number of independent restaurants in the area including a stretch of decent eateries at Pantai Mengiat near Bualu village, and more at the Bali Collection mall, which is home to expensive boutiques and a department store.

Tanjung Benoa

For many years the fishing village of **Tanjung Benoa ⑨** (Harbour Cape), on a long peninsula off the eastern-most end of Bukit Badung, was over-looked by developers. This oversight has actually worked to the benefit of the area, which still retains its traditional Balinese village atmosphere. Smaller hotels incorporating local building styles and materials line the shore. The white-sand beach can be disappointingly calm as the waters are sheltered by a ribbon of coral reefs in the distance. It is, how-ever, ideal for water sports. Although Benoa village doesn't have any grand sights, a walk north up the peninsula

will reveal a multicultural community, dating from its years as a trading centre, reflected in the Hindu, Buddhist, Islamic and Christian religious sites.

Both Tanjung Benoa and Nusa Dua are now accessible via a new scenic highway, a tolled causeway bridge stretching across the Gulf of Benoa, 12.7 km (8 miles) in length and completed in 2012.

Pura Luhur Uluwatu

At the western tip of Bukit Badung peninsula, where rocky precipices drop almost 100 metres (330ft) to the turbulent ocean below, is **Pura Luhur Uluwatu ⑩**, or Temple above the Headstone (daily daylight hours; charge). This small but very important sacred site sits on top of a dramatic promontory; the short path left of the temple leads along the cliff top to breathtaking views.

Originally dating from the 10th century, Pura Luhur Uluwatu is one of the major sea temples revered by many Balinese. The legendary 16th-century Javanese priest Danghyang Nirartha helped to establish this

Keep a close eye on the monkeys when visiting Pura Luhur Uluwatu – their cuteness can be deceiving.

BELOW: Pura Luhur Uluwatu is perched on a dramatic cliff side.

Bukit Badung's famous surfing beaches are best tackled by more experienced surfers.

BELOW: a quieter moment on Kuta beach, usually a hotbed of tourists and commercialism.

temple, and it is said that he achieved enlightenment here.

The temple's *candi bentar* (split gate) is flanked by carvings in the shape of wings. The entrance to the second courtyard is an arched gateway guarded by statues of Ganesha, the elephant-headed god revered as the remover of obstacles. The innermost sanctuary is off limits to those who are not praying. Beware of the aggressive monkeys residing here.

Part of the temple actually fell into the sea during the early 1900s, which was an omen of the impending destruction of the royal courts that soon followed. More recently, lightning struck some shrines during the late 1990s, again an omen of the economic and political troubles that befell Bali and Indonesia in 1998. The temple was renovated soon after these events.

Surfing beaches

Just north of the temple, the western end of Bukit Badung is well known among surfers. Due to the dangerous reefs and strong currents, however, only experienced riders should attempt

the tricky waves that swell from April to September. Viewers can watch the action from the shore, but the beaches are not ideal for swimming.

Among the famous surfing beaches stretching along the dramatic northwest coast of the peninsula are **Uluwatu**, **Suluban**, **Padang Padang**, **Impossibles**, **Bingin**, **Dreamland** (renamed New Kuta Beach) and **Balangan**.

Garuda Wisnu Kencana Cultural Park

Return to the middle of Bukit Badung and head north, turning right at the entrance road to the **Garuda Wisnu Kencana Cultural Park ⓫** (daily 8am–10pm; charge; tel: 0361-703603; www.gwk-culturalpark.com). This grandiose monstrosity, started during the mid-1990s and which may never be completed, is supposed to showcase Balinese art and culture.

The focus of the 250-hectare (618-acre) site will be a 66-metre (200ft) high bronze statue of the Hindu god of life, Wisnu (Vishnu), riding upon his Garuda sunbird, built on a hill that rises to 146 metres (450ft). Today,

only the armless head and torso of Wisnu sticks out from the ground; on a nearby cliff protrudes the head of Garuda, the winged messenger. Rarely used amphitheatres, along with a few galleries, shops and restaurants that are mostly empty and overpriced, are found at this hot and unappealing site. Huge blocks of limestone with walkways carved between them create a completely artificial atmosphere. It is best avoided unless one has a lot of time and the inclination to see a classic case of wasted resources.

Jimbaran

North of Bukit Badung is the stretch of beach known as **Jimbaran** ⑫, an exclusive luxury resort area that hugs the coast south of Kuta. This lovely crescent-shaped bay bordered by grey-sand beaches is pounded by the same thundering surf as Kuta. Its southern end is anchored by the deluxe Four Seasons Jimbaran, from where the Ngurah Rai International Airport is clearly visible (but thankfully not close enough to hear the noise of jets landing and taking off).

Go to the beach early in the morning to watch fishing boats bringing in their daily catch. The village is justly celebrated for its open-air restaurants that open around sunset right on the beach, all serving delicious and freshly grilled seafood. In October 2005, however, Jimbaran's peace was shattered when bombs were set off by Javanese terrorists at two of its beach-side eateries. The restaurants have been rebuilt and business is, thankfully, booming again.

Pura Ulun Siwi

Just across from the main market in Jimbaran village is the stately **Pura Ulun Siwi** ⑬ (daily daylight hours; donation), a large irrigation society temple dominated by a towering *meru* (pagoda). Inside, the shrines are oriented to the west, in the direction of the former kingdom of Mengwi that once owned the sacred site, the holy mountain of Gunung Batukau *(see page 197)* and the distant Gunung Semeru, far away in East Java.

KUTA AREA

The Kuta area comprises Tuban at its southern end and continues

TIP

Jimbaran village has a very important set of Barong and Rangda sacred masks, along with their attendant figures. Performances occur fairly regularly in the street in front of Pura Ulun Siwi, with men in trances violently stabbing themselves with sharp daggers.

LEFT: Wisnu statue at the Garuda Wisnu Kencana Cultural Park.
BELOW: waxing a surfboard on Kuta beach.

Kuta Bay

0   500 m
0   500 yds

The Samaya
La Lucciola
The Legian
Kerobokan

Bali Oberoi
Ko de ta
BASANKASA
PADANGSUMBA
SUMBA

Breezes
Resort

Anantara Seminyak
Resort
Dhyanapura
Resort
Jl. Dhyanapura

SEMINYAK

Rama Garden Hotel
Gang Arjuna
LEGIAN
KAJA

Puri Naga

Kumala Pantai Hotel
Jl. P. Bagus Taruna
Jayakarta

Puri Tantra Bungalows
Maharta Beach Hotel
Sari Beach Hotel
All Seasons Resort

Bali Sani
LEGIAN

Legian Beach

Padma Resort Bali

Casa Padma Suites

Bali Mandira
Jl. Padma

Legian Beach Hotel

Legian Nirwana
Jl. Melasti
Bank
BNI

Alam Kul Kul
Un's Hotel
Legian
Paradiso

Adhi Jaya
Benesari
Matahari
Bungalows

Grand Istana Rama Hotel
Pt Central
Currency
Exch.
Agung
Cottages

Barong
Bali
M-Bar-Go

Beachwalk Shopping Mall
Gang Poppies II
Sky
Garden
Lounge

Kuta Seaview
Maharani Hotel
Satriya Cott.

Gang Poppies Cott.

Kuta Beach
Poppies
Yulia Beach
Inn

Hotel Mercure Kuta
Poppies
Bemo Stn.
(Bus Stn.)

Hard Rock Hotel
Jl. Raya Pantai Kuta

Inna Natour
Kuta Beach Hotel
Matahari
Kuta Square
BCA Bank

Jl. Singasari
Chinese
Temple

Kuta Paradiso
Agung
Beach
Bungalows

Discovery Shopping Mall
Waterbom
Park
Mad Lange
Tomb

Discovery Kartika Plaza
Bali Dynasty
Bali Rani Hotel

Santika Beach
Ramada Bintang Bali
Kimia
Farma
Pharmacy

Sandi Phala

Risata Bali
Resort
J Boutique Hotel

Holiday Inn
Resort Baruna
Hotel
Mandara
ABIAN KUTA

Bali Segara
TUBAN

Patra Bali Resort

Airport Ngurah Rai

Teluk

Kuta

LEGIAN

KUTA

Pyramid

Jl. Raya Seminyak

Sunset Road

Jl. Tanjung Mekar

Jl. Legian

Jl. Kartika Plaza

Gang Nandir

Jl. Raya Tuban

Jl. Raya Kuta

north into Kuta proper, then Legian, Seminyak and Kerobokan. In reality, however, the borders in between these villages are invisible, as one area merges into the other.

The original villagers of **Kuta** ⑭ were farmers, fishermen and metalsmiths. Very few visitors today are aware that in former times Kuta was also a leper colony and slave station, with poor soil. Cynics might suggest that there are parallels to be drawn with the hordes that flock today to this tourist enclave for the combination of sun, sand, sea, surf (and sex). For many, Kuta is a veritable garden of pleasures, while others decry its plunge into rampant commercialism.

Danish entrepreneur Mads Lange (1806–56) was the first to put Kuta on the map in 1839 when he opened a trading centre that soon developed into a thriving port. In 1937, an American couple, Robert and Louise Koke, built the first bungalow-style hotel on the beach, attracting many visitors until the Japanese forces invaded in February 1942 during World War II.

Kuta once again fell into obscurity until the advent of mass tourism during the 1970s. At first, villagers looked askance at the nearly naked foreigners romping on the beach, a place which the Balinese traditionally viewed as close to the underworld. But they saw profits to be made and so converted their homes into cheap *losmen* (guesthouses) for tourists.

Both Balinese and tourists can be found along the broad sandy beach day after day, swimming, surfing – the waters off Kuta are among the best places to learn this sport – sunbathing and strolling. Countless touts hawking cheap souvenirs roam the beach while women offering nail painting, hair braiding and massages huddle beneath umbrellas and trees. Inland Kuta is packed with a jumble of bars, souvenir shops, surf shops, tattoo parlours, travel offices, accommodation, restaurants and fast-food

joints. Unregulated street hawkers are an increasing annoyance, and the congested streets and confusing one-way traffic is mayhem, banishing all traces of an island paradise. Still, if one stares out to sea and forgets the commercial swirl behind, the legendary Kuta sunset – when the conditions are right – is just as beautiful as it was a century ago.

Crime has escalated, so don't get too starry-eyed and romantic on the beach at night. On 12 October 2002, bombs planted by Indonesian Muslim terrorists exploded at two packed nightclubs, killing more than 200 people, mostly foreign tourists. A memorial across the street from the bomb site at Sari Club opened in late 2002. The area was slowly recovering when three bombs exploded again barely three years later on 1 October 2005, one at a busy restaurant in Kuta Square and two on Jimbaran Beach. Fortunately, the casualty rate was much lower this time.

Shopping at Kuta

Shopping options abound along Kuta's main street, **Jalan Legian**, and just about every side street all the way up to **Jalan Melasti**. At its southern end, near the Bemo Corner (Stasion Bemo) intersection, Jalan Legian turns right into **Jalan Pantai Kuta** where the **Matahari Kuta Square**, a shopping area centred around a department store, is found. Jalan Pantai Kuta and its slew of commerce then continues north, parallel to the beach, taking in the open-air Beachwalk Shopping Mall with its eco-friendly design incorporating a wide choice of shops and restaurants, the digital-format **Cinema XXI**, and the **Museum Kain** displaying rare batik cloth.

Tuban

Southern Kuta is known as **Tuban**. Presided over by the modern Discovery shopping mall, the atmosphere here is less frantic with many large family-oriented hotels, of which nearly all have direct access to the beach. The area therefore boasts family restaurants and attractions such as Waterbom Park and Bali Slingshot.

The hotels along this stretch are mainly mid-range to expensive. If looking for budget accommodation, head to Kuta proper. For a shopping

Surfboards for rental at Kuta. The waters here are among the best places to learn surfing, but it is believed that the god of the sea claims at least one victim each year. Women who work here leave "canang" (coconut leaf tray) offerings at the high-tide mark daily to pacify spirits.

LEFT: stylish homeware for sale in Seminyak. **BELOW:** making lace in Seminyak.

Introduced to Asia by the Portuguese and Spanish, chillies are frequently planted between paddy fields. They range from plump and fiery to slender, milder ones, and appear in several typical Balinese dishes.

excursion, visit the beachfront **Discovery Mall**. Fully air-conditioned, the three-floor mall attracts plenty of custom with two department stores, global lifestyle branded boutiques, local retailers, beachside cafés, and more.

Waterbom Park

Along Jalan Kartika Plaza in Tuban is the **Waterbom Park** (daily 9am–6pm; charge; tel: 0361-755676; www.waterbompark.com) with spiralling slides, thrilling ramps, a meandering river and play areas, along with restaurants and a spa. There are lifeguards on duty all the time, although adults must accompany children under 12 years old (the Bombastic Aquatic Playground is specially designed for the latter). It can get crowded later in the day and especially at weekends with long queues. Be prepared to climb lots of steps to get to the top of the rides, but it's well worth it. Lockers and towels can be rented.

Legian

North of Jalan Melasti, the loud and obnoxious chaos of Kuta drops off perceptibly. The beach at **Legian** is the main centre of activity; although a bit more sedate than Kuta, don't

BELOW: football at sunset, Legian beach.

expect it to be completely free of traffic and commercialism. This is the preferred beach for many of Bali's expatriate population, although increasingly, residents are turning to the charms of Seminyak beach.

Seminyak

Further north is hip **Seminyak** ⑮, blessed with a wide sandy beach and thundering surf to frolic in. This once distant Kuta suburb is both the home of exclusive hotels like The Legian and The Oberoi Bali, and chic beach side restaurants like La Lucciola and Ku dé Ta. Accommodation ranges from modern budget hotels to toprange hotels and villas.

Seminyak's **Jalan Kayu Aya** (Laksmana) and **Jalan Abimanyu** (Dhyana Pura) are both action-packed streets: the former has a clutch of restaurants ranging from Italian to Japanese, together with a collection of enticing boutiques, while the latter is home to a string of live music bars, gay bars and clubs. A number of chic home furnishing and decor stores have also flourished along **Jalan Raya Seminyak** in recent years, selling silk cushion covers, coconut-wood artefacts and lamps made of indigenous materials.

Pura Petitenget

Pura Dalem Petitenget ⑯ (daily daylight hours; donation) in Seminyak is a small but key temple by the beach where many ceremonies are held. It was built in honour of a visit by the 16th-century Javanese priest Danghyang Nirartha, who came to Bali to escape from the then encroaching Islam. He left his box of betel-chewing ingredients here, which explains the name, "Temple of the Awesome Box". During the late 1990s, a nearby sacred tree fell on the temple and damaged its structures, which had to be rebuilt. Although the temple looks new, it has a rather haunting atmosphere because of its lonely location.

Kerobokan

The main road does not run near the coast, so getting to places along the southwest shore is via long but paved access roads through rice fields. As development creeps further up along the coast, the next village in line becomes the scene for future speculation. **Kerobokan ⓗ** now has a growing number of fine restaurants, furniture and antique stores, lavish expatriate homes and exclusive villas for holiday rentals, complete with the service of housekeepers, chefs and personal butlers.

Canggu

Further up the coast are beaches at **Batubelig** and **Berawa**, followed by **Canggu ⓘ**, a dark sand beach blessed with great ambience in what is becoming a fast developing area, favoured by expatriates, and presenting a wide choice of restaurants and cafés. It's also a popular surfing spot and known for its great surf breaks. More beaches at **Batu Mejan**, **Pererenan** and **Selasih** stretch all the way up to the border with the Tabanan region.

Pura Tanah Lot

Although located across the Badung border in the Tabanan region (*see page 191*), **Pura Tanah Lot ⓙ** (daily daylight hours; charge) is more easily reached from south Bali. Located on a picturesque rocky islet just offshore and with its shrines and tufts of foliage spilling over the cliffs, the temple is reminiscent of a Chinese painting. Sadly, the endless rows of souvenir stalls on the approach road diminish both the image and mood.

The founding of Pura Tanah Lot is attributed to the 16th-century high priest Danghyang Nirartha, who fled to Bali from Java because of the rise of Islam. During his travels, he was attracted to a light emanating from a point on the west coast where he stopped and meditated. Locals became entranced with Nirartha and began studying with him. However, a local leader became jealous and challenged the high priest. Unperturbed, Nirartha simply moved the place where he was meditating to the sea, thus giving its name – "Temple of the Land in the Sea". He tossed his sashes into the waves, which became transformed into venomous sea snakes; they supposedly still dwell in caves located in the base of the temple. The sacred snakes are considered as living guardians of the temple and prevent evil forces from trying to enter.

There are many other temples scattered around the area, among them **Pura Batu Bolong** (Temple of the Perforated Stone) that sits on a rocky outcropping with waves surging through a large opening below.

Visitors are not allowed into Pura Tanah Lot but can get a dramatic view of it from the opposite coast, especially at sunset (*see margin tip*).

Nearby **Pan Pacific Nirwana Bali Resort** has an excellent Greg Norman-designed golf course (open to the public), with spectacular views of rice fields, the ocean and Pura Tanah Lot. ❑

TIP

For maximum serenity, it's best to visit Pura Tanah Lot during the early morning hours. This way you'll avoid the hordes of tourists in search of the legendary sunset backdrop of the temple. In the evening, some strategically positioned cafés along the cliff top, just where the best sunset views are, charge inflated prices.

BELOW: Pura Tanah Lot is a major tourist magnet.

BEST RESTAURANTS, BARS AND CAFÉS

Restaurants

Price for a two-course meal for one including a non-alcoholic beverage:

$$$$ over Rp 300,000
$$$ Rp 200,000– 300,000
$$ Rp 100,000– 200,000
$ below Rp 100,000

Denpasar

The capital city sees mostly locals and domestic tourists, hence the many small Indonesian and Chinese restaurants in Denpasar, particularly along Jalan Teuku Umar. Don't expect much in terms of Western fare.

Feyloon
Jalan Raya Puputan, Renon, Denpasar. Tel: 0361-265733. Open: daily L & D. **$$$**
Arguably Bali's best Chinese restaurant specialising in seafood, Cantonese in style with a few Szechuan flourishes. Meat and vegetarian dishes also on offer.

Sanur

This still remains Bali's largest expatriate area today. The variety is expanding rapidly and new restaurants open regularly.

Arena Pub & Restaurant
Jalan By Pass Ngurah Rai 115, Sanur. Tel: 0361-287255. Open: daily 4pm (kitchen closes at 10.30pm), drinks till late. **$$$**
An Austrian/German and Central European menu accompanied by a big range of beers. A must for meat lovers but there are some seafood options as well.

Beach Café
Sindhu Beach, Sanur. Tel: 0361-282875. Open: daily B, L & D. **$**
Great breakfasts: eggs Benedict or Florentine, or ask for a real English breakfast. Salads and sandwiches can be enjoyed either on the sands or inside.

Café Batujimbar
Jalan Danau Tamblingan 75, Sanur. Tel: 0361-287374. **$$$**
This is a popular streetside café and long-time favourite of people who know Sanur. Dining takes place in an opensided pavilion or alfresco under the trees. Italian and Mexican dishes grace the menu, together with salads, homemade breads and cakes, herbal teas and booster fruit juices. Organic vegetables and herbs are grown at the owner's farm near Bedugul.

Massimo il Ristorante
Jalan Danau Tamblingan 206, Sanur. Tel: 0361-288942. Open: daily L & D. **$$$** www.balimassimo.com
This is a great Italian restaurant, set in an attractive open pavilion. The menu offers authentic specialities from Lecce in southeast Italy, where the owner-chef Massimo hails from. The pasta dishes and thin-crust wood-fired oven pizzas are delicious. Massimo does an excellent risotto with mushrooms and Italian sausage, as well as chicken, duck and fish specialities, and the best Italian ice cream in Bali.

Sanur Harum
Sanur Paradise Plaza, Jalan Hang Tuah 46, Sanur. Tel: 0361-281781. Open: daily L & D. **$$–$$$** www.sanurparadise.com
Classy, air-conditioned Chinese restaurant, serving mostly Cantonese and Szechuan dishes. Eat-asmuch-as-you-want dim sum is available daily.

Stiff Chilli
Jalan Kesumasari 11, Semawang, Sanur. Tel: 0361-288371. Open: daily B, L & D. **$$**
www.stiffchilli.com
A rustic open-sided pavilion beside the beach, serving Italian cuisine with an Asian twist. This highly respected restaurant is famous for its crispy-skinned, grilled sausages, freshly baked ciabatta bread, authentic Italian pizzas and pasta delights, such as the tricoloured fettuccine topped with creamy smoked marlin sauce.

Nusa Dua and Tanjung Benoa

The restaurant pickings are slim in this area and mainly confined to the large luxury hotels. The Bali Collection shopping mall has more than a dozen restaurants that offer a good range of eating options, but all are quite expensive when compared to elsewhere in Bali.

Bumbu Bali
Tanjung Benoa. Tel: 0361-774502. Open: daily L & D. **$$$**. www.balifoods.com
Beautifully presented and authentic Balinese dishes cooked by the former executive chef of the Grand Hyatt Bali. A multi-course *rijsttafel* meal comprising tiny portions of three appetisers, seven main courses and three desserts is a good introduction to the food of Bali. You can also sign up for cooking classes (see page 259).

The Italian Restaurant
Amanusa, Nusa Dua. Tel: 0361-772333. Open: daily D. **$$$$**
www.amanresorts.com
Rather unimaginative name but all is forgiven when you try its wellexecuted elegant Italian dishes either inside in air-conditioned comfort or on the romantic garden terrace.

Maguro Asian Bistro
Nusa Dua Beach Hotel.
Tel: 0361-771210. Open:
daily L & D. $$$
www.nusaduahotel.com
Open-air beach side dining with an array of inventive Asian dishes. Also has a selection of sushi and sashimi as well as *yakitori* (grilled skewered meats).

Raja's
Nusa Dua Beach Hotel.
Tel: 0361-771210.
Open: daily D. $$$$
www.nusaduahotel.com
An elegant, fine-dining Balinese restaurant, with *bebek betutu* (whole duck marinaded in spices, wrapped in palm leaves and slow-cooked) as the signature dish.

Spice
Conrad Hotel, Jalan Pratama Raya 168, Tanjung Benoa. Tel: 0361-778788.
Open: daily D. $$$$
www.conradhotels.com
The highlight here is the sensational seven-course menu of bite-sized portions. An à la carte menu is also available.

Jimbaran
Try any one of the grilled seafood restaurants that open around sunset all along the beach. Expect lots of smoke from the open-air barbecues but the setting is pleasant, and the food usually good. Apart from these, the choices are generally slim outside of the hotels.

Kuta
The haven for surfers, originally the only food choices here were cheap eats in the two lanes near the Poppies Hotel and uninspiring food served at hotels on the beach front and along Jalan Legian. These days, the professionals are moving in and the quality (and prices) fast rising, but the backpacker cheapies still exist along the many lanes that wind around Kuta.

Kori Restaurant and Bar
Gang Poppies 2, Kuta.
Tel: 0361-758605. Open:
daily L & D. $$$
www.korirestaurant.co.id
There's great atmosphere here to accompany Kori's wide range of Western and Balinese dishes, which place an emphasis on simple but flavourful tastes. Its grilled seafood is among its strengths.

Made's Warung Kuta
Jalan Pantai Kuta.
Tel: 0361-755297. Open:
daily B, L & D. $$
One of the original Kuta restaurants from the early 1980s and the first stop for many nostalgia-seekers revisiting Bali. Also has a second outlet, Made's Warung Seminyak (tel: 0361-732130), which is much nicer in terms of atmosphere.

TJ's Mexican Restaurant
Gang Poppies I, Kuta.
Tel: 0361-751093. Open:
daily B, L & D. $$
www.tjsbali.com
The first Mexican restaurant (actually Tex-Mex) in Bali, and still the best, serving large portions, margaritas, ice-cold beer and desserts. Nice garden setting.

Tuban
Sometimes referred to as South Kuta, this area has suddenly come to life with the opening of a slew of good restaurants.

Batan Waru
Bali Garden Hotel, Jalan Kartika Plaza, Tuban.
Tel: 0361-766303. Open:
daily L & D. $$$
www.baligoodfood.com
Branch of the famous Ubud eatery, serving excellent and delicious, value-for-money Indonesian, Balinese and Western favourites. Recommended are chilli prawns; *tum ayam* (spiced chicken steamed in a banana leaf); and *sop buntut* (Javanese oxtail soup).

Golden Lotus
Dynasty Hotel, Jalan Kartika Plaza, Tuban. Tel: 0361-752403. Open: daily L & D. $$$$. www.balidynasty.com
Quality Chinese (mainly Cantonese) food, with an extensive dim sum range served every day, and an eat-all-you-can buffet on Sundays and public holidays (11am–2.30pm).

Kunyit Bali
Hotel Santika, Jalan Kartika, Tuban. Tel: 0361-751267.
Open: daily L & D. $$
www.santikabali.com
Any one of its special menus offers a taste of indigenous Bali. Specials include green papaya and snail soup, pork stewed in turmeric and sweet soy, and *ayam panggang kalasan*, – chicken cooked in spiced coconut milk.

Ma Joly
Kupu Kupu Barong Beach Resort, Tuban. Tel: 0361-753780. Open: daily B, L & D. $$$$
www.kupubarong.com
Chic beachside French restaurant – sit indoors or on the beach. Try the fricassée of garoupa with prawns or toro tuna black pepper steak. Daily lunch specials a bargain.

Mama's
Jalan Raya Legian 99, Legian. Tel: 0361-751805.
Open: daily 24 hours. $$
www.bali-mamas.com
A German restaurant with four varieties of draught beer. Favourite dishes include *schlachtplatte*, made up of blood sausage, *liverwurst* and pork shoulder draped over a pile of sauerkraut and boiled potatoes.

Seminyak and Kerobokan
There is some blurring of boundaries between the Seminyak and Kerobokan areas, but here you'll find a mix of late-night bars and excellent restaurants. The so-called "Eat Street" – the loop from Jalan Laksmana/Kayu Aya through Jalan Petitenget – offers a huge range of cuisines at great prices.

Baku Dapa
Jalan Abimanyu, Seminyak.
Tel: 0361-731148. Open:
daily 24 hours. $

Price for a two-course
meal for one including a
non-alcoholic beverage:
$$$$ over Rp 300,000
$$$ Rp 200,000–
300,000
$$ Rp 100,000–
200,000
$ below Rp 100,000

Amazing small *warung*
serving many dishes from
Manado, such as the
breakfast porridge *bubur
Manado*. House speciali-
ty is *sop buntut* (oxtail
soup), the best in Bali.

Biku
Jalan Petitenget 888, Semi-
nyak. Tel: 0361-8570888.
Open: daily B, L & D. **$$$**
www.bikubali.com
Housed in a charming
150-year-old Javanese
teak building, Biku spe-
cialises in colonial Indo-
nesian dishes and after-
noon tea, as well as a
great selection of deli-
cious homemade cakes
and pies.

Breeze
The Samaya, Jalan Kayu
Aya, Seminyak. Tel: 0361-
732567. Open: daily L & D.
$$$$
www.thesamayabali.com
This fine dining restau-
rant has received rave
reviews for both its Asian
-accented Continental
cuisine and idyllic beach-
side setting. Start the
evening at about 6pm
with sunset cocktails at
the adjoining bar.

Café Marzano
Jalan Double Six, Seminyak.
Tel: 0361-733671. Open
Mon–Sat: B, L & D. **$$**
Busy Italian café with a
large antipasti selection,
also home-made pastas

and a selection of wood-
fired pizzas and calzones.

Chat Café
Jalan Kunti I 18, Seminyak.
Tel: 0361-732303. Open:
daily B, L & D. **$$**
www.chatcafebali.com
Hearty breakfasts, and a
large variety of Indone-
sian and Western snacks
and mains. Free Wi-fi.

Chez Gado Gado
Jalan Abimanyu 99, Semin-
yak. Tel: 0361-730955.
Open: daily B, L & D. **$$$**
Sit on the terrace under
the trees and watch
Bali's famous sunset
and the surf rolling in.
The lunch-time crisp-
skinned *wasabi* chicken
breast on a bed of
spiced Thai noodles is
fusion food at its best.

Gateway of India
Jalan Abimanyu. Tel: 0361-
732940. Open: daily L & D.
$$
Authentic northern Indi-
an food and a tandoori
oven in operation in the
evening. Branches in
Kuta (Jalan Pantai Kuta
11, tel: 0361-754463)
and Sanur (Jalan Danau
Tamblingan 103, tel:
0361-281579).

Grocer & Grind
Jalan Kayu Jati 3X, Ker-
obokan. Tel: 0361-730418.
Open: daily B, L & D. **$$$**
www.grocerandgrind.com
Stylish, perennially busy
bistro. Sandwiches, sal-
ads and the tapas tast-
ing plates are popular for
lunch; dinner has more
options. Free Wi-fi.

The Junction
Jalan Kayu Aya, Seminyak.
Tel: 0361-735610. **$$**
The Junction features

funky architecture in a
stylish interior. Specialis-
es in organic salads
made with gourmet
ingredients with tasty
sandwiches in the form
of panini, pitta pockets,
crêpes and baguettes.

Kaizan
Jalan Kayu Aya 33, Semin-
yak. Tel: 0361-742324.
Open: daily D. **$$$**
An air-conditioned area
downstairs serves Japa-
nese food – the speciali-
ty is *shabu-shabu* (select
two different broths and
then the ingredients) –
while an open-roof area
upstairs is dedicated to
Korean barbecue.

Khaima
Jalan Kayu Aya, Seminyak.
Tel: 0361-7423925. Open:
daily L & D. **$$$**
Atmospheric Moroccan-
style restaurant where
meats and vegetables
are steamed slowly in
spice-infused *tagine* cas-
seroles. Occasional belly
dance performances.

Ku De Ta
Jalan Kayu Aya, Seminyak.
Tel: 0361-736969. Open:
daily B, L & D; drinks till
late. **$$$$**
www.kudeta.net
Located right on Semin-
yak beach, Bali's hippest
and most famous restau-
rant and beach club is
upmarket and Australian-
managed with indoor and
outdoor dining areas. The
food is Modern Austral-
ian, and the sunset views
over the ocean are gor-
geous.

Kura Kura
Bali Oberoi, Jalan Kayu Aya,
Seminyak. Tel: 0361-

730361. Open: daily D. **$$$$**
www.oberoihotels.com
The venerable Bali Oberoi
can always be counted on
for its reliablity and old
world charm. Expect crea-
tive twists on the usual
Continental staples.

La Lucciola
Jalan Petitenget, Seminyak.
Tel: 0361-730848. Open:
daily B, L & D. **$$$$**
Come here for Mediter-
ranean-inspired food in a
laid-back setting – a big,
two-level thatched struc-
ture looking out over the
beach. A great place for
sunset cocktails.

La Sal
Jalan Drupadi 100, Semin-
yak. Tel: 0361-738321.
Open: Mon–Sat L, daily D.
$$$
www.lasalbali.com
Expect an excellent
selection of inventive
tapas and main courses.
An Argentinian-style
churrasco meal of grilled
meats is served nightly.

Made's Warung II
Jalan Raya Seminyak; Tel
0361 732 130. Open: daily
L & D. **$$$**
www.madeswarung.com
Famous for it's delicious
Indonesian food. This
restaurant is always
busy and traditionally-
styled building and large
open courtyard is partic-
ularly atmospheric.

Mannekepis
Jalan Raya Seminyak 2,
Seminyak. Tel: 0361-
8475784. Open: daily
10–1am. **$$$**
www.mannekepis-bistro.com
International jazz and
blues café with some
Belgian specials, such as

gentse waterzooi (creamy soup with chicken, potatoes and vegetables).

Mama San
Jalan Raya Kerobokan 135, Seminyak. Tel: 0361-730436. Open: daily D. $$$$
www.mamasanbali.com
Mama San serves elegant Asian comfort food in fine-dining style within a purpose-designed retro-vintage industrial warehouse. Enjoy a pre-dinner cocktail on tan leather chesterfields in the chic upstairs lounge, then dine downstairs on Chinese, Indonesian, Indian, Malay, Singaporean, Thai, Cambodian and Vietnamese cuisine.

Métis
Jalan Petitenget 6. Tel: 0361-737888. Open: Mon–Sat L, daily D. $$$$
This large and sophisticated fine dining restaurant, bar, lounge and gallery beside the rice fields serves French Mediterranean cuisine, including pan-seared foie gras with port and raspberry reduction, morello cherry and roasted apple.

Mykonos Taverna
Jalan Laksmana 57. Tel: 0361-733253. Open: daily L & D. $$
www.mykonos-bali.com
A small, simple, traditional Greek taverna with *bouzouki* music to match. Wonderful Greek dips, plus fish and lamb dishes all at reasonable prices can be ordered off the dinner menu.

Naughty Nuri's
Jalan Batubelig 41, Ker-obokan. Tel: 0361-847 6722. Open: daily B, L & D. $$ www.naughtynurisbali.com
On Jalan Batubelig not far from the beach end, you'll find Naughty Nuri's (an offshoot of the legendary establishment of the same name in Ubud) with nightly barbecues including delicious pork ribs and extraordinarily potent Martinis.

Panterai
Jalan Raya, Seminyak 17. Tel: 0361-732567. Open: daily L & D. $$$
www.pantarei-restaurant-bali.net
Stylish restaurant that serves a wide range of Greek specials, including mezze items like *krasato*, octopus sautéed in red wine and olive oil. Live music every evening.

Queen's Tandoor
Jalan Raya, Seminyak. Tel: 0361-732770. Open: daily L & D. $$$
www.queenstandoor.com
Both mild North Indian and spicy South Indian dishes cooked by Indian chefs, so expect the real deal. Upstairs is air-conditioned while downstairs is open air.

Ryoshi
Jalan Raya, Seminyak 17. Tel: 0361-731152. Open: daily L & D. $$
www.ryoshibali.com
Excellent-value Japanese food, such as sushi, sashimi, tempura and teppanyaki, an array of rice and noodle dishes and many veggie choices.

Sardine
Jalan Petitenget, Kerobokan.

Tel: 0361-738202. Open: daily D. $$$$
www.sardinebali.com
A bamboo pavilion where the emphasis is on gourmet fresh fish and seafood. More than half the restaurant's space is dedicated to a working rice field, ensuring that guests are always guaranteed gorgeous rural views.

Sarong
Jalan Raya Petitenget 19X, Kerobokan. Tel: 0361-737809. Open: daily D. $$$$
www.sarongbali.com
This stylishly chic restaurant and bar venue is packed full even on weeknights. Expect a palette of taste sensations from all over Asia.

Sate Bali
Jalan Kayu Aya. Tel: 0361-736734. Open: daily L & D. $$
For a superlative introduction to Balinese food, order the multi-course *rijsttafel* dinner. Sate Bali also runs an excellent cooking class – the owner and chef has a background in leading five-star hotels.

Taco Beach
Jl Kunti, Seminyak. $$
Small and simple restaurant beside the street with a cheerful colourful decor serving superb Californian-style Mexican food, including Balinese fusion dishes such as the Babi Guling burritos and Babi Guling tacos. Ingredients are fresh and prices are low.

Trattoria
Jalan Kayu Aya. Tel: 0361-737082. Open: daily D. $$

Packed almost every night of the week. Good pastas, excellent pizzas and salads as well as authentic Italian beef and seafood dishes.

Wah Wah Burger
Jalan Kayu Aya, Seminyak. Tel: 0361-736585. Open: daily B, L & D. $$$
www.wahwahburger.com
This is not any old burger joint. Specialising in sassy gourmet burgers, their top of the range is a burger topped with seared foie gras in a berry reduction. There's a stylish cocktail bar here too.

Warisan Restaurant
Jalan Raya Kerobokan 38, Br Taman, Kerobokan. Tel: 0361-731175/7492796. Open: daily L & D. $$$
www.warisanrestaurant.com
The former Kafe Warisan serves French and Mediterranean inspired cuisine and fine wines in a charming open air setting with a terrace that wraps around a lush central courtyard planted with frangipani trees. Try the chicken stuffed with goats cheese wrapped in bresaola served on a bed of quinoa.

Wild Orchid
Anantara Resort, Jalan Dhyana Pura, Seminyak. Tel: 0361-737773. Open: daily D. $$$$
www.bali.anantara.com
This chic restaurant overflows to the swimming pool, and the beach and sea are just beyond. Traditional Thai with a few modern touches.

BALI BEACH ACTIVITIES

As well as surf, sand and sun, beaches offer impromptu shopping, outdoor massage and a variety of sports.

Bali's beaches are unfortunately not blessed with the archetypal white sands and gin-clear aquamarine waters that one associates with tropical island havens, in fact many of its beaches have black or grey sand due to the volcanic origins of the island. The only true white-sand beaches are the surf beaches on the south of the Bukit Peninsula, as well as Nusa Dua, Tanjung Benoa and Sanur.

Meanwhile the beaches at Kuta, Legian and Seminyak on the southwest coast have grey sand but make up for it with thundering surf, fabulous mango-streaked sunsets and a broad, flat expanse of shore that is perfect for long walks and sports such as volleyball, frisbee and soccer. They're a hive of activity, with people surfing, swimming and sunbathing while warding off the hawkers. At around four or five o'clock in the afternoon, especially on Sundays, Balinese families join the throng; their children paddle naked in the shallows and build sandcastles more reminiscent of miniature Taj Mahals than of Norman fortresses.

ABOVE AND LEFT: Sanur is bounded by a 5-km (3-mile) long shoreline within a gentle reef-sheltered lagoon. Swimming is safe off this golden-sand beach, and surfers can take a boat out to the nearby reef. Head to Tanjung Benoa for jet-skiing, water-skiing, windsurfing, wake-boarding, para-sailing and Flyfish – an experience involving a floating bed being dragged behind a speedboat, causing it to fly up in the air.

BELOW: surfer on Kuta beach and a dive instructor at Pulau Menjangan. The breaks and barrels off the south coast attract surfers from around the world, while the coral reefs around Pulau Menjangan in northwestern Bali teem with rich aquatic life.

ABOVE: horse riding on the beach at Seminyak. The sweeping coast beyond Kuta and Legian beaches, stretching into Seminyak, Petitenget, Batubelig and Canggu, has long, flat expanses of smooth sand that are great for relaxed horse rides. Small and gentle ponies can be hired, and lessons, along with guides for novices, are available. Experienced riders will enjoy the freedom of galloping near the shoreline with waves rolling in and breaking at the horses' hoofs.

LEFT: hair braiding at Kuta beach. Women roam the beach looking for those with suitably long hair. Once you've agreed on a price, nimble fingers will skilfully braid thin cornrows of hair into artistic patterns across the head and thread small, colourful beads onto the ends of the strands. This can take nearly an hour, so remember to protect yourself from the sun or have it done under the shade of a tree.

BELOW: the beach at Tanjung Benoa – the slender peninsula that juts into the bay north of Nusa Dua – is the domain of water sports operators.

RIGHT: fishing at Nusa Lembongan. Special boats and yachts take visitors for a day of fishing in the waters near one of Bali's offshore islands in the southeast. Longer live-aboard expeditions to fishing sites further afield can be arranged by chartering a vessel that includes fishing gear, the services of a cook and accommodation on board.

UBUD AND SURROUNDINGS

The Gianyar region, to which Ubud belongs, is Bali's undisputed cultural enclave. This is where to find artists' studios and galleries – together with lush rice fields, ornate temples and ancient historical sites. Ubud is where visitors gravitate to when they want to escape the tourist hordes of the south.

Denpasar

Driving northwards from Denpasar into the Gianyar region, the cacophony of south Bali recedes a little, depending upon exactly where one is headed. Shrines and temples dot landscapes of verdant rice paddies, soothing one back to sanity. The richly cultural Gianyar region was home to ancient kingdoms, extending from the centre of Bali down to the southern coast.

Gianyar has given the island much of its reputation as a centre of creativity, born literally from the incredible fertility of its spring-fed, lava-enriched soil. With such bountiful harvests, the people had time to cultivate their artistic talents; the result is a high level of aesthetic excellence that extends even to the commercial arts and crafts industry. Ubud is one of Gianyar's main tourist centres and is easily accessible from all parts of the island.

DENPASAR TO UBUD

The roads leading to Ubud are lined with countless villages, once isolated but nowadays nearly indistinguishable from one another in the continual sprawl. Non-stop driving might take just over an hour from Denpasar, but doing so would be a great pity as many villages along the way specialise in some kind of art form and are usually worth lingering at.

Batubulan

The first large village of note upon entering the region of Gianyar is **Batubulan ❶** (Moonstone), stretching for about 2km (1 mile) and distinguishable from urban Denpasar only by the numerous *paras* stone-carving shops lining the road sides. *Paras* is composed of compressed clay and volcanic ash found in nearby ravines.

Main attractions

TAMAN BURUNG BALI BIRD PARK
CELUK
UBUD MARKET
NEKA ART MUSEUM
MONKEY FOREST
HERONS ROOSTING AT PETULU
TEGALLALANG
ELEPHANT SAFARI PARK
GUNUNG KAWI
PURA KEHEN AT BANGLI

LEFT: holy spring at Pura Tirtha Empul.
RIGHT: a stone carver at work in Batubulan.

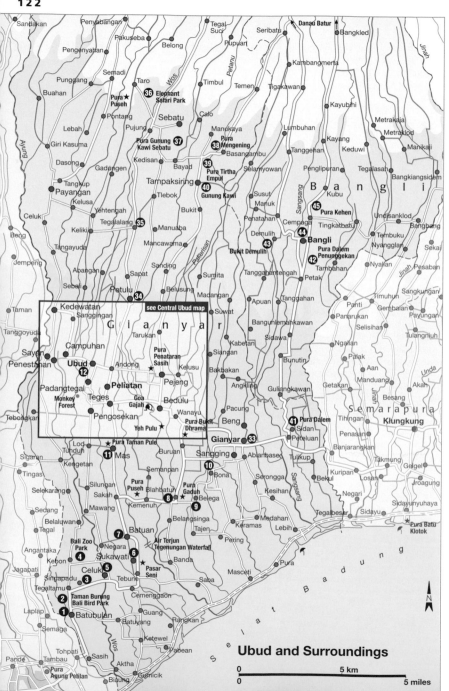

Ubud and Surroundings

Santlakan
Penyabangan
Pakuseba
Belong
Tegal Suci
Pupuari
Seribatu
Danau Batur
Bangkled
Jinah

Pengenyatran
Semadi
Taro
Timbul
Temen
Tigakawan
Kambangmerta

Punggang
Buahan
Pura Puseh ★
36 Elephant Safari Park
Sebatu
Calo
Manukaya
Lumbuhan
Kayubihi
Metrakaja
Metraklod

Lebah
Pontang
Pujung
Kedisan
Bayad
37 Pura Gunung Kawi Sebatu
38 Pura Mengening
Basangambu
Selamyowan
Tanggenan
Kayang
Keduwi
Manikali

Giri Kasuma
Dasong
Gadungen
Tampaksiring
39 Pura Tirtha Empul
B a n g l i
Penglipuran
Tegalasah
Bangkiangsidem

Tangkup
Payangan
Kelusa
Yehtengah
Tlebok
40 Gunung Kawi
Susut
Manuk
Kubu
45 Pura Kehen
Undisanklod
Bangbang

Celuk
Keliki
Tegalalang
35
Bukit
Manuaba
Penatahan
Cempaga
44 Bangli
Tingkatbatu
Tembuku
Nyanggian
Sekai

Beng
Tangayuda
Jempeng
Abangan
Mancawama
Sanding
Demulih
43
42 Pura Dalem Penunggekan
Tambahan
Nyalian
Pesaban

Sebali
Patulu
Sapat
Belusung
Bukit Demulih
Tanggahantengah
Petak
Nyajan
Sangkungan

34
Madangan
Apuan
Tanggahan
Timuhun
Gembalan
Payungan

Kedewatan
Sangginggan
G i a n y a r
Suwat
Bangunlemahkawan
Sidawa
Panti
Panarukan
Selisihan

Tanggoyuda
Tarukan
Kabetan
Siangan
Ngallan
Palak
Tulangniuh

Campuhan
Pura Penataran Sasih
Andong
Kelusu
Bakbakan
Bunutin
Aan
Manduang
Unda
Akah

Sayen
Penestanan
Ubud
12
★
Pejeng
Angkling
Guliangkawan
Getakan
Jinah
Besang
S e m a r a p u r a

Padangtegal
Peliatan
Teges
Goa Gajah
Bedulu
Pacung
Tihingan
41 Pura Dalem Sidan
Klungkung

Monkey Forest
Pengosekan
Wanayu
Pura Bukit Dharma
Beng
Peteluan
Penasan
Banjarangkan

Tebongkan
Yeh Pulu
Gianyar **33**
Buruhan
Sangging
Ablanbasen
Tulikup
Kuripan
Losan
Takmung
Galgel
Jroagung

Sigaran
Tunduh
Pura Taman Pule ★
11 Mas
Semanpan
10
Bona
Serongga
Sangsang
Bekul
Negari
Sidayunyuhaya

Tingas
Selekarang
Kengetan
Silungan
Sakah
Pura Puseh ★
Blahbatuh
8
Pura Gaduh ★
9
Belega
Kesihan
Tegalbesar
Sidayu
Pura Batu Klotok

Sedang
Belaluwan
Tegal
Mawang
Kemenuh
Belangsinga
Medahan
Lebih

Angtakara
Jagapati
Bali Zoo Park
4
Negara
7 Batuan
Tajen
Keramas
Pura

Kebon
6 Sukawati
Air Terjun Tegenungan Waterfall
Banda
Pering
Masceti

Laplap
Singapadu
Tegaltamu
3
Celuk
5
Tebune
Pasar Seni ★
Cemenggaon
Saba
S e l a t   B a d u n g

Taman Burung Bali Bird Park
2
1 Batubulan
Guang
Batuyang
Rangkan
Ketewel
Pabean

Semaga
Tohpati
Tambau
Sasih
Pura Agung Petilan
Aktha
Biaung
Gumicik
Pande

N

0   5 km
0   5 miles

It's so soft and porous that the tropical climate wears it down, making it necessary for temple carvings to be replaced every few decades. Men usually carve in groups, copying in stone what their ancestors carved before them, and increasingly, what appeals to visitors.

Also in Batubulan is the **Seniwati Gallery of Art**, a showcase for female Indonesian artists and a source of income and empowerment (entry by appointment only; tel: 081-338 453006, www.seniwatigallery.com).

Taman Burung Bali and Rimba Reptile Park

North of Batubulan is the **Taman Burung Bali Bird Park ❷** (daily 9am–5.30pm; charge; tel: 0361-299352; www.bali-bird-park.com). Paved paths lead through landscaped gardens where more than 1,000 specimens of over 250 exotic bird species live in well-designed aviaries. It is dedicated to the protection of mostly Indonesian birds; the endangered *jalak putih* (white Bali starlings) have been bred here in captivity for the first time in Bali.

Ticket includes entry to the adjacent **Rimba Reptile Park**, which is home to one of the biggest collections of rare reptiles and amphibians in Indonesia, all living among lush tropical gardens.

Singapadu

Continue about 1km (½ mile) north on the main road and turn right at a T-junction into **Singapadu ❸** (Fighting Lions) village. Numerous wood-and-stone carving shops are interspersed among the houses, but the village is more famous for producing some of Bali's talented musicians and dancers. Take time to visit the workshop-home of **I Wayan Tangguh** (tel: 0361-298685), one of Bali's best mask makers, and his son, I Made Sutiarka. Look for the sign with his name on the right side of the main road. Here you will see a chunk of wood evolve into a beautiful work of art in addition to viewing his collection of exquisite masks.

Bali Zoo Park

Further along the road in Singapadu, on the left, is the family-friendly

Batubulan is noted for performances of the Barong *and* Rangda *dance (see page 62). Tourists are brought in by bus to see this dramatic struggle between good and evil.*

BELOW: barong masks and costumes in the old royal palace, Puri Saren Agung, which hosts traditional dance performances nightly.

TIP

At Banjar Babakan in Sukawati, you can watch leather puppets being made at the home of the puppeteer I Wayan Nartha, located at the very end of a side street about 100 metres/yds south of the market. It's best to call ahead on tel: 0361-299080 to see if the house is open to receive visitors.

Bali Zoo Park ❹ (daily 9am–6pm; charge; tel: 0361-294356). This 3.5-hectare (9-acre) landscaped zoo is where you will find animals other than birds – like tigers, deer and camels – including the beast after which Singapadu was named. *Singa* (lion) refers to the two royal brothers who *padu* (challenged) each other for the right to rule.

Celuk

From Singapadu, turn right at the T-junction and travel east to **Celuk ❺** (Cove), synonymous with silver- and goldsmiths, and one of the wealthier villages in Bali. Shops along the way, less crowded and often cheaper than those along the main road, offer all kinds of sterling silver and gold jewellery and decorative objects. Stop to have a look in the artisan workshops which are usually small and dimly lit rooms crowded with workers, some not even in their teens. The intricate details obtained from using simple hand tools are amazing. As with most Balinese crafts, silversmithing is largely an art passed down from one generation to the next.

Sukawati

From Celuk, head east, then north to **Sukawati ❻** (Beautiful Joy), once the centre of a powerful kingdom during the 18th century. *Kain prada* cloth, gold-leafed by hand in the past, is silkscreened by the metre by Sukawati's villagers for costumes and shrines, and made into lovely temple parasols and dance fans. Look out for the road side shops selling these items.

Sukawati, however, is more famous for producing some of Bali's best *dalang* (puppeteers), who make their own *wayang kulit*, or leather puppets, delicately carved from thin cattle hide and then painted *(see pages 65–6)*. The *dalang*'s work is very complicated and it takes years to master the craft. A number of puppeteers live in **Banjar Babakan** neighbourhood behind the market but one of the better known ones is I Wayan Nartha *(see margin tip)*.

Sukawati's **Pasar Seni** (daily 9am–5pm) is a big two-storey building at the centre of town. In the past, it used to be filled with hundreds of vendors selling every imaginable kind of arts and crafts; these days there seem to be as many vendors hawking clothing and knick-knacks. Items vary in quality, but all are much less expensive than at the larger art shops and even at stalls in Kuta. Bargaining is expected.

Batuan

Another 1km (½ mile) north of the Sukawati market is the village of **Batuan ❼** (Boulder), where some of the finest *topeng* masked dancers *(see page 63)* in Bali live. This dance is an essential part of most religious events. Full of anecdotes and bawdy jokes, and depicting a wide range of different characters, a good dancer can completely engage onlookers.

A more modern dance with its roots in Batuan is the Frog Dance, performed by children wearing frog

BELOW: shadow puppet in the making, Sukawati.

masks and costumes. It is usually done only for tourist shows at hotels. The music is a unique ensemble of jew's harps, reeds, flutes and drums.

Batuan is also known for its distinctive style of painting, which evolved in the 1930s. Using mainly black or dark green ink, Batuan painters fill their canvases with dense scenes drawn from everyday life – villagers, ceremonies and the supernatural. Quite often, modern and quirky elements are introduced into these traditional Balinese scenes, like surfers and long-nosed Western tourists pointing long camera lenses at everything.

Another of Batuan's attractions is the **Pura Puseh** (daily daylight hours; donation). The temple dates back to the 11th century and has many fine carvings. Regular performances of *gambuh (see page 64)* are held on the 1st and 15th of every month (7–9pm; charge). Although efforts have been made to revive this dance form (there are fewer than a dozen remaining venues on the entire island), it is not popular among the Balinese because of its slow pace, archaic language

that is not understood by many, and near absence of humour.

Blahbatuh

After another 2km (1 mile) north up the main road to **Sakah**, turn right at the big, ugly statue of Brahmarare (Brahma as a Baby) to the village at **Blahbatuh ❽**. Here is the temple of **Pura Gaduh** (daily daylight hours; donation), associated with Kebo Iwo, the legendary giant from the 14th-century kingdom of Bedulu. After entering the temple, have a look at the main gate's balustrades, with carvings of women performing some rather erotic acts with horses.

In a pavilion is a huge stone head said to be in the likeness of Kebo Iwo. According to legend, Gajah Mada, prime minister of the Javanese Majapahit kingdom, realised he couldn't conquer Bali as long as Kebo Iwo was alive. Gajah Mada then hatched a plan. Knowing the giant was a bachelor because no woman could match his size, Gajah Mada had a huge female puppet constructed with a warrior hidden inside to trick Kebo Iwo into think-

Batuan's delightful frog dance is mainly performed by children.

LEFT: mask-makers in Batuan. **BELOW:** head of legendary giant Kebo Iwo at Pura Gaduh.

Gamelan *gongs at the Sidha Karya Gamelan Foundry.*

ing that she would become his wife. Gajah Mada told Kebo Iwo to dig a well for his future house, which the eager giant did with his bare hands in the porous limestone. When he was deep down inside, still unable to find water, Gajah Mada ordered his soldiers to fill in the hole, burying him alive. With his dying breath, Kebo Iwo swore that since he was covered with chalky white dust, he would return as a giant albino *kebo* (water buffalo), the animal in his name, and subjugate the Javanese for 300 years. The curse came true with Dutch colonial rule of Java from the 17th to 20th centuries.

While in Blahbatuh make a stop to visit **Sidha Karya Gamelan Foundry** (tel: 0361-942798). Here, you can see men pump the bellows to fire up the heat for metal forging. Others use large mallets to hammer the heated bronze into the desired shapes for musical instruments. Instrument cases also are carved and gilded here. An entire *gamelan gong kebyar* (costing over US$10,000) may be purchased; orders must be placed far in advance.

Belega, Bona and Mas

On the back road 1km (½ mile) east from Blahbatuh is **Belega** ❾ village, where bamboo furniture of all sorts is produced. Another 1½km (1 mile) northeast is **Bona** ❿, which specialises in products woven from dried fan-palm leaves. Bona is also the place where the dramatic *kecak* dance was born (*see page 64*).

From Bona, continuing another 2km (1 mile) northeast will lead to **Gianyar** town (*see page 140*), the capital of the Gianyar district. Otherwise, backtrack to the Brahmarare statue near Sakah and head north to the village of **Mas** ⓫ (Gold), best known for its intricate woodcarvings and masks. Today, Mas also hosts a large number of workshops producing teak furniture. A string of galleries and souvenir shops line Mas' main road and side alleys for the next 3km (2 miles). One of the best-known artists for new designs in masks here is **Ida Bagus Anom** who has a woodcarving workshop and showroom, along the main road (tel: 0361-975292). He has carved masks for pantomimes as well as performance artists from all over

the world and his distinctive yawning masks have been widely copied throughout the island.

On the west side of the main road near the main market in Mas is **Njana Tilem Gallery** (daily 9am–4.30pm; tel: 0361-975099). The late Ida Bagus Njana and his son Ida Bagus Tilem were two of Bali's most talented wood sculptors. Many of their innovative and intricate pieces are on display along with a large collection of antique pieces.

Many of the inhabitants of Mas are *brahmana*, the priestly caste who trace their roots back to Danghyang Nirartha. This 16th-century Javanese high priest founded **Pura Taman Pule** (daily daylight hours; donation), located just beyond the field north of the market and named after the *pule* tree (*Alstonia scholaris*) which is used for making masks.

UBUD

The name **Ubud** ⓬ comes from the Balinese word *ubad* (medicine) because of the healing properties of plants growing by the Campuhan River on the western end of town. Blessed with a picturesque location that inspired the arts, the village (actually Campuhan specifically) became the adopted home of Western artists like Walter Spies and Rudolf Bonnet in the 1920s.

During the 1930s, together with a local nobleman named Cokorde Gede Agung Sukawati, they founded an artists' association known as Pitamaha *(see page 72)*. This initiative inspired a renaissance, transforming the sleepy village of Ubud into a centre of artistic activity. The masses that followed in the ensuing decades naturally led to commercialisation, but the money from tourism has benefited the arts here.

A few minutes away from the souvenir outlets, art galleries, cafés and persistent dance performance ticket salesmen lies a gentler, calmer Ubud unaltered by the tourists zooming about on their rental scooters. However, this is fast disappearing: like Kuta in the south, neighbouring villages have lost some of their geographical distinctiveness to Ubud's expanding sprawl.

Bearing in mind the size of Ubud and its population of around 80,000, the vast range of accommodation and restaurants competing for the attention of tourists – not to mention the rampant commerce – may seem overwhelming. Visitors hoping to escape the area entirely will do well to head for the surrounding villages – like Campuhan, Sayan, Peliatan or Pengosekan – which provide better opportunities for experiencing life in a Balinese village community.

Ubud's favourable location makes it an ideal base for excursions. You can visit some of the oldest temples on the island or explore the delights of the local countryside just by walking *(see page 134)*. The area is crisscrossed by a network of narrow but mostly well constructed roads, linking the many villages in the vicinity of Ubud with each other.

TIP

In 2006, the new **Bali Botanic Garden Ubud** opened (daily 9am–5pm; charge; tel: 0361-970951; www.botanicgardenbali.com). Located just north of Ubud town in the village of Kutuh Kaja, the garden is a lush sanctuary, although sadly it hasn't been so well maintained since the death of the founder.

BELOW: Pasar Ubud (Ubud Market).

Statue at Puri Saren Agung, the former palace of the Ubud royal family.

CENTRAL UBUD

The main east–west artery is **Jalan Raya Ubud**; the centre of town is where it intersects with the north–south **Monkey Forest Road** (Jalan Wana Wana). Most of the following sights can be covered by starting at the main market in the centre of town.

Ubud Market

Located at the main crossroads of Jalan Raya Ubud and Monkey Forest Road is the main market, **Pasar Ubud** ⑬. The recently renovated complex is a two-storey building, with an annexe just to the right. At the back is a fresh produce market (daily 6am–2pm), while the side facing the main road is stocked with clothing, fabrics, handicrafts and souvenirs, and is aimed more at tourists (daily 9am–5pm).

Puri Saren Agung

Across the road from the market is **Puri Saren Agung**, the palace of the royal family that ruled from the late 1800s until World War II. Most of the buildings were designed by I Gusti Nyoman Lempad (1862–1978), Bali's most famous architect, artist and carver, and were erected following a devastating 1917 earthquake. There are seven pavilions inside, each with four-poster beds and spacious verandahs, available for guests who want to experience life in a Balinese palace (tel: 0361-975057 for bookings). The front courtyard is open to the public during daylight hours, and traditional dance performances are held here every evening at 7.30pm; tickets are available at the courtyard reception desk. Just across the road is the unremarkable **Pura Desa**, which is the main place of worship for the people of Ubud.

Yayasan Bina Wisata

Close to the intersection along Jalan Raya Ubud is **Yayasan Bina Wisata** (Tourism Development Foundation; daily 8am–8pm; tel: 0361-973285),

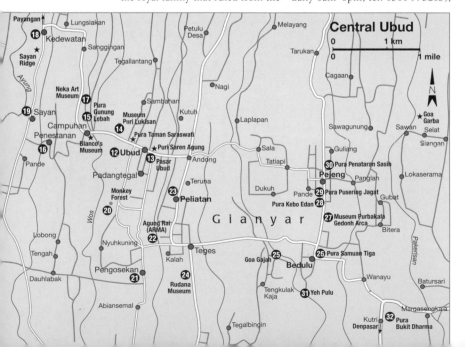

tasked with the job of preserving Ubud's natural and cultural beauty Instead of simply encouraging mass tourism, the foundation strives to unify the needs of both visitors and local people. Visitors are asked, for example, to respect the local ceremonies and wear traditional clothing when appropriate, and are encouraged to learn more about the special qualities of Ubud.

The multilingual staff are helpful in answering questions and planning journeys. A message board has details of performances and ceremonies in the area and tickets to dances can also be bought here.

Threads of Life

Around 100 metres/yds west of the main Jalan Raya Ubud and Monkey Forest Road intersection heading north is **Jalan Kajeng**, a side street paved with blocks bearing the names of local people and places. Continue a little further up to the interesting **Threads of Life Indonesian Textile Arts Centre** (daily 10am–7pm; tel: 0361-972187; www.threadsoflife. com) on the right, where beautiful

natural dyed and handmade textiles from throughout the archipelago are on display and for sale. The centre encourages traditional weaving skills and also offers courses in textile appreciation and weaving. You might want to enquire about its tours to Balinese villages which specialise in *ikat* and *songket* weaving.

Pura Taman Saraswati

Back on Jalan Raya Ubud, turn right at the corner; next to the Lotus restaurant is a path leading to a large pond of pink lotuses. Behind the sculpted animals, out of whose mouths gush water, stands **Pura Taman Saraswati**, the Lotus Garden Temple of Saraswati, the Hindu goddess of learning, knowledge and the arts. This architectural masterpiece was designed by the famous Balinese architect and artist I Gusti Nyoman Lempad. Inside is an incredible stone throne to Saraswati carved by the master himself.

Museum Puri Lukisan

A short walk west of Pura Taman Saraswati is the **Museum Puri Lukisan** ⓮ (daily 9am–5pm; charge; tel: 0361-

Batik scarves for sale at Ubud Market. Gianyar region has a major centre of batik textile production at Tampaksiring.

BELOW: Pura Taman Saraswati.

971159; www.mpl-ubud.com). Descend a long flight of stairs and up again to a peaceful setting of beautiful gardens and lotus pools. Opened in 1956 (and renovated in the mid-1990s), the excellent collection showcases the richness of traditional and modern Balinese art.

The main building features Balinese paintings and sculptures from the 1930s, including works by the Pitamaha artists and fine drawings by the great I Gusti Nyoman Lempad, whose fluid classical scenes gained him the most recognition.

A second gallery displays works by the Young Artists from the 1960s as well as traditional and contemporary paintings. A third building is mainly used for temporary exhibitions. Would-be purchasers of serious art will find this place a useful introduction to the principal genres of art practised in Bali. Some of the paintings on display are for sale.

Neka Art Gallery

Stay on the main road, Jalan Raya Ubud, and turn left (north) a few metres to the **Neka Art Gallery**

(daily 9am–5pm; tel: 0316-975034), one of the first to open in Ubud in 1967. Individual galleries feature the different styles of Balinese painting. Be sure to go up to the top floor where a special room displays works by the famous Dutch-born Indonesian artist Arie Smit; another section has contemporary Balinese and Indonesian paintings. All the works here are for sale, unlike in the associated Neka Art Museum.

WEST FROM UBUD

Although some of these sights are within walking distance from the centre of town (on a cool day), the roads are narrow and congested with traffic. Public transport in *bemo* (minivans) provides access to most places daily; otherwise hire a car with a driver.

Campuhan and Pura Gunung Lebah

Jalan Raya Ubud, heading west from Ubud's main crossroads, leads to the **Campuhan River** (Confluence of Two Rivers) and the **Campuhan** district, a spiritually powerful site. Just down a small road is the important **Pura Gunung Lebah** ⓯ (daily daylight hours; donation) the Low Mountain Temple, dedicated to the goddess of Danau Batur *(see page 149)*. Extensively renovated during the early 1990s, this picturesque temple is believed to have been the 8th-century residence of the legendary Javanese priest Resi Markandeya. Several important purification rituals take place here, especially the bathing of sacred temple relics and the dispersing of ashes of the cremated dead.

Blanco Renaissance Museum

The late Spanish artist Antonio Blanco (1926–99) built a garden home-studio with a towering *meru* (pagoda) at the top of a steep driveway on the left just after the short

Campuhan Bridge. The flamboyant Blanco is most well known for his rather erotic paintings of his favourite models: his Balinese wife and their daughter. Blanco was also a poet of sorts, and often combined verses into his visual art.

Just behind the home is the **Blanco Renaissance Museum** (daily 9am–5pm; charge; tel: 0361-975502). Adorned with gold painted statues and stained-glass windows, it displays many of his drawings and paintings.

Penestanan

Up a steep road just on the left is **Penestanan ⑯**. This area arose from obscurity when the Dutch-born Arie Smit, who lived and worked here as an artist, encouraged some local youths during the early 1960s to paint. With Smit's encouragement and freedom of choice on subject matter and style, the artists produced imaginative, naive-style scenes of village life and rituals that became eventually known as the Young Artists style. This genre uses oil paints thinned with turpentine for a matte effect, applied in flat, bright areas of colour with dark outlines. Lighting and shadow are absent, there is little perspective, sometimes no facial features, and decorative foliage dominates the scenes. Although there is no one main Young Artists studio in Penestanan, its streets are dotted with numerous galleries selling these works.

Nothing to do with the Young Artists style but full of verve and colour are the artworks with a gay theme at **Symon Gallery** (daily 9am–7pm; tel: 0361-974721; www.symonstudios. com) just across the road from the Hotel Tjamphuan. The American painter, who has lived in Bali since 1978, also exhibits his works at the more remote Art Zoo in the north *(see page 174)*.

Neka Art Museum

Another 1km (½ mile) further up the main road along Jalan Raya Sanggingan is the **Neka Art Museum ⑰** (daily 9am–5pm; charge; tel: 0361-975074; www.museumneka.com). Housing one of the finest collections of art on the island, it was founded in 1976 by former school teacher Suteja Neka,

The entrance to Blanco Renaissance Museum.

BELOW: an *odalan* (temple festival) at Pura Gunung Lebah.

Door detail at the Neka Art Museum. The museum is one of Bali's finest in terms of quality of work. Try to visit before noon when bus loads of tourists take over the place.

BELOW: *Waiting to Dance* (1983), by Abdul Aziz, at Neka Art Museum.

one of Indonesia's foremost art connoisseurs. The collection is housed within several Balinese-style buildings set amid gardens. Nearly 400 artworks are chronologically displayed and well-documented with descriptive labels in English (and Japanese), providing an excellent background to the development of painting in Bali. The multilingual staff are both friendly and knowledgeable.

The Balinese Painting Hall contains Balinese works ranging from the classical narrative *wayang* (puppet) style to the Ubud and Batuan styles. The large Arie Smit Pavilion is devoted to the work of this Dutch-born artist along with works by his students of the Young Artists school, plus contemporary Balinese art in a wide range of styles.

Works by Indonesian artists, some of whom have lived in Bali, are displayed in the Contemporary Indonesian Art Hall, while the East-West Annexe has works by foreign artists like Miguel Covarrubias, Rudolf Bonnet, Han Snel and Donald Friend. A special display features black-and-white photographs of Bali during the late 1930s and early 1940s, taken by Robert Koke, an American who built the first hotel on Kuta beach. The important Lempad Pavilion has one of the largest collections of drawings by I Gusti Nyoman Lempad, Bali's most renowned artist. Adding to the atmosphere are numerous traditional and modern sculptures in wood and metal scattered throughout the galleries and grounds.

Views from the open-air café are spectacular and overlook a lush river valley. The museum has an extensive research library, large bookstore and a gift shop. A wide selection of high-quality paintings are for sale at fairly steep prices.

Kedewatan, Payangan and Sayan

From Sanggingan, the main road climbs some 3km (2 miles) north to **Kedewatan** ⓲ (Divine Place), a village blessed with outstanding views and sweet *rambutan* fruit trees. This area and **Payangan**, further north and more rural, is where you will find a clutch of ultra-expensive luxury resorts like Amandari, Alila Ubud and Como Shambhala Estate. Even if you can't afford to stay here, have a meal at any one of the hotels' highly rated restaurants and sneak in views of breathaking architecture.

South of Kedewatan is **Sayan** ⓳. This village hugs the edge of a beautiful gorge with the **Ayung River** tumbling through the valley below. The scenery here is some of Bali's most dramatic. One of the best ways to take in the area's stunning beauty is on a white-water trip down the Ayung River *(see margin tip)*. The Canadian ethno-musicologist Colin McPhee (1900–64), who documented Balinese *gamelan* music, built his home here during the 1930s. A more modern intrusion is the lovely Four Seasons Sayan resort, with a reception area resembling a space pod.

SOUTH FROM UBUD

Monkey Forest Road (Jalan Wanara Wana), going south from the centre of town and all the way down to Pengosekan village, is an almost continuous stretch of shops, art galleries, restaurants, hotels and guesthouses. At the beginning of the 1980s, it was just a quiet village street, but now it demonstrates all too clearly the extent to which rapid development has taken a toll on the Ubud environment.

Pondok Pekak Library

Just down Monkey Forest Road on the east side of the football field is the **Pondok Pekak Library and Learning Centre** (Mon–Fri 9am–9pm; Sat, Sun 9am–5pm; tel: 0361-976194). For a small fee, users can borrow books from the only children's library in Bali and from a general section. There is a restaurant and a breezy upstairs reading room. Courses in Balinese art and culture are offered, and the centre also has a children's music and dance group staging regular performances, and a club for expatriate women.

Monkey Forest

Continuing your walk south will bring you to Ubud's well known **Monkey Forest ⑳** (daily 8am–6pm; charge; www.monkeyforestubud.com), best done early morning or late afternoon when the sun isn't so scorching. Follow a paved path in the forest and be sure to conceal your cameras, jewellery, keys, sunglasses or any other shiny object, for the mischievous and fearless macaques will snatch them and run off in a flash. The Balinese regard the monkeys as the sacred descendants of the monkey general Hanoman. You'll see ladies selling bananas at the entrance but, unless you want to be pounced on, it's best not to feed the monkeys as they can become aggressive *(see margin picture page 135)*.

Descending the steps into the forest, past the sacred *waringan* tree, you reach the cemetery and eerie **Pura Dalem Agung** (Great Temple of the Dead), dedicated to the goddess of death, Durga. She often takes the form of the widow-witch Rangda.

TIP

White-water rafting down the Ayung River is more exciting during the rainy season from Nov–Mar. The two best operators are **Sobek**: tel: 0361-287059; www.balisobek.com, and **Bali Adventure Tours**: tel: 0361-721480; www.bali adventuretours.com.

BELOW: macaques in Monkey Forest, regarded as sacred by the Balinese.

Ubud Walks

You will see rural vistas of farmers tending rice fields, flocks of ducks being herded, and women with temple offerings on their heads.

For most of these walks, you'll need to either take a public *bemo* (mini-van) or ask your hotel to arrange transport (there are no taxis in Ubud) to take you to the starting point for your walk. Set off early in the morning when it's cooler and bring along a bottle of water, some snacks, insect repellent, a hat and a small foldable umbrella (during the rainy season). Alternatively, take a guided walk *(see page 255)* of Ubud's rice fields.

Penestanan to Monkey Forest: (10km/6 miles). Start at the flight of stairs opposite the **Hotel Tjampuhan**. Climb the stairs and walk 1½km (1 mile) through **Penestanan**. Continue 3km (2 miles) south down through **Katik Lantang** to **Singakerta**. Turn left at the crossroads to **Dangin Labak** and continue east over a bridge to **Nyuhkuning**. Turn left at the first road and

follow it 1km (½ mile) north to **Monkey Forest** and back to Ubud.

Kutuh to Petulu: (9km/6 miles). Start in the mid-afternoon, go east from the centre of Ubud and take the side road to **Kutuh**. Continue uphill for 4km (2 miles) to **Junjungan**. At a T-junction, turn right and walk east, then north to another T-junction, again turning right. Go downhill 2km (1 mile) to **Petulu** to watch thousands of white herons roosting in the trees before sunset. Head downhill to a Y-junction, and if there's a late-running *bemo*, hop on to get back to Ubud. Otherwise, continue 2km (1 mile) south to Ubud.

Bedulu to Pejeng: (6km/4 miles). Ride a *bemo* to opposite the **Goa** community hall on the main road in **Bedulu**, and turn left up a lane going north and then east to the main road to **Pejeng**. Continue uphill to the first side road on the left leading to **Pura Pusering Jagat**. Walk west to the **Pande** community hall and turn right, heading north, then turn left at a small temple at a T-junction. Follow the road, then:

a) either continue straight to **Pura Batan Bingin** with its beautiful carvings and huge trees in the courtyard. Don't miss scenes from the *Ramayana* epic carved in bas-reliefs on the outer walls. Follow the road around the temple to a Y-junction and veer right.

b) turn left at first T-junction to **Tatiapi**, continuing south to **Candi Tebing Kelebutan**. Follow a path down through the cemetery to this rock-cut temple facade, and swim in the river below. As the road continues through **Dukuh**, other places to cool off are **Pura Beji Bun** 1km (½ mile) west and then south along a lane, and at **Pura Beji Taman Sari**, a further 1km (½ mile) northwest down a path. Both temples have water gushing out of spouts into separate bathing pools for men and women. Follow the road up to a Y-junction and turn left.

Both routes lead to **Sala**. Turn left at the community hall, and continue 1.5km (1 mile) west down a river gorge and up the other side to the statue of Arjuna and back to Ubud. ❏

Left: ducks in rice paddy near Ubud.

Nearby **Padangtegal** (Grassy Fields) village is home to many of Ubud's painters, and has a number of pleasant guesthouses fronting lush rice fields.

Pengosekan

As Monkey Forest Road bends east, turn right at the Y-junction and head south to **Pengosekan** ㉑. Villagers here make beautiful baskets from dried *lontar* (fan-palm) leaves. The leaves are first buried in the ground to produce different shades of brown before being spirally plaited into traditional basket shapes. Pengosekan is also known for its particular style of painting, dense with birds, butterflies and blossoms.

Agung Rai Museum of Art

At a T-junction in Pengosekan, turn left to the main entrance of the **Agung Rai Museum of Art** ㉒ (daily 9am–6pm; charge; tel: 0361-975449; www.armabali.com). Opened in 1996 by art dealer Anak Agung Rai, the grand buildings are set in landscaped grounds. The upper floor of the main gallery is dedicated

to Balinese paintings, some of them from the 1930s.

The lower floor features classical *wayang* (puppet) style works from the early 1900s, antique textiles and contemporary Indonesian art. Labels are in English, Indonesian and Japanese.

Another building displays works by famous artists, including the only paintings on Bali by the Javanese Raden Saleh and the German Walter Spies. Paintings by other foreign-born artists who lived and worked in Bali are shown too. The museum also promotes the performing arts with regular dance presentations and a children's *gamelan* music and dance group (*check website for details*).

Peliatan

Continue west on the main road, and turn left to enter **Peliatan** ㉓ village, which gained international fame for its *legong* dancers who took New York and Paris by storm while on tour during the 1950s. Today, the daughters of these performers, along with their cousins and friends,

The creatures at Ubud's Monkey Forest are tourist-savvy and expect remuneration in the form of bananas and peanuts for their antics. Vendors conveniently sell such treats to bribe the monkeys in return for snatched objects.

LEFT: painting at Agung Rai Museum of Art.
BELOW: Pura Dalem Agung at Monkey Forest.

Woodcarving at the Rudana Museum.

BELOW: Peliatan is famous for its talented *legong* dancers.
RIGHT: painter at the Rudana Museum.

continue the tradition. The original dancers were all trained under the discerning and critical eyes and ears of the late Anak Agung Gede Mandera. For decades, Gung Kak, as he was affectionally called, groomed both dancers and musicians alike, and his legacy lives on today in Peliatan. One of the few all-women *gamelan* troupes (*gamelan wanita*) in Bali rehearses here; many of them are relatives of Gung Kak.

At the main crossroads, stop for a look at **Puri Agung Peliatan**, the palace of the royal family. The *kecak* dance is held in the front courtyard every Friday night.

Rudana Museum

From Peliatan, continue south on the main Mas–Denpasar road to the **Rudana Museum** ㉔ (daily 9am–5pm; tel: 0361-975779; charge; www.museumrudana.com). Opened in 1995, it is owned by Nyoman Rudana, a local politician and art enthusiast. There are over 400 pieces of fine art and sculpture exhibited here. Start at the top floor of this three-storey museum, which features works in the traditional Balinese styles. The first and the lower floors display works by well-known Indonesian contemporary artists, including a big display of exquisite wooden sculptures. Regular exhibitions are held here, with the biggest one in August to commemorate the museums anniversary.

EAST OF UBUD

East of Ubud is a region heavy with ancient archaeological sites and old temples. The history and origins of some of these sites are vague, adding to their mystery. Most of them are concentrated in **Bedulu** and **Pejeng**, once the realm of Bali's earliest kingdom. Most of the sites can be done on a day trip out of Ubud, but pick and choose the ones that most interest you as there are too many to squeeze into a single day. Temples in each cluster are within walking distance of each other, but getting to some of those further away requires transport. Many small *warung* along the way sell snacks and bottled water, but eating places are almost non-existent here.

Goa Gajah

Follow the main road south out of Ubud and head east towards Gianyar. Stop in Bedulu at the **Goa Gajah** ㉕ (Elephant Cave;) daily 9am–5pm; charge) – recognised by the many stalls flogging cheap souvenirs to tourists on the approach road. Dating back to the 11th century, reference to a Lwa Gajah (Elephant River) in Bali, the supposed dwelling place of a Buddhist priest, is made in a 14th-century Javanese court poem.

At the entrance of the cave are six large stone figures, spouting water from pots held at their bellies into two holy pools. The heads and torsos once stood in front of the cave before the bathing pools were excavated by Dutch archaeologist, JC Krijgsman in 1922.

To the left of the man-made cave is a 1,000-year-old statue of the demonic goddess Hariti, who once devoured children but later converted to Buddhism and became their protector. The Balinese call her Men Brayut, the woman who had 18 children. Villagers pray here to be blessed with offspring of their own.

Just above the cave entrance is a monstrous head with its hands appearing to push apart its fanged gaping mouth. The demonic face, with bulging eyes and large earplugs, is a Boma figure that frightens away evil. All around it are fantastically carved animals and humans running away in fear.

The dark and musty interior contains several niches, which may have been sleeping places or meditation alcoves. At the left end of the T-shaped corridor is a four-armed statue of the elephant-headed god of obstacles, Ganesha, son of Siwa (Shiva). At the cave's right end are three *lingga* (phalluses), the attribute of Siwa, carved from a single block of stone.

Outside on the other side of the cave are a series of shrines, plus a small one in the middle of a pond fed by a holy spring. A flight of stairs by the towering *kepuh* (kapok) tree leads down to the river, where lie the remains of a Buddhist shrine carved in bas-relief and another meditation niche near a small bathing place. There were once a few seated Bud-

TIP

There are elements of both Hinduism and Buddhism found at Goa Gajah, derived from the 8th to the 14th centuries. The cave may be an early precursor of the Hindu-Buddhist character that to a large degree defines Bali today.

BELOW: the entrance to Goa Gajah.

TIP

During the full moon in April or May, dozens of villages bring their deities to visit Pura Samuan Tiga during a 13-day temple festival. There are ceremonial dances, ritual battles with hundreds of devotees, and long processions of offerings.

dha statues; only a headless one remains as the other statues were stolen in 1992.

Pura Samuan Tiga

Continuing east, a left turn at the T-junction leads to **Pura Samuan Tiga** ㉖ (Tripartite Meeting Temple; daily daylight hours; admission charge), one of the most important temples in Bali. In the late 10th century, the Balinese religion lacked cohesion. A number of separate sects were in constant conflict with each other, and so a meeting was held at this temple to merge the three elements of Shivaism, Buddhism and animism, which is still practised today. Pura Samuan Tiga was also the state temple of the Bedulu kingdom from the 9th to the 14th centuries.

Unusual among temples is the descent upon entering it. Built on terraces, the immense complex looks like a small village of gates, shrines and pavilions, most of which were refurbished during the mid 1990s. A trio of stone *meru* (pagodas) for the deities of the lakes, material wealth and sea are shaded by a huge banyan tree. Down by the river is a sacred spring.

Museum Purbakala

From Pura Samuan Tiga, head out west to the main road, turn right and go uphill about 500 metres/ yds to visit **Museum Purbakala** ㉗ (Mon–Thu 8am–3pm; Fri 8am– 12pm; admission charge; tel: 0361- 942354). There are four buildings on this site which display megalithic and Bronze Age artefacts from all over Bali, including huge stone sarcophagi from 300 BC; look out for the turtle-shaped ones that were found in Bangli.

Pura Kebo Edan

A little further uphill on the other side of the road towards Pejeng is **Pura Kebo Edan** ㉘, (Crazy Buffalo Temple; daily daylight hours; donation). Inside the temple is a fascinating figure over 3 metres (10ft) tall. Restored in 1952, the Pejeng Giant, whose face is covered by a stone mask with horns and fangs, is depicted trampling on a wide-eyed and dead

BELOW: artefacts at Museum Purbakala.

demon. More notable, however, is the giant's pierced penis, which swings to the left, a sign of the "left-handed" practices of the Tantric Bhairawa cult who used magical and perhaps even erotic practices in their worship of the Hindu god Siwa (Shiva) in his terrifying form.

Everywhere around the temple are carved stone skulls, demons and the temple's namesake figures of water buffaloes with their heads crazily turned back on their bodies.

Pura Pusering Jagat

Further north on the main road, turn left at the next side road to the **Pura Pusering Jagat** ㉙, (Navel of the World Temple; daily daylight hours; donation). Inside is a shallow oval pit in the ground, the "navel" that gives rise to the temple's name. Offerings placed here are said to miraculously appear at Pura Penataran Agung Ped on the offshore island of Nusa Penida (see page 160), home to Ratu Gede Mas Mecaling, the great fanged lord of supernatural forces. A cylindrical vessel called Naragiri (Mountain of Men) is carved with the story of the deities and demons churning the ocean of milk to produce the elixir of immortality. The reliefs are rather worn, but the vessel is sacred and miraculously produces holy water during the temple's anniversary ceremony during the full moon in July.

Pura Penataran Sasih

Another 100 metres/yds north on the other side of the main road is **Pura Penataran Sasih** ㉚, (State Temple of the Moon; daily daylight hours; charge), which was the state temple of the ancient Pejeng kingdom from the 9th–14th centuries. The shrine contains many carvings from this time but the oldest and most famous is the **Moon of Pejeng**. This great 190cm (75in) bronze gong in the shape of an hourglass drum dates back to Indo-

nesia's Bronze Age, which began in 300 BC. It is said to be the largest kettle gong in the world. The head is decorated with eight stylised faces and other motifs, indicating that the relic originated from the Dong Son culture, which was based in the Tonkin region of present-day northern Vietnam.

Legend has it that the gong was a wheel of the chariot that carried the moon on its nightly journey across the sky. One night, one of the wheels fell and landed in a tree. A thief was disturbed by the brilliant light, so he climbed up and urinated on it in the hope of extinguishing it. The wheel exploded and lost its shine, and the thief lost his life from the blast. A piece of the base broke off when it fell to the ground. The gong is never sounded, even during the temple's anniversary ceremony in the full moon of February, which features beautiful offerings, sacred dances and ritual battles.

Yeh Pulu

Head back about 1km (½ mile) south and then east along a paved path that

Working on the Tegalalang rice terraces where indigenous Balinese rice is cultivated.

BELOW: the Moon of Pejeng shrine at Pura Penataran Sasih.

Dyed cotton threads ready for weaving into endek fabric (see page 70). Gianyar is a major centre for this type of weaving.

BELOW: posing in front of one of Yeh Pulu's rock wall carvings.

goes through scenic rice fields to **Yeh Pulu** ㉛ (Rice Container Water Temple; daily daylight hours; charge). Aside from a statue of the elephant-headed god Ganesha, the carvings in deep bas-relief show scenes from daily life. They begin with a *kakayonan*, the cosmic tree of life that is the first to appear in a *wayang kulit* (shadow puppetry) performance. Next to it is a man gesturing in welcome. Other scenes include that of a woman at her house, some men on horseback, a boar hunt, and a woman pulling at the tail of a horse with a rider.

Some scholars say that they tell the story of Kresna (or Krishna) as a youth, but this tale of the Hindu god was not known in Bali when the bas-reliefs were carved during the 14th century. Locals say the legendary giant Kebo Iwo *(see page 125)* carved them with his fingernails.

A small temple at the end has a holy spring with *yeh* (water) trickling out of a small stone shaped like a *pulu* (traditional rice storage bin) in the middle, thus explaining the name of the site.

Pura Bukit Dharma

On the main road past Bedulu to Gianyar, turn right at the **Semabaung** junction, with a statue of a goddess surrounded by snakes. Head south to **Kutri**, where on the left side is **Pura Bukit Dharma** ㉜ (daily daylight hours; free). After visiting the temple, climb up the forested hill for some nice views and to see an ancient stone figure of the multiple-armed goddess Durga slaying a buffalo demon. She is believed to represent the Javanese queen Mahendradatta, wife of the Balinese king Udayana.

Gianyar

From Bedulu, travel east along the main road to **Gianyar** ㉝ (New High Priest Residence). Once the capital of a kingdom, it is now an overgrown town and the administrative capital of the Gianyar region. Wander around the market and commercial centre. Try some of Gianyar's famous *babi guling*, a plate of spicy roasted pork, crispy skin and blood sausage served with mounds of rice; not for those who

keep tabs on their cholesterol levels. A night bazaar with local food and wares begins around 4pm in the parking area of the market.

The speciality of this area is the *endek* cloth *(see page 70)* that the Balinese use as part of their traditional temple attire. There are a number of factories that hold informal tours, and it's intriguing to watch the process of turning white threads through a complex dyeing process into patterns of vibrant colour.

At the centre of town is **Puri Agung Gianyar**, the palace of the local royalty. In the late 1800s, the Dutch saved Gianyar from attack by its hostile neighbours and made it a protected state. During Indonesia's war of independence from 1945–9, the royal family supported the Dutch. The palace is well maintained but not open to the public, so peer through the gates for some views.

NORTH FROM UBUD

Escape from the hustle and bustle of Ubud by heading north for scenes of natural beauty and the Tampasiring area, where a cluster of ancient temples is the main focus of interest.

Petulu

About 6km (4 miles) north of Ubud is **Petulu** ❷. Every morning at dawn, huge flocks of *kokokan* (white **Javan pond herons** and **plumed egrets**) fly off in search of food and then noisily return to roost at sunset (around 6pm). Thousands of them cover the trees like snow and splatter the roadsides with their droppings, so view them from a safe distance. Locals say that the birds are manifestations of souls of people killed in the aftermath of the failed Communist coup against the Indonesian government in Jakarta in 1965. Soon after some 100,000 people connected with the Jakarta coup were massacred in Bali, the egrets mysteriously appeared in Petulu in 1966. It's a spectacular

sight, as the flocks of birds fill the sky before landing, squabbling over prime perches and turning the tree tops white. Village tradition dictates that the birds should not be disturbed during their roosting, but you can sit at a simple viewing platform, and drink cold Bintang beers or soft drinks as you watch.

Tegalalang

Back on the main road, another 7km (4 miles) north in the wood carving village of **Tegalalang** ❸ (Grass Fields) are pretty rice terraces worthy of a stop. A winding river valley is carved into steep embankments, and the long-stemmed *padi Bali* (indigenous Balinese rice) is grown here. Workshops and simple wholesale outlets line the road for 5km (3 miles), selling all sorts of wooden handicrafts and bamboo wind-chimes at half the price you'd pay in Kuta.

Elephant Safari Park

Continue north past Pujung to **Taro** where children will enjoy the family-friendly **Elephant Safari Park** ❸ (daily 9am–6pm; charge; tel: 0361-

The best place to see the kokokan, or white egrets, of Petulu is to bag a table at one of the nearby viewing stations, order a drink, sit back and watch the spectacle at sunset.

BELOW: rice terraces at Tegalalang.

Koi carp reside in the spring-fed pools at Pura Tirtha Empul.

721480; www.baliadventuretours.com). The elephants here were mostly rescued from the effects of deforestation in Sumatra. At the park, children will be able to touch, hand feed and interact with these amazing creatures. For an extra fee, you can take the safari ride tour through the jungles of Taro, perched in a teakwood chair on top of an elephant. The 25-room **Elephant Safari Park Lodge** at the park offers visitors the chance to interact more closely with the elephants (www.elephantsafariparklodge.com).

Pura Gunung Kawi Sebatu

Return on the road towards Pujung and turn left into **Sebatu** (Stone), following it all the way to **Pura Gunung Kawi Sebatu** ❸ (daily daylight hours; charge). This picturesque temple, with colourful shrines and pavilions, is dedicated to the goddess of Lake Batur. Water cascades down a cliff and fills a sacred pool with a shrine in the centre. In the front of the temple, the water gushes out from spouts into two pools that were previously used for

bathing. Newer bathing pools (for men and women) have been constructed nearer the exit, and there is an extra charge to use these.

Pura Mengening

The main road through Sebatu continues 3½km (2 miles) to the village of **Tampaksiring**, the centre for intricate carvings in coconut shells and cattle bones. Filigreed designs of mythological figures, animals and plants are painstakingly cut into these fragile materials.

Continue across the main road, and nearby on the right is a side road that leads to **Pura Mengening** ❸ (daily daylight hours; donation), which has a holy spring to one side. A reconstructed stone *candi* (temple monument) similar to those found in central Java from the 9th century, dominates the inner sanctum of the temple. This may be the commemorative shrine of the 10th-century Balinese King Udayana.

Pura Tirtha Empul

Further up the main road in Tampaksiring is another holy spring at **Pura**

BELOW: holy springs at Pura Tirtha Empul.
RIGHT: bananas for sale within the grounds of the holy springs.

Tirtha Empul ❸❾ (daily daylight hours; charge), bubbling up through black sand within a sacred enclosure inside. It is the source of the Pakerisan River. The Balinese believe that the spring was created by the Hindu god Indra, who pierced the earth to create *tirta* (holy water) in order to revive his soldiers who were poisoned by the demon king Mayadanawa. The temple was built during the 10th century, and the waters gushing through its many spouts are said to have magical curative powers. People often journey here from near and far to purify themselves in the pools after presenting a small offering to the spring's deity. Sacred Barong dance masks and costumes are also spiritually recharged here.

Gunung Kawi

Back on the main road and 1km (½ mile) downhill, turn left and go east to the end of the small road. A very long flight of steep stone steps descends to the ancient site of **Gunung Kawi** ❹❶ (daily daylight hours; charge), an amazing complex of rock-hewn *candi* (shrines) facades and monks' alcoves nestled in a scenic valley overlooking the Pakerisan River.

Dating back to the 11th century, the carvings are remarkably preserved royal memorials for members of Bali's Warmadewa dynasty. One theory holds that the main group of five *candi* across the river honours King Udayana, his queen, Mahendradatta, his concubine and his two sons. Another theory suggests that they honour Udayana's son Anak Wungsu, who ruled Bali during the 11th century, and his wives.

Next to these five monuments are a cluster of niches and rooms hewn out from solid rock. Footwear must be removed before you enter, so be careful of the rough ground. Just outside is a more usual type of Balinese temple with open-sided pavilions, shrines and carved gates. South

of this temple is an isolated group of stone meditation alcoves.

Four more *candi* on the west side of the river are for queens or royal concubines. A tenth one with monks' cells stands alone some distance away through the rice terraces, and may have been for a high court official. Ask the vendors at souvenir shops lining the staircase for directions.

BANGLI

Heading north from the town of Gianyar leads to the region of **Bangli**, a former kingdom founded in the 18th century by a prince from Klungkung in east Bali. From Bangli, it is possible to travel all the way north to Gunung Batur *(see page 148)*.

Pura Dalem Sidan

Head east out of Gianyar and after 2km (1 mile) is the turn-off that leads to **Peteluan**. Go uphill and continue 1km (½ mile) to the **Pura Dalem** ❹❶ (Temple of Death) at **Sidan**. The *kulkul* (wooden gong) tower is decked with bas-reliefs showing underworld demons punishing sinners. The carved gate is equally mag-

Pay heed to signage at all Balinese temples and shrines.

BELOW: shrines carved into solid rock at Gunung Kawi.

Statue at Pura Kehen.

BELOW and **RIGHT:**
the terraced mountain
sanctuary of Pura
Kehen.

nificent. Across the road are some nice views of rice terraces above a river valley.

Pura Dalem Penunggekan

Further uphill, you come shortly to a large stone gateway marking the entrance to the Bangli region. Continue for another 7km (4 miles) to a Y-junction. The left side goes uphill into the town of Bangli. Around 400 metres/yds up on the right side, going out of town, is **Pura Dalem Penunggekan** ㊷; either walk to this Temple of Death from the road going into town, or visit it on your way out. The outer walls of the temple are carved with vivid scenes of sinners being punished in hell.

Bukit Demulih

Continue further west and at a Y-junction veer left and follow the road, turning right at the crossroads to **Bukit Demulih** ㊸ (Hill of No Return). Be warned that it may take a while to find the right vantage point, but when you do it makes the 500-metre (1,600ft) climb well worth it: the view of central Bali from the top is superb. In fact it's all so peaceful and relaxing that you won't want to leave – as the name indicates.

Bangli

The capital of **Bangli** ㊹, which has the same name as the region, stretches out for over 3km (1¾ miles) and is a pleasant, laid-back mountain town with the towering *meru* (pagodas) of temples and palaces lining the main road. Take some time to explore the local market. Dried palm-leaf crafts are the speciality of this town.

Pura Kehen

At the northern end of town, less than 1½km (1 mile) from the centre of Bangli, turn right at a T-junction and continue east to **Pura Kehen** ㊺, (daily daylight hours; donation) a terraced mountain sanctuary and the state temple of Bangli. A long flight of stairs leads up to a towering gate. An enormous banyan tree with a hut for a *kulkul* (warning drum) below it shades the first courtyard, where the walls are inlaid with pieces of Chinese porcelain. The highest level has a 11-tiered *meru* (pagoda) to Siwa (Shiva) and an elaborately carved throne with three compartments for the Hindu trinity of Brahma, Wisnu (Vishnu) and Siwa (Shiva). From here, the main road continues 15km (9 miles) uphill to the volcano of **Gunung Batur** and its adjacent lake *(see page 148)*. ❑

Restaurants

Price for a two-course meal for one including a non-alcoholic beverage:

$$$$ over Rp 300,000
$$$ Rp 200,000–300,000
$$ Rp 100,000–200,000
$ below Rp 100,000

Ubud

Ary's Warung

Jalan Raya Ubud, Ubud.
Tel: 0361-975053.
Open: daily L & D. **$$$**
www.dekco.com
This restaurant calls its food "Contemporary Asian Cuisine", which artfully blends Western food and techniques with Asian spices and ingredients. The tasting menu is a good way of sampling food that you might otherwise not have ordered, with a shorter luncheon tasting menu also available. An interesting selection of hors d'oeuvres is served at the smart cocktail bar.

Bali Pesto Café

Jalan Monkey Forest, Ubud.
Tel: 0361-7424076. Open:
daily B, L & D. **$$**
Tasty Indonesian cuisine with an Italian touch. Good value breakfasts and thin and crispy pizzas. Good to try are the daging bumbu Bali (tender slices of beef tenderloin sautéed with Balinese spices) or pork spare ribs served with a

tangy tomato, ginger and chilli sauce.

Barberkyu

Jalan Monkey Forest.
Tel: 0361-976177. Open:
daily L & D. **$$**
Serves a mix of international and Indonesian food, with an emphasis on barbecued meats. Many types of sausages (chorizo, bratwurst and the Balinese urutan) plus ribs, steaks, kebabs and prawns.

Batan Waru

Jalan Dewi Sita, Ubud.
Tel: 0361-977528. Open:
daily B, L & D. **$$$**
www.baligoodfood.com
Exceptional Indonesian and Western dishes, refreshing drinks and tasty desserts are served here in big portions, representing excellent value for money. Try the Indonesian specials ayam rica-rica (chicken in chilli and coconut gravy) or ayam panggang Bali (Balinese-style grilled chicken). Tuesday evening is chilli crab night (plus fish, prawns and other shellfish).

Bebek Bengil (Dirty Duck Diner)

Jalan Hanoman, Padang Tegal. Tel: 0361-975489.
Open: daily L & D. **$$$**
Large restaurant set among the rice fields and cooled by refreshing breezes. Most well-known for its deep fried crispy duck, which sells

out quickly. Other dishes like the bebek betutu (duck marinaded with spices and cooked over hot coals) and the Asian spiced spare ribs are also good. Western dishes, such as chicken Kiev and fish and chips, are well prepared. Expect reasonably priced food matched by friendly service.

Café Lotus

Jalan Raya Ubud, Ubud.
Tel: 0361-975660. Open:
daily B, L & D. **$$$**
www.lotusrestaurants.com
The menu includes a good mix of Western staples, home-made pastas, Indonesian-style dishes and tempting cheesecakes. You can eat right next to a huge lotus pond with views of Pura Taman Saraswati temple and the adjoining stage, which features Balinese music and dance performances in the evening.

Casa Luna

Jalan Raya Ubud, Ubud.
Tel: 0361-977409. Open:
daily B, L & D. **$$$**
www.casalunabali.com
A large restaurant serving tasty Balinese (and Indonesian) food, which is usually very good; the international offerings are much less consistent in quality. A bakery at the front of the restaurant sells good breads, cakes and pastries.

Café des Artistes

Jalan Bisma 9X, Ubud.
Tel: 0361-972706. Open:
daily L & D. **$$$**
www.cafedesartistesbali.com
One of Ubud's best-value restaurants with a pleasant garden setting; reservations are essential on most evenings. Offers Belgian specialities such as carbonades à la flamande (beef stewed in black beer) and steaks, as well as some Indonesian and Thai dishes thrown in for good measure. Order a Belgian beer too, the perfect accompaniment to your meal.

Cinta Grill

Jalan Monkey Forest, Ubud.
Tel: 0361-975395.
Open: daily B, L & D. **$$$**
www.baligoodfood.com
Restaurant with attached terrace and garden courtyard offering a menu of international and local dishes. Eclectic menu of salads, soups, sandwiches, pastas, curries, stir fries and delicious desserts.

Ibu Oka

Jalan Suweta, Ubud.
Tel: 0361-976345. Open:
daily 11am–2.30pm. **$$**
The most famous outlet in Bali for babi guling, this island's most revered dish – from opening till about 2.30pm there is a constant queue. When the street is closed for royal ceremonies, the warung

Price for a two-course meal for one including a non-alcoholic beverage:

$$$$ over Rp 300,000
$$$ Rp 200,000–300,000
$$ Rp 100,000–200,000
$ below Rp 100,000

operates from the owner's house at Jalan Tegal Sari 2 nearby.

Indian Delites
Jalan Raya Pengosekan, Pengosekan. Tel: 0361-7444222. Open: daily L & D. **$$$**

Affiliated to the famous Gateway of India restaurants (in Seminyak, Kuta and Sanur) and serving virtually the same menu of tasty and reasonably priced Indian fare. Try the wonderful *kathi* rolls (chicken or vegetarian); *kadai* chicken curry; *malai kofta* (cottage cheese and vegetable croquettes); and *aloo mattar* (potato and green pea curry).

Indus
Jalan Raya Sanggingan. Tel: 0361-977684. Open: daily B, L & D. **$$$**

www.casalunabali.com/indus-restaurant

An Ubud favourite, with stunning views of the Tjampuhan River valley and Mt Agung from its open-air terraces ont two levels, and cool open-sided interior. Serves healthy Asian cuisine, and there is a small art gallery on the premises.

Kakiang Café
Jalan Raya Pengosekan, Pengosekan. Tel: 0361-

978984. Open: daily B, L & D. **$$**

www.kakiang.com

A very small but excellent air-conditioned café with great breads, pastries and cakes, as well as fine Illy coffee. The best croissants in Bali are also found here, but they sell out quickly.

Kokokan Club
Arma Resort, Jalan Raya Pengosekan, Ubud. Tel: 0361-976659. Open: daily L & D. **$$$**

www.armaresort.com

Extensive Thai menu at this hotel restaurant set in a lush garden. Recommended starters include *yam wonsen* (noodle salad tossed with prawn, minced chicken, squid and a potent chilli sauce) and *por peh sod* (spring rolls stuffed with shredded vegetables and glass noodles, and drenched in a sweet soy sauce). The mains are all above average but particularly outstanding is the *gaeng ped fucthong* – roast duck and pumpkin bathed in a wonderful fragrant and coconut-rich red curry. Good selection of vegetarian dishes too.

Lamak
Jalan Monkey Forest, Ubud. Tel: 0361-974668. Open: daily L & D. **$$$$**

www.lamakbali.com

Designed by the highly regarded Made Wijaya, this is one of Ubud's most professional restaurants. Serves excellent fusion food like duck breast in Asian spices,

and lamb rack cutlets coated with a tangy Hunan sauce. Lamak also has one of the most stylish cocktail bars in Bali. Offers complimentary guest pick-up from local hotels.

Pignou di Penyu
Jalan Goutama, Ubud. Tel: 0361-972577. Open: Mon–Sat 9am–10pm. **$$$**

This small and intimate French eatery offers genuine French fare at down-to-earth prices. Starters like the Marseillaise fish soup or Parisienne onion soup, and mains like the prawns flambéed in aniseed liqueur will satisfy any hankerings for Gallic food.

Ryoshi
Jalan Raya Ubud. Tel: 0361-972192. Open: daily L & D. **$$$**

www.ryoshibali.com

A traditional Japanese restaurant with a small sushi and sashimi bar upstairs, and a pleasant window-lined room with a jungle and river setting downstairs. Excellent-value tempura and *teppanyaki*, rice and noodle dishes, and vegetarian choices are served here.

TeraZo
Jalan Suweta, Ubud. Tel: 0361-978941. Open: daily L & D. **$$$**

www.baligoodfood.com

An unassuming eatery with good International and Asian dishes served in big portions. Ask to see the daily specials, which are usually worth trying. TeraZo's 8-layer pie (lunch only) of mush-

rooms, leeks, red peppers, ricotta cheese, spinach, parmesan cheese, smoked marlin and pumpkin, is fabulous.

Tut Mak
Jl Dewi Sita; tel: 0361-975754. Open daily B, L & D. **$$**

www.tutmak.com

This friendly café-style restaurant and coffee shop offers a variety of eating areas and is popular with expats. It serves great breakfasts, and its omelettes are a highlight, but sandwiches, burgers, dips, snacks and full meals, including Indonesian specialities, all put in an appearance too. There is also a children's menu. Coffee is Tut Mak's true specialty so try a hot, steamy café latte with a flaky croissant or oversized cinnamon roll.

Waroeng
Jalan Monkey Forest Road, Ubud. Tel: 0361-970928. Open: daily L & D. **$$**

www.thewaroeng.com

This little gem of an eatery serves a variety of Asian cuisines, plus a few Western options. Highlights include the chicken and chive curry tartlets, shrimp wontons with a sweet soy dip, and Indonesian specialities like the excellent *soto ayam*, a spicy chicken soup with egg, bean sprouts and a crisp potato cutlet, and *opor ayam*, chicken in a tamarind and lemongrass coconut curry.

Warung Enak
Jalan Raya Pengosekan, Pengosekan. Tel: 0361-972911. Open: daily L & D. **$$**
www.warungenakbali.com
Sensational Indonesian dishes from all over the archipelago served in a Made Wijaya-designed building that combines a series of Balinese pavilions and garden courtyards. Try the 18-course *rijstaffel* or select from among many specials on the regular menu. Guest pick-up from local hotels is available.

Outside Ubud Centre
CasCades
The Viceroy, Jalan Lanyahan, Nagi. Tel: 0361-971777. Open: daily L & D. **$$$$**
www.theviceroybali.com
Among Bali's best restaurants, overlooking the Lembah Valley. Both the à la carte and degustation menus change regularly but items like foie gras, sweetbreads, Alaskan crab and the best quality meats and seafood feature consistently. An excellent wine list and gracious service complement the wonderfully executed dishes.
Glow
Como Shambhala Estate at Begawan Giri. Tel: 0361-978888. Open: daily B, L & D. **$$$$**
cse.comoshambhala.bz
Occupying a magnificent position up above the Ayung River, this exquisite restaurant features a menu based on mainly organic and vegetarian

ingredients, plus a few meat and seafood dishes for non-vegetarians. It's amazing how the chef has created delicious and healthy food pleasing to both the eye and the palate.
Ibu Mangku
Kedewatan, Ubud. Tel: 0361-974795. Open: daily L. **$**
A popular *warung* thronged with both locals and tourists. Busy all day, it sells one dish, the *nasi ayam Kedewatan* – mixed plate of grilled chicken, Balinese *tum ayam* (minced chicken and spices wrapped in banana leaf), vegetables, egg, fried peanuts and rice. Simple but oh-so-satisfying and at a rock-bottom price.
Jazz Café
Jalan Sukma, Tebesaya, Ubud. Tel: 0361-976594. Open: Tue–Sun D from 6pm. **$$$**
www.jazzcafebali.com
Ubud's main entertainment venue features live jazz nightly. The bistro-style food is surprisingly good too with a fine selection of salads, pastas, pizzas and more substantial main courses such as the grilled prawns with basmati rice and Indian curry sauce.
Kemiri
Uma Ubud, Jalan Sanggingan, Sanggingan. Tel: 0361-972448. Open: daily L & D. **$$$$**
www.uma.como.bz
Surprisingly good value food at this up-market

hotel restaurant, which includes many healthy (and interesting) treats from their Shambala Spa menu – such as grilled prawns with pomelo and apple salad with tamarind dressing; or seared baby snapper wrapped in pastry with cardamom sauce. Garden setting overlooking the pool.
Maya Sari
Maya Ubud, Jalan Gunung Sari, Peliatan. Tel: 0361-977888. Open: daily L & D. **$$$$**. www.mayaubud.com
Pleasant dining area overlooking the valley and a small river. The menu is mainly international, but many Asian fusion items also feature.
Mozaic
Jalan Raya Sanggingan. Tel: 0361-975768. Open: Tue–Sun D. **$$$$**
www.mozaic-bali.com
This is one of Bali's most up-market restaurants and it's easy to see why. The decor is stylish without being over the top and its Modern French cuisine is divine. A 6-course tasting menu is offered at dinner. Advance reservations absolutely essential.
Plantation
Alila Ubud, Payangan. Tel: 0361-975963. Open: daily B, L & D. **$$$$**
www.alilahotels.com
One of the better hotel restaurants serving a mix of international and Indonesian dishes in an open-air pavilion with coconut wood pillars. Excellent service and food (the breakfast

options are exquisite). Lunch and dinner throw up many inventive choices, including an excellent roasted spring chicken with black rice risotto and chilli jam.
Pizza Bagus
Jalan Raya Pengosekan, Ubud. Tel: 0361-978520. Open: daily L & D. **$$**
www.pizzabagus.com
The busiest pizza place in Ubud offering a huge selection, some of them more unusual than others – such as the Tirolese (ham and gorgonzola), the Veneta (smoked turkey, mushroom, capsicum, parmesan and basil) and Pizza Bagus Special (minced beef, chilli sauce, mushroom, carrot, cream cheese, basil and parmesan). Also does home/hotel delivery.
Siam Sally
Jalan Hanoman, Pengosekan, Ubud. Tel: 0361-98077. Open: daily L & D **$$$**
This friendly restaurant is designed along the lines of a Thai shop house within the frame of a contemporary Balinese structure. Downstairs are comfy sofas and tables and upstairs is an open-air pavilion with giant paper lanterns, as well as two terraces. Dishes include curries cooked with house-ground spice pastes and fresh coconut milk, market-style noodle dishes and delicious wok-seared creations.

GUNUNG BATUR AND SURROUNDINGS

Aboriginal Balinese known as the Bali Aga reside on the shore of Bali's largest freshwater lake, Danau Batur, located at the base of the active volcano Gunung Batur. On a clear day, the viewpoint at nearby Penelokan offers magnificent panoramas.

Main attractions
GUNUNG BATUR
DANAU BATUR
PENELOKAN
BATUR VOLCANO MUSEUM
PURA ULUN DANU BATUR
PURA PUNCAK PENULISAN

BELOW: worshippers making offerings at Pura Ulun Danu Batur.

As the road climbs steadily out of **Bangli** town *(see page 144),* the terrain gradually changes from thick bamboo forests to open windswept slopes. Temperatures drop perceptibly and visibility is often reduced by dense mists that roll in during the late afternoon. Colourful fruit stalls line the final approach to the crater rim overlooking the active volcano of **Gunung Batur ❶**. At 1,717 metres (5,600ft), the volcano sits in a vast caldera measuring 11km (7 miles) in diameter and 200 metres

(600ft) in depth. This active volcano last had a minor eruption in 1994, although it sends out clouds of ash from time to time. Legend tells of Siwa (Shiva) dividing the mythological Hindu Mount Meru and placing the two halves in Bali as Agung and Batur. To the east, **Gunung Abang** towers at some 2,150 metres (7,065ft). It is best to visit this area before noon when the rolling mists descend.

At the foot of Gunung Batur lies **Danau Batur ❷**, Bali's largest freshwater lake measuring 7km (4 miles) long and 2km (1 mile) wide. Its depth has never been measured, but this is the source of the rivers and springs for the entire eastern half of Bali, and irrigates most of the island's fertile rice fields. Few people swim in the calm but chilly waters, although it's not forbidden.

Penelokan

The road uphill from Bangli finally emerges at Gunung Batur's crater rim at **Penelokan ❸** (Looking Place). Ribbons of black lava ripple down the sides of Gunung Batur, while Danau Batur resembles a blue or silver sheet of glass – depending on the time of day. The hawkers here can be aggressive and persistent. If arriving during daylight hours, note that entrance fees are charged for a vehicle and each passenger; this allows you access to the entire Gunung Batur area. Keep the tickets while travelling around the area and show them at checkpoints to avoid being charged again.

While here, you might like to visit **Batur Volcano Museum** ❹ (Jl Kintamani, Penelokan, tel: 0366-51152; daily 8am–4pm), where you can learn all about the secrets and mysteries of volcanic phenomena through various panels, interactive games and computer simulations as well as three 20-minute film shows (for groups) in the theatre. Kids love it.

Pura Ulun Danu Batur

Follow the main road 4km (2½ miles) northwest along the crater rim to Bali's second most important temple after Pura Besakih, **Pura Ulun Danu Batur** ❺ (daily during daylight hours; charge). This complex of more than 100 shrines sits on a spectacular and peaceful site overlooking the mountain and lake below. The rituals at this temple venerate Ida Betari Dewi Danu,

the goddess of Danau Batur, who blesses most of Bali with her water.

In 1917, Gunung Batur erupted violently and sent out powerful tremors, destroying thousands of homes and temples, and claiming more than 1,000 lives. Lava engulfed the village of Songan *(see page 151)* below the volcano but miraculously stopped at the foot of the temple at the northern end of the lake. The people took this as a good omen and continued to worship here.

In 1926, another eruption nearly buried the temple. This time, the villagers moved everything up to the crater rim and built the temple where it stands today. Towering gateways open into courtyards covered with black gravel. Rows of *meru* (pagodas) in the inner sanctum stand silhouetted against the open sky overlooking the crater. The main one in the middle is for the lake goddess; others flanking it are for deities of the mountains and royal houses.

Sunrise at Danau Batur at the foot of Gunung Batur.

BELOW: effigy at Pura Ulun Danu Batur.

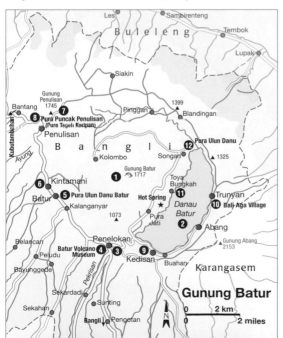

Instead of using the public hot pools, head for the Natural Hot Springs in Toya Bungkah (daily 8am–7pm; charge; tel: 081 338 325 552; www. baturhotspring.com). The mineral pools are set in gardens and there are spa facilities.

BELOW: praying at one of Pura Ulun Danu Batur's shrines, which venerate the goddess of the lake, Danau Batur.

Kintamani and Penulisan

Just beyond Pura Ulun Danu Batur lies **Kintamani** village. Inscriptions from the 10th century indicate that this area was one of the earliest kingdoms. It is a rather plain town today, with hardly any evidence of its ancient glory. On every third morning, the main street comes alive with a fresh produce market.

Continue 5km (3 miles) north along the main road to a forested area often enshrouded by clouds. On a clear day during the dry season (May–Oct), the vista from the viewpoint at **Gunung Penulisan** ❼, some 1,745 metres (5,780ft) high, takes in vistas of the northern coast, Lombok to the east, the island of Nusa Penida to the south, as well as the three great mountains of Bali – Gunung Batur, Abang and Agung.

Closer to the road junction, a long flight of steps leads to **Pura Puncak Penulisan** ❽, also known as **Pura Tegeh Koripan** (daily during daylight hours; charge). This is Bali's highest temple, a complex of terraced sacred sites. The sparse pavilions shelter sculptures of deities and

royalty from the 11th to 15th centuries, including that of Batari Mandul, an 11th-century Chinese princess. If the clouds haven't descended yet, the views from here are incredible.

Kedisan and Trunyan

From Penelokan, a steep, winding road leads 3km (2 miles) downhill to **Kedisan** ❾, on the shore of Danau Batur where boats make the trip to **Trunyan** ❿, the Bali Aga (aboriginal Balinese) village known for its ancient ancestral rites. Trunyan is named after the *taru menyan* (frankincense tree) that grows in the nearby cemetery.

Departing from Balinese tradition, cremation is not practised at Trunyan; instead, the dead are left in open graves. There is no odour of decaying flesh due to the presence of the *taru menyan* tree, which is believed to produce a fragrant smell, while its roots – beneath the bodies – bafflingly prevent putrefaction. If venturing to the shadowy *kubutan* or cemetery (situated about 500 metres/yds outside the village, and accessible only by boat), don't expect to see

piles of dead bodies. Instead there are 11 open graves hidden by bamboo lattices. The most recent dead body replaces the oldest one, whose skull is cleaned and placed with others on a stone platform nearby. Secretive and protective of their customs, the villagers keep the 4-metre (13ft)-tall image of Dewa Ratu Gede Pancering Jagat hidden in a pagoda; tourists are forbidden to see it.

Proceed with caution if visiting Trunyan (there have been cases of boatmen wanting to renegotiate rates in the middle of the lake). Settle on a price for the boat from Kedisan to Trunyan, Kuban, Toya Bungkah and back to Kedisan.

Most visitors are discouraged by tales of touts demanding extortionate boat fares that increase halfway across the lake. However, the village is now accessible by a narrow, winding and incredibly-steep road; it is possible to negotiate the road by car but probably safer by *ojek* (motorcyle taxi), which can be arranged in Toya Bungkah. Be prepared to pay a donation of anything up to Rp 600,000 to the head of the village.

Toya Bungkah

If skipping Trunyan, travel from Kedisan by the winding 7km (4-mile) road past an arid landscape strewn with lava boulders to **Toya Bungkah ⑪**, on the west bank of Danau Batur. (Watch out for trucks carrying sand and gravel.) Toya Bungkah is known for its hot springs, said to be imbued with medicinal properties. The free public bathing pools are polluted since people use soap for bathing and laundry; recommended is the **Natural Hot Springs** just beside the lake (*see margin page 150*). Nearby are a few restaurants and small hotels. Toya Bungkah is also the start of the trek up to Gunung Batur (*see pages 77 and 260*).

Pura Ulun Danu

At the northern end of Danau Batur at **Songan** is the original **Pura Ulun Danu ⑫**, nearly engulfed by lava in 1926 but later rebuilt on the same site. Legend tells of a deity here who meditated underground and caused a great flood. The villagers prayed for the water to be channelled underground and it did so, eventually emerging again as the source of Danau Batur. ❏

The original Pura Ulun Danu at Songan, destroyed by the eruption of Gunung Batur in 1926 and later rebuilt.

RESTAURANTS

Lunch buffets – strictly Indonesian fare – are served in the many restaurants along the ridge at Penelokan. For evening meals, go to the small hotels, or the simple *warung* down by the lake at Toya Bungkah.

Gong Dewata
Penelokan. Tel: 0366-51036. Open: daily B & L. **$$**
Breakfast and lunch buffets and also à la carte,

which includes Indonesian Chinese food. Eat on the front terrace facing the mountain or inside by the picture windows.

Grand Puncak Sari
Penelokan. Tel: 0366-51073. Open: daily L. **$$**
Two-level restaurant with open terrace upstairs and indoor dining room downstairs. Buffet comprises a wide spread of dishes, priced slightly higher than the usual. Indonesian Chi-

nese and local versions of Western dishes available à la carte.

Gunung Sari
Penelokan. Tel: 0366-52365. Open: daily L. **$$**
Split-level building, half glassed-in, half open terrace. Standard buffet lunch with better variety than most. Vegetarian options. À la carte features Balinese dishes such as *pepes ikan* (fish in banana leaf).

Lakeview Restaurant
Lakeview Ecolodge, Penelokan. Tel: 0366-51394. Open: daily 8am–

10pm. **$$**
www.lakeviewbali.com
Mountain side restaurant serving breakfast and lunch buffets, specialising in Indonesian and Balinese cuisine, sourcing its ingredients within a 15km (9 mile) radius of Lake Batur. International dishes also on the menu.

• • • • • • • •
Price for a two-course meal for one including a non-alcoholic beverage:
$ = below Rp 100,000,
$$ = Rp 100,000–200,000.
$$$ = Rp 200,000–300,000.
$$$$ = over Rp 300,000.

EAST BALI

In the Balinese world view, the east is an auspicious direction. Not surprisingly, Bali's pre-eminent temple, Pura Besakih, is here. Vestiges of former grandeur – such as the palace remnants at Taman Gili – remain, and there are startling black-sand beaches with hundreds of fishing outriggers moored onshore.

Neither as developed nor as rich as the southern part of the island, the eastern side of Bali has a different ambience, defined by its lava-strewn landscapes and high, bare hills ribbed with ancient rice terraces. Partly hidden by the eastern coastal ranges is the colossal cone of the active volcano **Gunung Agung**, which at 3,014 metres (9,796ft) high, dominates this drier, sparser side of Bali. The coastal strip along the eastern shore, lined with fishing and salt-producing villages and black-sand beaches, has become a tourist destination in its own right. Unfortunately, the gathering of coral to make lime for local construction has irreparably damaged some of the reefs and led to the erosion of many beaches. Further inland, a few villages, set in lush valleys, still retain their archaic traditions.

Pura Besakih

The access point to Pura Besakih is via **Menanga**. From here, follow the road another 5km (3 miles) as it ascends to **Pura Besakih ❶** (daily daylight hours; charge, camera fees extra). This is Bali's largest and most important place of worship, often referred to as

the "Mother Temple". Opinions are divided on whether it's worth visiting, mainly because of the overt commerce (there are souvenir shops and persistent vendors everywhere) and the hard-sell tactics of the "official guides" (see margin tip, page 155).

Pura Besakih began as an ancient terraced mountain sanctuary as early as the 8th century AD. Over time it was enlarged, until it grew to its present size of more than 30 public temples with hundreds of shrines, most of which were added between

Main attractions
PURA BESAKIH
TAMAN GILI
NUSA LEMBONGAN
TENGANAN
PASIR PUTIH BEACH
TAMAN UJUNG
TAMAN TIRTAGANGGA
PURA LEMPUYANG
AMED
TULAMBEN MARINE RESERVE

LEFT: seaweed farmers at sunset over Jungutbatu Bay, Nusa Lembongan island.
RIGHT: visiting Pura Besakih.

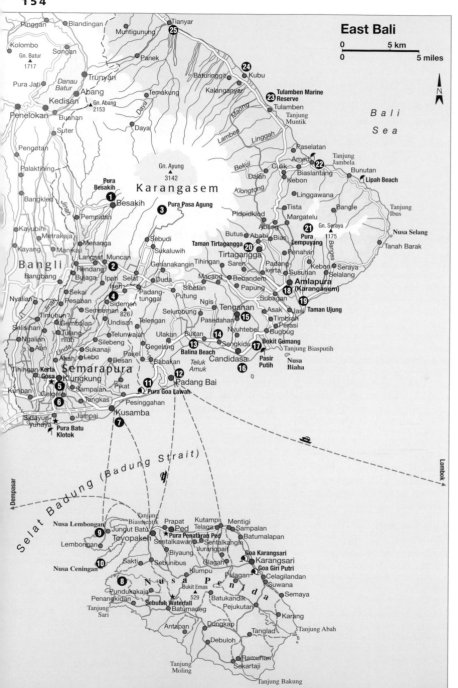

East Bali

0   5 km

0   5 miles

N

Bali Sea

Pinggan   Blandingan   Muntigunung   Tianyar **25**

Kolombo   Songan   Panek

Gn. Batur 1717

Pura Jati   Danau Batur   Trunyan   Abang   Temakung

Kedisan   Gn. Abang 2153

Penelokan   Buahan   Daya

Suter   Daya

Pengotan

Palaktihing

Bangkled

Kayubihi   Metrakaja   Menanga

Kayang   Mankaji   Langsat Muncan

Bangli

Bangbang   Rendang **2**

Bujaga   Ipah   Selat   Duda

Nyalian   Sekai   Pesaban   Iseh **4**

Selisihan   Timuhun   Gembalan   Sidemen

Ngalian   Tulang nliuh   Undisan

Aan   Lebu   Silebeng   Telunwajah

Tihingan Kerta   Sukanaji   Pakel

Gosa **5**   Klungkung   Besan   Babakan

Kuripan   Gelgel   Pikat

6   Sampalan

Sidayu-   Jumpai   Tangkas

yuhaya   Pesinggahan

Pura Batu Klotok   Kusamba **7**

Tanyar **25**

Baturinggit   Kubu **24**

Kalangapyar

23 Tulamben Marine Reserve

Tulamben

Tanjung Muntik

Raselatan

Amed **22**

Culik   Biaslantang

Daiah   Kebon

Linggawana

Tista   Bangle

Margatelu

21 Pura Lempuyang

Gn. Seraya 1175

Abang

Butus   Bias

Taman Tirtagangga **20**

Tirtagangga

Saren   Penahan

Padang-kerta

Macang   Bebandem   Susunan

Papung   Kebon   Seraya

Subagan

Tenganan   Asak   Jasi **19** Taman Ujung

15 Nyuhtebel   Timbrah

Pasedahan   Perasi

Buitan   Bugbug

14 Sengkidu   Bukit Gumang

Ulakan **13**   **17**

Gegelang   Balina Beach   Tanjung Biasputih

Candidasa   Pasir Putih   Nusa Biaha

16

Teluk Amuk

12 Padang Bai

11 Pura Goa Lawah

Amlapura (Karangasem) **18**

Tanjung Jambela   Bunutan

Lipah Beach

Tanjung Ibus

Nusa Selang

Tanah Barak

Gn. Ayung 3142

Karangasem

Pura Besakih **1**   Besakih

Pura Pasa Agung **3**

Pempatan

Sebudi

Sukaluwih

Genanakangin   Tihingan

Pura Besakih

Pidpidklod

Klongtong

Bekul

Maong

Lambeg   Linggah

Gulik   Biaslantang

Ababi

Padang-tunggal

Putung   Ngis

Selumbung

Pasedahan

Telengan   Sibetan

Semarapura

Selat Badung (Badung Strait)

Selat Badung

◄ Dempasar

Lombok ►

Nusa Lembongan

Tanjung Biasmentik   Prapat   Kutampi   Mentigi

Jungut Batu   Ped   Telaga   Sampalan

Toyopakeh **9**   Sentalkawan   Batumalapan

Lembongan   Biyaung   Jurangpait   Sentalkangin

Sakti   Sebunibus   Glagah   Goa Karangsari

10   Klumpu   **Karangsari**

Nusa Ceningan   Pulagan   Goa Giri Putri

8   *Nusa Penida*   Celagilandan

Pundukakaja   Bukit Emas   Suwana

Penangkidan   Batukandik   Semaya

Sebuluh Waterfall   Pejukutan

Tanjung Sari   Batumadeg   Karang

Antapan   Dungkap   Tanglad   Tanjung Abah

Debuloh

Ramunan Sekartaji

Tanjung Moling

Tanjung Bakung

Pura Penataran Ped ★

the 14th and 18th centuries. From the 5th to the 17th centuries, Pura Besakih became the state sanctuary of the Gelgel dynasty. Today, the temple is overseen by the descendants of the Klungkung royal family who are direct heirs of the Gelgel kingdom.

In 1917, Pura Besakih was almost levelled by a massive earthquake and was rebuilt. In 1963, however, the temple miraculously suffered minimal damage during the eruption of Gunung Agung (*see box below*), even though it is located only 6km (4 miles) from the crater.

Pura Penataran Agung

Within the complex is the all-important **Pura Penataran Agung**, built on a series of terraces. A long flight of steps leads to an austere *candi bentar* (split gate) made of granite. The setting is magnificent, with the peak of Gunung Agung looming overhead and panoramic views of south Bali below. Non-worshippers are not allowed into the temple even if properly dressed, but one can see the inner sanctum through the gates or by walking around the complex and peering over the walls.

Inside the main courtyard, which interestingly is not the highest one, is a large *padmasana tiga* (triple lotus shrine) of dark volcanic stone with three high seats on a single base for enthroning three aspects of the supreme god: Siwa, Sadasiwa and Paramasiwa. Many Balinese interpret this shrine as the more familiar Hindu trinity of Brahma, Wisnu (Vishnu), and Siwa (Shiva). The other temples that make up Pura Besakih are not worth seeing, although each one has a symbolic importance.

The main festival at Pura Besakih, Batara Turun Kabeh, when "the gods descend together", takes place during the full moon in March or April. Thousands of worshippers come by bus and truck loads from all over Bali during this 11-day event.

Muncan

Back on the main road and 2km (1 mile) downhill from Menanga, turn left at the T-junction in **Rendang** village to **Muncan ❷**. Follow the road as it winds 4km (2½ miles) east through spectacular rice terraces. On the eve of

Appeasing the Gods

In 1963, devotees at Pura Besakih were preparing for Eka Dasa Rudra, the greatest sacrifice that occurs only once every 100 years, when Gunung Agung began to rumble to life after over 120 years of being dormant. This was seen as a good sign, and activities continued. By the time the ceremony took place in March, thick columns of dark smoke were rising from the summit. Shortly after, Agung exploded violently. More than 1,600 people were killed and 100,000 were left homeless, most losing their livelihoods as entire villages were engulfed. To most Balinese, the eruption was punishment for doing the ritual at the wrong time. In 1979, a properly timed ceremony to mark the end of a Balinese century went without incident.

BELOW: Pura Besakih – the long flight of steps leading to the granite split gate.

TIP

The easier way to climb up Gunung Agung is from Pura Pasar Agung, since the temple is already halfway up the slopes. This approach, however, does not reach the peak, which can only be done by a very difficult hike from Pura Besakih. Either way you should hire the services of a guide.

the lunar-solar New Year in March, a special ceremony takes place in Muncan, when two large male and female figures fashioned from special trees enact an ancient fertility rite with a simulated public mating. Afterwards, the figures are thrown into the river; it is believed that using the river water to irrigate the rice fields will result in bountiful harvests.

Pura Pasar Agung

Some 4km (2½ miles) east of Muncan, in **Selat**, a paved road winds 12km (7½ miles) uphill through **Sebudi** and lava fields to **Pura Pasar Agung** ❸ (daily daylight hours; donation). This is the start point of one of the trekking routes up the mountain. Completely destroyed during the 1963 eruption of Gunung Agung *(see box page 155)*, the temple was rebuilt and expanded during the late 1990s. Located at the top of a long flight of stairs, the setting is spectacular with the summit of Agung up close and stunning panoramas of east Bali peeking out from the clouds below. Inside is a triple lotus shrine similar to the one found at Pura Besakih.

Iseh and Sidemen

Back on the main road, just 1½km (1 mile) east in **Selat-Duda** is a T-junction. Turn right and follow the road as it winds 12km (7½ miles) downhill through scenic rice fields in **Iseh** – where German artist Walter Spies built a home in 1937 to escape from his increasingly hectic social life in Campuan – to **Sidemen** ❹. This village is a centre for handwoven *songket* (gold or silver thread brocade) and *endek* (weft-*ikat* cloth). Hikes through Sideman's idyllic surroundings can be made by contacting guesthouses in the area.

Also in the village is **Yayasan Siddhamaha** (Great Accomplishments Foundation), a Swiss-sponsored school for teaching local adolescents Balinese language, literature, palm-leaf inscribing, painting, music and dance in addition to the regular curriculum.

Klungkung (Semarapura)

About 10km (6½ miles) downhill from Sideman, turn right into **Satria**, where colourful gold-leafed parasols line the streets. These and other temple and ceremonial paraphernalia are made here. Follow the road 1km (½ mile) west as it crosses a bridge over the Unda River into **Klungkung** ❺, also known as **Semarapura**.

During the late 17th century, the kingdom of Gelgel, based in Gelgel *(see page 159)*, lost a series of battles and allegiances. One of the king's ministers revolted and put himself on the throne, and a long battle ensued to regain it. In 1710, a new court was built at Klungkung because the old site at Gelgel was considered cursed. As the seat of the Dewa Agung, the highest of the Balinese kings, Klungkung holds a special place in the island's history and culture; many of Klungkung's kings and noblemen supported and developed styles of music, drama and art that flourish today in Bali.

Just east of the main crossroads

BELOW: women weaving double Ikat fabric, Sideman.

in Klungkung is the shopping area. Explore the handful of antique shops on the main street and the multistorey **Pasar Klungkung** market (daily 7am–4pm) at the back for local items and wares. Towering over the town centre is the **Puputan Klungkung Monument**. This sombre black stone tower commemorates the massacre of the Klungkung royal family by the Dutch in 1908.

Taman Gili

Today, the remains of the old palace are found across the street within the grounds of **Taman Gili** (daily 9am–5pm; charge for all pavilions and museum). **Bale Kerta Gosa** (Pavilion of Peace and Prosperity) to the right of the main entrance has exquisite examples of painting and architecture in the traditional Klungkung style.

Often mistakenly referred to as the Hall of Justice because of its ceiling paintings (although no criminal cases would have been tried in such a grand place), different animal-headed armrests on the chairs indicate that the king (lion), his priests (bulls) and advisers (serpents) met here to consult on affairs of the realm. The ceiling paintings, arranged in several tiers, are in the *wayang* (puppet figure) style of Kamasan, named after the village where artists still paint such works.

Reading from bottom to top and going clockwise, they mostly tell the story of *Bima Swarga* (Heavenly Bima) from the *Mahabharata* epic. The hero Bima searches for the souls of his parents in the underworld, battling first with demons and the god of hell, and then against the heavenly deities to allow their souls to enter paradise. Other levels show the *Tantri* animal fables, the story of the mythological *Garuda* bird, events caused by earthquakes, and the grisly punishments that await sinners in hell.

The adjacent **Bale Kambang** (Floating Pavilion), built in the middle of a pond, was mainly used by the royal family as a place to rest and be entertained. The ceiling paintings show Balinese astrological signs along with the Buddhist tales of the Men Brayut family, with 18 children, and the bodhisattva *Sutasoma* battling demons.

At the base of the Puputan Klungkung Monument are some statues of the Klungkung royal family who were massacred by the Dutch in 1908.

LEFT: ceiling paintings at Bale Kerta Gosa.
BELOW: Bale Kambang, the "floating pavilion".

Below: a Kamasan-style painting.

Semarajaya Museum

On the left-hand side of Taman Gili stands the red-brick gate of the **former palace**, now fenced-off as a shrine. According to local lore, the palace doors mysteriously sealed shut by themselves after the royal family was massacred, and no one has dared to open them since. Look for figures of Chinese, Portuguese and Dutch figures scrambling up the sides of the gate.

At the back of the grounds lies **Semarajaya Museum** (daily 9am–5pm; charge for Taman Gili includes museum), mostly filled with artefacts of the Klungkung region such as traditional weapons, puppet-style painting, and tools for weaving and salt-producing. Some old photos of the former court are also on display. An adjoining section houses a collection of paintings and sculptures by the Italian artist Emilio Ambron (1905–96), who lived and worked in Bali during the 1930s.

Tihingan

Head 2½km (1½ miles) west out of town on the main road to the interesting *gamelan*-making village of **Tihingan** (Bamboo). Families in this village keep furnaces burning to melt bronze for the keys and kettles of Balinese *gamelan* musical instruments. Go during the cooler morning hours when most of the work is done at the small foundries located behind homes. Listen out for rhythmic pounding – although as forging is not done every day, it's mainly a matter of being there at the right time. The wooden instrument cases which hold the *gamelan* keys are also carved and gilded here.

Nyoman Gunarsa Museum

From the Tihingan crossroads, head 2½km (1½ miles) downhill to the **Nyoman Gunarsa Museum** (daily 9am–4pm; charge; tel: 0366-22255; www.gunarsamuseum.com). The four-storey building houses a collection of traditional Balinese paintings, masks (look out for the giant Barong image), carvings and other antiques, including contemporary semi-abstract works by I Nyoman Gunarsa, founder of the museum (who hails from Klungkung) and other modern Balinese artists.

Kamasan

About 2km (1 mile) south of Klungkung is **Kamasan**, where artists use natural pigments to illustrate episodes from Indian epics, Javanese-Balinese romances, legends, and astrological and agricultural charts in the *wayang* (puppet-figure) style. Workshops are found along the main street; although Kamasan-style paintings are sold all over Bali, better quality works are found here at lower prices. One of the leading practioners of this art form, I Nyoman Mandra, still lives in Kamasan.

Be sure to stop by the **Kamasan Art Centre** in the village to see some fine examples of Kamasan painting. The centre also runs classes in painting, dance and *gamelan* playing.

Gelgel

Just south of Kamasan is **Gelgel** ❻ (pronounced ghell-ghell), the former capital of the Klungkung dynasty. In the late 1400s and 1500s, the Balinese kings here wielded immense power during the golden age of art, culture and religion. Today there is little evidence of its former glory; the town feels more Islamic in character and is dominated by a large mosque. Exquisite handwoven *songket* (brocade with gold or silver threads) and *endek* (weft-*ikat* cloth) are made in many homes in Gelgel.

Gelgel's **Pura Dasar** (daily daylight hours; donation) is a large and important temple for members of the *pasek* commoner clans. The temple has ancient megalithic stone seats and rows of beautiful *meru* (pagodas) built in the local style. During the full moon in October, dozens of villagers come here to take part in an extremely colourful temple ceremony.

Kusamba

Leave Klungkung and head towards the coast at **Kusamba** ❼ where numerous colourful *jukung* or fishing outriggers with painted faces line the black-sand shores of its beach.

Apart from fishing, salt production is the other main activity in this region, evidenced by the thatched huts and wooden troughs lined up along isolated stretches of the beach near Kusamba and sections of the northeastern coast around Amed and Tianyar. To produce salt, villagers splash seawater onto plots of sand, a process repeated many times. The dense salt-infused sand is then placed in conical wooden vats in the thatched huts and seawater is poured over it. Concentrated salt water filters into pots, and is then poured into long wooden troughs outside to partially evaporate into sludge. The wet crystals are then scooped into bamboo baskets to let the liquid drain out, then and left to dry completely.

Sea salt produced at the coastal villages of east Bali is mainly used for processing dried fish.

Nusa Penida

Across from Kusamba off the southeastern coast lie three sparsely populated islands – Nusa Penida, Nusa Lembongan and Nusa Ceningan – which can be accessed by boat from the mainland (either Kusamba, Benoa harbour in the south, or Padang Bai

BELOW: producing sea salt near Kusamba

Pura Segara, part of Pura Penataran Ped complex, Nusa Penida Island.

BELOW: Crystal Bay, Nusa Penida Island.

in the east). The largest of the islands is **Nusa Penida 8**, which covers 240 sq km (95 sq miles) and has around 47,000 people who subsist largely on fishing and seaweed farming.

Originally a penal colony for the Klungkung kingdom on the mainland, Nusa Penida is dry and austere. Many of its inhabitants are considered to be experts in black magic, for this is the home of the great fanged lord of supernatural forces, Ratu Gede Mas Mecaling. *Kain cepuk*, weft-*ikat* cloths with geometric designs on red backgrounds, sacred to the queen of black magic Rangda, are woven in many villages, as are the ritual *kain keling* striped cloths.

Nusa Penida gets very little tourist traffic, and is ideal if you want to escape the hordes of south Bali and experience something out of the ordinary. Boats from Nusa Lembongan drop passengers off at Toyopakeh in the north, where public *bemo* and rental vehicles with drivers can be used for an exploration of the island. About 3km (1½ miles) east of Toyopakeh is the temple complex at **Pura Penataran Ped** (daily daylight

hours; donation). It comprises **Pura Segara**, dedicated to the sea deity, **Pura Taman**, honouring Wisnu (Vishnu), **Pura Ratu Gede**, dedicated to the lord of sorcery, and **Pura Dalem Ped**, to the deities of death. All the temple walls and gates are made of local white limestone.

Past the main town at Sampalan, continue down the eastern coast to **Goa Giri Putri** (Cave of the Mountain Princess), near the village of Suwana. Here, steep stairs lead to the cave dedicated to Parwati, consort of Siwa (Shiva). Guides with pressure lamps wait at a small temple near the mouth of the cave. After a short but steep descent down a tiny opening with a low ceiling, the cave opens up to 15 metres (50ft) in height. Diesel-powered lights barely show the way, so walk carefully around the small holes and protruding rocks covered with slippery droppings from bats. Shrines dot the interior, and it is possible to climb a ladder to the upper niches. After about 300 metres (1,000ft), sunlight shines through a large opening overlooking a valley.

Other sights on the island worth

seeing are **Tanglad**, where weaving is the mainstay, and the waterfall at **Batukandik**. Further inland a rough road leads to the highest point, **Bukit Emas** (Golden Hill) at 521 metres (1,700ft), which has stunning panoramas from its temple, **Pura Puncak Mundi**.

Nusa Lembongan

The island of **Nusa Lembongan ❾**, although much smaller at 10 sq km (4 sq miles), far outstrips its sister island in terms of visitor numbers. The white-sand beaches at **Jungutbatu** and **Mushroom Bay** along its western coast are ringed with cosy guesthouses and boutique resorts, ideal for extended stays, while beach clubs offer snorkelling and diving facilities for day trippers arriving on catamarans from Tanjong Benoa. Apart from diving (*see page 256 for operators*), for which the waters around these islands are famous, there is also a lively surf scene along the south coast at **Dream Beach** during the dry season. The surf breaks, which go by names such as Shipwreck, Lacerations and Playground, can be dangerous and are not meant for novices.

Visitors can travel around the island (which is small enough to be covered on foot or mountain bike) to seaweed farms and mangrove swamps. In **Lembongan** village, the bizzare **Rumah di Bawah Tanah** (Underground House) was built more than 40 years ago by a local priest acting upon divine inspiration. It has a living room, bedrooms and kitchen with a well carved out of natural limestone, but no one actually lives here. Local guides take visitors around for a small fee.

Nusa Ceningan

East of Lembongan village, a 1km (½-mile) suspension bridge connects to the smallest island in the group, **Nusa Ceningan ❿**. You can climb 65 metres (200ft) up the island's highest hill for some great views. The lagoon is filled with bamboo frames used to cultivate seaweed, which is exported and used as an emulsifying agent in cosmetics and processed food. Seaweed cultivation is also a major activity on Nusa Penida and Nusa Lembongan, employing over 80 percent of the local population.

> **TIP**
>
> The waters around Nusa Penida and Nusa Lembongan are particularly noted for clear waters and rich diversity of marine life; the area is frequented by migratory sunfish in October.

BELOW: seaweed cultivation and porters at Jungutbatu Bay, Nusa Lembongan.

TIP

It's difficult to predict Tenganan's Usaba Sambah festival dates, but it is usually held at full moon in June or July. A similar but smaller festival occurs at the same time in the neighbouring village of Tenganan Dauh Tukad.

Pura Goa Lawah

Back on the mainland, about 2½km (1½ miles) east of Kusamba is the bat cave temple of **Pura Goa Lawah** ⓫ (daily daylight hours; charge). Be forewarned that the hawkers here are extremely pushy. The walls of the cave literally vibrate with thousands of bats – their bodies packed so close together that the upper surface of the cave resembles undulating mud. Occasionally a python, believed to be a manifestation of the mythological underworld serpent Basuki, appears and feeds on them. In 2004, one snake died and was respectfully cremated.

Lining the entrance are several small shrines covered with smelly bat droppings. The temple is very important for post-cremation rites: on the beach across the street, the soul is called in from the sea and a container is symbolically filled with seawater and brought to the cave. After rituals are performed, it's then brought to Pura Dalem Puri, which is part of the Pura Besakih complex *(see page 153)*. The cave is said to extend via a lava tube all the way to Pura Goa, also in the Besakih complex.

Padang Bai

Some 1½km (1 mile) east along the road, a scenic point by the shore with huge regional symbols marks the exit from Klungkung and the entrance to Karangasem. A further 5km (3 miles) east is a T-junction; veering right leads to **Padang Bai** ⓬. This picturesque bay cradled by hills is the main port for the Bali–Lombok ferries and fast boats as well as the public boats to Nusa Penida. Passenger and cargo vessels, yachts and international cruise liners stop by here, and there is a range of tourist facilities. Beyond the ferry terminal is the white-sand **Bias Tugal Beach**, also referred to as Pantai Kecil (Little Beach). To get there, follow the road from the police station for 100 metres/yds up the hill, turn left at the sign for the beach, head up the steep hill and then descend via the hillside track through the bush.

At a headland east of Padangbai is **Pura Silayukti**, built in honour of the great Javanese priest Empu Kuturan, who lived in this area at the beginning of the 11th century. The temple occupies the site of his former home. From its vantage-location are good views of the bay below.

Beyond the temple on the other side of the headland are **Blue Lagoon** and **Teluk Jepun** (Japan Bay), both good for snorkelling and diving. At Blue Lagoon, the snorkelling areas are easily accessible from the beach, while getting to the snorkelling sites in Teluk Jepun requires a short boat trip. The coral reefs are varied, as is the marine life, but the waters can be cold and cloudy at times. Diving trips can be arranged through local operators at Padangbai.

Balina and Manggis

Beyong Padangbai comes the broad sweep of **Teluk Amuk** (Amuk Bay), the site of a controversial oil terminal. At its eastern end, after the coastal road crosses an iron bridge, a track

BELOW: the harbour at Padang Bai.

Sri Sadia Rahayu 01

leads down to **Buitan** village and **Balina** ⓭ beach. Apart from simple guesthouses, this is where you'll find the fabled Amankila resort (which is blessed with a surprisingly picturesque sandy beach) and the more modest but still stylish Alila Manggis.

Nearby is the fishing village of **Manggis**, which takes its name from the delectable mangosteen fruit (look for the giant statue of this purple-skinned fruit along the road).

Sengkidu

Further east along the main road is **Sengkidu** ⓮. The **Pura Puseh** (daylight hours; free) temple has a colourful ceremony during the full moon in November with men in trance stabbing themselves with sharp daggers and hundreds of villagers joining in ritual dances. Small hotels and guesthouses line the beach at Sengkidu, which is another place that has been affected by erosion.

Tenganan

Continue east on the main road, and at a junction before Candidasa turn left up an asphalt road to the Bali Aga (aboriginal Balinese) village of **Tenganan** ⓯ (daily daylight hours; charge). The village is surrounded by a wall, and houses line both sides of a long, stone-paved terrace with ritual pavilions in the centre. Until the 1970s, Tenganan was a closed society, visited only by the occasional ethnologist. An entrance fee is now charged, a sign of how much that times have changed. The villagers practise unusual rituals, many of which date from Bali's pre-Hindu animist days. The dead, for instance, are not cremated in this village; instead, the bodies are buried naked face down.

By one account the inhabitants originally came from East Java, but another legend from the 14th century tells of the king of Bedulu in Gianyar whose favourite horse ran away. He sent his subjects to search for it; some went east and found the corpse of the animal. When the king offered to reward them, they asked for the land wherever the decaying horse could be smelled. For several days one of the men led the court official around, yet the air remained pungent with the odour of rotting horse. When the

Purchase a puppet as a souvenir from the walled village of Tenganan.

BELOW: local women preparing for a festival in Tenganan.

Detail of pattern from geringsing *fabric. The cloth is said to be imbued with magical properties.*

BELOW: Bali Aga women pounding rice the traditional way in Tenganan.

tired official decided that too much land had been given up and left, the gleeful man who led him pulled out a piece of smelly horse flesh hidden inside his clothes.

The village still owns these large tracts of land, making it one of the richest in this area. By tradition, the men do not work the fields but hire people from the surrounding areas to cultivate them in return for a share of the harvest. The men instead spend their time inscribing dried fan-palm leaves to make illustrated *lontar* (manuscripts), or crafting basketry from smoked *ata* (liana vines).

The village women weave the famous double-*ikat* cloth called *geringsing (see page 71),* which means "illness-free". A single high-quality cloth can take up to five years to complete. A finely woven piece can cost several thousand dollars, and they are in great demand by Balinese for rituals and by foreign collectors and museums overseas. In the village souvenir shops, you will mostly find inferior quality fabrics for sale at lower prices.

During ceremonies, girls wear *geringsing* and adorn their hair with gold

flowers for ritual dances, accompanied by men playing the *gamelan selonding,* an archaic and rare music ensemble with iron-keyed metallophones.

In June or July during the annual Usaba Sambah festival, which lasts a month, creaky wooden *ayunan* (ferris-wheels) are set up and manually operated by men. Unwed village maidens ride these as part of ancient fertility rites; the turning symbolises the descent of the sun to the earth.

Another Tenganan practice during the Usaba Sambah festival is the *makare,* where men engage in a fight using thorny pandanus leaves, accompanied by *gamelan selonding* music. Both opponents must draw blood as offerings to the demons, warding off attacks with rattan shields. After the battles, the wounds are treated with a stinging mixture of turmeric and vinegar that, miraculously, leaves no scars.

If you have time visit Tenganan Dauh Tukad (West Tenganan), for which you will see the turning signposted on the right as you drive back to the main road. This village was once part of the original Tenganan but became separated by a river following a flood. Quieter and much less visited, West Tenganan is similar to East Tenganan but not bound by such strict *adat* (customary law) practices.

Candidasa

On the main road just past the Tenganan junction is the beach side resort area of **Candidasa** ⓰, which has a good range of hotels and restaurants and is an excellent base from which to explore eastern Bali. Unfortunately, the shore is blighted by ugly jetties protruding into the water, too little and too late to stop the erosion caused from years of unbridled coral removal for construction. As a result the beach here is very narrow, although golden and sandy. **Pasir Putih** beach, however, is gorgeous, blessed with soft silvery-white sand (access is via a steep rough track signposted "Virgin Beach",

negotiable by car, which leads off the main road 6km/3½ miles to the east of Candidasa).

Across from Candidasa's man-made lotus lagoon is **Pura Candi Dasa** (daily daylight hours; donation), a 12th-century complex built on several levels on the hillside. One of the upper temples is for Hariti, originally a child-eating ogress who converted to Buddhism and became a protector of children. The Balinese call her Men Brayut, from the folktale of a mother who had 18 children. Women who want to conceive come here to pray and make offerings to her.

Bukit Gumang

After Candidasa, the road climbs and winds for 5km (3 miles) through the hills to **Bukit Gumang** ⑰ and you'll see monkeys hanging around the roadside. On every even-numbered year by the light of the full moon in October, the *perang dewa* (Battle of the Gods) takes place here. Thousands of people from four surrounding villages ascend 300 metres (1,000ft) to the peak, carrying offerings of suckling pigs, which are then

hung from frangipani trees. Men bearing images of the village deities in portable shrines fall into trance, causing the palanquins to collide and battle with each other.

From Bukit Gumang, the road descends to **Bugbug** (pronounced *boog-boog*), where long narrow lanes, wide enough only for a single person to pass through, run perpendicular to the village's one main road.

Amlapura

Continue along the main road to **Amlapura** ⑱, the capital of the Karangasem region. This former kingdom was founded during the weakening of the Gelgel court in the 17th century. By the late 18th and early 19th centuries, it was the most powerful state in Bali, and had extended its domain to the neighbouring island of Lombok.

Amlapura's main attraction is the old palace complex of **Puri Agung Karangasem** (daily 9am–5pm; charge), a fusion of European and Asian architectural styles and design dating back to the turn of the 20th century. Now unoccupied, the main palace build-

Entrance to Puri Agung Karangasem.

BELOW: Bale Maskerdam at the old palace complex of Puri Agung Karangasem in Amlapura.

Water-lily pond in the water gardens at Taman Ujung.

BELOW: Taman Ujung, a former royal summer retreat.

ing with a wide verandah is the **Bale Maskerdam**, named after Amsterdam in Holland and in deference to the Dutch who allowed the king of Karangasem to retain his royal title and some of his powers in return for his cooperation. Inside is some furniture donated by the Dutch royal family. Opposite is the ornate **Bale Pemandesan**, a pavilion used for tooth-filing ceremonies and embellished with Chinese features. The third pavilion, **Bale Kambang**, appears to float in the middle of a large artificial pool. It was used by the royal family mainly for relaxing and entertainment.

Taman Ujung

The kings of Karangasem created delightful water gardens to escape the heat of eastern Bali. **Taman Ujung** ⑲ (daily 8am–5pm; charge), the "Eternal Happiness Park" at **Ujung**, about 8km (5 miles) south of Amlapura, is a vast complex of pools, pavilions and a long bridge with archways, all artistically moulded in concrete *(see photo feature, pages 170–1)* Built in 1919, the water park was destroyed by an earthquake in 1976. After a drawn-out res-

toration, it reopened in 2004 and is once more worthy of a visit.

Ujung to Amed

From Ujung the road continues about 6km (4 miles) along the coast and uphill to **Seraya**. A vehicle with very good brakes (preferably a four-wheel-drive) is necessary, especially for continuing further along the northeastern coast to Amed. The views of the ocean along this route are breathtaking, with black-sand beaches filled with hundreds of colourful *jukung* (outrigger fishing boats), and the route is worthwhile for those seeking adventure. From Seraya, it winds another 25km (15 miles) or so along a narrow road filled with sharp bends around the base of **Gunung Seraya** (1,175 metres/3,855ft), and on to the beach side resort area of **Amed**.

Taman Tirtagangga to Amed

An easier and just as picturesque route to **Amed** continues 6km (4 miles) northwest of Amlapura to **Taman Tirtagangga** ⑳ (daily 8am–5pm; charge, with additional fees for different pools), the "Water of the Ganges Park", another royal water park. Local people flock here just before sunset to bathe in pools fed by natural springs gushing out from animal statues and fountains. Parts of this water park were destroyed by the eruption of Gunung Agung in 1963 and subsequently repaired. Some recently added architectural elements, however, don't do justice to the site.

Pura Lempuyang

From Taman Tirtagangga, the road leads 4km (2½ miles) to **Abang**, with spectacular views between two mountains, Gunung Agung to the west and Gunung Seraya to the east. Back in the late 1960s (or so the story goes), before electricity reached this part of Bali, a space satellite reported the observation of a blue beam emanating from

earth; the precise location was plotted and the source confirmed as the temple of **Pura Lempuyang** ㉑ (daily daylight hours; donation).

Just east from the main road is a white structure nestled on the hillside: this is the split gate of the lower temple. Drive up to this point by turning right at Abang, and on a clear day you will see a breathtaking view of Gunung Agung, perfectly framed within the boundaries of the gate. The temple guardians – three pairs of colossal sea serpents, complete with scales and ferocious teeth – border a trio of towering steps, but this is only the beginning. Further on, a stairway of 1,700 steps winds through the forest up to the temple itself, 768 metres (2,520ft) above sea level. The intense spiritual energy of this place is almost tangible.

From Abang, it's another 14km (9 miles) along a winding road, forking right first at **Culik**, to Amed.

Amed

Although **Amed** ㉒ refers to the fishing village, it is also the name given to a series of gravelly beaches tucked into coves and stretching several kilometres along the coast, like Jemeluk, Lipah, Lehan, Selang and Aas. Out to sea are views of Lombok while those inland are of Gunung Agung. All along the beach are colourful fishing outriggers and thatched huts where salt is produced. It is an idyllic setting and perfect for those who shun crowds. Village life is simple here, but there's enough tourism infrastructure in the way of small hotels and restaurants along the coast to keep visitors occupied for a few days. There are also ample opportunities for diving, snorkelling and mountain treks.

Tulamben Marine Reserve

To reach the northeastern coast, return to Culik and turn right. About 10km (6 miles) from Culik is the **Tulamben Marine Reserve** ㉓. Diving and snorkelling is the main activity at the site of the wrecked American navy cargo ship *Liberty*, which was sailing in the Lombok Strait in January 1942 when it was torpedoed by the Japanese. The ship was towed to Bali and beached. Shockwaves from the 1963 eruption of Gunung Agung broke it in half and pushed it 50 metres (150ft) offshore to its present location. There, over the years, it has become home to a wide variety of tropical fish and coral.

Northeast coast

A long stretch of well-paved road runs along the northeast coast, which still displays evidence of the 1963 eruption of Gunung Agung in the form of dark lava flows on the mountain sides. It's a stark, raw and dramatic drive through mostly dry hills covered with scrub and lava boulders and punctuated by fan palm and coconut trees.

Along the way are the salt-making villages of **Kubu** ㉔ and **Tianyar** ㉕, with wooden troughs for evaporating seawater lining black-sand beaches like those found at Kusamba. There is little of interest till you reach Tejakula *(see page 174)*. ❑

Colourful outrigger (jukung) boats on a black-sand beach at Amed.

BELOW: Amed with Gunung Agung in the background.

BEST RESTAURANTS

Restaurants

Price for a two-course meal for one including a non-alcoholic beverage:

$$$$ over Rp 300,000
$$$ Rp 200,000–300,000
$$ Rp 100,000–200,000
$ below Rp 100,000

Nusa Lembongan

Most eateries are found within hotels, although there are some decent *warung* (local stalls) in the Jungutbatu area.

Manggis

Like most places on the east coast of Bali, the best restaurants are those found within hotels. The following are recommended.

Seasalt

Alila Manggis, Buitan, Manggis. Tel: 0363-41011. Open: daily B, L & D. **$$$$**
www.alilahotelo.com
Stylish restaurant housed in an open-air Balinese pavilion overlooking lotus ponds. The food is contemporary with international, Balinese and Indonesian dishes. Salads, sandwiches and light meals during the day and more elaborate dinners at night. The restaurant is well known for its cooking courses, which are either half-day, or longer 2- or 5-day programmes.

Candidasa

Most restaurants here serve grilled seafood along with other standard Indonesian dishes. Like Ubud, this is another area that is beginning to see foreign professionals opening up more international-style restaurants. There are a number of options outside of the hotels.

Candi Agung

Jalan Raya Candidasa. Tel: 0363-41672. Open: daily B, L & D. **$$**
Small clean *warung* that features a Balinese dance performance every evening at 8pm, when one of the waitresses changes into costume and performs on a small stage at the front. Simple, well-executed Indonesian Chinese dishes, many featuring chicken and fish. Especially good Is *udang goreng*, or grilled prawns with Balinese *sambal*.

Garpu

Rama Candidasa, Candidasa. Tel: 0363-41974. Open: daily B, L & D. **$$$**
www.ramacandidasahotel.com
Air-conditioned restaurant with ocean views across Padang Bai attached to Rama Candidasa Resort & Spa. Its resident French chef cooks some of the best food in this area. Try his *feuilleté de crevettes à*

l'Américaine, sautéed shrimps served in a light puff pastry case and smothered with a lobster sauce, and the most perfect duck terrine served with Cumberland sauce. A variety of delectable breads are baked in-house daily.

Kafé Watergarden

Jalan Raya Candidasa. Tel: 0363-41540. Open: daily B, L & D. **$$$**
www.watergardenhotel.com
A part of the impressive Watergarden hotel, this English-managed restaurant serves quality and value-for-money food. Dishes are Indonesian with some international favourites (even some Thai-inspired meals). Vegetarian options are also available, spring rolls, guacamole and samosas are on the menu.

La Rouge

Jalan Raya Candidasa. Tel: 0363-41991. Open: daily L & D. **$$$**
This partially open-air restaurant will surprise you with its visual pleasures and sumptuous fabrics. Tables spill out into a candlelit garden, while the menu presents Western, Balinese and Indian food, with lots of seafood and a blackboard of daily specials.

Lotus Seaview

Jalan Raya Candidasa. Tel: 0363-41257. Open:

daily B, L & D. **$$**
www.lotusrestaurants.com
Another restaurant from the well-regarded Lotus chain, this is a pleasant place with prime sea views, serving a mix of Balinese food and Western dishes with Italian accents. The famous *bebek betutu* does not have to be pre-ordered.

Temple Café

Temple Bungalows, Jalan Raya Candidasa. Tel: 0363-41629. Open: daily B, L & D. **$$**
www.bali-seafront-bungalows.com
Australian-owned eatery featuring some home-style German dishes, cabbage rolls among them, excellent big breakfasts and many unusual items – such as curried shepherd's pie. For a quick snack, try the spicy chicken and salad wrap. Great value for money.

Vincent's

Jalan Raya Candidasa. Tel: 0363-41368. Open: daily L & D. **$$$**
www.vincentsbali.com
Smart Dutch-owned restaurant with lounge and romantic garden dining. Serves a mix of local and European food. The latter includes dishes such as Cyprus Halloumi cheese wrapped in puff pastry with a homemade ginger compote, or chicken pot pie served

with mashed potatoes. Dutch-style breakfasts (uitsmijter) and good Illy coffees are also available. Cool jazz music is often played in the background.

Amed

The district referred to as Amed actually comprises more than 10 small fishing villages spread out to the south of Amed. Most of the action centres around Lipah beach.

Café Indah
Lipah Beach, Amed. Tel: 0363-23437. Open: daily L & D. $$
Small warung right on the edge of the beach. Simple, cheap and well prepared Indonesian food. Try the fish in black bean, the excellent sate, chilli prawn and sweet and sour chicken.

Restaurant Gede
Lipah Beach, Amed. Tel: 0363-23517. Open: daily B, L & D. $$$
Probably the best Indonesian Chinese cuisine available in the Amed area, although more expensive than the norm. Seafood dishes include slipper lobster, king prawn and whatever is locally caught. The chicken or fish mandarin is a favourite on the lengthy menu.

Life in Amed
Life In Amed Resort, Lean, Amed. Tel: 0363 23152, Mobile: 081 338 501555. Open: daily B, L & D. $$
www.lifebali.com

Small, clean restaurant serving a mix of Western and local cuisines, all impressively presented. Recommended are the salad of goat's cheese (served with figs and toasted pine nuts); chicken salad with Dijon cream dressing; prawn and pineapple in coconut milk curry; and whole baby red snapper perfectly grilled and served with a Balinese lawar salad.

The Pavilion
Baliku Resort, Banyuning, Amed. Tel: 081-338 209173. Open: daily L & D. $$
Large open terrace on hillside with magnificent views across to Lombok and the surrounding mountains; located just opposite the Japanese shipwreck (popular for snorkelling). The herb cheese filo parcels are very popular, as is the Tuscan baked chicken.

Puri Wirata
Bunutan, Amed. Tel: 0363-23523. Open: daily B, L & D. $$
German-managed bungalows and restaurant, sited at the edge of the ocean among palm trees, where the usual mix of Indonesian and Western cuisines is offered. Also available in the mornings is a German breakfast, bratkartoffekn – pan-fried mix of sliced potato, bacon and onion, all topped with a fried egg.

Sails
Horizon Resort, Lean,

Amed. Tel: 0362-22006. Open: daily L & D. $$$
www.sailsrestaurantbali.com
With a magical position on the mountain side of the main road and blessed with stunning ocean views of the Lombok Strait, the Kiwi-owned Sails restaurant serves local and Western dishes but all done a little differently from the norm. The chicken or pork mandarin with star anise, lamb medallions, barbecued pork ribs and freshly caught fish all rate highly.

Santai
Santai Bungalows, Bunutan, Amed. Tel: 0363-23487. Open: daily B, L & D. $$$
www.santaibali.com
The chef prepares arguably the best selection of international food in the Amed area. Top favourites are the couscous salad with tandoori chicken, roasted garlic soup with king prawns, ginger-glazed barracuda fillet with vegetable noodles and cashew nuts, and the traditional Balinese ikan pepes – fish minced with coconut and spices then wrapped in banana leaf and grilled.

Warung Brith
Lipah Beach, Amed. Tel: 0363-23527. Open: daily L & D. $$
Very popular and friendly warung whose signature dish is ang shio hie, or Chinese-style sweet and sour fish – a total contrast to the usually sickly sweet offering dished up

by suburban Chinese restaurants around the world. Here it consists of big chunks of fresh fish, stir-fried with finely shredded onions, pineapple, red and green peppers and topped with a flavourful, tangy sauce. Traditional Balinese dishes like bebek betutu and babi guling are also available if pre-ordered.

Wayan's Warung
Lipah Beach, Amed. Open: daily B, L & D. $–$$
Small local warung serving freshly cooked, tasty and amazing-value meals. The fare is mostly Indonesian Chinese, like foo yung hai (vegetable and chicken omelette topped with a spicy sambal sauce), crisp tempeh in a sweet-spicy soy sauce, and chicken or fish rolls rolled in grated coconut. There is also grilled freshly caught fish and wonderful satay too.

Tulamben

Tauch Terminal
Tulamben. Tel: 0363-22911. Open: daily B, L & D. $$$
www.tauch-terminal.com
Pleasant seaside location at a popular site for scuba diving (the shipwreck Liberty is just offshore). A mix of homestyle European and Indonesian dishes are found on the menu. Thanks to its German management, dishes include a German-style breakfast (served 7–10am).

WATER PARKS OF EAST BALI

Pools, pavilions and gardens, once the preserve of royalty, offer a welcome respite from the heat.

ABOVE: Taman Ujung. Previously used as a royal summer residence, the Bale Kambang (floating pavilion) sits in the midst of a large reflecting pond full of water-lilies.

Taman Ujung, or Taman Sukasada (Eternal Happiness Park) was built in 1919 by the last Raja of Karangasem, Anak Agung Anglurah Ketut Karangasem. The water palace was formally used from 1921 as a place for the Raja to entertain as well as being a retreat for the royal family. It was shattered by an earthquake in 1976 but restored in 2004.

The renovated park isn't as atmospheric as the original but it is still extremely beautiful, graced with water-lily-filled reflecting pools, airy pavilions and bridges with decorative arches.

More evocative is **Taman Tirtagangga** (Water of the Ganges Park), built by the same king in 1948 and modelled after Versailles Palace in France. Chilly, natural spring water gushes out from spouts and fountains into large pools in which you can swim. Accommodation is also available in the park.

RIGHT: statue at Taman Ujung.
A contemporary Balinese rendition of the Ganges river goddess Dewi Gangga, seen pouring water from her pot.

ABOVE: fountain at Taman Tirtagangga. Water pours down the sides of an 11-tiered pagoda fountain and gushes out from the mouth of a large boar into a swimming pool.

LODGING AT TIRTAGANGGA

It's worth spending a relaxing night or two at Taman Tirtagangga, using it as your base to explore east Bali. The park itself is very pretty and is the perfect foil for the stunning surrounding landscape of hills and rice terraces. Guesthouses in the area have guides who can take you on interesting walks along back roads to remote villages.

Right on the grounds of Taman Tirtagangga, on the hill to the back, is Tirtagangga Water Palace Villas with lovely sweeping views of the park and the rice terraces beyond. Villa Tirta Ayu is a luxurious two-bedroom facility with its own resident housekeeper, cook and driver. The second villa, called Villa Djamrud (the Marble Suite Villa *pictured above*) has a living room furnished with antique furniture, dining pavilion and open-air garden bathroom on the lower floor, and a mosquito-net draped bedroom with attached bathroom upstairs.

For booking details, contact: tel: 0363-21383, e-mail: tgangga@indo.net.id, www.tirtagangga-villas.com.

RIGHT: posing for photos on stepping stones at Taman Tirtagangga water park.

BELOW: bull statue at Taman Tirtagangga. This is one of many whimsical figures with water pouring out of its mouth into the pools.

ABOVE: Bathers cool off in the chilly waters of one of several pools continuously fed by a natural spring from the hill behind Taman Tirtagangga.

NORTH BALI

North Bali is almost a world unto itself in terms of its people, terrain and architecture. You can linger at the peaceful coastal resort of Lovina or head inland to the foot of lofty mountains where the cool highlands are speckled with waterfalls, serene lakes and temples, as well as coffee, clove and vanilla estates.

eographically separated by a chain of towering volcanoes running from west to east across Bali, the northern part of the island is not only physically different from the south but has developed its own distinctive character over time. For centuries, the coastal communities of the north participated in the trade that traversed the calm Java Sea. The Dutch, too, conquered this part of Bali first in 1849, before moving south. All these have exposed the Balinese population to outside influences, making them much more cosmopolitan as a result.

Today, the highest educated Balinese are from the north coast, partly due to the early implementation of a Western-style educational system by the Dutch. Modern Balinese literature also had its beginnings in the north. With a softer variety of sandstone available from local quarries, carvers have been able to create intricate stone carvings for temples. As a result North Bali temple carvings are more three-dimensional and exuberant than anywhere else in Bali. The countryside, too, appears golden due to lower rainfall. Orchards of citrus fruits, grapes, spices, vanilla, coffee and cocoa replace the familiar rice fields, although non-irrigated rice is widely grown and prized by most Balinese for its delicious flavour.

Les

Travelling from east Bali along the main north coastal route, turn left towards the village of **Les**, and follow the road for about a kilometre to a small junction, where there is a sign indicating a waterfall, and a parking area outside a small group of shops. From there the journey

> **Main attractions**
> PURA MEDUWE KARANG
> PURA DALEM, JAGARAGA
> LOVINA
> BRAHMA ARAMA VIHARA
> AIR PANAS BANJAR
> AIR TERJUN GITGIT
> PURA ULUN DANU BRATAN
> BALI BOTANICAL GARDENS
> DANAU BUYAN AND DANAU
>   TAMBLINGAN

LEFT: thundering Air Terjun Gitgit is best seen during the wet season. **RIGHT:** Brahma Amara Vihara.

can only be continued by foot. Follow the beaten track south, away from the rice fields, for about 20 minutes. The spectacular **Borboran Yeh Mempeh** , meaning "Flying Water", is Bali's highest waterfall. You can bathe in the shallow pool right beneath the torrent.

Painting of a young Balinese man at the Art Zoo in Alas Sari.

Tejakula

Further along the main road at **Tejakula** ❷ the traditional musicians and dancers are very talented, and the village is home to Bali's most complete *wayang wong* troupe with its dozens of colourful human, monkey and ogre masks for dance drama performances of the *Ramayana* epic.

In the middle of Tejakula are the quaint **horse baths** fed by a natural spring. In the past, horses making the long and hot journey along the north coast made a stop here to be washed in the cool water. The elaborate structure with sculpted arches is now a gender segregated public bathing area.

BELOW: Tejakula village with the old horse baths on the right.

Pura Ponjok Batu

Further west about 12km (7 miles) along the coast is the dramatic **Pura Ponjok Batu** ❸ (daily daylight hours; donation), perched on a scenic hillside overlooking the sea. The temple marks the site where the 16th-century Javanese high priest Danghyang Nirartha who had stopped to admire the view when he saw a boat in trouble. He revived the unconscious crew with the waters from a spring that magically appeared on the beach. They were able to continue travelling even though the boat had no sail and the mast was broken. Just below the temple, a replica of the boat is found on a small rock battered by waves.

Art Zoo

At **Alas Sari** another 3km (2 miles) west of Pura Ponjok Batu is the funky **Art Zoo** ❹ (daily 9am–5pm; free; www.symonstudios.com), a fantasy homoerotic land created by Ameri-

North Bali

0   5 km
0   5 miles

N

Bali
Sea

Lovina
Lovina Beach ⑩
Wanu Kalibukbu nggang
Pengastulan Genit Pengayaman
Umaanyar Tangguwesia Dencarik
Seririt ⑳ Banjar
Johanyar ⑪ ★ Brahma Arama Vihara
Gilimanuk ★ Air Panas
Ringdikit 623 922
S. Saba Bangdu
Bestala
Mayong Tunjuk Kayuputih
Busungbiyu
Kekeran Banyuatis
Pelapuan Munduk Waterfall
Taman Nasional Bali Barat Kedis
(West Bali National Park) Subuk

can artist Symon. Stop by to see his life-size sculptures and colourful paintings of young Balinese men and other pop art themes. A similar set-up is found in Ubud (*see page 131*) if you don't get this far. Be sure to climb up to the top of the pagoda-like tower for stunning views of the coastline and surrounding hills and then enter its base to see the Buddhist sanctuary filled with images and incense.

Air Sanih

A further 5km (3 miles) west are the cool springs at **Air Sanih ⑤**, also known as Yeh Sanih (daily daylight hours; charge). The big spring-fed pool under spreading frangipani trees near the sea isn't terribly inviting but many local people flock here, especially around sunset, to swim or bathe. Accommodation, mostly budget-range places, and restaurants are available nearby if you decide to spend the night.

Pura Meduwe Karang

Just before the main road north from Gunung Batur meets the coastal road in **Kubutambahan** is a small side road towards the sea leading to the temple of **Pura Meduwe Karang ⑥** (daily daylight hours; donation). Built in 1890, the temple is filled with the elaborate carvings and decorations so typical of northern-style temple architecture, often depicting scenes that are humorous, highly animated and even erotic in character. Fertility motifs abound, including portrayals of various erotic acts. Other carvings show demons and humans, including Dutch artist W.O.J. Nieuwenkamp (1874–1950) riding a bicycle with flowery wheels – look for it on the ocean-side wall of the main shrine in the temple's inner courtyard. At the start of the 20th century, Nieuwenkamp travelled everywhere in Bali by bicycle, sketching scenes of what he saw.

Pura Meduwe Karang literally means "Temple of the Owner of the

Relief detail at Pura Meduwe Kawang depicting Dutch artist W.O.J. Nieuwenkamp on his bicycle.

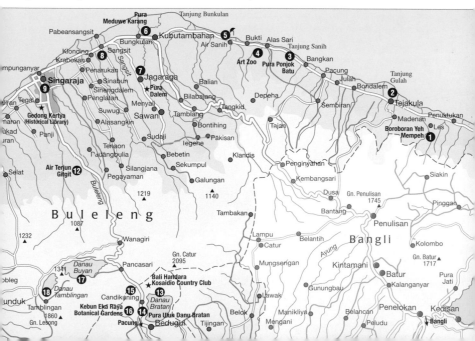

The Yudha Mandala Tama Independence Monument graces the waterfront at Singaraja.

BELOW: Pura Beji is built from sandstone, unlike most other Balinese temples.

Land", and it honours the deity of the crops of dry agriculture. Just as *subak* temples ensure harvests on irrigated rice fields, this temple assures blessings for plants grown on unirrigated land, including fruits, coconut and coffee.

Jagaraga

Another 2km (1 mile) east in Bungkulan, turn (left) uphill at the main T-junction and continue 4km (2½ miles) inland to **Jagaraga** ⑦. This is the scene of the bloody 1849 battle between the Balinese and the Dutch, which killed off most of the village's population and ended several years of fighting between the two sides. Today, Jagaraja is more famous for its interesting **Pura Dalem** (Temple of the Dead daily daylight hours; donation), where Siwa (Shiva), the Hindu god of destruction, presides. Highly animated bas-reliefs portray life before and after the Dutch arrival – armed bandits holding up two smug Europeans riding in an antique Ford car, World War II airplanes engaged in an aerial battle with some plunging into the sea, and a Dutch steamer sending out a smoky SOS signal while being attacked by a

sea monster. Even the widow-witch Rangda and the statue of a dazed mother buried under a pile of children are carved with a sense of humour.

Pura Beji

Back along the main northern coastal road in **Sangsit** ⑧ is the amazing **Pura Beji** (daily daylight hours; donation) built of pink sandstone during the 15th century. At this *subak* (irrigation) temple dedicated to Dewi Sri, intricate carvings of *naga* (serpents) and symbols of water and fertility adorn the balustrades, with fantastic beasts, demonic guardians, jawless birds and fierce tigers peering out from the entangled flora. Rows of slender towers jut up from the temple terraces, forming a labyrinth of stone. To counterbalance the overpowering motifs, the temple courtyard is unusually spacious and planted with frangipani trees.

Singaraja

About 9km (6 miles) west of Pura Beji Sangsit is **Singaraja** ⑨, Bali's second largest town (after Denpasar) and the north's main commercial centre.

In many respects, Singaraja is also the intellectual centre of the north, with two major universities. After the Dutch imposed direct colonial rule on the Buleleng region in 1882, Singaraja became the capital and chief port until 1953, when the administrative centre was moved to Denpasar in the south. But even before the Dutch showed up, Singaraja was an important shipping and trading centre. Today, Singaraja still has a bustling and cosmopolitan flavour. Its population comprises Balinese, Javanese, Arabs and Chinese.

Singaraja's old port was destroyed by rough waves during the early 1990s. Nearby is the **Ling Gwan Kiong Chinese Buddhist Temple** (daily daylight hours; donation), dating back to 1873 and filled with colourful murals of deities and mythological figures. Further up the waterfront is **Yudha Mandala Tama Independence Monument**, which commemorates Indonesia's struggle against the Dutch from 1945 to 1949.

Gedong Kirtya

On Jalan Veteran just two blocks east of the **Singa Ambara Raja**, a large statue of the winged lion-king that symbolises Singaraja, is the historical **Gedong Kirtya** library (Mon–Thu 8am–3.30pm, Fri 8am–12.30pm; free; tel: 0362-22645). This repository of old books and Balinese manuscripts was established by the Dutch in 1928 – partly to compensate for their bloody conquest of Bali. It has a fine collection of *lontar*, traditional books made from dried fan-palm leaves cut into strips, inscribed and preserved between two pieces of wood or bamboo. Some works are relatively newer copies of older ones that have disintegrated due to humidity, fungus and insect damage. The *lontar* manuscripts cover literature, mythology, historical chronicles and religion. Some even have miniature drawings, which are masterpieces in the art of illustration. The library also has several royal edicts

inscribed on thin sheets of bronze dating from the 10th century, among the earliest written documents in Bali.

West of Singaraja to Lovina

About 10km (6 miles) west of Singaraja is the low-key beach resort area of **Lovina** . Stretching over 8km (5 miles) of mainly black-sand beaches, the name Lovina (Lovely Indonesia) was given by Panji Tisna, the last king of Buleleng and a convert to Christianity, to the north coast's string of fishing villages with names like Kaliasem, Kalibukbuk, Anturan and Tukad Mungga.

Caressed by gentle waves, Lovina is much better suited for families because of the rather laid-back pace and lack of crowds. Accommodation ranges from simple guesthouses to mid-range resorts with restaurants and other facilities, mostly located on both sides of **Jalan Raya Lovina**.

Nearly every hotel, guide or fisherman in Lovina offers dolphin watching tours, very early in the morning in motorised traditional *jukung* fishing boats. Occasionally no dolphins are sighted, but about 90 percent of the time dolphin-watchers are treated to

Entrance to Ling Gwan Kiong Chinese Buddhist Temple in Singaraja.

BELOW: tourists set off for dolphin watching from Lovina beach.

the breathtaking spectacle of these graceful mammals vaulting out of the water in a remarkable aerial display. Diving and snorkelling are major activities in Lovina, although better options are found in the waters around Pulau Menjangan *(see page 185)* nearby.

Brahma Arama Vihara

Continuing west from Lovina, turn left at Dencarik and continue for about 3km (2 miles) to **Brahma Arama Vihara** (daily 8am–6pm; charge) in **Banjar** ⓫. This striking Thai-style Theravada Buddhist temple, with its bright orange roof and colourful statues of Buddha and other figures, was founded in 1958 by a Balinese monk and rebuilt in 1971. The views down to the coast are stunning, and visitors are welcome as long as they dress modestly, lower their voices and walk quietly and barefooted.

Air Panas Banjar

From Brahma Arama Vihara, it's another 3km (2 miles) to **Air Panas Banjar** (daily 8am–6pm; charge), a

natural sulphuric spring with slightly warmer than tepid water cascading out from the mouths of carved *naga* (serpents) into two pools. You can get a free massage from the water gushing out from the higher spouts at the third pool. There are changing rooms, toilets and a restaurant on site.

South of Singaraja to Gitgit

About 11km (7 miles) south of Singaraja, take the turn-off on the left for the waterfall, **Air Terjun Gitgit** ⓬ (daily daylight hours; charge). The thundering 40-metre (130ft) waterfall is impressive, especially at the peak of the rainy season between January and March. The deep pool at the bottom of the falls is good for swimming, but according to local lore, couples who use the pool together will separate (you have been warned). Like most scenic places in Bali, persistent guides and numerous kiosks selling kitschy souvenirs disturb the atmosphere. For more peace and quiet, 2km (1 mile) further up the hill another path along a river and through forests leads you to a series of multi-tiered waterfalls.

Canang sari (*offering of flowers in a woven coconut leaf tray) at Air Panas Banjar.*

BELOW: Naga (serpent) carvings spouting warm water at Air Panas Banjar.

Danau Bratan

Beyond the Gitgit waterfalls, the road south twists and turns as it climbs up the mountain side, finally emerging at a crest with a Y-junction. Veering to the left, the main road descends into the ancient crater of **Gunung Catur**, which soars to 2,095 metres (6,915ft) to the east. In this lovely landscape of vegetable and flower farms and the cooler temperatures of the Tabanan region *(see page 191)* sits serene **Danau Bratan ⑬**, a large lake surrounded by densely forested mountains topped by clouds. A wide range of tourist facilities are scattered around the area, including the spectacular **Bali Handara Kosaido Country Club** golf course *(see page 79 and 255)*.

Pura Ulun Danu Bratan

Because the lake is an essential water source for surrounding farmlands and rice fields in the southwest and northwest parts of the island, the Balinese worship the goddess of the lake, Dewi Danu, at **Pura Ulun Danu Bratan ⑭** (daily daylight hours; charge).

Built during the 17th century by a king of Mengwi, this sacred site,

dedicated to the lake goddess, is the second most important irrigation temple after Pura Ulun Danu Batur. The graceful 11-tiered *meru* (pagoda) appears to float upon the surface of the water. On the nearby shore are two other temples, and a stone *stupa* (memorial shrine) with four Buddha statues in niches facing the main compass directions.

Candikuning and Bedugul

On the western side of the lake, the colourful market town of **Candikuning ⑮** is where wild orchids and colourful flowers are sold alongside temperate and tropical food crops grown in the region's fertile soil. The farms here provide a constant supply of flowers for Balinese offerings, along with a wide variety of fruits and vegetables for restaurants.

At the southern shore of the lake is **Bedugul**, which is the name of the small town here as well as the entire mountain resort area. Because of the higher altitude, temperatures in this region are much lower than on the coast, giving it an alpine feel. There is nothing much of interest here except

The tiny, sweet strawberries for sale at Candikuning market are grown in farms around this high-altitude region.

BELOW: fishing boats on Danau Bratan.

Lake Transport

The pathways through the rainforest between lakes Danau Buyan and Danau Tamblingan *(see page 180)* lead to Pura Tahun, a temple with an 11 roofed *meru*. From here, you can arrange for one of the local villagers to row you across the tranquil waters in a *pedau akit*, a traditional double canoe – motorboats and water sports are forbidden here. The natural spring that feeds the lakes provides water for drinking and the waters are also a rich source of fish, evident from the offshore fishing platforms. On the far side of Danau Tamblingan is Pura Gubug, the Farmers' Temple, dedicated to the lake goddess, and the tiny village of Munduk Tamblingan where the locals rear cattle on the lotus that grows in the shallow water.

Cloves are green when picked, turning reddish brown and later almost black when completely dried. Look for them laid out on mats to dry in the area around Munduk.

Below: hydrangias are grown for use in offering trays, as here in Munduk.

for the **Taman Recreasi Bedugul**, which has noisy jet-skis for hire.

Bali Botanical Gardens

Near the Candi Kunung market, up a small side road, is the lush **Bali Botanical Gardens** N (daily 8am–6pm; charge; tel: 0368-21273). This cool, shady park covers 132 hectares (325 acres) of tropical rainforest on the slopes of Gunung Pohon (Tree Mountain), with more than 650 different species of trees and nearly 500 varieties of wild and cultivated orchids.

The Botanical Gardens is also home to **Bali Treetop Adventure Park** (daily 8.30am–6pm, charge; tel: 0361-852 0680), where adults and children can venture from tree to tree through suspended bridges, spider nets, Tarzan jumps, flying swings and flying-foxes.

Danau Buyan and Danau Tamblingan

From Danau Bratan, head northeast along the road that curves around **Danau Buyan** N, a quiet lake embraced by hillsides covered with coffee plantations. A narrow strip

of land separates it from the smaller **Danau Tamblingan** N to the east. Each has a temple on its shore dedicated to the lake goddess *(see box page 179)*. Both bodies of water were one until 1818, when a landslide divided them into two. The drive is very picturesque as it passes through small villages along the road, with vantage points to stop and enjoy the stunning views. The surrounding area is ideal for trekking.

Munduk

Beyond Danau Tamblingan the road winds its way down 6km (4 miles) west to **Munduk** N, an old mountain settlement with coffee, vanilla and clove plantations started by the Dutch during the late 1890s. The views down to the north coast are spectacular, the air crisp and clear. The main road passes through remote villages and continues for 26km (16 miles) all the way down to **Seririt** N, a town that was completely rebuilt after it was destroyed by an earthquake in 1976. Turning right takes you back to Lovina while going left along the coastal road leads to remote West Bali. ❑

BEST RESTAURANTS, BARS AND CAFÉS

Restaurants

Price for a two-course meal for one including a non-alcoholic beverage:

$$$$ over Rp 300,000
$$$ Rp 200,000–300,000
$$ Rp 100,000–200,000
$ below Rp 100,000

Lovina

Adirama
Adirama Hotel, Lovina.
Tel: 0362-41759. Open: daily B, L & D. **$$**
Hotel restaurant right at the water's edge serving everything from fish and chips to Indonesian butter fried chicken. Also features a good selection of Mexican dishes (tacos, enchilladas, quesadillas and crunchy taquitos).

Damai Restaurant
Jalan Damai, Lovina.
Tel: 0362-41008. Open: daily L & D. **$$$$**
www.damai.com
Lovely up-market resort whose fine-dining restaurant offers exquisite *nouvelle* and fusion Indonesian and Western cuisines, together with sweeping views, excellent wines and desserts. Try the 5-course gourmet dinner.

Jasmine Kitchen
Gang Bina Ria, off Jalan Bina Ria, Kalibukbuk, Lovina.
Tel: 0362-41565. Open: daily L & D. **$$**
Small Thai eatery whose vegetarian spring rolls,

served with sweet chilli sauce, are perfect; also recommended is *massaman* curry with coconut milk, potatoes and peanuts, either with prawns or vegetables.

Kakatua
Kalibukbuk, Lovina.
Tel: 0362-41344. Open: daily B, L & D. **$$**
Comprising two open-sided pavilions linked by a fish pond and pots of flowering plants, Kakatua cooks up a storm in its simple open kitchen. Delicious offerings range from pizza, pasta and cauliflower cheese to Indian curries, Mexican fare, Thai dishes, and home-made puddings.

Khi Khi Seafood Restaurant
Kalibukbuk, Lovina.
Tel: 0362-41548.
Open: daily B, L & D **$$$**
An old favourite, this long-established, large seafood restaurant is very popular with the locals. Serves Indonesian and Japanese cuisine as well as grilled fresh fish, prawns, calamari and a variety of Chinese specialities.

Kubu Lalang
Pantai Tukadmungga, Lovina.
Tel: 0362-42207. Open: daily B, L & D. **$$**
www.kubu.balihotelguide.com
Set right on the beach, this restaurant has a large menu consisting of Balinese, European, Ara-

bic and Indian dishes, priced very reasonably and accompanied by pleasant service.

Kwizien
Jalan Raya Kaliasem, Lovina.
Tel: 0362-42031. Open: daily L & D. **$$**
Special-occasion restaurant, with both an air-conditioned section and open terrace, offering European and local dishes. The barbecued chicken wings, lamb medallions and pork spare ribs are to be recommended.

Le Gong
Bali Paradise Hotel, Jalan Kartika, Kalibukbuk. Tel: 0362-41432. Open: daily B, L & D. **$$$**
This hotel restaurant is a gem. Sit indoors if you want the air conditioning; otherwise ask for an outside table overlooking the swimming pool and landscaped gardens. The Steak Diane (fillet mignon with a sauce made of mustard, onion, mushrooms, cream and red wine) is a favourite.

Villa Agung
Villa Agung Bungalows, Jalan Singaraja, Lovina.
Tel: 0362-41527. Open: daily B, L & D. **$$**
www.agungvilla.com
Beach side bungalow restaurant with a menu of good international and Indonesian dishes.

Warung Aria
Jalan Raya Lovina 18, Kalibukbuk, Lovina.

Tel: 0362-41341. Open: daily L & D. **$$**
Perenially busy small *warung* on main road serving simple (and cheap) Cantonese-style dishes such as a superlative fried rice studded with shrimps.

Bedugul/Pacung

Café Teras
Jalan Raya Denpasar-Singaraja, Lempuna.
Tel: 0362-29312. Open: daily B, L & D. **$$**
Located just outside the Bali Handara Kosaido Golf Club entrance. Sit in the garden terrace or inside in a colonial-style dining room as you tuck into *miso* soup, grilled chicken with a teriyaki sauce, and *okonomiyaki*, a Japanese-style pizza.

Kamandalu
Bali Handara Kosaido Golf and Country Club, Bedugul.
Tel: 0362-22646. Open: daily B, L & D. **$$**
www.balihandarakosaido.com
Fine restaurant serving a variety of Japanese, Indonesian and Balinese dishes. Dining area overlooks the golf course.

Pacung Indah
Pacung. Tel: 0368-21020.
Open: daily B, L & D. **$$**
Just south of Begugul. As you gaze at lovely rice terraces, dine on Indonesian specialities and a few Western dishes prepared with local produce.

WEST BALI

Remote west Bali sees few visitors because the attractions are so widespread. Those who make the trek west will be amply rewarded with vineyards heavy with bunches of grapes, dramatic windswept coastal temples, isolated Christian communities, some of Bali's best diving and a massive national park.

Travellers fed up with the congested roads of southern Bali will greet the seemingly empty roads of western Bali with euphoria. Not only are there fewer vehicles, but also fewer people here. A national park, a refuge for endangered wildlife, takes up much of this part of the island, while black-sand beaches mostly unprotected by offshore reefs along the southwest coast are usually empty except for diehard surfers. This is the region called Jembrana, Bali's "wild west" that was once home to the island's earliest prehistoric inhabitants. Hindu high priests and aristocrats from Java first stepped foot on this part of Bali to spread the faith or lay claim to the island. Over the centuries, migrants from more populated areas in Bali, Java, Madura, Sulawesi and even distant Malaysia established communities here. This ethnically, culturally and geographically diverse area offers surprises to visitors who make the effort to explore it.

Celukan Bawang

Located 16km (10 miles) west of **Seririt**, the small and sheltered harbour of **Celukan Bawang ❶** (Onion Cove) has replaced Singaraja as the main port for the north coast. Occasionally, a distinctive *pinisi* (wooden sailing ship) of the Bugis people from south Sulawesi drops anchor here.

West to Pulaki

Continuing west, the land takes on a drier texture and the agricultural diversity becomes apparent. All along here past Pantai Gondol to **Pulaki** and further west, grapes are cultivated, both for eating and making wine. Vines loaded with

Main attractions
PEMUTERAN
PULAU MENJANGAN
WEST BALI NATIONAL PARK
BELIMBINGSARI AND PALASARI
BUNUT BOLONG

LEFT: fishing boats in Perancak harbour in the west of the island. **RIGHT:** the unique Bunut Bolong tree near Manggissari village.

Vineyard at Hatten Wines.

bunches of dark purple fruit hang from raised trellises during the dry season from June to September. Near **Grokgak** ❷ are the vineyards of **Hatten Wines** (tel: 0361-286298; www.hattenwines.com), which cultivate both the Alphonse-Lavallée red and the Belgia white varieties. The processing, however, takes place at its winery in Sanur. Although generally not open to the public, you can visit both the Hatten vineyards in north Bali and the winery in the south as part of a tour organised by **Bali Discovery** (tel: 0361-286283; www.balidiscovery.com), with wine tastings and lunch included.

Pulaki

Another 5km (3 miles) along the road, just past **Banyupoh** village in **Pulaki** ❸, is an interesting pair of temples originating from an incident in the 16th century, when the Javanese high priest Danghyang Nirartha came here to escape from the rise of Islam in Java. One day Nirartha's youngest daughter became lost in the forest and was violated by some men from a local village. When the priest found her she was nearly dead; he purified and transformed her into a goddess called Dewi Melanting. Her temple, set against forested hills, is called **Pura Melanting** (daily, daylight hours; donation).

Nirartha cursed those responsible for the crime, making them invisible, and ordered these *wong gamang* to serve his wife whom he deified at **Pura Pulaki** (daily, daylight hours; donation), about 2km (1 mile) to the west. The temple, rebuilt in the 1980s, hugs a ledge cut out of the mountain side that overlooks the ocean and is guarded by a band of frisky monkeys. According to the villagers, the invisible *wong gamang* are said to still roam the island, causing dogs to howl for no apparent reason.

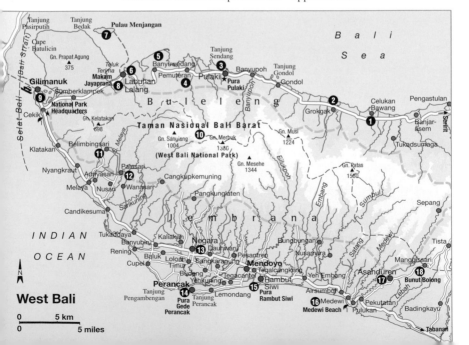

West Bali

0 ___ 5 km
0 ___ 5 miles

Part of the Pura Pulaki complex is **Pura Pabean** (daily, daylight hours; donation), just opposite and strikingly perched on a hill overlooking the coast. Unusually blending both Chinese and Balinese design elements, this is where fishermen come to pray for safe passage.

Pemuteran

A further 3km (2 miles) west of Pulaki is **Pemuteran** ❹, with its quiet beaches and great diving and snorkelling at coral reefs offshore. There is an increasing number of cottage-style hotels here that can arrange hikes into the West Bali National Park and dive trips to nearby Pulau Menjangan. More low-key yet more upmarket than Lovina beach to the east, Pemuteran sees many repeat visitors who enjoy its relaxed and understated air. Right in front of the **Taman Sari Cottages**, an experimental reef regrowth programme is underway, using low-voltage current to encourage the growth of coral around artificial reef frames. So far the results have been fruitful, as evidenced by the number of snorkellers in Pemuteran Bay.

Banyuwedang

Another 10km (6 miles) west at a bend in the road is **Banyuwedang** ❺ (Hot Water), which has natural hot springs with medicinal properties, said to heal skin diseases. The springs are a little grubby so a better option is the nearby **Mimpi Resort** where for a modest fee visitors can take a dip in the hot pools that pump in mineral water from the springs at Banyuwedang.

Pulau Menjangan

Next along the road is **Labuhan Lalang** ❻, the jump-off point for Pulau Menjangan. It has a visitors' centre (daily 8am–3pm) and car park with simple food stalls. Snorkelling equipment can be rented here for boat trips to the tiny and uninhabited **Pulau Menjangan** ❼ (Deer Island). Dive trips are better arranged from Pemuteran. A part of the West Bali National Park and located less than 10km (6 miles) offshore, it has some of Bali's best diving sites, with diverse marine life, good visibility and pristine coral reefs extending deep into the ocean floor.

TIP

At Pemuteran, turtles are raised at Reef Seen Aquatics (tel: 0362-92339; www.reefseen.com), and for a small donation visitors can sponsor the release of these endangered creatures into the sea. Reef Seen, which pioneered the reef protection plan in Pemuteran and Menjangan, also organises dive and snorkel trips.

BELOW: temple festival at Pura Pulaki.

BELOW: the jetty for the ferry to Menjangan island, Labuhan Labang. **BELOW RIGHT:** the Catholic church in Palasari village.

The legendary Javanese high priest Empu Kuturan is said to have arrived here during the 10th century, when a deer led him around Bali. The island's name is a misnomer now as the rare Java deer are rarely spotted, but it is a protected sanctuary for the endangered *jalak putih* (white Bali starling).

Makam Jayaprana

Just 1km (½ mile) beyond Labuhan Lalang and located high up a steep hillside with lovely views is **Makam Jayaprana ❽**, the gravesite of the 17th-century local folk hero called Jayaprana. The handsome orphan Jayaprana, who was raised by the lord of Kalianget, near Banjar, had wed the beautiful Layonsari. The lord became jealous and desired Layonsari for himself, so he hatched a ruse to lure Jayaprana to a distant bay and had him murdered. In despair, Layonsari committed suicide rather than submit to the treacherous lord, and was reunited with Jayaprana in heaven. The shrine has a glass case which contains images of the ill-fated couple. Women pray here for divine assistance in matters of love.

Gilimanuk

At a T-junction in the main road in **Cekik**, 14km (9 miles) from Labuhan Lalang, turn to the right to **Gilimanuk ❾**. This nondescript town on a small peninsula is marked by a distinctive arch towering above the road, depicting four serpents with their tails entwined. Beyond the commercial stretch is a modern terminal for ferries that shuttle passengers, buses and cars (operating 24 hours daily) between Bali and Java, a distance of only 3km (2 miles) and covered in 30 minutes.

The only attraction worth seeing in Gilimanuk is **Museum Situs Purbakala** (Museum of Prehistoric Man; Mon–Fri 8am–3pm; donation), which displays the excavated prehistoric remains from a small settlement said to be 4,000 years old. In fact some of Bali's earliest evidence of human life has been found in this area, with artefacts like stone adzes and pottery fragments dating back to 1000 BC. Given the narrow strait, it must have been easy enough for people from East Java to make the crossing to Bali. In fact, geologists maintain that Java and Bali were once part of the same land mass.

West Bali National Park

Cekik is also the location of the headquarters of **Taman Nasional Bali Barat**  (West Bali National Park; Mon–Thu 7.30am–3.30pm, Fri 7.30am–11am, Sat 7.30am–1pm; tel: 0365-61060). Printed information is limited, but the staff are quite helpful. Obtain the necessary permits for hiking in the park here or at the visitor centre in Labuhan Lalang. An official guide is compulsory as visitors are not allowed to trek on their own. Established in 1984, the 760 sq km (300 sq miles) of forested mountains, coasts and offshore reefs are the last remaining pristine areas on the island. The gentle slopes of **Gunung Prapat Agung** at 375 metres (1,230ft) anchor the western tip of Bali and the national park. A trail of 24km (15 miles) goes partway around the foot of the mountain.

The park is the home of civet cats, several species of deer, birds and monkeys, and a few dozen rare Java buffalo. The last sighting of a Bali tiger was in 1937, when it was shot dead by a Dutch official. The area is also a refuge for the endangered *jalak putih*, the small white Bali starling or Rothschild's mynah (*Leucopsar rothschildi*), with brilliant blue patches around its eyes and black-tipped wings. Poaching has left fewer than a dozen of these birds in the wild, although zoos around the world maintain several thousand specimens.

Belimbingsari and Palasari

From Cekik, travel 15km (9 miles) to **Melaya** and turn inland to the village of **Belimbingsari** . Home to Bali's largest Protestant community, its impressive church has distinctly Balinese design elements and a *kulkul* (warning drum) instead of a bell signalling the start of service. Sunday services are at 9am (tel: 0365-42192 to check).

Palasari  with its 1,500-strong Catholic community is a short drive south. As with Belimbingsari, the early converts settled in remote West Bali by choice as they were shunned by the Hindu Balinese. The cathedral, adorned with Balinese touches like *meru* temple roofs, is a stunning piece of architecture in the middle of nowhere. The original structure dates back to 1958, with the present church built in 1991. Friday mass at 5.30pm and Sunday mass at 6.30am are good times to visit but call ahead to check first (tel: 0365-42201).

Negara and Loloan Timur

Part of the road southeast follows the coast, before turning inland at Candikesuma to the next port of call at **Negara** . There is little tourist development along this 30km (19-mile) long road, punctuated by orchards and coconut trees, and the occasional mosque (Jembrana region has a large Muslim migrant population from Java and elsewhere). There is nothing of much interest in Negara even though it is Jembrana's largest town and the main administrative centre.

Just 1km (½ mile) south of Negara is **Loloan Timur**, a small village

Statue of Christ in the forecourt of Palasari's Catholic church.

BELOW: the Catholic church in Palasari village.

Medewi's black-sand and pebble beach.

populated by Muslim Bugis people from south Sulawesi who settled here many generations ago. A number of their wooden homes retain the unique traditional Buginese style and are elevated on posts.

The Jembrana region's other claims to fame are the renowned bull races *(see blue box below)* and the unique *gamelan jegog*, a music ensemble using only bamboo instruments, some of which are gigantic tubes 3 metres (10ft) long and 15 cm (6in) in diameter. *Jegog* music is very fast, rhythmic and precise; the instruments are played in specific sequences and produce some wonderful sounds, while also being visually attractive. Some have likened the resonant sounds to roaring thunder as the music can be heard and even felt from quite a distance away. *Gamelan jegog* accompanies traditional dances like *tari silat* (self-defence dance) and newer ones such as the *tari makepung* (bull racing dance). Today, there are nearly 50 ensembles, mostly located around the towns of Sangkar Agung, Mendoyo Dangintukad and Tegal Cangkring.

Below: *makepung* (bull racing) at Perancak.

Pura Gede Perancak

From Loloan Timur, follow the road northeast to **Dauhwaru**, then turn right and continue zigzagging all the way to the coastal town of **Yeh Kuning**. From there, go west along the coast to the mouth of **Perancak River**, believed to be the place where 16th-century Javanese high priest Danghyang Nirartha first landed in Bali. While he was resting in the shade of an *ancak* (a kind of banyan), a local ruler ordered him to pray in the temple there. After the priest did so, it collapsed and was rebuilt by villagers as the small and simple **Pura Gede Perancak ⑭** (Great Temple of the Ancak Tree).

Pura Rambut Siwi

Return to the main road and continue east. At **Yeh Embang**, a side road on the right leads towards a spectacular stretch of black-sand beach where stands **Pura Rambut Siwi ⑮** (The Lock of Hair Temple; daily daylight hours; donation). Stop at one of several pavilions perched on a cliff overlooking the ocean to the west of this temple and admire the panoramic views.

Bull Races

The *makepung*, or water-buffalo races, of Negara were introduced about a century ago by migrants from Madura, in Java. Wearing colourful banners and crowns, their horns decorated and wooden bells tied around their necks, the bulls race down the erratic 2km (1¼-mile) -long track. It's remarkable to see such docile creatures thunder across the finish line at speeds of up to 60kmph (37mph). The daredevil charioteers often ride standing up on a chariot, twisting the bulls' tails to give them extra motivation. The races take place every second Sunday from July to November. Contact the **Jembrana Tourist Office** (tel: 0365-41060) for race dates.

In the 16th century, the Javanese high priest Danghyang Nirartha is said to have stopped at the village, and put an end to an epidemic that was devastating the population. Before moving on, he presented the people with a gift of his hair, thus explaining the name of the holy site. Nirartha's hair and some of his personal belongings are enshrined within a *meru* (pagoda) in the inner courtyard of the main temple.

Medewi

Further east along the main road is Medewi , a rather undistinguished village but with a black-sand and pebble beach; the stretch on the other side of the river mouth is good for surfing. Be aware that the waves can be rough and the undercurrent strong here. Food can be bought from beachside vendors, or restaurants at one of the modest hotels near the beach.

Bunut Bolong

Just beyond Medewi at **Pekutatan**, veer left at the Y-junction and begin a steady climb up into the mountains. The narrow, twisting and paved road, just 10km (6 miles) long, passes through rainforest and plantations of coffee, cocoa and cloves, and the mountain side-hugging village of **Asahduren** ⑰. Stop to have a look at Balinese village life scarcely affected by the demands of tourism.

Heading north, the road passes right through the base of a gigantic *bunut* (a type of banyan) tree in **Manggissari** village. The road used to wend around this grand old tree, but as it continued to grow larger the only choice was to create a tunnel through it. Cutting down the tree would have left its resident spirit without a place to stay. Called **Bunut Bolong** ⑱ (Hole in the Bunut Tree), a small shrine with two tiger figures sits on its right-hand side. This is where drivers sometimes stop to ask for permission to continue on their journey by making offerings to the spirit.

The road continues past isolated mountain villages like Tista to **Pupuan** in Tabanan region (see page 193). Stop here to admire the rice terraces and breathtaking views of southwest Bali before continuing either to north Bali or south to Tabanan proper. ❏

Surfer at Soka beach.

RESTAURANTS

Most eating places in this area are in hotels.
Dewi Ramona
Matahari Beach Resort.
Tel: 0362-92312.
Open: daily 7am–10.30pm.
$$$$
www.matahari-beach-resort.
com
A perfect blend of Asian and Western cuisines is served at this up-market hotel restaurant. Highlights include the unique varieties of spring rolls and the

Balinese special, fish cooked in banana leaf.
Taman Selini
Taman Selini Resort.
Tel: 0362-94746.
Open: daily B, L & D. **$$**
www.tamanselini.com
Delightful beach side restaurant with surprisingly good Greek dishes in addition to the usual local and international fare. The *mezze* plate, *moussaka* and prawn *saghanaki* are delicious.

Negara
Very limited choice, mostly small *warungs*.
Wira Pada Restaurant
Jalan Ngurah Rai 107. Tel: 0365-42669. Open: Mon– Sat L & D. **$$**
Serves Indonesian food, including *tepung* dishes (various meats coated in breadcrumbs and pan fried) and some Chinese-style food, like sweet and sour chicken or fish.

Medewi
Most eating places in this area are in hotels.

Medewi Beach Cottages
Tel: 0365-40029, Open: daily 7am–10.30pm. **$$**
Situated on a black-sand beach, at this beach-side area popular with surfers. The pickings are slim and the Indonesian and Western dishes are very run-of-the-mill.

• • • • • • • •
Price for a two-course meal for one including a non-alcoholic beverage:
$ = *below Rp 100,000.*
$$ = *Rp 100,000–200,000.*
$$$ = *Rp 200,000–300,000.*
$$$$ = *over Rp 300,000.*

TABANAN REGION

Tabanan, famed for its rice, has vast expanses of terraced rice fields. But there are also historically important towns that are centres for music, dance and religion, and the mountain sanctuary of Pura Luhur Batukau, an ancestral temple still maintained by descendants of Bali's royalty.

The fertile plains of the Tabanan region were once home to the powerful Mengwi kingdom, which emerged around 1700 after the fall of Gelgel. At one time, it controlled Bukit Badung in the south and areas as far away as east Java. Mengwi rule ended in 1891 when it was defeated by its neighbours, and its realm divided between Tabanan and Badung. Unlike the kings of Gianyar, Bangli and Karangasem to the east, the raja of Tabanan had no agreement with the Dutch, and in 1906, the Dutch took control of his land, which was later distributed among the villages in the area. Rice was the choice crop, and Tabanan today is known as the Rice Basket of Bali.

Despite being deprived of political power by the Dutch, Tabanan's royalty remained leaders among their people. Palaces continued to serve as centres for the arts, and royal families retained their role of presiding over temple ceremonies. In the forests near Gunung Batukau lies the remote mountain sanctuary of Pura Luhur Batukau, a royal temple where thousands journey to pay homage.

The central mountains of northern Tabanan rise steeply through some of the more isolated parts of the island, where deer and wild boars roam dense forests. The region's southwest coast still remains fairly undeveloped, with rough waves pounding quiet stretches of black-sand beaches. The famous Pura Tanah Lot *(see page 113)* sits on a rocky islet off the coast of Tabanan, but is more easily accessed from tourist centres in South Bali.

Tabanan

The town of **Tabanan ❶** is the region's administrative capital and a bustling

Main attractions
KRAMBITAN
PURA TAMAN AYUN
SANGEH MONKEY FOREST
PURA LUHUR BATUKAU
JATILUWIH

LEFT: fertile rice terraces at Jatiluwih.
RIGHT: Statue of Mario (left) at the Gedong Mario Theatre.

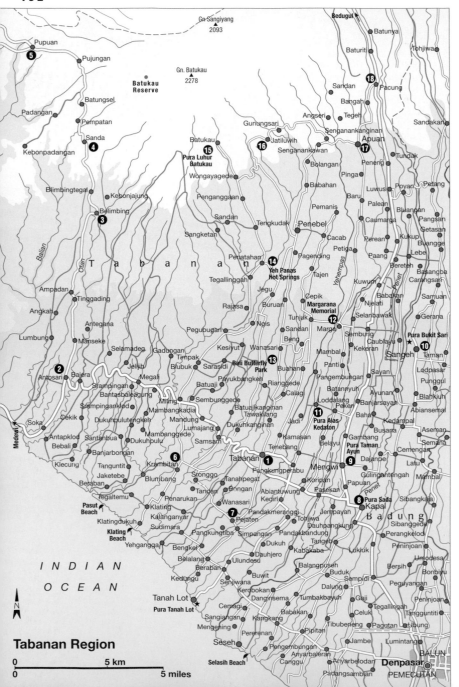

Gn Sangiyang
2093

Gn. Batukau
2278

**Batukau
Reserve**

Pupuan **5**

Pujungan

Batungsel

Padangan

Pempatan

Sanda **4**

Kebonpadangan

Blimbingtegal

Kebonjajung

Belimbing **3**

Ampadan

Tinggading

Angkah

Antegana

Lumbung

Manseke

Selamadeg

Gadungan

Antosari **2**

Bajera

Jelijih

Srampingan

Timpak

Blubuk

Megati

Bantasbaleagung

Srampingankiod

Miling

Mambangkadia

Soka

Cekik

Dukuhpulutengkeh

Mandung

Antapklod

Santanbua

Mambanggede

Dukuhpulu

Lumajang

Dukuhkanginan

Bebali

Samsam

Klecung

Banjarbongan

Tanguntit

Krambitan **6**

Jaketebe

Blunjbang

Sronggo

Beraban

Tangan

Tegaltemu

Penarukan

Klating

**Pasut
Beach**

Klatingdukuh

Kalanganyar

**Klating
Beach**

Sudimara

Yehganggat

Pangkungtiba

Bengkel

INDIAN

OCEAN

Belalang

Kedungu

Tanah Lot

Pura Tanah Lot

Cemagi

Sangiangan

Mengening

Tabanan Region

0   5 km

0   5 miles

Batunya

Bedugul

Baturiti

Tohjiwa

Sandan

Bangah

Pacung **18**

Tegeh

Angseri

Gunungsari

Batukau

15

**Pura Luhur
Batukau**

Jatiluwih **16**

Senganankawan

Senganankanginan

Apuan

17

Tundak

Sandakan

Wongayagede

Penanggaan

Bolangan

Peneng

Pinga

Babahan

Baru

Luwus

Poyan

Petang

Sandan

Pemanis

Palean

Buangan

Pangsan

Tengkudak

Penebel

Caumarga

Kukup

Getasan

Sangketan

Cacab

Perean

Paang

Lebe

Buangge

Petiga

Beretek

Penataran

Pagending

14

Tajen

Kuwum

Babakan

Basangba

Carangsari

Tegallinggah

**Yeh Panas
Hot Springs**

Njelati

Samuan

Jegu

Cepik

**Margarana
Memorial**

Selanbawak

Gerana

Rajasa

Buruan

Tunjuk

12

Sembung

Caublayu

Pura Bukit Sari

Pegubugan

Ngis

Sandan

Marga

Kekeran

Sangeh **10**

Kesiyut

Wanasari

Beng

Mambal

Taman

Timpak

13

Buahan

Panti

Sayan

Lodpasar

Sarasidi

**Bali Butterfly
Park**

Rianggede

Pangembungan

Ayunan

Punggul

Batuaji

Payukbangket

Calag

Batannyuh

Peken

Banjarsayan

Blahkiuh

Sembunggede

Batuajikanginan

Loddalang

Baha

Abiansemal

Tawakilang

Jadi

11

**Pura Alas
Kedaton**

Kedampal

Kamasan

Busara

Aseman

Tenebang

Belayu

Gambang

Semana

**Pura Taman
Ayun**

Dalanpe

Cemengan

Latu

Tabanan **1**

Mengwi **9**

Pangkungperabu

Koripan

Papuan

Gulingantengah

Mambal

Sronggo

Tanahpegat

Abiantuwung

Pasekan

Sibangkaja

Bongan

Kediri

8

Pura Sada

Wanasari **7**

Pandakmerangti

Tohjiwa

Jempayan

Kapal

B a d u n g

Pejaten

Simpangan

Dauhpangkung

Pandakbandung

Tangeb

Lukluk

Sibanggede

Perangkelod

Dukuh

Kabakaba

Peninjoan

Dauhjero

Balangpuseh

Buduk

Bersih

Limodesa

Ulundesu

Buwit

Dalung

Sempidi

Bonbiyu

Peguyangan

Beraban

Senjiwana

Kerobokan

Danginsema

Tumbakbayuh

Gaji

Tegallingan

Peninjoan

Babakan

Celuk

Tangguntiti

Kangkang

Tibubeneng

Pagutan

Ubung

Pipitan

Jambe

Lumintang

Seseh

Pengembungan

Anyarbaleran

BALUN

Selasih Beach

Canggu

Anyarbelodan

Denpasar

Padangsambian

PEMECUTAN

place with many businesses but few tourist attractions. Near the centre of the city is **Gedong Mario Theatre**, which is used for performances of music and dance. The Theatre was built in 1974 to honour the region's late, great male dancer I Ketut Marya, better known simply as Mario. Born at the end of the 19th century, Mario was already dancing at the age of six. During the early 1920s, he developed and perfected the spectacular solo dances of *kebyar duduk* and *kebyar trompong* (*see page 65*), which began in north Bali during the 1910s. Mario's grace and movement enraptured European audiences who saw him dance on a tour of Europe during the 1930s.

At the eastern end of Tabanan town is the **Museum Subak** (Mon–Sat 7.30am–5pm, Fri 7.30am–1pm; charge; tel: 0361-810315), dedicated to the cultivation of rice, the mainstay of Tabanan's economy. Although rice is such an important part of Balinese life, visitors rarely come to see the museum's well documented displays of agricultural tools that trace the history and process of rice from paddy field to kitchen. Ask to see the

adjacent traditional Balinese house with a *lumbug* (rice storehouse).

Scenic drive to Pupuan

Armed with information about rice growing in Tabanan, head west along the curving road wending its way to **Antosari 2**. From here and at vantage points north at villages like **Belimbing 3** and **Sanda 4** are spectacular rice terraces carved from hillsides on either side of the road as far as the eye can see. Continuing north leads to **Pujungan** where a track on the right leads to a scenic waterfall. From this point onwards clove and coffee plantations are interspersed with rice fields until the road reaches **Pupuan 5**.

From Pupuan, there are two options. Heading north for 12km (7½ miles) will lead to Mayong and all the way to the coast at Seririt. Continuing south, the twisting road descends via Tista, Manggissari and Asahduren villages to Pekutatan in west Bali.

Krambitan

Some 3km (2 miles) southwest of Tabanan town is **Krambitan 6**,

Museum Subak has well-documented displays on the cultivation of rice in Bali.

BELOW: planting rice on the terraces at Belimbing.

Pura Sada with its 11-tiered tower.

BELOW: detail of Boma image at Pura Sada.

where a branch of the Tabanan royal family owns the atmospheric 17th-century **Puri Anyar** (New Palace) and **Puri Agung** (Great Palace), both with beautiful architecture and ambience of the past. The latter, where Tabanan royalty still live today, doubles up as a guesthouse and restaurant (tel: 0361-812668). Krambitan village has a unique style of traditional *wayang* (puppet figure) painting that depicts episodes from epics, myths and romantic tales. The men also maintain large *tektekan* ensembles, playing giant wooden cattle bells and rhythmically striking bamboo tubes to create exciting music.

Pejaten

Southeast of Krambitan, a road zigzags through rice fields to the village of **Pejaten** ❼, where traditional pottery is a home industry. Terracotta roof tiles, decorative wall plaques, whimsical figures and tableware are often glazed and painted with colourful accents. Stop by **Tanteri Ceramics** (daily 8am–4.30pm, tel: 0361-831948; www.tantericeramicbali.com) to see a good selection of products. The range of vases, bowls, teapots, soapdishes and candle holders in greenish glaze are embellished with frogs, dragonflies and leaves.

Pura Sada

Southeast of Tabanan, the main road leads 10km (6 miles) to **Kapal** (Boat), where the road sides are lined with temple shrines, guardian statues, and other temple paraphernalia. Much more important is **Pura Sada** ❽ (daily daylight hours; donation), an ancestral shrine honouring the deified spirit of Ratu Sakti Jayengrat (Powerful World Conquering Lord), whose identity still remains uncertain.

The original foundations may date to the 12th century, but the temple was rebuilt by one of the early kings of Mengwi during the 17th century and is the oldest of the kingdom's state shrines. It was destroyed in the great earthquake of 1917 and was restored in 1949. A large brick and stone *prasada* (tower) with 11 tiers dominates the inner courtyard, giving the temple its name.

Pura Taman Ayun

Travel north 4km (2½ miles) to **Mengwi**, turning right at the crossroads to **Pura Taman Ayun** ❾, built in the 18th century by a king of Mengwi as a royal family temple. The surrounding moat gives the impression of a garden sanctuary with soaring *meru* (pagodas) resembling the masts of a majestic ship in the middle of a pond. Only worshippers are allowed inside, so you must admire this architectural masterpiece from behind the low temple walls.

This temple is a place to worship the gods of other sacred sites, with individual shrines to the mountain deities of Batukau, Agung and Batur, as well as to the resident god of Pura Sada temple. Important kings of Mengwi are also venerated here. Note the small and beautifully carved doors of the shrines.

Sangeh

From Pura Taman Ayun, travel east to Latu and then head north uphill to **Blahkiuh** and the sacred "monkey forest" at **Sangeh** (daily daylight hours; charge). According to the Indian *Ramayana* epic, the monkey general Hanoman broke off a Himalayan mountain peak laden with magical plants to revive the fallen heroes of Rama's forces. When this feat was accomplished, Hanoman returned the peak but part of it fell to earth at Sangeh along with some of his monkey soldiers. Today, the forest is home to three clans of mischievous monkeys, so take the same precautions as you would at Ubud's Monkey Forest *(see page 133)*. Towering 40-metre (130ft) tall *palahlar (Dipterocarpus Trinervis)* trees, said to be 300 years old, make up this forest and are incorrectly assumed to be nutmeg trees. The place is a protected sanctuary and no one is permitted to chop down any of the trees or harm the monkeys.

In the heart of the forest lies **Pura Bukit Sari ⑩**, a moss-covered 17th-century holy site originally built as a meditation temple and then con-verted to an agricultural temple. In the central courtyard, a large statue of the mythological *garuda* bird symbolises freedom from suffering.

Pura Alas Kedaton

Alternatively, to get to a more accessible "monkey forest", head north out of Mengwi for some 5km (3 miles) and turn left at the junction to **Belayu**, a small village where beautiful handwoven *songket* (brocade) cloths are made. Continue past Belayu to **Pura Alas Kedaton ⑪** (daily daylight hours; charge). Besides the usual souvenir stalls, many fruit bats and mischievous monkeys – again, take heed – inhabit the surrounding trees.

Margarana Memorial

Return to the crossroads at Belayu, turn left uphill and travel 6km (4 miles) to **Marga**, the site of the important **Margarana Memorial ⑫** (daily 9am–5pm; charge). In 1946, the commander of Indonesian nationalist troops in Bali, Lt Col. I Gusti Ngurah Rai, and his company of 94 guerrilla fighters were surrounded and out-numbered by Dutch forces in Marga.

TIP

While in Tabanan area, spend a few languid days at Puri Taman Sari near Marga. This lovely home of a descendant of the Mengwi royal family is open to guests who wish to experience authentic life in a Balinese village *(see page 248 for more details)*.

BELOW: the monkey forest at Sangeh's temple.

Yeh Panas' hot springs are said to have healing properties. After soaking in the hot pool, cool off in the adjacent fresh-water swimming pool.

BELOW: zooming past Jatiluwih's rice terraces. **RIGHT:** worshipper at Pura Luhur Batakau.

As an added measure, the Dutch also bombarded them from the air. Ngurah Rai and his men refused to surrender. Instead, they attacked the Dutch positions and died to the last man in a suicidal assault reminiscent of the royal *puputan* ("finishing off") 40 years earlier in Badung, also in defiance of the Dutch.

The Margarana Memorial was built to honour these valiant soldiers. It is a five-sided pillar 17 metres (55ft) tall, inscribed with a courageous letter written by Ngurah Rai stating his refusal to surrender until freedom was won. Nearby are 94 stone markers, each bearing the name and home village of a fallen hero. The anniversary of the massacre is remembered in a solemn ceremony every 20 November; Bali's airport and a university in Denpasar are named in honour of Ngurah Rai.

Bali Butterfly Park

From Marga, return to the main road and go west to **Tunjuk**, then head downhill to **Wanasari**. Just down the main road is the **Bali Butterfly Park** ⓭ (daily 8am–5pm; charge; tel: 0361-814282/3). Around 15 species of but-

terflies flutter in an enclosed area; they are more active on warm, dry days, but you won't see them if it's raining.

Yeh Panas

Head north uphill for another 9km (6 miles) to get to **Penatahan**, where hot water surges from a river bank at **Yeh Panas** ⓮. The Balinese believe that such an unusual natural phenomenon is inhabited by spirits, so a small temple was built at the site. During World War II, occupying Japanese forces made the first additions to the place when they tried to create a Japanese-style outdoor bathing place here. The hot springs are now a part of the **Yeh Panas Hot Springs Resort** (daily 8am–6pm; tel: 0361-262356 or 484052 reservation office), where for a fee non-guests can take a relaxing soak in its waters – there are nine private and semi-private pools here.

Pura Luhur Batukau

Continue north up the road 10km (6 miles) via **Wongayagede** to one of Bali's most venerated temples, the **Pura Luhur Batukau** ⓯ (Temple of the Stone Coconut Shell; daily day-

light hours; charge), on the slopes of Gunung Batukau. The modest structures are devoid of ornate carving and gilding, blending in well with the surrounding forests. Although the 1991 renovations have detracted from the temple's mystique, it is still a quiet and beautiful place for reflection.

The main temple in the complex is dedicated to the god of **Gunung Batukau**, second highest mountain on the island at 2,278 metres (7,475ft). It's so important that every temple in southwest Bali has a shrine dedicated to this exalted deity. As the ancestral temple of the royal families of Mengwi and Tabanan, there are also shrines for their deified ancestors. In the inner courtyard, the seven-tiered *meru* is dedicated to the ruler who established the Mengwi kingdom around the end of the 17th century; a three-tiered one is dedicated to the 18th-century founder of Tabanan. Descendants of both dynasties still maintain the temple today.

Jatiluwih

Back down the road 3km (2 miles) in Wongayagede is a T-junction. Turn left and follow the twisting road uphill to the mountain village of **Jatiluwih ⑯**, since 2008 a Unesco World Heritage Site for its preservation of traditional Balinese farming techniques. True to its name, which means extraordinary or truly marvellous, this scenic point at 850 metres (2,700ft) above sea level offers one of the most breathtaking panoramic views imaginable, with rice terraces stretching all the way to southern Bali. *Padi Bali* (indigenous Balinese rice) with long graceful stalks is grown here, and during harvest time women bear heavy bundles of the ripe yellow grains home on their heads while men carry yet more on each end of bamboo shoulder poles.

Apuan and Pacung

The road twists and turns further east to **Apuan ⑰**. This small mountain village is the spiritual home of sacred *barong* masks from all over Tabanan. From a T-junction in Apuan head 5km (3 miles) uphill where the road joins the main route at **Pacung ⑱**. Stop to admire the views of beautiful rice terraces from this vantage point. Taking the road north leads to the Bedugul area (see page 179). ❑

TIP

The Sarinbuana Eco-Tower is a 20-metre (65ft) high steel construction near Sarinbuana village, on the slopes of Gunung Batukau, with a truly breathtaking view from the top. The surrounding area is known to have the greatest biological diversity in Bali. Local guides will lead visitors on treks through lush forests to the summit of Batukau. Contact: Sarinbuana Eco-Lodge, tel: 0361-7435198, www.baliecolodge.com.

RESTAURANTS

These villages at the foot of Gunung Batukau are known for their stunning views and cooler weather.

Cempaka Belimbing
Belimbing. Tel: 0361-745 1178. Open: daily B, L & D. **$$** www.cempakabelimbing.com
In an open-air restaurant (part of a villa complex) with rice field and spectacular mountain views, the food plays s econd fiddle. Still, expect very decent Indonesian and Western fare.

Plantations
Sanda Butik Villas, Sanda. Mobile tel: 0828-373 0055. Open: daily B, L & D. **$$$** www.sandavillas.com
Magnificent views from this Danish-owned mountain-side terrace restaurant. It is the perfect transit spot between Bali's north and south coasts. Chilli-garlic prawns, chicken breast stuffed with Brie, and curry bags – shredded chicken curry and vegetables wrapped in pastry

– are just some of Plantations' options.

Big Tree Farm
Jatiluwih. Tel: 0361-461978. Open: daily D May–Oct. **$$$$** www.bigtreebali.com
American couple Blair and Ben Ripple, who run this large organic farm, feature the torchlit Firefly Supper Series from May–Oct: seasonal produce almost straight from their fields to your plate. Cost includes a 6-course dinner, wine and transport. By reservation only.

Café Jatiluwih
Jatiluwih. Tel: 0361-815245. Open: daily B & L. **$$** Indonesian dishes amid stunning rice terraces.
Prana Dewi
Wongayagede. Tel: 361-736654. Open: daily B, L & D. **$$$**. www.baliprana.com
Serves Asian and Western food using organically grown ingredients.

• • • • • • • • •
Price for a two-course meal for one including a non-alcoholic beverage:
$ = below Rp 100,000,
$$ = Rp 100,000–200,000.
$$$ = Rp 200,000–300,000.
$$$$ = over Rp 300,000.

LOMBOK

Lombok charms visitors with its unspoilt natural beauty of pristine white-sand beaches, forests and mountains as well as its largely untouched culture. Tourism impacts lightly on the traditional lifestyle.

L ying to the east of Bali and accessible by a 25-minute flight or two-hour fast boat ride from that better known island, Lombok is a haven for those seeking the unspoilt beauty of the old Bali. Indeed, many people refer to it as "Bali 20 years ago", which isn't an apt description considering the landscapes and cultures that are unique to Lombok.

At roughly 5,300 sq km (2,380 sq miles), Lombok is slightly smaller than Bali, and has a wide range of natural attractions and outdoor activities to suit more adventurous travellers. The main tourism areas are in Senggigi on the west coast, the three Gili islands off the northwest coast, and Kuta on the south coast.

The beaches surrounding Lombok are pristine, with clean waters bordered by long stretches of sand and usually fringed by coconut palms. The west of the island is especially green and lush, with a series of beautiful bays skirting the entire coastline and the lovely Gili islands within easy reach. The southern coast is even more stunning: long stretches of deserted beaches, cliffs and bays facing a vast ocean that provides some of the best surfing in Indonesia. Large parts of the island are still heavily forested and embellished with waterfalls, rivers, hills and mountains, providing myriad opportunities for exploration. Dominating north Lombok is a mountain range of 13 peaks, crowned by the magnificent volcano, Gunung Rinjani. To the south, agriculture is the mainstay. Many fields are still tilled using water buffalo and antiquated equipment, and the villages there are timeless.

For those seeking authentic cultural experiences, the ancient traditions of the local Sasak people, largely undisturbed by outside influences, are endlessly fascinating. The Sasak still live in traditional villages, farm, fish and produce handicrafts. Colourful ceremonies, dance and music are an authentic part of local life and not staged for tourists. Lombok pottery, made by hand and fired in simple wood kilns, is exported all over the world, while old weaving, thatching and woodworking techniques are still handed down through the generations.

Lombok may not have the spit and polish of Bali, but it does have the tropical paradise atmosphere which many expect to find on the larger island. ❏

PRECEDING PAGES: snorkelling off Gili Meno, Gili Islands. **LEFT:** sunset, Gili Twanangan.
ABOVE RIGHT: Balinese food hamper containing chillis, garlic, onion and macadamia nuts.

WEST LOMBOK

West Lombok has a tourism infrastructure that almost rivals South Bali – but thankfully it doesn't overwhelm. The wide sandy beaches of Senggigi invite some serious chilling-out, but the more active can also explore old temples, markets and the trio of quaint little towns, Ampenan, Mataram and Cakranegara.

Denpasar

The Sasak, a Malay race inhabiting Lombok for at least 2,000 years, probably settled on the island's coastal areas as long as 4,000 years ago. For much of the last 600 years, Lombok was a feudal state with many small kingdoms, some of which followed animistic beliefs, while others practised a combination of animism with Hinduism or Buddhism. Over the centuries, Java influenced Lombok in varying degrees, eventually conquering it in the 14th century and incorporating it into the Majapahit empire. Several small kingdoms on Lombok were once ruled by Javanese nobles who had been exiled to Lombok; in fact Sasak aristocracy today still claims Javanese ancestry. Java introduced both Hinduism and Islam to Lombok, but its religious and political influence waned by the 17th century. Islam gradually spread through eastern and central Lombok, while the west coast, being closer to Bali, was predominantly Hindu.

From the mid-17th century onwards, the Balinese Karangasem kingdom colonised Lombok, ruling the island until 1894. Balinese influence always centred in the west, where

Balinese still constitute at least 10 percent of the population today. The Balinese king, Anak Agung Ngurah Gede Karangasem, gained extensive influence over western Lombok during the mid-1800s and oversaw development of the arts and the construction of an impressive number of temples. He also restricted the land rights of the Sasak aristocracy on Lombok, introduced an inflexible taxation system, and demanded forced labour of Sasak peasantry. Revolts erupted several times in the 19th century, with Islam

Main attractions
MAYURA WATER PALACE
BANYUMULEK
GUNUNG PENGSONG
TAMAN NARMADA
PURA SURANADI
PURA BATU BOLONG

LEFT: Sasak fisherman repairing his boat on the west coast.
RIGHT: Malimbu fishing beach, along the coastal road between Senggigi and Bangsal.

A traditional rice store, lumbung, raised off the ground on posts.

the rallying cry among the Sasak.

Sasak leaders approached the Dutch for help in overthrowing Balinese rule in the early 1890s. The Dutch, mistakenly believing that Lombok was rich in tin, assisted and the Sasak War broke out in 1894. The Balinese were eventually defeated, and a number of temples and palaces on Lombok were destroyed. Many of the final confrontations ended in *puputan*, the mass suicides of Balinese palace nobles, their families and followers.

With the defeat of the Balinese, the Sasak leaders believed they had the right to rule. Instead, the Dutch took over the island, banishing the king and his family and offering only minor government positions to Sasak and Balinese leaders. Colonialism intensified land use and taxation until the Japanese took control of the island in 1942. When the Japanese left in 1945, the Dutch returned briefly but were repelled by nationalist guerrillas. Lombok has remained independent ever since.

Religion in Lombok

There are two main groups among the Sasak: Wektu Lima and Wektu Telu. The Wektu Lima are orthodox Sunni Muslims, while the Wektu Telu are nominal Muslims who combine a belief in Allah and some Islamic observances with a mosaic of animism, ancestor worship, Hinduism and Buddhism. The Wektu Lima have adopted the Islamic identity of Muslims throughout Indonesia, while the Wektu Telu are generally uninterested in the world at large, focusing instead on their strong ties to ancestral lands.

Both Wektu Lima and Wektu Telu Muslims observe Islamic religious practices, especially fasting during the month of Ramadan. Other religions, particularly Hinduism and Buddhism, peacefully co-exist alongside the local Muslim population, and there are a variety of mosques, churches and temples to visit on the island.

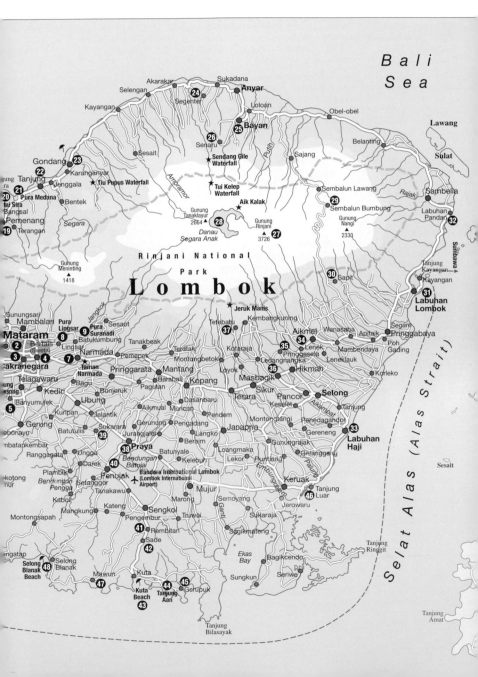

Bali Sea

Akarakar
Sukadana
Selengan
24
Segenter
Anyar
Kayangan
Loloan
Obel-obel
Bayan
25
Lawang
26
Belanting
Sesait
Senaru
Sajang
Sulat
Gondang **23**
Karanganyar
★ Sendang Gile
Waterfall
gung Tanjung
22
Jenggala ★ Tiu Pupus Waterfall
★ Tui Kelep
Waterfall
Sembalun Lawang
Rajak
Sambelia
20 **21**
Pura Medana
Bentek
Aik Kalak
29
Sembalun Bumbung
Labuhan
Pandan **32**
lai Sira
Bangsal
Pemenang
Segara
Gunung
Tanaklayur
2664 ▲
28
Gunung
Rinjani
▲ 3726 **27**
Gunung
Nangi
▲ 2330
Sumbawa
19
Terangan
Danau
Segara Anak

Gunung
Meninting
▲ 1418

R i n j a n i   N a t i o n a l

Tanjung
Kayangan
30 Sapit
Kayangan

P a r k

L o m b o k

31
**Labuhan
Lombok**

Gunungsari
Mambalan
Pura
Lingsar
Pura ★ Sesaot
9 Suranadi
Tanakbeak
Jeruk Manis
Tetebatu
Kembangkuning
Aikmel Wanasaba
Apitaik
Segare
Pringgabaya
Mataram
8
Batukumbung
Terutak
Kotaraja
34
Lenek
Mambendaya
Poh
Gading
Bertais **2**
Sweta
Lingsar **7**
Narmada Pemepek
Montongbetok
Layok
35
Ledangnangka
Leneklauk
3
4
Taman
Narmada
Pringgarata
Mantang Barabali
Kopang
36
Hikmah
Korleko
akranegara
Bagu
Pagutan
Masbagik
Sikur
Pancor
Selong
Telagawaru
Kedin
Bonjeruk
Dasanbaru
Terara
Keselet
Tanjung
sjong
Ubung
Aikmual Muncan
Pendem
Montongtangi
Penedagandor
33
**Labuhan
Haji**
5
Banyumulek
Kuripan
Jelantik
Gerunung
Pengadang
Langko
Janapria
Gereneng
Gerung
Batutulis
Sukarara
Jurangjaler
Beraim
Gunungrajak
Kabanjahe
ebonayu
39
Loangmaka
Lekor Puntiang
mbatankembar
Ungga
Darek
38 Praya
Batunyale
Kelebuh
Keruak
46
Tanjung
Luar
Ranggagata
Bendungan
Batujai
40
Penujak
Bandara International Lombok
(Lombok International
Airport)
Mujur
Marong
Semoyang
Jerowaru
kotong
Plambik
Benningan
Pengga
Setanggor
Tanakawu
Sengkol
Truwai
Sukaraja
Tanjung
Ringgit
Kabol
Mangkung
Kateng
Pengembur
41
Rembitan
Sagikmateng
Montongsapah
42
Sade
Ekas
Bay
Bagikcendo
ngatap
Selong
Blanak
48
Selong
Blanak
Beach
Mawun
47
Kuta
44
45
Gerupuk
Sungkun
Seriwe
**Kuta
Beach**
43
Tanjung
Aan
Tanjung
Bilasayak
Tanjung
Amat
Sesait

S e l a t   A l a s   (A l a s   S t r a i t)

TIP

The sellers on the streets and beaches around Senggigi will offer pearls at what seem to be very low prices. These are genuine pearls, although usually of low quality, so be sure to bargain hard. A better selection of pearls can be found in the many gold and pearl shops in Ampenan and Cakranegara and, in particular, in the myriad specialist retail outlets in Sekarbele (in Mataram).

BELOW: two Sasak children ride in a tumbrel (two-wheeled cart), pulled by a pony, in Nusa Tenggara.

Today, Lombok retains many traits and customs similar to those of Java and Bali, and the Sasak language has many words from Javanese and Balinese (although Bahasa Indonesia is widely spoken). However, Sasak culture is distinct from that of Java and Bali, with many traditions and beliefs specific only to Lombok.

WEST LOMBOK TOWNS

The west coast of Lombok is the most developed area of the island with small towns, relatively good roads, shops, restaurants and hotels, and the island's only airport.

Senggigi is the main beach resort and is located approximately 20 minutes, drive from Selaparang Airport. The west coast of Lombok faces Bali across the Lombok Strait and affords wonderful sunsets with the sacred volcano, Gunung Agung on Bali, silhouetted against the orange-tinted evening sky.

The west is also lush and green, with mountains inland and the wide Lombok Strait forming a series of picturesque bays and beaches along the western and northwestern coast-line. West Lombok, being closest to Bali, has a long history of Hindu settlement. Traces of the old empires are still very much visible in its large Balinese-Hindu population, and its many Balinese-style temples and ceremonies.

Ampenan

The three main cities in western Lombok – Ampenan, Mataram and Cakranegara – meld together to create what is, for Lombok, an urban sprawl. **Ampenan ❶** is the old port town and some Dutch colonial architecture is still visible in the buildings closer to the beach to the west. This area becomes a boisterous market at night, filled with *warung* and *kaki lima* (food carts) hawking cheap and tasty food.

There are occasional performances of the *gandrung* dance or the shadow puppet play known as *wayang Sasak* on special holidays. With its numerous shops, cheap hotels, dusty roads, plentiful *cidomo* (horse-drawn carts), gold and pearl shops, and its quaint Arab quarter, Ampenan is a colourful town to explore on foot.

Mataram

The city of **Mataram ❷** is the main administrative centre for Lombok and Sumbawa part of NTB (Nusa Tenggara Barat) province, and has government offices, banks, mosques, the main post office and Mataram University.

Mataram's **Nusa Tenggara Barat Museum** (Tue–Sun 7am–2pm; charge; tel: 0370-632159) houses historical and cultural artefacts from Lombok and Sumbawa, and it occasionally hosts special exhibits. Displays cover geology, history and culture.

Another interesting stop is the cultural centre, **Taman Budaya** (tel: 0370-622428) on Jalan Majapahit, where there are regular performances of traditional music and dance.

Cakranegara and Bertais

Just to the east of Mataram town is **Cakranegara ❸**, Lombok's main shopping area. It is also home to many Chinese and Balinese, who make up over 50 percent of the town's population. Many of Lombok's weaving and basketry industries are located near Cakranegara. Turn left at the main traffic lights and look for the market on the right near the bridge; the baskets made here are sold in Bali at many times what you pay in Lombok.

Further east, near the bus terminal, is **Bertais ❹**, the next large town east of Cakra. Also sometimes called **Sweta**, it has a huge daily market which sells everything that is made or produced on the island, from foodstuffs to clothing, exotic birds, handicrafts and more. However it is not recommended that you visit this market alone.

Pura Meru

There are several important sights in Cakranegara, foremost of which is **Pura Meru** (daily 8am–5pm; donation) at Jalan Selaparang. Built in 1720 by Balinese prince Anak Agung Made Karang, this is the largest temple on Lombok. Its three main *meru*

(pagoda) represent the Hindu trinity – Shiva (Siwa in Bahasa Indonesia), Vishnu (Wisnu) and Brahma.

On Lombok, this is the most important temple for the Balinese, and its annual Pujawali festival, held over five days during the September or October full moon, is the biggest Balinese-Hindu celebration. The outer courtyard hall has drums that call the devout to ceremonies and festivals. Two buildings with raised offering platforms are found in the central courtyard, while the interior enclosure has 33 shrines and the three multi-tiered *meru*.

Pura Mayura

Just across the street from Pura Meru stands **Pura Mayura** (daily 8am–5pm; donation), built in 1744 as the court temple of the last Balinese kingdom in Lombok. Part of the **Mayura Water Palace**, a large artificial lake here, holds an open hall or *bale kambang* (floating pavilion), used as a meeting and relaxing place. Today, the palace gardens are a playground for children and grazing livestock. The temple sits behind the water gardens.

The daily market at Bertais (Sweta), east of Cakranegara, is a hive of activity, with traders from the surrounding villages converging on this small town.

BELOW: Balinese-inspired Pura Meru.

The water gardens of Pura Mayura.

Banyumulek and Gunung Pengsong

About 7km (4 miles) south of Cakranegara is **Banyumulek ⑤** village, a major centre for the production of the distinctive terracotta pottery that Lombok is so famous for. In the mornings, visitors can watch the women potters at work. The eye-catching pots, plates, saucers, bowls, lamps, planters and goblets are decorated, etched and engraved in unique traditional and contemporary designs with paints, textiles and other finishes.

Just 3km (2 miles) west of Banyumulek village is **Gunung Pengsong ⑥**, where a holy shrine (daily 8am–5pm; donation) sits on a hilltop and has lovely vistas of rice fields, the coast and Gunung Rinjani. Populated by monkeys, this is the hill the Balinese aimed for in the mythical account of their initial arrival in west Lombok.

Narmada

Continuing some 10km (6 miles) east of Cakranegara is **Narmada ⑦**. The structures and pool at **Taman Narmada** (daily 7am–6pm; donation) were reportedly built in 1805

BELOW: view of the pool at Taman Narmada.

as a replica of Gunung Rinjani and Danau Segara Anak (*see page 220*), the crater lake within Gunung Rinjani's caldera. When the ruling king, Anak Agung Ngurah Gede Karangasem, became too old to make the long and mandatory trek to Segara Anak, he built Taman Narmada – comprising terraced gardens, pools, a large lake and a temple called **Pura Kalasa** – as a replica where he could perform his annual rituals. The annual pilgrimage to Segara Anak, where pilgrims throw gold pieces into the lake as offerings, still exists to this day, and the festival at Taman Narmada coincides with this pilgrimage during the full moon of either October or November.

The gardens at Pura Narmada are splendid, and on special occasions performances of *gandrung*, *gendang belek* and other traditional dances are held here. The two swimming pools at Narmada, where you can splash around (separate admission charge), are very popular with local children.

Pura Lingsar

Northwest of Narmada is **Pura Lingsar ⑧** (daily 8am–5pm; donation),

with two shrines, one Hindu and the other for Wektu Telu followers. This is the temple where people of various religions – Hindus, Buddhists, Christians and orthodox Muslims – come together to pray for prosperity, rain, fertility and health. The temple is associated with irrigation and rice, and the annual festival here features a ritualised mock battle called the *Perang Topat*.

Built around 1714, Pura Lingsar was originally based on the prevailing animist beliefs of the time, and some of the original animist statues still remain today. While the main courtyard symbolically unites the deities of Bali and Lombok, the second courtyard, called Kemaliq, contains sacred pools and unique altars of rocks, reminiscent of ancient megalithic worship. These rocks, brought down from the top of Gunung Rinjani and dressed in ceremonial cloths, are believed to contain the spirits of the ancestors of the land.

Pura Lingsar has a spring-fed pool which contains large freshwater holy eels. Visitors are welcome to accompany a temple priest who will feed the eels hard-boiled eggs, purchased at nearby stands.

Pura Suranadi

Located a few kilometres northeast of Narmada in **Suranadi** is **Pura Suranadi** **9** (daily 8am–5pm; donation), a complex of three temples. Pura Suranadi is among the oldest and holiest of the Balinese temples in Lombok, founded by the 16th-century Javanese high priest, Danghyang Nirartha. Underground streams bubble up into restored baths used for ritual bathing; this is also where locals obtain the holy water for cremation ceremonies.

Huge sacred eels live in the pools and streams here and, as at Pura Lingsar, can sometimes be lured out with an offering of hardboiled eggs, purchased from a nearby stall. The eels are considered holy (to see a sacred eel is

deemed lucky) and it is taboo to eat them or to contaminate the waters.

Beyond Suranadi, on the main road before the temple, is **Hutan Wisata Suranadi** (daily 8am–5pm; charge). Stroll through this small botanical forest with labelled specimens and observe birds, monkeys and butterflies.

WEST COAST

The main road starts at Ampenan and winds its way up the entire west coast, around the north of the island and down the east coast, making orientation and travelling around easy. Heading north from Ampenan is **Pura Segara**, a Balinese sea temple. The Chinese cemetery on the main road has interesting sea-facing graves painted in bright colours with Chinese decorations.

Batu Layar **10**, on the hill a few kilometres before Senggigi, has an important ancestral grave *(makam)* where Muslims come to picnic and to pray for health and success. There are many such *makam* all over Lombok (the graves of key religious leaders generally become shrines).

BELOW: temple structures at Pura Lingsar.

Capes for ritual dancers.

Nearby **Pura Batu Bolong** (daily 8am–5pm; donation) meaning "hollow rock" is an interesting Hindu temple on a cliff facing Bali across the Lombok Strait. Built on a large rock outcrop with a hole at the base, from which the temple takes its name, it is said that beautiful virgins were once sacrificed to the sea from the seat-like rock at the outermost point. Colourful Hindu ceremonies are held here every month at the dark and full moons, and also at Hindu festival times. This is a great place to watch the sunset, with fantastic vistas across to Gunung Agung on Bali.

Senggigi

About 10km (6 miles) north of Ampenan is **Senggigi** , the main tourist centre on Lombok. Nowhere near as large or as busy as its Bali counterparts, Senggigi is a very good base for exploring the rest of the island. The pace here is laid back, with activities centred around the beaches and day trips to places of interest within a few hours' drive.

Senggigi beach is the large bay that forms the centre of Senggigi, with the main road running parallel and slightly inland, and large resorts occupying the space between. The beach provides picturesque views of Bali's Gunung Agung.

Just off the spit of land at the south end of Senggigi beach is **Senggigi Point**, a good spot for snorkelling and, in the right conditions, some decent surf breaks. The main road is lined with small shops, an art market, tour agencies, restaurants, bars and low-key nightclubs. There are also supermarkets, moneychangers, a post office and all the usual tourist facilities. Senggigi is a popular place to stay, with a good range of deluxe hotels and resorts, as well as budget accommodation.

North of Senggigi

Tourism development runs north along the coastal road for about 10km (6 miles), with many hotels and restaurants along the beautiful beaches that line the entire west coast. About 2km (1 mile) north is **Kerandangan**, with a popular beach nearby and some nice hotels slightly out of town in a pretty valley.

Further north, **Mangsit** has developed as an accommodation alternative to Senggigi, with boutique-style hotels positioned along the breathtaking bays of this section of coast. Further north again is **Lendang Luar**, with two hotels perched on the long stretch of pristine beach here.

Deserted white-sand beaches flanked by coconut groves and untouched by development continue all the way north along the coastal road. **Malimbu** and **Nipah** are two pretty bays good for snorkelling. **Teluk Nara** and **Teluk Kodek** are on a large bay about 25km (15 miles) north of Senggigi. All the main dive operators have boats here to transfer guests to the **Gili Islands** (*see page 212*) as an alternative to nearby **Bangsal Harbour**, the main jumping-off point (*see page 217*). ❑

BELOW: Senggigi beach.

BEST RESTAURANTS

Restaurants

Price for a two-course meal for one including a non-alcoholic beverage:

$$$$	over Rp 300,000
$$$	Rp 200,000–300,000
$$	Rp 100,000–200,000
$	below Rp 100,000

Cakranegara

Seafood Nikmat

Jalan Panca Usaha 1, Cakranegara. Tel: 0370-634330. Open: daily L & D. **$$**

Features many types of fresh fish and seafood, including lobsters, prawns and crabs, most of which is kept in the tanks and fished out (literally) when you order. The fish and seafood can be cooked in any style you wish, either Indonesian or Cantonese (XO sauce, sweet and sour, black pepper, and more).

Mataram

Ali Baba

Jalan Catur Warga 4, Mataram. Tel: 0370-640800. Open: daily L & D. **$$**

Small traditional Arab kebab house (the owner is from Yemen). Dishes are eaten with unleavened Lebanese bread or *kebuli*, traditional Arabian rice cooked with herbs, spices and coconut milk. The shish kebab (beef or lamb) is excellent.

Dua M

Jalan Transisto 99, Mataram. Tel: 0370-622914. Open: daily L & D. **$**

A long-time favourite among locals, Dua M serves traditional Sasak food. Try the spicy *pelecing ayam* – grilled chicken with a piquant red sauce – or the popular *pelecing kangkung*, using water spinach.

Senggigi and Mangsit

Asmara Restaurant

Jalan Raya Senggigi, Senggigi. Tel: 0370-693619. Open: daily B, L & D. **$$$**
www.asmara-group.com

This is one of Senggigi's best restaurants. German-owned, it has a good range of international dishes, fresh seafood and pastas, and arguably the best steaks in town. The menu also includes local Sasak-style food and a selection of vegetarian dishes. Well-stocked library, bar area and billiards table for adults, a playground and wading pool for children.

Bumbu

Jalan Raya Senggigi. Tel: 0370-692236. Open: daily L & D. **$$$**

Serves a mix of Asian cuisines but the Thai menu is the best. Lip-smacking fish cakes, tom *kha gai* (chicken soup in coconut milk) and an array of curries: red, green, yellow and massaman, with a choice of chicken, beef, seafood or vegetable.

De Quake

Art Market, Senggigi. Tel: 0370-693694. Open: daily L & D. **$$$**. www.dequake.com

In a relaxing location overlooking the beach, with a bar downstairs and the restaurant upstairs. Serves a delicious variety of Asian and international cuisine, with dishes such as Vietnamese chicken salad, fish ginger caramel, Malay-style chicken laksa, and cashew beef.

Quali

Qunci Pool Villas & Spa, Mangsit. Tel: 0370-693800. Open: daily B, L & D. **$$$**
www.quncivillas.com

The main restaurant at this extension of the Qunci resort specialises in Asian cuisine, with everything from Indian samosas to Thai soups, noodles dishes, curries, fresh seafood and Lombok's famous fried chicken, *ayam taliwang*.

Square

Jalan Raya Senggigi. Tel: 0370-664 4888. Open: daily L & D. **$$$**
www.squarelombok.com

Lombok's classiest independent restaurant. Three separate areas offer both standard Indonesian Chinese and an exceptional international menu. The fare, such as roasted tomato and goats' cheese terrine, pan-seared foie gras with apple chutney and sweet and sour tamarind sauce, and king prawn and mushroom risotto with Madras curry beurre meuniere sauce, is inventive.

Sunset Beach Restaurant

Puri Mas Boutique Resort & Spa, Mangsit. Tel: 0370-693831. Open: daily B, L & D. **$$$**. www.purimas-lombok.com

Overlooks the palm-fringed Mangsit Beach. The menu specialises in fresh seafood and the traditional Indonesian "Rijstaffel" assortment of meat, fish, and vegetable dishes accompanied by rice and spicy sauces. There is also a good selection of international dishes. Delicious desserts include a good old-fashioned apple crumble.

Taman

Jalan Raya Senggigi. Tel: 0370-693842. Open: daily B, L & D. **$$$**

Right in the centre of town, this popular two-storey restaurant has both indoor and outdoor seating. Classic jazz tunes and occasional live bands set the atmosphere. Large menu features international dishes, pizzas, a good selection of fish and seafood, and some Indian curries.

THE GILI ISLANDS

Denpasar

Tropical island aficionados declare these islands perfect for snorkelling and diving, or just plain lolling about. If picture-perfect, white-sand beaches lapped by aquamarine waters harbouring colourful coral reefs and fish are not sufficient draws, head for Gili Trawangan, the "party island".

Main attractions
GILI AIR
GILI MENO
GILI TRAWANGAN

BELOW: a perfect view of the beach from Villa Julius, Gili Twanangan.

The three Gili islands lie just off the northwest coast of Lombok. For years they have attracted visitors from around the world for their pristine waters, great diving and snorkelling, and for their funky, laid back charm, with no cars, motorbikes or dogs to disturb the peace. The word "Gili" means "small island", in fact, there are 26 Gili islands surrounding the mainland of Lombok, and so the three most famous have come to be known as the "Gilis" by travellers. Tropical island aficionados have long considered the Gilis to be on par with the appeal of Thailand's south coast island havens and the coral atolls of Maldives.

Over the past decade, each of the Gilis has developed a unique personality. Although previously the domain of backpackers and more intrepid travellers, word has got around and the Gili islands now attract a diverse range of both upmarket and budget visitors, from serious diving enthusiasts to families and couples of all ages. The Gilis are small, flat coral islands with sparse vegetation and rainfall, and it can seem much hotter here than on the mainland. There is no fresh water on the Gilis, so be prepared for salt-water showers. Water is drawn from wells or shipped from the mainland, hence the need to conserve the islands' limited water resources. Drink only bottled water, eat well-cooked food, and, if staying in budget hotels, choose places with mosquito nets. There have been several fatal cases of methanol poisoning on the Gili Islands, the best advice is not to drink alcohol apart from beer. The only form of transport, apart from bicycles and walking, are the delightful *cidomo* (horse-drawn carts).

A good number of reputable and internationally accredited dive operators based in Lombok organise dive trips to the Gili islands. While much of the coral in the shallow waters has been destroyed by dynamite fishing and coral bleaching caused by El Niño in 1997, there is still an interesting array of fish to see in the waters directly off the beaches. At greater depths and at the specific dive locations around the three islands, the pristine waters are home to an abundant variety of corals, aquatic life and thousands of species of tropical fish.

The Gilis are easily reached from the mainland by boats from Bangsal Harbour *(see page 217)*, or through the tour and dive operators in Senggigi.

Gili Air

Gili Air ⑯ is the island closest to the mainland and the most easily accessed of the three Gilis. This island has the largest local population of the three and combines the charm of a tropical island with easy access to the people and culture that has made Lombok so special.

Much of the development is on the east coast, facing Lombok and the towering Gunung Rinjani, which provides spectacular sunrises; sunsets over Gunung Agung on Bali are visible from the south and western coasts of Gili Air. The best beaches are also found on the east side, with clear turquoise waters and soft white sand.

Diving facilities abound and there is good snorkelling directly from the shore, particularly from the east and northeast beaches. **Air Wall**, off the west coast, is a popular dive site, with soft corals that gleam yellow and orange in the sunlight, and harbour scorpion fish and thousands of glassfish. In the deeper waters are whitetip reef sharks and schools of larger fish species.

Dream Divers (tel: 0370-634547; www.dreamdivers.com), a PADI operation with experienced Western and local instructors, can take you out to some of the best spots for diving.

A good range of accommodation is to be had on Gili Air, from simple guesthouses to more expensive hotels with all the attendant creature comforts. Dining opportunities range from good-quality restaurants to simple *warung* on the beach and, while the bars aren't as loud as on Gili Trawangan, there are still plenty of opportunities to have fun.

Although the Gilis are generally laid-back, it's important to remember that the local people are mostly Muslim. Nude and topless sunbathing is offensive to the islanders. Please respect local customs and keep your clothes on.

BELOW: fire dancing at Paradise Sunset bar, Gili Twanangan.

The waters around Gili Meno are home to hawksbill (pictured) and green turtles.

BELOW: snorkelling off Gili Meno.

Gili Meno

Gili Meno ⑰ is the middle and smallest island of the three, with the lowest population. It is not as developed as Gili Trawangan or Gili Air, and the pace is slower. Small hotels and basic beach side huts provide accommodation for those seeking less crowded beaches, clean waters and quiet walks under the star-filled skies.

The landscape is flat, with coconut groves inland and a small lake in the west from which the locals harvest meagre supplies of salt. **Meno Wall**, off the west coast, is a popular dive site, with many varieties of marine life found at depths of 18 metres (60ft). Hawksbill and green turtles call the waters around Gili Meno home and are a common sight, particularly on the northwest corner, while the reefs just offshore feature outcrops of brilliant blue coral.

On the east side lies the main development, which has a stunning wide beach. The string of beachside bars and *warung* along this stretch provide plenty of opportunities for viewing spectacular sunrises and sunsets over the volcanoes.

Gili Trawangan

Gili Trawangan ⑱ is furthest from the mainland and the largest, most famous island of the three with a reputation as "the party island" – thanks to the wild parties held at its bars and restaurants. In recent years the scene here has evolved rapidly, whereas Gili Meno and Gili Air are developing at a slower pace. Trawangan still maintains its timeless tropical paradise charm, but now has a wider range of facilities to cater to a broader spectrum of travellers.

Backpackers flock here to enjoy the gorgeous white-sand beaches, cheap accommodation, and (naturally) the parties held at different locations every night, while more up-market travellers stay at the better hotels and boutique villas. There is good snorkelling just off the shore with waters that teem with a still abundant variety of tropical fish species. Strong currents are sometimes a bother, especially in the strait with neighbouring Gili Meno. Further out are vast gardens of coral, regarded as one of the best dive spots in Lombok, particularly **Shark Point** to the east of the island, which is home to a fascinating array of marine life.

The small hill in the south of the island is a great lookout from which to enjoy the spectacular sunsets across the ocean to Bali; or, the brilliant sunrise over Gunung Rinjani on Lombok. At the far southern end of the hill are remnants of old World War II Japanese gun emplacements and crumbling bunkers, but the hand-dug tunnels have been blocked up.

The main development is on the east coast, particularly southeast in the area called "Sentral" where boats dock. There are also hotels on the north coast, offering peaceful alternatives. Gili Trawangan has the best tourism infrastructure of the Gilis, including shops, tour agencies, moneychangers, ATMs, a non-emergency 24-hour medical clinic, and internet cafés. ❏

BEST RESTAURANTS

Restaurants

Price for a two-course meal for one including a non-alcoholic beverage:

$$$$ over Rp 300,000
$$$ Rp 200,000–300,000
$$ Rp 100,000–200,000
$ below Rp 100,000

Gili Air

Coconut Cottages
East Coast, to the north of the main restaurant strip. Tel: 0370-635365. Open: daily B, L & D. **$$**
www.coconuts-giliair.com
Set back from the beach in a cool coconut grove, this very popular hotel serves good seafood dishes, as well as European and Indonesian meals in the restaurant and the pavilions in the garden. During peak seasons an excellent buffet makes an appearance, with tasty curries and Sasak food at a very reasonable price.

Restaurant Gili Air
Gili Air Hotel. Tel: 0370-643580. Open: daily B, L & D. **$$**
www.hotelgiliair.com
Expect the usual mix of local and Western dishes at this casual, laid-back eatery, but with a slightly higher standard than elsewhere on the island. In addition, there is a nightly barbecue of either seafood or meat.

Gili Meno

Bibi's Café
Villa Nautilus, East Coast. No telephone. Open: daily B, L & D. **$$**
www.villanautilus.com
Small stylish restaurant at Gili Meno's most luxurious resort. Serves the usual mix of local and Western food with an emphasis on freshly caught seafood.

Blue Marlin Dive & Café
East Coast. Tel: 0370-639979. Open: daily B, L & D. **$$**
This popular dive shop near the harbour is open for breakfast and has a good selection of Western and Indonesian dishes for lunch and dinner. It also serves good-value sandwiches and burgers, steaks and seafood dishes, as well as a full range of drinks and cocktails.

Gili Trawangan

The Beach House
Sentral, East Coast. Mobile tel: 0813-3974 7459. Open: daily B, L & D. **$$$**
www.beachhousegilit.com
A very popular bar and restaurant, located directly on the beach front. The nightly barbecue features a delicious array of fresh fish, lobster, prawns, crab and squid, in addition to imported steaks from Australia. The great atmosphere and full bar

and cocktail facilities make this one of the best on Gili Trawangan.

Horizontal
Sentral, East Coast. Tel: 0370-639248. Open: daily L & D. **$$$**
In a prime location overlooking a beautiful beach, this bar has upmarket decor, a chill-out lounge and a fantastic range of cocktails. Delicious and innovative food is served, including tapas and gourmet pizzas. Late night, the lounge grooves to chill-out tunes and the beautiful people come out to play. You'll be forgiven for thinking you're in Bali's Seminyak beach.

Ko Ko Mo
Sentral, East Coast. Tel: 0370-642352. Open: daily B, L & D. **$$$$**
www.kokomogilit.com
Gili Trawangan's first and only fine-dining restaurant, with indoor and outdoor beach side seating and the best wine cellar on the island. Here you can enjoy a delectable feast of freshly-shucked oysters, beef carpaccio or thinly sliced Australian "Harvey Beef" tenderloin, Peking duck, medallions of bamboo lobster, and more. Wicked desserts include Strawberry Dacquoise and Fallen Chocolate Cake.

Pesona Restaurant
Pesona Resort, Sentral,

East Coast. Tel: 0370-6607233. Open: daily L & D. **$$**
www.pesonaresort.com
Beachfront restaurant with a romantic setting and a wide range of Indian dishes, some Western dishes and a nightly seafood barbecue. Attached is the Sheesha Lounge and Cocktail Bar.

Scallywags
Sentral, East Coast. Tel: 0370-631945. Open: daily B, L & D. **$$$**
Popular all-day British-owned café with a variety of seafood and other dishes. Have your fish, prawn or lobster either grilled plain or cooked Continental style. Delights include the grilled grouper fish with artichoke salad and lombok sambal, and the fillet steak gorgonzola with creamy potatoes. A seafood barbecue features nightly. Free Wi-fi.

Wrap a Snapper
Sentral, East Coast. Tel: 0370-642217. Open: daily L & D. **$$**
Originally from Seminyak, Bali, and now a firm part of the local eating out scene, this restaurant specialises in English-style fish and chips: fresh fish filleted and coated in a light batter and then deep-fried, served with perfect French fries. Other seafood is available too.

NORTH AND EAST LOMBOK

Trekking in the Rinjani National Park and its vicinity brings you to awesome forests and waterfalls. More adventurous spirits may prefer climbing Gunung Rinjani, an internationally recognised ecotourism site, or teeing-off on the world-class Kosaido Golf Course.

Denpasar

North Lombok is reached by two main roads. The coastal road that runs from Ampenan all the way up the west coast to the north provides stunning views of the many beautiful bays and beaches that line this coast, as well as vistas over the Gili islands and Bali to the west. The **Pusuk Pass**, a winding mountain road, starts in Gunungsari, north of Mataram, and runs through the mountains inland, terminating at Pemenang in the north. The drive up the pass provides wonderful views of valleys and gorges, with rivers running through the tropical forests and small villages scattered among the trees. Families of grey monkeys live in the jungle and sometimes hang out beside the road. Beyond Pemenang, the northern coastal road winds past stunning seascapes and sparsely populated villages. Heading inland from Anyar leads to the lofty Gunung Rinjani, the main attraction in this area.

Pemenang and Bangsal

Pemenang ⓳ is the crossroads where the coastal road meets the Pusuk Pass road with Jalan Raya and continues north around the island. The road to the west runs only about 1km (½ mile) to **Bangsal Harbour**, which is the main point of departure for public boats to the beautiful Gili Islands. The road is blocked roughly halfway down at a parking area, and you must continue on foot about another 400 metres 450yds to the beach. *Cidomo* (horse cart) drivers will entice you to pay high prices for the ride to the beach, but it isn't that far. The harbour area is rife with persistent touts who hang around trying to force travellers to charter boats and buy

LEFT: Mount Rinjani volcano rising high above the clouds. **RIGHT:** hiking up to the volcano.

goods before going to the islands. All the supplies found on the mainland can be purchased on the Gili Islands, so ignore the overpriced mosquito repellent and water bottles sold here. Don't let anyone touch your bag and if you do use a porter, negotiate a price beforehand of around Rp 5,000 per bag. Tickets for the public boats out to the islands can be purchased from the large white building directly to the left on the beach, and boat charters can also be organised from here, with fixed prices clearly displayed inside the building.

Pantai Sira and Tanjung Medana

Further north, a small signposted road branches off from the main road to **Pantai Sira ⑳**, a beautiful, long, whiter-than-white sand beach. This is also the site for the **Kosaido Golf Course**, a stunning world-class 18-hole golf course with magnificent views from the manicured greens. A scattering of luxurious new holiday villas rest beside the beach, already the location of the funky-fantastic, antique-chic Hotel Tugu Lombok.

On the tip of the next peninsula north at **Tanjung Medana** is a small temple, **Pura Medana ㉑** (daily 8am–5pm; donation), with wonderful sunset views and a peaceful atmosphere. On the road out to the temple is the lovely Medana Resort and, at the very end, the luxurious Oberoi Lombok, in a breathtaking beach side location.

Tanjung and Gondang

About 4km (2 miles) north of Pura Medana is **Tanjung ㉒**. Muslims, Hindus and Buddhists live here and, as a result, a wide variety of ceremonies originate from this area. Tanjung has an interesting daily market and on Sundays a cattle market where cows, goats and horses from all over the island are bought and sold.

Up the coast is **Gondang ㉓**, a small town near a good beach. **Tiu Pupus Waterfall** is a 20-minute walk beyond the end of a rocky road. The spring-fed falls are disappointing during the dry season, but otherwise flow into a deep pool where you can swim. Alternatively, trek to the traditional Sasak village of **Kerurak**.

BELOW: the beautiful white-sand beach at Pantai Sira.

Another 30-minute trek leads to the **Kerta Gangga Waterfalls**, with three beautiful falls set in the jungle.

Segenter

Travel about 20km (13 miles) from Gondang and head inland at **Suka-dana** to find the dusty, traditional village of **Segenter ㉔**, which provides a glimpse into the harsh reality of life on the island's dry side. The 300 villagers in this northern interior village eke out a living growing corn and beans, yet they welcome visitors with a smile and proudly share their simple life with tours through the village.

Bayan

Back on the coastal road, turning right at **Anyar** leads to **Bayan ㉕**, a village that maintains old dance and poetic traditions, as well as *kemidi rudat*, a theatre based on the fables, *The Thousand and One Nights*. The village is also the site of the phenomenal Alip festival held once every three years. Bayan is the home of the Wektu Telu religion, which combines the practices of Islam with Hinduism, Buddhism and animist beliefs. The adherents of Wektu Telu (meaning "three times") pray at three different periods and acknowledge three types of important ceremonies: human rites (birth, marriage, death), Islamic ceremonies (Maulid, Lebaran) and cyclical rites associated with agriculture and farming.

Most of the Wektu Telu festivals are at the start of the October–December rainy season or else the April–May harvest. One of the island's oldest and most important Wektu Telu mosques is in Bayan.

Senaru

The inland road from Bayan leads to **Senaru ㉖** village, the gateway to **Rinjani National Park** (daily 8am–6pm; charge; guide fees extra), a nature reserve of 41,330 hectares (100,000 acres) that surrounds

Gunung Rinjani volcano. The whole area is a picturesque haven, featuring magnificent waterfalls, lush and accessible jungle treks, traditional villages, and plantations of tobacco and cashew nuts, tended alongside verdant rice terraces. Tropical animal species and rare tropical birds like the black-naped oriole live in the surrounding jungle, as well as abundant varieties of plants and flowers.

The **Sendang Gile Waterfall** at Senaru is spectacular. The water cascades in a steep vertical drop down the hillside into a rocky stream below. Guides can be hired from the restaurant near the car park for the gentle 30-minute trek through the jungle to the awesome **Tiu Kelep Waterfall**, dominated by a projectile jet of pure white energy. At the base of the falls is a deep pool. If you feel like having a dip in the refreshingly cool water, you should allow yourself to drift in a circle behind the main waterfall. It is believed to be blessed with youth-enhancing properties and, according to local legend, each time you circle it, you will emerge one year younger.

The Gili Islands can be reached easily from this part of Lombok – the main departure point is at Bangsal Harbour.

BELOW: thundering Sendang Gile Waterfalls.

Trekking Gunung Rinjani requires hardy hiking boots.

Climbing Gunung Rinjani

Senaru is the usual starting point for climbing Lombok's famous volcano, **Gunung Rinjani** ㉗. Other options, for a slightly shorter route to the summit, are the villages of Sembalun Lawang and Sembalun Bumbung to the east.

Rinjani soars some 3,726 metres (12,224ft) above sea level and is the second highest volcano in Indonesia, attracting thousands of trekkers and climbers annually. The huge crater near the top contains a beautiful crescent-shaped lake, **Danau Segara Anak** ㉘ (Child of the Sea Lake). A smaller volcanic cone, **Gunung Baru Jari**, juts out from one side of the crater. There are a number of caves, small waterfalls and hot springs scattered around the volcano, most important of which is **Air Kalak** on the northeast of the crater, where the volcanically heated waters are said to cure illnesses, particularly skin diseases.

In 2004, the Rinjani Trek won the prestigious World Legacy Award and the volcano is recognised internationally as an important ecotourism destination. The trek, funded by the New Zealand government, has set up a series of programmes for climbing the volcano and for trekking in the Rinjani National Park, all of which involve the local communities. It is always prudent to use an authorised guide (preferably equipped with two-way radio), deal with a reputable trekking business and carry as few valuables as possible with you.

For details, contact the **Rinjani Trek Organisation** at the Hotel Lombok Raya in Mataram (Jalan Usaha No. 11, tel: 0370-641124) or the office in Senaru (daily 7am–5pm; mobile tel: 081-9331 67395; www. rinjaninationalpark.com).

Sembalun Bumbung and Sembalun Lawang

Branching off the main coastal road from Bayan, a smaller road runs inland through the mountains with wonderful scenery of dense forests opening up to valley vistas and towering mountain ranges. **Sembalun Bumbung** ㉙ is located in a high, cool valley on the slopes of Gunung Rinjani, along with a neighbouring village, **Sembalun Lawang**. Both

are surrounded by lush fields and valleys planted with garlic, fruit and vegetables, which thrive in the cooler climate. Here, the NZODA (New Zealand Official Development Assistance) project provides assistance to women weavers in the form of technical and marketing support. The aim is to produce a new and sustainable source of income for the local people by reviving the weaving industry. The traditional weaving interests of the village were abandoned many years ago at a time when cultivating garlic proved to be a more attractive source of income. In recent years, however, the demand for garlic has decreased and life has become much tougher for the people of this once relatively prosperous village.

Both villages are alternative points to Senaru for climbing Gunung Rinjani and there are a number of tourist agencies that organise treks in the region, as well as several small guesthouses.

The road through the mountains is steep and rough in places, and eventually ends in **Sapit ㉚**, a pleasant mountain village to the southeast.

EAST LOMBOK

Continuing on the main road around the island, the route passes coastal scenery on the left and mountain vistas on the right, eventually traversing the north coast and descending to the east. In comparison to the west coast, this part of Lombok receives few visitors, and many of the villages in eastern Lombok are strongly Islamic. There have been reports of harassment in the past and Westerners are viewed with suspicion in some of the more remote areas.

The coastline is extremely beautiful, with many pristine beaches and wonderful views across the water to neighbouring Sumbawa. **Labuhan Lombok ㉛**, also sometimes called Kayangan, is the eastern port, with regular ferries departing for Sumbawa and the islands to the east. Although transport and lodging are difficult to arrange, worth visiting are **Labuhan Pandan ㉜** on the east coast, with some stunning deserted beaches and fine snorkelling, and **Labuhan Haji ㉝**, with its beautiful beach, on the southeastern coast. ❑

RESTAURANTS

North Lombok
Medana Resort
Jalan Medana, Tanjung.
Tel: 0370-628000,
628100. Open: daily B, L & D. **$$$**
www.lombokmedana.com
The open-air restaurant of this beach side hotel has some lovely views and serves European dishes and Indonesian specialities.
Oberoi Lombok
Jalan Medana, Tanjung.
Tel: 0370-643602.
Sunbird Café: open daily B

& D. **$$$$** Lumbung: open daily D. **$$$$**
www.oberoihotels.com
This world-class resort, commanding fantastic views from its beach front location, has some of the best up-market dining in Lombok, offering innovative Continental and Asian cuisine and a romantic atmosphere.
Pondok Senaru & Restaurant
Rinjani National Park, Senaru.
Mobile tel: 0812-622 868.
Open: daily B, L & D. **$$**

Attractive restaurant with fine views over the rice terraces and foothills. Serves a variety of sandwiches for snacks, and more substantial Indonesian meals at lunch and dinner.
Hotel Tugu Lombok
Tel: 0370 620111. Open: daily B, L & D. **$$$$**
This fascinating hotel, full of antiques, old stone carvings, artworks and artefacts, presents a choice of unique and authentic dining experiences, each following a historical theme complemented by the ambi-

ence, venue, cuisine, costumes, tableware and rituals.

East Lombok
Pondok Matahari
Labuhan Pandan, East Lombok. Mobile tel: 0812-374 9915. Open: daily B, L & D. **$$**
The restaurant at this small hotel serves simple Indonesian meals.

• • • • • • • •
Price for a two-course meal for one including a non-alcoholic beverage:
$ = below Rp 100,000,
$$ = Rp 100,000–200,000.
$$$ = Rp 200,000–300,000.
$$$$ = over Rp 300,000.

CENTRAL AND SOUTH LOMBOK

Isolated villages in the cooler central zone produce handicrafts such as *ikat* cloth, ceramics and baskets. As you head south, there is magnificent coastal scenery, including splendid beaches better than any you will find in neighbouring Bali.

Denpasar

C entral Lombok, located on the southern slopes of Gunung Rinjani *(see page 220)*, is cooler and lusher than the south, receiving much rainfall in the wet season and protected by forests and jungle throughout the year. Traditional villages dot the slopes, their livelihoods centred on handicrafts such as pottery, textiles, woven grass and bamboo crafts, and woodworking. Continuing south, away from the mountains, the landscape becomes much drier and fields of tobacco, corn, cassava and peanuts become the norm. On reaching the south coast, the landscape opens up to reveal a long coastline with some of the most sublime beaches and views in Indonesia.

Around Lenek

Heading from the east coast on the main road from Labuhan Lombok is **Lenek** ㉞. This whole area has many small villages whose people still practise *adat* Sasak (traditional customs). Well known as a source of traditional Sasak music and dance, Lenek also offers *tari pepakon*, a medicinal trance dance. A local cultural patron of the arts has established an organisation to reinvigorate the performing arts, based in Lenek. To the west is **Pringgasela** ㉟, a village steeped in tradition and a major centre for *ikat* weaving. Visit the small houses and shops to purchase traditionally woven fabrics.

Southeast of Lenek is **Bonjeruk**, a village of *dalang* (puppeteers) for the shadow play *wayang sasak*; many of the puppets are made here. Past Bonjeruk is **Masbagik** ㊱, best known as a centre of pottery and ceramic crafts; the pottery made here has distinctive geometric patterns.

Main attractions

LOYOK
SUKARARA
PENUJAK
REMBITAN AND SADE
KUTA
TANJUNG AAN
TANJUNG LUAR
SEKOTONG
GILI NANGGU

LEFT: craftsman at work in Penujak pottery village.
RIGHT: Kuta Beach.

Traditional thatched lumbung (rice barns) at Rembitan village.

Loyok and Tetebatu

Following the main road another few kilometres further west, a road leads north to **Loyok**, a small dusty village where families make traditional woven products using rattan, grasses and bamboo. The baskets, boxes, mats and other weavings are of good quality and often sent to Bali, where they fetch much higher prices. Visit the shops and the family compounds out at the back, where often several generations of the same family weave.

Continuing north is **Tetebatu ㊲**, on the southern slopes of Gunung Rinjani. This is a cool mountain retreat with beautiful rice terraces, forests and bright green fields of tobacco. It is wet and misty during the rainy season, and cool and lush during the dry. To the north of Tetebatu, about an hour's trekking through a monkey-filled forest, is the **Jeruk Manis** waterfall. It's best to take a local guide with you for security.

Praya, Sukarara & Penujak

BELOW: songket weaving at Sukarara village.

About half-an-hour's drive southeast of Cakranegara, **Praya ㊳** is a crossroads, the location of Lombok's new international airport, which opened in 2011, and the hub of the south. Home of the Saturday market, it is close to many handicraft villages.

Some 5km (3 miles) to the west of Praya is the weaving village of **Sukarara ㊴**, where traditional *ikat* fabric is made. Weavers work outside many of the shops, using antiquated back strap looms to produce works of art. Some of the larger pieces can take several months of painstaking work to weave, and collectors from around the world visit this village to purchase the blankets, sarongs and cloth.

South of Praya is **Penujak ㊵**, one of Lombok's main pottery making centres. Shops and workshops line the main road, and local children will run out to greet you and guide you into the shops when you arrive. Penujak pottery uses mainly animal motifs, including frogs and geckos, as decoration.

Rembitan and Sade

Travelling down to the south coast, you pass small farming villages and a drier, flatter landscape then in the north. You'll reach **Rembitan ㊶** vil-

lage first, on the right, and then **Sade** ㊷, on the left along the main road just before Kuta. These are traditional Sasak villages sandwiched between the main road and the rice fields. Rembitan is a popular tourist stop with clusters of thatched *lumbung*, or rice barns. Sade is a more authentic hilltop village with the oldest mosque in Lombok, **Mesjid Kuno**. This ancient, thatched-roof house of worship can only be entered by Muslims. Both villages are interesting examples of traditional Sasak architecture and communal living. Residents, who act as guides for a small fee, encourage walks through both villages.

Kuta

Kuta ㊸, on the south coast, lags behind Senggigi in development, but still has a decent variety of mainly budget accommodation and restaurants. It has a beautiful white-sand beach, and is located about 45km (28 miles) from Cakranegara or 1½ hours' drive from Senggigi; it is a good base for exploring the beautiful southern coastline. Kuta and the surrounding region have gained a reputation for

having some of the best surfing spots in Southeast Asia. It is here that the gentle waters of Lombok meet the currents of the Indian Ocean, forming great surf breaks and fantastic vistas of cliffs, headlands and beaches carved out of the rugged southern coastline.

The stylish Novotel Coralia on **Mandalika** beach is in an excellent location and is reasonably priced; smaller Kuta hotels and guesthouses are cheaper options. Mandalika beach is also the site of the annual Bau Nyale festival. This unusual event, which is primarily a secular gathering, attracts more than 100,000 people every year *(see box below)*. Kuta market (Wed and Sun mornings) is a lively cacophony of chickens and friendly local people, brightened by an array of colourful fruits and woven baskets.

Tanjung Aan and Gerepuk

East of Kuta are a series of beautiful, untouched beaches. **Tanjung Aan** ㊹ has spectacular scenery off the peninsula, with a few vendor shacks and a virtually undisturbed white-sand beach. Another 3km (2 miles) east is the beach and fishing village

In a peresean, *two men, armed with rattan sticks and shields made of cowhide, duel with each other.*

LEFT: spice tray in the market at Nusa Tenngara.

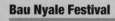

Bau Nyale Festival

The Bau Nyale festival commemorates the legend of the beautiful Putri (Princess) Mandalika, who was much sought after as a bride by every king in Lombok. According to local lore, the princess was so torn between the suitors that she threw herself into the sea, crying out "Kuta" ("Wait for me here") in the local Sasak language. When she disappeared into the waves below, hundreds of *nyale* – sea worms – floated to the surface.

Thus, every February, when the conditions are right, the *nyale* worms return to the site. People come from all over Lombok to collect the ugly sea worms, which are fried and eaten (the worms are said to be an aphrodisiac). A *dukun* (priest) will wade into the sea to observe the spawning *nyale* and predict the impending rice harvest based on the number of worms that appear.

Bau Nyale is the only time of the year when young people on this staunch Muslim island are permitted to strut and flirt openly. When night falls, the youngsters will compete with each other by singing pantun, an improvised poetry of rhyming couplets, and watch men fighting the *peresean*.

Freshly caught fish at Tanjung Luar.

BELOW: Kuta Beach.

of **Gerupuk** , located on the spit of land that juts out into the ocean, with stunning views of the sea and the surrounding islands and bays. Gerupuk is well known as a surf location and ideal for windsurfing or bodysurfing.

East of Gerupuk

Further east, just beyond **Batu Nampar** village, is the little-visited village of **Batu Rintang**. With traditional thatched rice barns and huts, it's an honest look at local life. Outside Batu Nampar are salt works and floating seaweed frames, farmed by migrants from South Sulawesi and Madura.

Continuing around the bay, northeast of Batu Nampar is **Jerowaru**, site of a Thursday market. To the south is **Ekas**, a magnificent bay framed by cliffs overlooking the breathtaking coast. A little further up on the east coast is **Tanjung Luar** , site of a vibrant fish market; it's fascinating to observe the activity here. The village is inhabited by Bugis fishermen from Sulawesi, who arrived here during the early 1600s. The beach front is lined with typical Bugis-style houses painted in the same strong colours as the fishing boats and constructed on high stilts, with shutters instead of windows.

Mawun and Selong Blanak

Returning to the south coast, about 30 minutes drive to the west of Kuta, the beach at **Mawun** rings a perfect half-moon bay, popular for swimming and picnicking. There are good right- and left-hand barrels for surfing when the swell is large enough. This deserted beach, flanked by massive headlands, has very few trees, thus accentuating the spectacular scenery and sound of crashing waves. Apart from the occasional fisherman, it is likely that you'll have this fine beach all to yourself. It also can be reached by bicycle from Kuta, although the road is a bit steep.

Further west, a picturesque little fishing village lies on the fringe of **Selong Blanak** beach. Instead of detracting from the beauty of the sweeping beach, the village adds to its charm. Colourful fishing outriggers rock in the gentle waves at the bay's east end and buffaloes are herded along the beach daily. The villagers make their living from fishing, especially for squid. White, sugary sand skirts the gorgeous bay, but what makes this place so stunning is the scale of the surrounding landscape – which is of continental proportions.

Southwest coast

The road to the southwest coast is in very poor condition and has had a problem with road side robberies in the past. This coast is best accessed by returning to Praya and taking the main road west from there.

Lembar , about an hour south of Ampenan on the southwest coast, is the centre of Lombok's shipping transport and the harbour for boats arriving from Bali and the west.

Gerung, inland to the east, is the village of the famous *cepung*, a men's social dance during which they read and sing from the *Lontar*

Monyet (Monkey Manuscript), drink *tuak* (palm wine), dance and vocally imitate *gamelan* instruments. After **Lemar**, the road south winds first around the wide natural harbour and through small villages set in valleys, where natural clay is harvested from the hillsides and used to manufacture bricks. The small coastal villages rely mainly on fishing and you will see floating fishing platforms made of bamboo, known as *bagan*, sitting in the shallow tidal waters.

Finally, the road opens out into the breathtaking scenery of **Sekotong**. The large calm bay just before **Taun** ➐ (Sekotong Barat) is one of the most beautiful on Lombok, reminiscent of the Caribbean. Investors are snapping up real estate in the area, with at least one major resort development occupying the hillside overlooking the sea.

Just off the coast lie three small islands: **Gili Nanggu** ➑ with its soft white sand and sparkling clear waters, **Gili Sudat** and **Gili Tangkong**. Gili Nanggu has a small basic hotel and the island is perfect as a castaway escape, with reasonable snorkelling off the beach. There is a signposted parking area at Sekotong Barat where small boats can be chartered to explore these lovely islands.

Winding down the coast, the road hugs the bays and beaches that make up the magical southwest, with views of the many small, undeveloped islands sitting just offshore and the outline of Bali on the horizon. At **Pelangan** is a small hotel, and boats can be chartered here to explore the numerous islands off the coast, including the huge **Gili Gede** island, which is currently being developed with a marina resort.

The road southwards deteriorates dramatically, although it is still passable in the dry season. Winding through tiny villages, it continues to the southwesternmost point of Lombok – a sheer cliff framing **Bangko Bangko** ➒ beach. Bangko Bangko juts into the sea, forming a junction with the Indian Ocean and creating incredible surf breaks that attract serious surfers from around the world. It regularly rates as one of the top five surf destinations in Southeast Asia. Wild and desolate, the limestone cliffs here have been carved by the tides, and the surrounding scenery is dramatically beautiful. ❑

TIP

There is some wonderful snorkelling and great scenery around the islands off the southwest coast. Charter boats near the Bola-Bola Resort (mobile tel: 0817-578 7355) in Pelangan to explore Gili Gede and the other nearby islands.

RESTAURANTS

Central Lombok
Wisma Soedjono
Tetebatu, Central Lombok. Mobile tel: 0818-544 265. Open: daily B, L & D. **$$**
Set high on the hillside with beautiful views of the surrounding countryside, this restaurant is the most popular in the area. Serves inexpensive Indonesian and Sasak food (*nasi campur* and *sate*); some Western-style snacks are also available.

South Lombok
Family Café
Jalan Raya, Kuta. Tel: 0370-653748. Open: daily B, L & D. **$$**
Right on the main street of Kuta, this café is good for meeting people. A good range of Western dishes and the usual Indonesian and Sasak specialities are served.
Laut Biru Café
1 Jalan Seempiak, Selong Belanak Beach. Tel: 0821-4430 3339 Open: daily B & L. **$$$**

Asian and international delights created from the choicest ingredients. Favourites include pumpkin soup, Thai curries, and lemon cheesecake. Fully licensed bar. Guests are entitled to use the adjacent beachclub.
Novotel Coralia
Mandalika Beach, Kuta. Tel: 0370-653333. Open: daily B, L & D. **$$$$**
www.novotel-lombok.com
With two restaurants, the Novotel offers the best dining in the south and lovely views of the ocean. **Kafe Chilli** is the less expensive of the two and serves good Western meals. **Empat Ikan**, the resort's main dining restaurant, serves beautifully prepared seafood, including fresh lobster. During peak seasons theme dinners are often held beachside, with Sasak entertainment.

• • • • • • • •

Price for a two-course meal for one including a non-alcoholic beverage:
$ = below Rp 100,000,
$$ = Rp 100,000–200,000.
$$$ = Rp 200,000–300,000.
$$$$ = over Rp 300,000.

INSIGHT GUIDES **TRAVEL TIPS**
BALI & LOMBOK

TRANSPORT · ACCOMMODATION · ACTIVITIES · A – Z · LANGUAGE

TRANSPORT: BALI

GETTING THERE AND GETTING AROUND

GETTING THERE

By Air

Ngurah Rai International Airport in Bali (sometimes referred to by the city, name, Denpasar) is served by direct flights from cities in Europe, US, Australia and Asia. In addition, there are daily flights from several key Indonesian cities like Jakarta, Yogyakarta and Surabaya. Some international airlines fly only to Jakarta's Soekarno-Hatta International Airport, from where domestic flights to Bali (flight time: 80 minutes) are frequent.

Foreign airlines serving Bali include: Aeroflot (seasonal), AirAsia, Air New Zealand (seasonal), Cathay Pacific, Cebu Pacific, China Airlines, EVA Air, Hong Kong Airlines, Japan Airlines, Jetstar Airways, KLM, Korean Air, Malaysia Airlines, Philippine Airlines, Qatar Airways, Singapore Airlines, Thai Airways and Virgin Australia.

Indonesian airlines serving Bali include: Batavia Air, Citilink, Garuda Indonesia, Indonesia Air Asia, Lion Air, Sriwijaya Air, Trans-Nusa Air Services, Trigana Air and Wings Air.

The airport, which was extensively renovated in 2013, has 17 gates: 3 in the domestic terminal, and 14 in the international terminal. The international terminal has a Balinese architectural theme and has separate departure and arrival halls. The departures area has 62 check-in counters that are equipped with electronic scales and luggage conveyors. Eight of the international gates have aerobridges and automated aircraft parking systems. The international terminal also has prayer rooms, showers and a massage service. Various lounge areas are provided, some including children's play areas and movie lounges, broadcasting movies, news, variety and entertainment and sport channels.

The contact details for **Ngurah Rai International Airport** are: tel: 0361-751025, 751011.

If leaving Bali by air on a domestic airline, you are advised to reconfirm your reservation. Some local airlines tend to overbook. Reconfirmation is usually not required for international airlines.

Check in two hours before flight time. The **international departure tax** is Rp 200,000; **domestic tax** is Rp 75,000. These can be purchased at designated counters at the airport. Only cash (in rupiah) is accepted so be sure to set enough rupiah aside, although you can change foreign currency at the airport.

KEY AIRLINE OFFICES

Key Indonesian Carriers:
Garuda: tel: 0804-1807807; www.garuda-indonesia.com
Batavia Air: tel: 021-3899 9888 (call centre), 0361-767633; www.batavia-air.co.id
Lion Air: tel: 0361-751011; www.lionair.co.id

Key International Carriers:
Air Asia: tel: 0361-760116; www.airasia.com
Cathay Pacific: tel: 0361-766931; www.cathaypacific.com
China Airlines: tel: 0361-754856; www.china-airlines.com

EVA Air: tel: 0361-759773; www.evaair.com
Japan Airlines: tel: 0361-757077; www.jal.com
Jetstar Airways: tel: 001 803 61 691; www.jetstar.com
Malaysia Airlines: tel: 0361-764995; www.malaysiaair.com
Singapore Airlines: tel: 0361-768388; www.singaporeair.com
Qatar Airways: tel: 0361-752222; www.qatarairways.com
Thai Airways: tel: 0361-288141; www.thaiair.com

Flying from UK and US

From the UK (and European cities), the easiest direct service with the most options into Bali is with Singapore Airlines. The plane will land in Singapore first, from where there are three daily flights to (and from) Bali. Malaysia Airlines also connects to Bali via Kuala Lumpur, Thai Airways via Bangkok, Qatar Airways via Doha and Cathay Pacific via Hong Kong. Check the UK-based travel agency, **Trailfinders** (www.trailfinders.co.uk) for good flight deals.

From the US connections can be made by using international carriers such as Japan Airlines, which flies from the US to Tokyo and then direct from Tokyo to Bali. Also convenient is Singapore Airlines, which flies out of Los Angeles, San Francisco and New York to Singapore, and then connects daily to Bali. Qatar Airways also connects to Washington and New York via Doha. It is also possible to fly from the US to Asian cities like Kuala Lumpur, Bangkok and Hong Kong, and then connect to Bali *(see above)*.

By Minivan or Car

In Java families or small groups can hire an air-conditioned minivan with driver for about US$50 per day, plus fuel, food and accommodation. This costs about the same as flying, but you get to see more if you plan stopovers and side-trips. Remember that prices are always negotiable. You can rent a car in Java and drive to Bali yourself, but the cost will be about the same as hiring both a driver and car, and there is the added hassle of returning the vehicle.

By Bus

Budget travellers who plan to take the public *bis malam* (overnight bus) from Java to Bali should be wary of drivers who speed on dark roads (some have been known to fall asleep at the wheel). In addition, professional thieves operate on some buses, stealing your belongings while you are sleeping. In isolated areas, road gangs are known to hold up buses and rob the passengers, perhaps even working in cahoots with the drivers.

Air-conditioned buses to Denpasar from Jakarta (with a ferry connecting the two islands) take 24 hours, from Surabaya 10–12 hours, and from Yogyakarta 15–16 hours. Restaurant and toilet stops are made along the way. Be sure to specify that you want an air-conditioned bus, but be forewarned that there are no non-smoking buses and onboard video entertainment is very loud. There are numerous operators and fares vary considerably, depending on the level of comfort you require.

From Jakarta to Bali, expect to pay around Rp 350,000; from Yogyakarta Rp 300,000, and from Surabaya Rp 200,000. Premium tourist services, such as **Perama**, will bus you direct from major cities in Java right through to Kuta, Sanur and Ubud.

Perama buses travel daily from the Mandalika terminal in Bertais, Lombok, to Sumbawa, Bali and Java. The cost from Lombok to Bali is Rp 150,000 (including the ferry crossing), or Rp 500,000 with the fast boat. There are also connections direct to the Gili Islands. **Perama Tours:** Jalan Legian No. 39, Kuta, tel: 0361-751551, 0361-751875, fax: 0361-751170, www.peramatour.com.

By Ferry

From Java: Ferries make the 30-minute trip between Gilimanuk in West Bali and Ketapang in East Java. The fares are Rp 6,000 per person, Rp 95,000 per car and Rp 19,000 per motorbike; you won't have to pay for a person if you pay for a motorcycle (2 people + 1 motorcycle = Rp 19,000. Note: the cost of the ferry ride is included in the service offered by most of the bus services.

From Lombok: From Lembar, Lombok, the regular ferries take 4 hours to reach Padangbai in East Bali. The ticket costs Rp 40,000.

Contact **Perama** *(see By Bus)* for transport packages that include land transfers and ferry tickets.

There are two fast boat services: **Gili Cat** (www.gilicat.com), daily to Padangbai, Rp 600,000 one-way; and **Blue Water Express** (www.bwsbali.com), daily to Padang Bai or Serangan, Rp 690,000 one-way. Note: all departures are from Teluk Kode (mainland Lombok) and Gili Trawangan.

OFFICIAL TAXI RATES

The official fixed taxi rates from the airport to key destinations are currently in the region of:

Tuban	Rp 45,000
Kuta I	Rp 55,000
Kuta II	Rp 65,000
Legian	Rp 70,000
Seminyak/	
Dhyana Pura	Rp 80,000
Oberoi/Kerobokan	Rp 90,000
Umalas/Br Semer/	
Kuwum	Rp 100,000
Denpasar I	Rp 90,000
Denpasar II	Rp 100,000
Denpasar III	Rp 120,000
Gatsu/Ubung	
Bus Station	Rp 120,000
Gatsu Timur	
Tohpati	Rp 125,000
Ayana Resort	Rp 125,000
Sanur	Rp 125,000
Nusa Dua	Rp 125,000
Kedonganan	Rp 65,000
Jimbaran I/	
Intercontinental	Rp 80,000
Jimbaran II/	
Jl Uluwatu II/	
Four Seasons	Rp 100,000
Amanusa/Mulia/	
Tanjung Benoa	Rp 135,000
Nikko Bali	Rp 140,000
Ungusan/Banyan	
Tree	Rp 150,000
Pecatu/Uluwatu	Rp 165,000
Batubulan	Rp 140,000
Canggu	Rp 165,000
Tanah Lot	Rp 250,000
Ubud Centre	Rp 250,000
Padang Bai	Rp 350,000
Candidasa	Rp 375,000

GETTING AROUND

From the Airport

From the airport, depending on the traffic, which can be bad, it takes approximately 15 minutes to reach Tuban and Kuta, 20–25 minutes to Legian, 30 minutes to Seminyak, 40 minutes to Kerobokan, 45–50 minutes to Canggu, 25 minutes to Sanur, 20 minutes to Nusa Dua, 10 minutes to Jimbaran, 75 minutes to Ubud, and 3 hours to Lovina.

If you have not made prior arrangements with your hotel to pick you up, there is a reliable taxi service from the airport that you can use; fixed rates to various destinations are clearly posted on a board at the counter outside the arrival hall *(see page 231)*. Pay the cashier at the desk and you will receive a coupon to hand to your designated taxi driver.

There are no other forms of public transport from the airport apart from airport taxis and hotel pick-up services.

The fixed rates are about 50 percent more expensive than metered taxi rates. If you are on a tight budget and are prepared to haul your luggage outside the airport gates, you will be able to flag down a taxi and pay the metered fare.

Orientation

Roads in Bali are heavily used, not only for traffic but also as a parade ground for escorting deities to the sea and cremation processions. Many roads are not regularly maintained and are speckled with potholes or sometimes partly blocked by piles of gravel dumped at the sides. Traffic jams in the tourism-dense south can be horrific, caused by ceremonial processions, by rush-hour congestion, floods, a truck stuck in a storm drain, or a gaggle of geese – the reasons for gridlocks are manifold.

Congestion on Jalan Legian and Jalan Seminyak, however, has

BEACHES OF SOUTH BALI

People who have seen the blinding white-sand beaches and clear aquamarine waters of Thailand are invariably disappointed by Bali's beaches. Because of the island's volcanic origins, most of the beaches are either grey or black sand, and often pebbly.

Nusa Dua is among the few stretches of white sand beach on Bali (nicer and wider along the stretch where the Grand Hyatt and Ayodya are located, and a bit narrow and a little less pleasant past the little spit of sand where the Melia hotel is located, all the way to the Nusa Dua Hotel). North of Nusa Dua is **Tanjung Benoa**, which has white sand but is disappointingly calm (for those who like some surf) due to a ring of coral reefs in the distance.

The beach at **Sanur** is more of a golden hue but only swimmable at high tide; at low tide the water recedes to your waist (or sometimes knees) and is littered with coral and rocks.

The broad stretch of grey sands along **Kuta**, **Legian** and **Seminyak** sees gorgeous mango-streaked sunsets when the conditions are right. They are great for beach walks and for frolicking in the surf, boogie boarding, and if you venture far out enough, for surfing – albeit a bit rough for children and with a strong undertow at times. The sand bed is relatively flat and firm, and free of rocks and other debris. Much of the same also applies to the beach at **Jimbaran**.

South of Jimbaran are the stunning white-sand beaches of **Uluwatu**, **Suluban**, **Padang Padang**, **Impossibles**, **Bingin** and **Balangan**. They produce fabulous breaks for surfers but are not safe for swimmers.

been considerably eased by the opening of the Sunset Road, which bypasses Kuta, Legian and Seminyak. Likewise, the 2013 construction of a new underpass at Simpang Siur and a new toll road to Tanjung Benoa and Nusa Dua has also helped to alleviate traffic problems, as has the Sunrise Road highway along the east coast, which gives access to the ruggedly beautiful beaches and traditional fishing villages of this area.

Although it is possible to get around Bali in a couple of days, this is not a good idea; it's far better to explore the area you are in rather than make long treks across the island. Half-day outings are best accomplished by starting early, which leaves the rest of the day for relaxing on the beach or in a restaurant, taking a stroll through a nearby village or market, and then attending an evening festival or performance.

The main tourist hub is the southern triangle formed by the frenetically busy **Kuta/Legian/Seminyak** stretch, with quieter **Jimbaran** on the west and the slightly more sedate **Nusa Dua/Tanjung Benoa** and **Sanur** areas on the east. If you're a beach lover, enjoy dining out at a different restaurant every night and like lively nightlife, then stay in these areas.

Those who prefer something quieter but still close to the beach, should head for **Candidasa** and **Amed** on the east coast, **Lovina** in the north or **Pemuteran** in the northwest. Be aware, however, that outside of the south the beaches are pebbly rather than sandy, or black/grey sand and not white.

Those bent on seeing cultural attractions should base themselves in the **Ubud** area, where nearby villages in the Gianyar regency provide the opportunity to see arts and crafts, music and dance performances, as well as numerous ancient temples. **Denpasar** has little of interest, apart from the markets and the museum. If you like mountain scenery and cooler climes, consider spending some time in the **Bedugul** area near the lovely **Danau Bratan**, or to the east, **Danau Batur** at the foot of **Gunung Batur**.

Public Transport

Minivans

Minivans *(bemo)* operate on fixed routes from terminals or marketplaces in cities and major towns. Some transfer points are located at important crossroads. There are no marked stopping places, Just flag one down, and call out "stop" when you want to get out. Fares are based on distance travelled and always very cheap, ranging from one thousand to a few thousand rupiah. Always carry small change with you; you can't expect a *bemo* driver to give you change from a Rp 50,000, or even a Rp 20,000 bank note. Pay the fare just before getting off; establishing the correct fare is a different issue altogether as tourists are almost always overcharged.

As passengers and products of all sorts get loaded off and on, it can get hot and crowded. This mode of transport does take time but allows you to meet the locals; beware of pickpockets, though.

Buses

Major bus terminals are at Tegal in Denpasar (services to Kuta); Kereneng in Denpasar (services to points in the city, Batubulan and Sanur); Ubung (services to Tabanan, Singaraja and Jembrana); Batubulan (services to Gianyar, Singaraja, Bangli, Klungkung and Karangasem) and in Singaraja (services to Jembrana, Tabanan, Denpasar and Karangasem). Fares are approximately Rp 25,000 per 50km (30 miles) and buses operate out of the same terminals as *bemo*.

Tourist Shuttle Services

...ttle services operate daily ...een Kuta, Ubud, Sanur, ... and Candidasa. Although they cost a bit more than buses or *bemo*, they are faster and more comfortable. Tickets are available from most hotels and tourist agencies. The fares from both Kuta and the Airport to various other points in Bali are as follows:

Kuta–Sanur	Rp 35,000
Kuta–Ubud	Rp 50,000
Kuta–Lovina	Rp 125,000
Kuta–Padang Bai	Rp 60,000
Kuta–Candidasa	Rp 60,000
Kuta–Bedugul:	Rp 75,000
Kuta–Kintamani (min 2 people)	Rp 150,000
Padang Bai–Amed (min 2 people)	Rp 185,000

Taxis

Taxis are air-conditioned and charge metered fares. The only fixed rates are from the airport to the major hotels (*see page 231*). Check with the driver before you board as many drivers prefer to charge a flat rate instead of using the meter. To be sure you don't get ripped off, ask your hotel concierge what the going rate is for the destination you want to get to.

Few taxis outside of the Kuta-Legian-Seminyak area cruise the streets for passengers, so call one of the numbers below (or ask your hotel concierge for you). The best company is **Bali Taxi** (Bluebird Group), with light blue cabs and a reputation for providing reliable, safe and honest service. The meters run at approximately Rp 6,000 per kilometre with a flag fall rate of Rp 6,000. If you call a taxi, the minimum charge is Rp 15,000. Most drivers speak some English, especially Bali Taxi drivers.

Bali Taxi: tel: 0361-701111 (complaints tel: 0361-701621)
Komotra: tel: 0361-758855
There are very few taxis in Ubud. The only ones you will see are those that have brought passengers from other tourist areas and are hoping for a fare back. You can arrange private transport with your hotel or negotiate a fare with one of the many young men offering transport on the street.

Motorcycle Taxis

Young men operate motorcycle taxis known as *ojek*, and wait at designated places for customers. This is very convenient for locations not serviced by public transport. Agree on the price beforehand, and make sure you wear the helmet the driver provides, as it's required by law. The drivers do tend to weave in and out of heavy traffic but are usually very experienced. Fares are negotiable, usually just a few thousand rupiah for a short journey and no more than about half what you would pay for a taxi.

Private Transport

Vehicle with Driver

Chartering a car or minivan with driver can be done by the half-day or full-day. Rates are cheaper if negotiated on the street rather than from your hotel (look out for young men who call out "transpor transpor" and move their hands as if driving a car).

Rates vary according to the kind of vehicle, its condition, actual travel time, and total number of hours hired. This amount should include fuel. Full-day rates generally range from about Rp 300,000 –500,000, half day from Rp 150,000–300,000. Alternatively you can rent a car yourself and pay about Rp 100,000 extra per day for the services of an English-speaking driver.

It is courteous to give your driver money for a meal if you stop for lunch or dinner, or you may even invite him to eat with you (although some drivers may feel shy about doing this). If you are pleased with the driver, a tip of Rp 30,000 is appropriate. You will usually get a better rate if you arrange to use the same driver for all the trips during your stay.

If you're not comfortable chartering a vehicle off the street, ask a tour agency or your hotel (which can also arrange for a guide) to get you a vehicle and driver. Rates will be substantially higher though.

Reliable operators include:
Bali Trip Transport Service & Car Rental: Jalan Raya Sayan, Ubud, tel: 0361-974923.
Perama Tours: Jalan Legian 39, Kuta, tel: 0361-751551, 751875; www.peramatour.com.
Satya Dharma: Jalan Merta Ayu No. 9, Kerobokan, tel: 0361-735258.

Private Car Hire

Driving in Bali can be dangerous. Generally, drivers do not drive defensively, the roads are narrow and poorly maintained, and dogs and chickens frequently dart into the road. Street lighting at night is limited. If you collide with anything, you are responsible for all costs. It's safer to hire a driver while you relax and enjoy the sights.

Self-drive cars are available in Sanur, Kuta and Ubud, for which you must have an International Driving Permit. It's also advisable to pay the extra cost to ensure you have full insurance coverage. Petrol is not included. You can book a car through your hotel or from any of the companies listed below. They will deliver the car to you and pick it up at the end of the rental period. Always test-drive the car and check that it is in good working order before paying. Note: Drive on the left side of the road.

Prices (per day) range between US$20–$40 for a Suzuki Jeep to US$30–$50 for a larger Toyota Kijang. These rates still include collision insurance, unlimited mileage and pick-up and delivery service.

POLICE CHECKS

When riding a motorbike or driving a car, it is not uncommon to be flagged down by the police at a spot-check point. You will be asked to show your driving licence and vehicle registration papers. If you do not have these documents with you, you will be expected to pay a "fine", a negotiable bribe of usually around Rp 100,000.

The following rental agencies are recommended:
Kuta
Bali Happy Rent Car: Jalan Raya Kuta, Kuta, tel: 0361-751954.
Merpati Transport: Jalan Raya Kuta 67, Kuta, tel: 0361-752137.
Jimbaran
Golden Bird Bali: Jalan Bypass Nusa Dua 4, Jimbaran, tel: 0361-701621.
Astra: Jalan Bypass Ngurah Rai, Jimbaran, tel: 0361-703333.
Sanur
Avis: Jalan Danau Tamblingan 27, Sanur, tel: 0361-282635.
Bagus Car Rental: Jalan Duyung 1, Sanur, tel: 0361-287794.
Seminyak/Kerobokan
Satya Dharma Rent a Car: Jalan Merta Ayu 9, tel: 0361-735258.
Ubud
Three Brothers: Jalan Raya Ubud and Monkey Forest Road, tel: 0361-975525.
Denpasar
Bali Car Hire: Jalan Gunung Guntur XVII–No 20, Denpasar, tel: 0361-7460011; www.balicarhire.com.
Bali Car Rentals: Jalan Tunjung Sari 69, Denpasar, tel: 0361-411499, mobile 081-23830079.

Motorcycle Hire

Motorcyles are a convenient and inexpensive way to get around the island, but there are risks due to heavy traffic and poor roads. Helmets are required by law but the cheap ones provided by rental agencies offer little protection. Bring your own or buy a good one from a local shop, especially one with a face shield for protection from sun, rain, bugs and dust. Drive slowly and defensively, as more and more people are injured or killed every year in accidents.

The cost of motorbike hire varies according to the model, condition of the machine, length of rental, and time of year. Expect to pay around Rp 40,000–60,000 per day. Petrol is not included. Buy full insurance so that you are not responsible for any damage. Be sure to test drive it to check that everything is in working order, especially brakes and lights. Most

rental bikes are 125cc or smaller.
You must have an International Driving Permit valid for motorcycles, or else go to the Denpasar Police Office to obtain a temporary permit, valid for three months on Bali only. Normally the person who rents you the motorbike will accompany you to the police office. Bring your passport, driving licence from your home country, and three passport-sized photos.

Bicycles

Mountain bikes are available for rent everywhere, but before you pay for one, make sure the wheels are properly aligned, the brakes work well, and that there is a working light. Because of the hazardous main roads, stick to the quieter country roads for maximum enjoyment. When you are actually pedalling, you don't feel the heat, just a cool breeze. The real sweat begins when you stop, so be sure to carry a bottle of water and to drink frequently to replenish the fluid that is lost.

Wear a helmet for extra safety, and try not to ride at night because roads are very poorly lit, or not lit at all. Hire prices vary from about Rp 20,000 to Rp 60,000 per day.

On Foot

Once off the main roads, walking can be a pleasant way to see Bali. Remember a sunhat, sunscreen and good walking shoes, carry bottled water, food or snacks, insect repellent, and an umbrella in case of rain or too much sun.

Hitchhiking just isn't done and most people will not understand what you are doing. This doesn't mean that you can't ask for a ride, but trying to get a free ride from a stranger is unusual.

Dokars

Dokars (2-wheeled horse drawn buggies), extinct elsewhere in Bali, are a tourist attraction in the Kuta area. Expect to pay around Rp 10,000–20,000 in Kuta for short ride.

Accommodation: Bali

Some Things to Consider Before You Book The Room

Choosing a Hotel

There is a mind-boggling choice of accommodation in Bali, from exquisite luxury resorts to humble *losmen* (guesthouses) where you lodge with a local family. Bali's luxury hotels are among the best in the world and feature first-class service and facilities. Apart from international 5-star chains like Hyatt, Four Seasons and Conrad, there are also high-quality local chains and many boutique properties. Bali also has the distinction of being the only place in the world with three award-winning Aman resorts – where the super rich (and often famous) hide out.

Choosing a Villa

If the impersonality of a large hotel does not appeal, plump for a stay at a private villa. Many wealthy foreigners and Indonesians from Jakarta have built luxury homes in Bali which they rent out to visitors on a daily or weekly basis. A villa can be anything from a 1-bedroom beach side cottage to an exclusive 8-bedroom luxury villa with every conceivable comfort. Locations can be rice field, jungle, beach front, cliff top, river side or mountain side.

Villas can be rented on a daily or weekly basis. Nearly every private has a swimming pool and the majority accommodate between 2 and 10 people and come equipped with kitchen and dining facilities plus a full complement of staff, from housekeepers and cooks to drivers, gardeners, pool attendants and security guards.

Details of Bali's rental villas can be found on these websites:

The Villa Guide
www.thevillaguide.com
Elite Havens
www.EliteHavens.com
Private Homes & Villas
www.phvillas.com

Hotel Areas

Every area of Bali has something special to offer; over the years, distinct subcultures have evolved within each of the main tourist centres. The infrastructure in South Bali is geared towards tourists while the Ubud area attracts lively young visitors who prefer some calm. The more remote areas (east, north, west and the central mountainous region) have their own charm. The Places chapters and the introduction to each hotel area in the following pages briefly describe what to expect.

Prices and Bookings

Advance reservations are recommended during the peak July– September and Christmas–New Year periods. Almost all hotels add a 21 percent government tax and service charge to your bill. Some smaller ones just add the 11 percent tax.

Often, better prices and package rates are available on hotel websites. If you call directly, the unwritten rule is that you can negotiate prices, especially during the low season.

Note that many of the 5-star resorts in the following listings, categorised as expensive or moderate, often offer a broad choice of accommodation, from standard rooms to pricier up-market suites and private villas.

Below: luxurious Villa Asada near Candidasa.

SOUTH BALI

DENPASAR

There's no real reason to stay in Denpasar unless you have urgent business that can't wait the short (15-minute) commute from Kuta. There are scores of hotels for under US$20, most of them catering to domestic tourists.

Inna Bali Hotel

Jalan Veteran 3
Tel: 0361-225681
www.innabalihotel.com
A historic, centrally located hotel, built by the Dutch in 1927. Retains its old colonial atmosphere in spite of the heavy traffic zooming by. Moderately priced rooms in the main section are basic, but have air conditioning, hot water, TV and telephone. More comfortable executive suites are in a building across the street. Restaurant and bar plus swimming pool on the premises; 74 rooms. $

SANUR

A popular destination for foreigners since the 1920s, Sanur offers peace and quiet. There are both first-class and budget hotels. Sanur has an "international" ambience, but is far less cosmopolitan than frenetic Kuta.

Abian Srama Hotel

Jalan Bypass Ngurah Rai 23
Tel: 0361-288792
Just 10 minutes from the beach, this pleasant family-run place has air conditioning, hot water, laundry service, swimming pool and coffee shop. Massage service is available. 48 rooms. $

Griya Santrian Hotel

Jalan Danau Tamblingan 47
Tel: 0361-288181
www.santrian.com
Friendly, family-run hotel with private seaside bungalows set in a spacious garden with winding paths. All bungalows have air conditioning and a private terrace – some open into the garden, while others have a view of the ocean. There are two pools and two restaurants. 96 rooms. $$$

La Taverna Hotel

Jalan Danau Tamblingan 29
Tel: 0361-288497
www.latavernahotel.com
Old hotel with a good reputation. Rooms here are in the form of delightful thatched bungalows, with Italian stucco walls, antique furniture and elegantly styled decor. The hotel is set in a garden with a private beach, pool, bar and pizzeria. Good beach front restaurant. 22 rooms plus 9 more expensive suites. $$$

Mercure Resort Sanur

Jalan Mertasari
Tel: 0361-288833
www.accorhotels-asia.com
Beach side hotel with cottage-style accommodation set in tropical gardens. Recreational activities include tennis, volleyball and table tennis. Pandawa restaurant serves a mix of Asian and Western cuisines. 189 cottages. $$

Puri Santrian

Jalan Danau Tamblingan 63
Tel: 0361-288009
www.santrian.com
Your choice of stylish rooms, facing either the beach or lush tropical gardens, or individual bungalows. Also the upmarket Santrian Club with suites that are more luxurious. Hotel has all features including large swimming pools, tennis court, spa and the upmarket Mezzanine restaurant. 26 rooms overlook the garden and 67 the pool. $$$

Sanur Beach Hotel

Jalan Danau Tamblingan
Tel: 0361-288011
www.sanurbeachhotelbali.com
Quiet place known for its friendly staff and excellent service. Its bungalows, set in lush gardens, have a rustic charm while the new high-rise section is more luxurious. Facilities include two main restaurants, the South American Peppers and the Italian Basilico. Three swimming pools, watersports, tennis courts and shops. 426 rooms. $$$

Sanur Paradise Plaza

Jalan Hang Tuah 46
Tel: 0361-281781
www.sanurparadise.com
A popular hotel and venue for conventions, conferences and seminars.

Rooms and suites are luxurious, with the landscaped grounds housing a large swimming pool, poolside café, two restaurants and a fitness centre with fully equipped gymnasium. There is a regular shuttle bus between the Paradise Plaza Hotel and the Paradise Plaza Suites (1, 2 and 3 bedroom apartments), where Camp Splash is located, a fun water playground for children. 329 rooms. $$$

Sativa Sanur Cottages

Jalan Cemara 45
Tel: 0361-287881
Well-managed, peaceful and cosy, this congenial hotel represents very good value. It is only 5 minutes away from the beach, and all rooms are just steps away from a swimming pool with swim-up bar. 50 rooms. $$

Tandjung Sari Hotel

Jalan Danau Tamblingan 41
Tel: 0361-288441
www.tandjungsari.com
A charming and historical hotel. Choose between a traditional Balinese-style bungalow or a villa with pavilion. All are set by the sea in lovely gardens with meandering paths. Swimming pool and restaurant, but meals can

served privately in your own bungalow. This old-style and serene hotel is known for its excellent service and great views. 26 bungalows/villas. **$$$$**

TUBAN

Sometimes referred to as South Kuta, this area now has a very impressive hotel strip, some with direct beach front access and close to shops and restaurants; an ideal area for families.

Bali Dynasty
Jalan Kartika Plaza
Tel: 0361-752403
www.balidynasty.com
This family resort (with family room accommodation for up to five guests) has undergone extensive renovations. There are five restaurants and five bars – including the renowned Golden Lotus Chinese and Gracie Kelly's Irish Pub – as well as three swimming pools, and a spa villa. The Kupu-Kupu Kiddies club will look after your children while you relax. 312 rooms. **$$$**

Discovery Kartika Plaza Hotel
Jalan Kartika Plaza
Tel: 0361-751067
www.discoverykartikaplaza.com
Situated in the heart of Tuban next to Discovery shopping mall and close to Waterbom Park, this large beach side family resort includes a huge swimming pool, extensive gardens, tennis courts, Musro nightclub and karaoke, a Chinese restaurant, and private villas right on the beach. 312 rooms. **$$$**

Ramada Bintang Bali Resort
Jalan Kartika Plaza
Tel: 0361-753292
www.bintang-bali-hotel.com
Good, recently refurbished international-class hotel near the beach with a choice of room styles. Pool, jacuzzi, gym, spa, tennis courts, conference facilities and restaurants (including the 24-hour La Brasserie). 401 rooms. **$$$**

The Sandi Phala
Jalan Wana Segara
Tel: 0361-753780
www.thesandiphala.com
Contemporary and luxurious beach side suites set in beautiful gardens. Located within the grounds is the highly regarded Ma Joly French restaurant; get a seat at the terrace bar from where you can watch Bali's wonderful sunsets. 11 suites. **$$$$**

KUTA

Kuta is chaotic and noisy, but a great playground. Years of unplanned development has turned it into a jumble of closely-packed pubs, nightclubs, restaurants, shops and budget hotels. Even with many first-class hotels, the area still caters best to the economy traveller who likes to be in the thick of things.

Hard Rock Hotel
Jalan Pantai Kuta
Tel: 0361-761869
www.hardrockhotels.net/bali
Rooms and suites are right along the beach at this fun, high-energy hotel, incorporating a Hard Rock Café and sev-

eral other food and bar outlets. There's live entertainment daily, and facilities include Bali's largest free-form pool, a health club, children's club, spa, recording studio and karaoke, and retail outlets. This is not the place for quiet relaxation, but is great for families. 418 rooms. **$$$**

Mercure Kuta
Jalan Pantai Kuta
Tel: 0361-767411
www.mercurekutabali.com
A modern 4-storey hotel furnished in traditional Balinese style. Standard rooms are on the lower floors, superior ones higher up and the deluxe rooms overlook the sea. Across the road is Kuta beach, next door the Hard Rock Café and around the corner Kuta's main shopping strip. Well appointed rooms, including cable TV, and private balcony. 130 rooms. **$$**

Poppies Cottages
Gang Poppies I
Tel: 0361-751059
www.poppies.net
One of the first hotels to open when the Kuta surf began attracting tourists. with air-conditioned, well-designed bungalows set in a tropical garden. Pool, restaurant, and only 300 metres/yds from the beach. Essential to book. 20 rooms. **$$**

Un's Hotel
Jalan Bene Sari 16
Tel: 0361-757409
www.unshotel.com
A peaceful oasis located between the shops and the beach. Rooms offer the option of fan or air conditioning, and are all bordered by communal balconies and terraces set around a swimming pool and pretty gardens. Guests can order room

service from The Balcony Restaurant. 30 rooms. **$**

Yulia Beach Inn
Jalan Pantai Kuta 43
Tel: 0361-751893
Clean and well-maintained, this hotel is close to the centre of things as well as being located close to the beach; rooms at the back are quieter. Superior rooms may be basic but there are also some deluxe rooms and bungalows. Small restaurant and a swimming pool. 34 rooms. **$**

LEGIAN

The northern end of Kuta beach is known as Legian, a little quieter and more relaxed than teeming Kuta. Central Legian beach has become a key entertainment area that includes good-value restaurants and nightspots.

Alam KulKul
Jalan Pantai Kuta
Tel: 0361-752520
www.alamkulkul.com
Modern hotel rooms opening onto tropical gardens and small private villas, all luxuriously fitted with every modern amenity. There are two swimming pools, and across the road is the long stretch of beach

PRICE CATEGORIES

Price for a double room (subject to a 10–21 percent tax and service charge):

$$$$ = over US$200
$$$ = US$120–200
$$ = US$60–120
$ = below US$60

that joins Kuta and Legian. An Indonesian restaurant is within the grounds while Italian restaurant, Papa's, faces the street. 57 rooms and 23 villas. **$$**

All Seasons Resort
Jalan Padma Utara
Tel: 0361-767688
www.accorhotels-asia.com
Large modern budget hotel close to Legian beach whose swimming pool is surrounded by tropical gardens. All rooms have air conditioning, minibar and cable TV, while the Colours Café offers Indonesian and international dishes at amazingly cheap prices. 113 rooms. **$**

Casa Padma Suites
Jalan Padma
Tel: 0361-753073
www.casasuites.com
This small boutique hotel is virtually built around the elongated swimming pool and The Drops restaurant extends out over it. A mix of standard rooms and suites, some of which have their own terraces, and close to many restaurants, bars, shops and the beach. 6 rooms and 23 suites. **$$**

Hotel Kumala Pantai
Jalan Werkudara, Legian Kaja
Tel: 0361-755500
www.kumalapantai.com
One of Bali's most popular hotels in this class: regularly fully booked as it's great value for money, is well-managed and has a pleasant beach side position. Large 50-metre swimming pool plus beach side restaurant on site. 88 rooms. **$$**

Legian Beach Hotel
Jalan Melasti
Tel: 0361-751711
www.legianbeachbali.com

Rooms and bungalows here are set in a large garden complex near the beach, and there's a relaxed atmosphere. The hotel has two swimming pools, spa, fitness centre, tennis and squash courts, water sports facilities, four restaurants and three bars. 216 rooms. **$$**

Padma Resort Bali at Legian
Jalan Padma 1
Tel: 0361-752111
www.padmaresortbali.com
Five-star resort set within beautiful gardens beside Legian Beach. Facilities include a wonderful spa and a good choice of restaurants, including the fine dining Bella Rosa Italian restaurant. 409 rooms. **$$$$**

SEMINYAK

Seminyak lies to the north of Legian. Further north and inland it merges into Kerobokan but the borders are hazy. Seminyak has the same sweeping beach and surf as Kuta and Legian but mercifully not the pressing crowds and vendors. The area has several luxury and mid-price hotels but scant budget places. Nearby Jalan Laksmana heaves with restaurants offering diverse cuisines while Jalan Raya Seminyak has up-market shops.

Anantara
Jalan Abimanyu (Dhyana Pura)
Tel: 0361-737773
www.bali.anantara.com
Covering a compact area of prime beachfront land, this hip, contemporary hotel makes optimum use of space by packing

in 59 spacious suites, a Thai restaurant, the trendy SOS (Sunset on Six) rooftop terrace bar with gorgeous views of Seminyak's stunning sunsets, a spa, gym, and three swimming pools. 59 suites. **$$$$**

Favehotel Seminyak
Jalan Abimanyu (Dhyana Pura) 9A
Tel: 0361-739000
www.favehotels.com
Set in the heart of Seminyak's party street, Favehotel opened in 2011. Modern and clean, it offers a fun atmosphere, fresh attitude and friendly services, every room has a satellite-channel TV and Wi-fi. 251 rooms. **$**

The Legian
Jalan Laksmana
Tel: 0361-730622
www.ghmhotels.com
A top-class resort right on the beach with 67 enormous suites. The resort combines modern minimalism with Balinese architectural touches. Excellent restaurant serving both contemporary cuisine and Balinese food; infinity pool, gym and spa. Even more exclusive – if without the sweeping views – is the extension called The Club at The Legian: 11 luxury villas and facilities a 3-minute buggy ride across the street. **$$$$**

Mystique Apartments
Jalan Raya Petitenget 2000XX
Tel: 0361-737415
www.balimystique.com
A small block of 16 luxury apartments (5-minute walk to the beach) set around a giant banyan tree amid pools. Most have two bedrooms and all have modern fittings. Facilities include a spa, swimming pool and res-

taurant. **$$$**

Oberoi Bali
Jalan Laksmana
Tel: 0361-730361
www.oberoihotels.com
A luxury hotel surrounded by sprawling lush gardens along one of Bali's finest beaches. Sea-or garden-view rooms and villas have over-sized bathrooms and courtyards, while some villas feature private swimming pools. Designed by Peter Muller in 1972 and remarkably well preserved for its age, the Oberoi is visually reminiscent of a classic Balinese palace and features extensive use of coral rock. Nightly cultural performances, two restaurants, a bar, and a saltwater pool. 60 rooms and 14 villas. **$$$$**

Pelangi Bali Hotel
Jalan Dhyana Pura
Tel: 0361-730346
www.pelangibali.com
Right on the beach front and close to the highly regarded Gado Gado restaurant. This small two-storey hotel has decently furnished rooms (plump for the larger deluxe room with living area if you can afford it) and a swimming pool that overlooks the crashing surf of Seminyak beach. 89 rooms. **$**

Sentosa Private Villas & Spa
Jalan Pura Telaga Waja, Petitenget
Tel: 0361-730333
www.balisentosa.com
Luxurious pool villas, from one- to three-bedroom units. Stylish spa, fitness centre and the superb Blossom restaurant (Modern Australian and Thai cuisines) make up for the 7-minute walk to the beach. Lots of good restaurants within its

vicinity. 38 villas. **$$$$**

The Samaya
Jalan Laksmana
Tel: 0361-731149
www.thesamayabali.com

Intimate garden villas, each surrounded by a wall and gate for privacy, All have large bedrooms and outdoor sitting areas with private plunge pools, and in-villa spa treatment is available. Eat at the award-winning Alang-Alang restaurant or order from your villa which comes with butler service. A large swimming pool and gardens overlook the beach. 46 villas. **$$$$**

W Retreat & Spa
Jl Petitenget, Seminyak
Tel: 0361 738106
www.whotels.com/baliseminyak

Uber-stylish beachside hotel presenting a sensational swirl of high-energy interiors, vivid design, cutting-edge technology and uniquely modern amenities. There's an assortment of restaurants including Fire and Starfish Boo. Fitness centre and spa offering round-the-clock treatments. 158 rooms and suites. **$$$$**

CANGGU

As Seminyak spreads northwards it becomes quieter and more isolated. Canggu is a well-known surf spot, perfect for escaping the crowds.

Hotel Tugu
Jalan Pantai Batu Bolong, Canggu
Tel: 0361-731707
www.tuguhotels.com

A living museum of priceless antiques and rare cultural artefacts, this stunning boutique hotel and spa is set between rice fields and the quiet rugged beach of Canggu. Two suites contain replica studios of famous painters who lived in Bali in the 1930s, and one of the restaurants is housed in a 300-year-old Kang Xi period temple. 22 villas. **$$$$**

JIMBARAN

Jimbaran, south of Kuta and the airport, is a sweeping bay that curves for 5 km (3 miles) to the headland. There is a handful of luxury resorts and the beach remains unspoilt and tranquil. A string of beach side seafood restaurants at Jimbaran provide alternatives to hotel food.

Ayana Resort & Spa
Jalan Karang Mas Sejahtera
Tel: 0361-702222
www.ayanaresort.com

This exceptional resort, in modern Balinese architectural style, sits within a spectacular cliff top setting. It offers a wide variety of accommodation as well as a near-overwhelming choice of facilities, restaurants, spa venues, swimming pools and wedding venues, including two ultra avant-garde wedding chapels. Pools and waterfalls cascade towards the ocean, and a series of romantic open pavilions are encompassed by lotus ponds. 368 rooms. **$$$$**

Bali Inter-Continental
Jalan Uluwatu
Tel: 0361-701888
www.ichotelsgroup.com

Set in 14 hectares (35 acres) of landscaped gardens embellished with statues, lagoons and pools, this resort fronts a beautiful beach and is an ideal spot for viewing the sunset. Squash and tennis courts, spa, three swimming pools, sports facilities, gym, four restaurants, including exquisite Japanese cuisine at KO, and two bars on the premises. 425 rooms. **$$$$**

Four Seasons Jimbaran
Jalan Bukit Permai
Tel: 0361-701010
www.fourseasons.com

Accommodation here is in individual luxury villas, all with private splash pools, built on a terraced hillside with landscaped gardens – the resort has a spectacular view of the bay and Gunung Agung in the distance. Four restaurants including Sundara by the beach, an award-winning spa, infinity pool, tennis courts and water sports facilities. 147 villas. **$$$$**

Jimbaran Puri Bali
Jalan Uluwatu
Tel: 0361-701605
www.jimbaranpuribali.com

Part of the luxury Orient Express chain, this beach front property comprises luxurious bungalows set within private walled gardens. Large swimming pool and two restaurants, one of which is right on the beach. Also a library, boutique and spa. 41 rooms. **$$$$**

Karma Jimbaran
Jalan Four Seasons
Tel: 0361-708848
www.karmajimbaran.com

Each villa at this resort is a self-contained, beautifully appointed home with swimming pool and fully fitted kitchen. Also on site is a gymnasium, a fine-dining steak house, and the Chakra Balinese spa. The only drawback? The beach is a 5-minute walk away. 38 three- and four-bedroom villas plus the Grand Residence. **$$$$**

THE BUKIT

The Bukit (which means 'hill' in Indonesian) is the rugged limestone peninsula that dangles like a pendant upon a chain at the southern tip of Bali. Until recently, this remote windswept outcrop was home solely to seaweed farmers, fishermen and die-hard surfers. In recent years, it has reinvented itself to become the most up-market destination on the island.

Bali Bule Homestay
Jl Pantai, Padang Padang
Tel: 0361-769979
www.balibulehomestay.com

Popular with surfers, this family-run bungalow complex opened in 2012, clean and spacious, five minute's walk from the beach. Swimming pool, restaurant, Wi-fi. 10 rooms. **$**

The Beverly Hills
Jalan Goa Gong, Banjar Santhi Karya, Ungasan
Tel: 0361-8481800
www.balibeverlyhills.com

PRICE CATEGORIES

Price for a double room (subject to a 10–21 percent tax and service charge):

$$$$ = over US$200
$$$ = US$120–200
$$ = US$60–120
$ = below US$60

Glamorous, Korean-owned villa hotel located on a peaceful hill only 20 minutes' drive from the airport, with unbroken views extending across Jimbaran Bay and the Garuda Wisnu Kencana statue. One-, two- and three-bedroom villas each with enormous en-suite bathrooms, walled gardens and private pools. Spa facilities and restaurant – romantic candlelit dinners on carpets of rose petals are a speciality. 25 villas. **$$$$**

Blue Point Bay Villas & Spa
Jalan Lubuansit
Tel: 0361-7441077
www.bluepointbayvillas.com
Cliff top location close to Uluwatu temple. Four standards of accommodation. Restaurants are on the edge of the cliff, facing the ocean. Of the two large pools, one is kidney-shaped looking out over the southern cliff. 29 rooms. **$$$**

Bulgari
Jalan Goa Lempeh, Banjar Dinas Kangin, Uluwatu
Tel: 0361-8471000
www.bulgarihotels.com
Resting 160 metres/yds above the ocean at Bali's southernmost point, this designer resort is the second in a series to be built in prestigious locations around the world. Opened in 2006, the glamorous cliff edge villa retreat and spa fuses chic Italian modernity with Indonesian artefacts and textiles. Overpriced villas, but the food served at the two restaurants is excellent. 56 one-bedroom and three two-bedroom villas, all with private plunge pools. **$$$$**

Karma Kandara
Banjar Wijaya Kusuma, Ungasan
Tel: 0361-8482200
www.karmakandara.com
Blessed with an intoxicating view of the Indian Ocean, this luxury resort offers a choice of one to four-bedroom villas with swimming pools, as well as a main swimming pool, a Balinese spa, a Mediterranean fine dining restaurant, and a private cliff inclinator providing access to the pristine beach, beach club and bar. 54 villas. **$$$$**

Rocky Bungalows
Off Jalan Uluwatu
Tel: 081-7346 209
Surfer hangout, 3 minutes' walk from the sea at Padang Padang, with pleasant balconied rooms and a relaxing atmosphere. Simple restaurant; 10 rooms. **$**

NUSA DUA

Nusa Dua is rather isolated from the rest of Bali, but it is blessed with fine white-sand beaches. To make up for the area's somewhat sterile character, hotels here provide everything on the premises. A few restaurants line the road outside the hotel area; inside the area, the Bali Collection complex offers expensive restaurants, duty-free shopping, department stores and a supermarket.

Amanusa
Nusa Dua
Tel: 0361-772333
www.amanresorts.com
Part of the Amanresorts chain, with its signature

understated architecture and lush gardens, this hilltop resort overlooks the Bali Golf and Country Club and has spectacular views of the ocean and coast. Huge swimming pool, Italian and Thai restaurants, tennis courts, golf facilities and a shuttle service to a private beach club with water-sports facilities. 35 villas. **$$$$**

Ayodya Resort Bali
Nusa Dua
Tel: 0361-771102
www.ayodyaresortbali.com
This sprawling resort is set on a lovely stretch of Nusa Dua beach and offers luxurious accommodation and fine dining. Leisure facilities include a huge swimming pool, a health centre and spa, all-weather tennis and squash courts, and water sports facilities. 538 rooms. **$$$**

Grand Hyatt Bali
Nusa Dua
Tel: 0361-771234
www.hyatt.com
The largest resort in Bali, the spectacular Grand Hyatt is bordered by a lovely white-sand beach. Spacious rooms are set in four Balinese-style villages with six swimming pools, lush gardens, ponds and fountains. Full range of facilities, including putting green, children's club, five restaurants and the Kriya Spa. Accommodation includes beachfront villas and suites with garden and ocean views. 672 rooms. **$$$**

Laguna Resort and Spa
Nusa Dua
Tel: 0361-771327
www.luxurycollection.com/bali
Luxurious rooms here are

almost surrounded by a vast, meandering artificial lagoon and feature butler service. The hotel has a beautiful beach-side setting with gardens, pools, cascading waterfalls and swimming lagoons. Tennis courts, three restaurants and water sports complete the picture. 270 rooms. **$$$**

The Mulia Resort & Villas
Jl. Raya Nusa Dua Selatan, Kawasan Sawangan
Nusa Dua
Tel: 0361 3027777
www.themulia.com
Newly opened in 2013, this boutique lifestyle retreat is set on 30 hectares of land beside the beach, presenting top-level privacy, personalised butler service, and an exquisite spa. Also offers hydrotherapy pools in each villa and a jacuzzi on every guestroom balcony. Guests can enjoy The Lounge at The Mulia, a lifestyle concept combining a cosy library, lounge and dining room. The Café features all-day dining buffet options, ZJ's is a nightclub, and the Living Room has a library, lounge and restaurant. 526 room and suites, 108 villas. **$$$$**

Nikko Bali Resort
Jalan Raya Nusa Dua, Selatan
Tel: 0361-773377
www.nikkobali.com
Nikko Bali's dramatic clifftop setting is unique. Close to Nusa Dua but unencumbered by neighbours, the resort is built into the rock face with a private beach that would be inaccessible but for the elevator that transports guests up and down the 15 storeys between the lush gar-

dens and the rolling surf. Five restaurants, three bars, amphitheatre and spa. 390 rooms. **$$$**

Nusa Dua Beach Hotel
Nusa Dua
Tel: 0361-771210
www.nusaduahotel.com
The choice of visiting heads of state, this beachfront hotel has a grandeur worthy of Bali's kings. Accommodation is in luxurious suites and bungalows set in landscaped grounds; the Palace Wing even has private butler service. Huge swimming pool and complete range of facilities. Three restaurants including the fine-dining

Balinese Raja's and Maguro for Japanese delicacies. 380 rooms. **$$$**

St Regis Bali Resort
Kawasan Pariwisata
Tel: 0361-8478111
www.stregis.com/bali
Stunning property celebrating the Baroque in its bold collision of classic and modern, simplicity and opulence. Rich fabrics and cultural artefacts nest in high-tech surroundings. Oversized suites, private villas and two exclusive residences, as well as restaurants, wedding chapel, lagoon pool, and spa. 123 villas, suites, and residences. **$$$$**

TANJUNG BENOA

The northern end of Nusa Dua is a long finger-shaped peninsula with a white sand beach that is lined with upmarket hotels and watersports operations. Its waters can be as still as a mill pond at low tide because of the protective coral reef offshore.

Conrad Bali
Jalan Pratama 168
Tel: 0361-778788
www.conradhotels.com
A magnificient 5-star property set amid tropical

gardens and waterfalls. Most of its tastefully appointed rooms have sea views while the deluxe lagoon rooms have direct access to the lagoon pool. Spa; three restaurants; 313 rooms. **$$$$**

Novotel Bali Benoa
Jalan Pratama
Tel: 0361-772239
www.novotelbali.com
Natural materials are used creatively in this well designed hotel, whose 190 rooms are not large but are tastefully furnished. Three restaurants, spa, kids' club, and shuttle bus service. **$$$**

UBUD AND SURROUNDINGS

UBUD CENTRE

There are many mid-range and budget hotels in the centre of Ubud, all within walking distance of markets, art galleries, shops and restaurants. The main road (Jalan Monkey Forest) is lined with many small hotels.

Adi Cottages
Jalan Monkey Forest
Tel: 0361 975231
Centrally located in the heart of Monkey Forest Street, a short walk to the Monkey Forest and Ubud market, Adi Cottages are traditionally styled and set in lush tropical gardens, complete with swimming pool and restaurant, creating an ambience that is uniquely Ubud. **$**
Barong Resort & Spa
Jalan Monkey Forest

Tel: 0361-971759
www.barong-resort.com
A stylish resort in the cultural heart of Ubud. Built in the style of a traditional Balinese family compound, these luxury bungalows and villas are very private. Overlooking the rice fields yet only minutes from Ubud's markets and restaurants. Swimming pool, spa, massage room, and restaurant. There is a shuttle bus to Ubud. 8 bungalows and 3 villas. **$$$**

Komaneka Resort
Jalan Monkey Forest
Tel: 0361-976090
www.komaneka.com
Elegant interiors make use of natural materials, and all the bungalows are set in gardens away from the road – very romantic and peaceful. The resort also has a restaurant, pool, spa, boutique and fine art gallery. Staff are friendly

and helpful. 20 bungalows. **$$$$**
Oka Wati's Sunset Bungalows
Near Jalan Monkey Forest
Tel: 0361-973386
www.okawatihotel.com
Down a quiet lane and set in the rice fields, this hotel has cosy rooms, some with hot-water showers. The owner, Oka Wati, is one of Ubud's legends, having operated the famous *babi guling* stall near the palace many years ago. She still runs her hotel hands-on and will personally prepare her speciality, *bebek betutu*, on request. Small swimming pool. 19 rooms with large verandahs. **$**
Samhita Garden
Jalan Bisma
Tel: 0361-975443
e-mail: santikg@indosat.net.id
Boutique hotel located near the centre of Ubud, with Spanish-

speaking management. Traditional bungalows with all necessary amenities in a garden setting with swimming pool. Only breakfast is served here but other meals can be ordered and delivered from the next door restaurant, Café des Artistes. 14 rooms. **$$**

PRICE CATEGORIES

Price for a double room (subject to a 10–21 percent tax and service charge):

$$$$ = over US$200
$$$ = US$120–200
$$ = US$60–120
$ = below US$60

TRANSPORT

ACCOMMODATION

ACTIVITIES

A – Z

LANGUAGE

Ubud Village
Jalan Monkey Forest
Tel: 0361-975571
www.ubudvillagehotel.com
An elegant medium-priced hotel that offers comfortable rooms and a selection of small luxury villas at the rear of the property, set close to a small river. Large swimming pool in pleasant surroundings, and restaurant/bar. 23 rooms and 5 villas. **$$**

Uma Sari Cottage
Jalan Bisma
Tel: 0361-981538
www.umasari.com
A delightful little hotel beside the rice fields only 5 minutes' walk from the centre of Ubud. Traditional Balinese architecture, each room has a verandah, and some of the rooms are air-conditioned. There is also a swimming pool and a restaurant. Great value for money, and friendly staff. 8 rooms. **$**

PENESTANAN

Located up a long flight of steps or a narrow road near Campuhan, this area has a rural feeling with panoramas across rice fields.

Melati Cottages
Jalan Raya Penestanan
Tel: 0361-974650
www.melaticottages.com
In a quiet, idyllic and breezy setting, this place is set back in the paddy fields on a hilltop with great views. The complex has several two-storey bungalows all en suite, with double beds, ceiling fans, hot water and large verandahs.

There's also a pool, internet access and laundry service. 22 rooms. **$**

The Sungu Resort & Spa
Jalan Raya Penestanan
Tel: 0361-975719
www.thesunguresort.com
A small luxury resort with accommodation in the heart of Penestanan. Comprises several spacious *lanais* (private terraces for sitting and dining) and villas, all with opulent marble bathrooms featuring sunken baths and showers. Deluxe villas are built in the shape of traditional thatched rice barns. It has a spa, a good restaurant and attractive artwork is displayed on the walls. 3 *lanais* and 8 villas, some with pools. **$$$**

CAMPUHAN AND SANGGINGAN

Campuhan is located just west of the main Ubud centre and is where German artist Walter Spies lived for a while; Sanggingan is quieter still, and is found further north up the hill.

Ananda Cottages
Campuhan
Tel: 0361-975376
www.anandaubud.com
At this lovely hotel set in pretty rice fields you can rent a "house" with three bedrooms, two baths and a sitting room or choose to stay in a standard room. All have hot water and either air conditioning or fan. Swimming pool and restaurant on the

premises. 54 bungalows. **$**

Tjampuhan Hotel
Campuhan
Tel: 0361-975368/9
www.tjampuhan.com
Rustic bungalows, built on the site of the former home of German artist Walter Spies, hug the lush upper banks of the Wos River and enjoy spectacular views. Large spring-fed hillside swimming pool and restaurant. There are two room styles here: Raja with air conditioning, and Agung with ceiling fans. 66 rooms plus the Walter Spies House. **$$**

Uma Ubud
Sanggingan
Tel: 0361-972448
www.uma.como.bz
Overlooking the Campuhan valley, the Uma combines luxury with a holistic cultural theme (yoga retreats are a highlight here). Conceived by Japanese interior designer Koichiro Ikebuchi, the architecture may be minimalist but the rooms are outfitted with every conceivable luxury. Excellent restaurant and Shambala retreat centre offering yoga, meditation classes and spa treatments. 29 rooms and suites. **$$$$**

SAYAN, KEDEWATAN AND PAYANGAN

Sayan and Kedewatan are just 10–15 minutes north of Ubud. Payangan is further north, and much more rural. The area has a scenic ridge that overlooks the Ayung River, indeed

almost all hotels in this area have been built on its banks.

Alila Ubud
Payangan
Tel: 0361-975963
www.alilahotels.com
Atmospheric resort located in a spectacular setting. Rooms and villa suites are stylishly appointed with the ones on the ground floor featuring an outdoor shower area in a private garden. The hotel has a stunning green-tiled swimming pool (the subject of many a magazine layout), a fine restaurant serving both international and Balinese cuisines and a spa. A nice touch is the complimentary tea and Balinese cakes served from 3–5pm. 64 rooms. **$$$$**

Amandari
Kedewatan
Tel: 0361-975333
www.amanresorts.com
Designed by Peter Muller (of Oberoi Bali fame), this hotel overlooking the Ayung River is unparalleled in both beauty and price. The large swimming pool takes its inspiration from a Balinese rice terrace, the far edge appearing to drop off into infinity. The expansive suites, which offer solitude and elegance, have large bathrooms and terraces while some have private swimming pools. 30 pavilions. **$$$$**

COMO Shambhala Estate
Payangan
Tel: 0361-978888
cse.comoshambhala.bz
Truly breathtaking wellness retreat in one of Bali's most magnificent

settings, on a spur of land at the confluence of the Ayung River and a tributory. Designed by Malaysian architect Cheong Yew Kuan, the resort's two fine-dining restaurants (Kudus House and Glow) virtually hang off the cliff top, with the white water rapids way down below. This remarkable property conducts yoga retreats and wellness programmes to help you de-stress and recharge. 22 suites within 5 residences and 10 villas. **$$$$**

Four Seasons Sayan
Sayan
Tel: 0361-977577
www.fourseasons.com
The approach to Four Seasons is via a solid teak bridge leading to an awesome elliptical lotus pond. Functioning as the rooftop of the resort's central building, it appears to hover above the trees like a giant flying saucer. The exquisite rooms, suites and villas here are nestled on a lush hillside set along the Ayung River. 54 rooms. **$$$$**

Royal Pita Maha
Kedewatan
Tel: 0361-980022
www.royalpitamaha-bali.com
This luxury resort is owned and operated by members of Ubud's royal family. The design is romantic Rococo-Balinese, and every wall, door and cornice is richly decorated with the artistic expression of local craftsmen. Private villas, all with swimming pools and views of the river gorge. Two restaurants, more swimming pools, health centre and spa are spread throughout

the grounds. 92 villas. **$$$$**

Ubud Hanging Gardens
Buahan, Payangan
Tel: 0361-982700
www.hanginggardens.ubud.com
Unlike most of the other luxury resorts along the Ayung River, this intimate retreat has been built on the opposite bank, dramatically suspended upon a gravity-defying terraced hillside with a spectacular jungle backdrop. There are views of a temple on the opposite side of the gorge. The pool villas, riverside spa, large free-form swimming pool, restaurants, bars, boutique and library are all easily accessed by a private funicular. 38 villas. **$$$$**

This village is a centre of music, dance, painting and woodcarving just five minutes' drive east of Ubud.

Maya Ubud
Jalan Gunung Sari, Peliatan
Tel: 0361-977888
www.mayaubud.com
The largest hotel in Ubud and a cut above the rest, known for its excellent and unobtrusive service. Set in a sprawl of lush lawns and gardens there are both tastefully furnished hotel rooms and villas (some with private pools), all facing the river. A quiet retreat yet only five minutes by hotel transport to central Ubud with all its restaurants and shops. Three restaurants offer a variety of cuisines and

the spa centre is one of Ubud's best, nestled where the two small rivers meet and adjacent to the River Café. 48 rooms and 80 villas. **$$$$**

Just 10–15 minutes south of Ubud, this is a little quieter than Peliatan, and there are views of rice fields.

Arma Resort
Tel: 0361-976659
www.armaresort.com
This hotel is set in the rice fields with views of Gunung Agung. Large rooms with verandahs are tastefully furnished and have hot water, bathtubs, mini bars and air conditioning. There is a Thai restaurant and a large pool within the grounds, with an art museum next door. Free transport is provided into Ubud. 15 bungalows plus 6 villas. **$$**

Casa Ganesha Hotel
Jalan Raya Pengosekan
Tel: 0361 971488
www.casaganesha.com
Blending contemporary design and traditional Balinese architecture, the secluded courtyards and spacious terraces of Casa Ganesha combine to create a relaxing atmosphere. The hotel features 24 rooms with an array of facilities, as well as a swimming pool and a restaurant offering international and local cuisine. **$**

Tegal Sari
Jalan Hanoman
Tel: 0361-973318
www.tegalsari-ubud.com
One of the most popu-

lar budget locations in Ubud, as a result of which bookings must be made well in advance. Located just off the main road, set in the paddy fields, with attractive bungalows surrounded by nature, so expect total serenity. A large stone-bottomed swimming pool and a pleasant restaurant makes this the perfect escape. 21 rooms. **$**

This quiet and picturesque area is located east of Ubud.

The Viceroy
Jalan Lanyahan
Tel: 0361-971777
www.theviceroybali.com
Luxurious villas in an elevated picturesque setting. Enjoy the privacy of a villa complemented by the amenities of a top-class hotel. Experience a pampering massage or body treatment at its Lembah Spa, then float down to the superb Cascades restaurant to partake in some French-style fine dining. There is a helicopter pad for quick airport transfers to the airport – if you can afford it. 11 villas. **$$$$**

Price for a double room (subject to a 10–21 percent tax and service charge):

$$$$ = over US$200
$$$ = US$120–200
$$ = US$60–120
$ = below US$60

Gunung Batur and Surroundings

Penelokan

Most of the accommodation around Gunung Batur is basic. Penelokan has stunning views of the volcano and lake. Kintamani is quieter but has few lodgings.

Lakeview Eco Lodge
Penelokan
Tel: 0366-51394
www.lakeviewbali.com
The spacious and pleasant rooms are perched on the crater rim of the ancient volcanic caldera, each with a spectacular view of Mount Batur and the lake, making it a popular stopover. There are two restaurants and a bar. 20 rooms. **$$**

Toya Bungkah

Toya Bungkah, the village at the edge of Danau Batur, gets great sunrises; this is the main starting point for trekking up Batur.

Hotel Puri Bening
Toya Bungkah
Tel: 0366-51244
www.indo.com/hotels/puribening
hayato
Modern hotel with odd architecture. Its standard rooms have views of the lake. Restaurant and swimming pool on site. 38 rooms. **$**

Under the Volcano III
Toya Bungkah
Tel: 0366-51166/0813 3860 0081

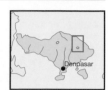

At this budget hotel, the rooms are basic but clean and come set in gardens near the crater lake. There is a small restaurant with pleasant service. There are two other nearby "Volcano" inns run by the same family. 6 rooms. **$**

East Bali

Nusa Lembongan

There is not much choice but the best hotels on Nusa Lembongan are situated on Mushroom Bay with its lovely crescent-shaped white-sand beach.

Hai Tide Huts
Mushroom Bay
Tel: 0361-720331
www.balihaicruises.com
Run by Bali Hai Cruises, it has *lumbung* (traditional rice barn) cottages. All enjoy panoramic ocean views and are located adjacent to the Bali Hai Cruises Beach Club where facilities include a swimming pool, ocean kayaks, snorkelling equipment, glass-bottom boat, banana boats, restaurant and bar. 6 cottages. **$$**

Nusa Bay Resort $$$
Mushroom Bay
Tel: 0363-723269
www.wakaexperience.com
A romantic resort with polished woods, natural floors and the distinctive *alang-alang* roofs, where each bungalow is set in private gardens. The restaurant offers alfresco dining on Balinese and Western cuisines and there's a swimming pool on site. 10 bungalows. **$$$**

Nusa Lembongan Resort
Mushroom Bay
Tel: 0363-725864
www.nusalembonganresort.com
This picturesque bayside island resort is reached by the Sails Sensation catamaran, owned by the same management group. Luxury villas surround the romantic restaurant where evening gourmet meals are served. During the day order yourself a picnic lunch for diving and exploration trips. 12 villas. **$$$**

Balina and Manggis

Buitan village is where you'll find Balina beach, a quiet stretch of black sand. Manggis is the nearby small village named after the mangosteen fruit.

Alila Manggis
Manggis
Tel: 0363-41011
www.alilahotels.com
A sprawling beach front site with contemporary styled rooms. The more expensive ones are on the top level and have large balconies facing the ocean. There is an excellent restaurant called SeaSalt which features both Indonesian and Western dishes; the hands-on cooking classes are very popular. Stunning pool makes up for the black pebble beach that

is almost unswimmable. 55 rooms. **$$$$**

Amankila
Manggis
Tel: 0363-41333
www.amankila.com
The most impressive of Bali's three Aman resorts, it is built on the side of a cliff and extends to the sea below. This is the ultimate in luxury, as are all Aman resorts, and offers fine dining at its two restaurants. A striking feature is the three-level swimming pool, which overlooks the breathtaking coastline. The beach is accessed by a flight of steep stairs (or ask for a buggy to take you there). In an area where most of the

Above: relaxing in Mushroom Bay, Nusa Lembongan.

beaches are pebbly, the Amankila has private access to a beautiful grey-sand beach. 33 rooms. **$$$$**

CANDIDASA

Don't expect much of a beach here: coral dredged over the years from the sea has led to serious erosion. Concrete barriers were built to halt this but it was too late. There are isolated patches of sand and a number of hotels have got around this by building over the water.

Amarta
Candidasa
Tel: 0363-41230
Bungalows and villas beside a small golden-sand beach, manned by friendly staff. Excellent value for money and a favourite with Bali's expats. The resort's rustic restaurant serves wholesome food and hearty breakfasts. Swimming pool. 16 rooms. **$**

Ida Beach Village
Candidasa
Tel: 0363-41118

www.idabeachvillage.com
Set in a garden with a beach side pool, accommodation ranges from simple cottages to rice barn bungalows with bedroom and balcony upstairs, and air conditioning or fan. Its 17 cottages are each named after a local village. **$**

Hotel Rama Candidasa
Candidasa
Tel: 0363-41974
www.ramacandidasahotel.com
Bungalows here have hot water, air conditioning and satellite television. All are set near the artificial white sand beach away from the main road, with a swimming pool and restaurant. Good range of activities including cookery lessons and snorkelling. 70 rooms. **$$**

Watergarden
Jalan Raya Candidasa
Tel: 0363-41540
www.watergardenhotel.com
The name of this delightful hotel says it all. The bungalows are scattered among lush gardens and ponds full of flora and fish. A favourite weekend retreat for many Bali

residents. The management (English) is very hands-on and the restaurant is excellent with a variety of vegetarian dishes and some Thai options. 12 rooms. **$$**

AMED

The district referred to as Amed, located in the shadow of Gunung Agung, is actually a group of about 10 small fishing villages south of Amed towards Seraya. Beaches are either black sand or pebbly.

Anda Amed Resort
Bunutan
Tel: 0363-23498
www.andaamedresort.com
Comfortable bungalows are fully equipped and tastefully furnished and there's an attractive swimming pool and restaurant. On the mountain side with great ocean views. 4 bungalows. **$$**

Good Karma Bungalows
Selang
Mobile tel: 081-2368 9090
Simple beach side thatched one- and two-bed bamboo bungalows shaded by banyan trees. Owned by a colourful character. Baba, who sings to his guests and promotes ecological awareness. 17 rooms. **$**

Life in Amed Resort
Lean
Tel: 081-3385 0155
www.lifebali.com
English-owned resort on the beach in the small fishing village of Lean, with landscaped gardens winding between the cottages and swimming pool. The rooms are up-market for this area and

have every facility. 8 rooms. **$$**

Puri Wirata
Bunutan
Tel: 0363-23523
www.diveamed.com
Pleasant Dutch-managed bungalows, sited at the edge of the ocean among palm trees. Rooms are excellent for this price range and have all the requisite amenities. Dive trips available and there's a good in-house restaurant. 30 rooms. **$**

Santai
Bunutan
Tel: 0363-23487
www.santaibali.com
One of the original boutique properties in this area comprising classic Balinese-style bungalows with main bedroom and extra bed in loft area. Swimming pool and fine restaurant. 10 rooms. **$$**

TULAMBEN

Tauch Terminal
Tulamben
Tel: 0363-22911
www.tauch-terminal.com
Pleasant seaside location at popular site for scuba diving. Modern rooms, most of which have balconies with ocean views. Restaurant serves local, international and German food. **$$**

PRICE CATEGORIES

Price for a double room (subject to a 10–21 percent tax and service charge):

$$$$ = over US$200
$$$ = US$120–200
$$ = US$60–120
$ = below US$60

NORTH BALI

LOVINA

Most hotels in the Lovina area have a stretch of black-sand beach. There is no surf as the beach is protected by the distant reef, so it is very safe for young children. Dolphin-watching is one of the main activities in Lovina.

Adirama
Jalan Raya Lovina
Tel: 0362-41759
www.adiramabeachhotel.com
This old beach front hotel has been completely renovated with attractive new furnishings and new bathrooms. Each room has a private balcony overlooking the swimming pool. Small spa and an attractive seafront restaurant on site. 16 standard rooms, 2 family rooms and 2 suites. $

Bali Paradise Hotel
Jalan Kartika, Kalibukbuk
Tel: 0362-41432
www.baliparadisehotel.com
New hotel hidden in the rice fields halfway between the main road and the sea. Excellent value for money. The expansive rooms all have great views and en suite bathrooms with walk-in showers and bathtubs. There's also a nice restaurant, bar and small spa. 8 rooms. $$

Damai Lovina Villas
Kayu Putih
Tel: 0362-41008
www.damai.com
Danish-owned luxury resort and spa perched high up on the mountain side and overlooking Lovina, the ocean and Java beyond. Immaculate bungalows are furnished and fitted with every necessity in either superior or deluxe categories. There's an attractive swimming pool as well as a poolside café and bar. Upstairs is a gourmet restaurant acclaimed for its food. 8 bungalows and 6 pool villas. $$$$

Puri Bagus Lovina
Lovina
Tel: 0362-21430
www.puribagus.net
A comfortable hotel right on the beach with spacious villas (either garden, sea or rice field views) featuring large marble bathrooms and outdoor showers. Good spa, Sarasawati restaurant and the Seafood Gazebo grill on site, plus large free-form swimming pool. The reception desk can book you on a variety of tours to north Bali. 40 villas. $$$

Villa Agung
Tukad Mungga
Tel: 0362-41527
www.agungvilla.com
The English-American owners live next door and run this efficient little place, whose charming budget-priced rooms are right on the beach. Pleasant restaurant with upstairs bar and lounge – the perfect viewing place to watch the dolphins at play. Some rooms with air conditioning, others have ceiling fan. 7 rooms. $

BEDUGUL AREA

Set within the crater of an extinct volcano, this small market town lies along the shores of the picturesque lake of Danau Bratan. There is also a spectacular golf course located in this area, while the neighbouring Danau Buyan and Danau Tamblingan lakes provide a flavour of rural Bali. Because of the altitude, the weather is refreshingly cool.

Bali Handara Kosaido Golf & Country Club
Tel: 0362-22646
www.balihandarakosaido.com
You don't have to play golf to stay here, but it is very convenient if you are a golfer. The championship course is a masterpiece of natural splendour with a dramatic backdrop. All the rooms look over the lush green fairways to the lakes, mountains and forest beyond, and are great value for this price. Hotel rooms, bungalows and villas. 77 rooms. $$

Pacung Indah
Tel: 0368-21020
Charming bungalow-style accommodation across the road from the Pacung Mountain Resort. The views are less impressive, but then again it is commensurately cheaper. Lovely on-site restaurant with very good food. 6 rooms. $

Pacung Mountain Resort
Jalan Raya Baturiti

Tel: 0368-21038
email: balipacung@telkom.net
Located in the Tabanan regency but easily accessed from the Bedugul area. Standard and deluxe rooms all have views of the stunning rice-terraced valley; the bungalows set at the bottom of the hill and reached by a funicular are more spacious and overlook the gardens and rice terraces. Swimming pool and restaurant. 39 rooms. $$

MUNDUK

Puri Lumbung Cottages
Munduk
Tel: 0362-92810
www.purilumbung.com
Idyllic mountain resort set in the beautiful countryside of Munduk, with its vanilla and clove plantations. The upper levels of the charming two-storey cottages, perched on stilts, have spectacular views of the area. Warung Kopi restaurant serves up delicious meals (and spectacular views of Mount Batukaru) and the hotel organises many excursions for its guests. Enjoy a body massage at the Arathi spa. 16 rooms. $$

PEMUTERAN

Idyllic beach area, away from the crowds and with a small number of boutique hotels. The beaches are a mixture of grey sand and pebbles but the good snorkelling offshore makes up for it. Plus Pulau Menjangan is a short boat ride away.

Matahari Beach Resort
Pemuteran
Tel: 0362-92312
www.matahari-beach-resort.com
Located near Pulau Menjangan, to which diving excursions can be arranged, this French-managed beach side resort has bungalows extending right up to the mountain behind. Two restaurants serving European and Indonesian food. 32 rooms. **$$$$**

Pondok Sari
Pemuteran
Tel: 0362-94738, 92337
www.pondoksari.com
With a quiet beach front location next door to Taman Sari Cottages (see opposite), this offers the same fine snorkelling just off its beach. All the lovely bungalows have two rooms, each with private terrace. Small pool, spa and good restaurant. Can organise a variety of excursions. 22 rooms. **$$**

Puri Ganesha Villas
Pemuteran
Tel: 0362-94766
www.puriganeshabali.com
Luxurious 2-bedroom villas with open-plan liv-

ing areas, antique furnishings, garden bathrooms, indoor and outdoor dining areas, kitchens, and private saltwater swimming pools. Ocean-facing verandahs have day beds to lounge on. Two staff are assigned to each villa and gourmet meals are served in Warung Sehat restaurant. Look for the adorable dalmatians which belong to the English owner of this resort. 4 villas. **$$$$**

Taman Sari Cottages
Pemuteran
Tel: 0362-93264
www.balitamansari.com
Charming small hotel facing a nice beach whose cottages and more expensive suites have lovely Balinese accents and indigenous furnishings. There is fine snorkelling just in front of the hotel, thanks to the hotel's eco-friendly conservation efforts, and dive trips to nearby Pulau Menjangan are also organised. Swimming pool and spa plus a great restaurant that serves international, Western and Thai dishes. 21 rooms and 8 suites. **$$**

Taman Selini Beach Bungalows
Pemuteran
Tel: 0362-94746
www.tamanselini.com
A great little beach front property, with clusters of coral reefs only 200 metres/yds from the hotel. On-site diving facilities and great-value rooms. The restaurant, which serves some Greek dishes – the

owner is a Sumatran lady married to a Greek – is popular with both local expats and in-house guests. 10 rooms. **$$**

NEAR MENJANGAN

There is no accommodation on Pulau Menjangan itself but there are several high-priced hotels on the northwestern tip of Bali that provide easy access to both the island and the West Bali National Park. Pulau Menjangan is also easily accessible from Pemuteran, where the hotels are cheaper and offer better value.

The Menjangan
Desa Pejarakan, Gerokgak
Tel: 0362-94700
www.themenjangan.com
Overlooking the serene Bajul Bay, Pulau Menjangan and the craggy folds of West Bali National Park's north facing ridges, this peaceful retreat is located within the boundaries of the national park, offering guests the chance to get close to nature and relax in exquisite surroundings. Activities include bird-watching and horse-riding. 12 rooms, 2 suites, 7 beach villas. **$$$**

Shorea Beach Resort
Telok Terima
Tel: 0362-94666
www.shoreabeachresort.com
Located on the doorstep of West Bali National Park and across from Pulau Men-

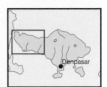

jangan, this isolated hotel in Teluk Terima bay can only be reached by a short boat ride from the hotel reception near Labuhan Lalang. Activities include diving, trekking and nature tours. **$$$**

MEDEWI

There is scant accommodation along the lonely western coast after the Pulau Menjangan area. Negara, the district capital, has little of interest. If you have to make a stop here, do so at Medewi beach where there are a few decent hotels.

Medewi Beach Cottages
Medewi
Tel: 0305-40029
Situated on a black sand surfing beach which is unfortunately fenced off except at the main entrance. Low key rooms clustered around a small pool. 20 rooms. **$$**

PRICE CATEGORIES

Price for a double room (subject to a 10–21 percent tax and service charge):

$$$$ = over US$200
$$$ = US$120–200
$$ = US$60–120
$ = below US$60

TABANAN REGION

TABANAN COAST

This area is relatively sparse for good accommodation. Most of Tabanan's attractions are undertaken as day trips from Ubud or Kuta.

Gajah Mina Beach Resort
Suraberata, Lalanglinggah, Selemadeg, Tabanan
Tel: 08123 882 438/08123 811 630
www.gajahminaresort.com
Charming Balinese-style villas, a superb restaurant serving fresh produce from the garden, and a swimming pool resting upon a headland above a beautiful black-sand cove. An ideal choice for those looking to escape from the main tourist areas. 11 suites and villas. **$$$**

Pan Pacific Nirwana Bali Resort
Jalan Raya Tanah Lot
Tel: 0361-815900
www.panpacific.com/Bali
This hotel, together with the accompanying Greg Norman-designed 18-hole golf course, was built to blend into the surrounding hills – you don't even see the low-rise building until you're actually standing at the

PRICE CATEGORIES

Price for a double room (subject to a 10–21 percent tax and service charge):

$$$$ = over US$200
$$$ = US$120–200
$$ = US$60–120
$ = below US$60

entrance. From the Pool Café and some of the rooms an unobstructed view stretches across the water to the sacred island temple of Tanah Lot. While golf and the temple are the two major attractions, many other activities are available. 278 rooms. **$$$**

BELIMBING AND SANDA

Northwest of Tabanan town in the foothills of Gunung Batukau are the pretty villages of Belimbing and Sanda. Spectacular rice terraces as far as the eye can see, punctuated by the odd coffee plantation.

Cempaka Belimbing Villas
Belimbing
Tel: 0361-7451178
www.cempakabelimbing.com
Located south of Sanda in the scenic area of Belimbing. The bungalows here are set in rice fields; some have views of the stunning rice terraces while others face the valley or the gardens and pool. It's a delight to sit on the spacious verandah and just chill. Restaurant, large swimming pool and a tour desk that organises excursions in the local area. 14 villas. **$$**

Sanda Butik Villas
Sanda
Mobile tel: 081-33851 8836
www.sandavillas.com
The slightly cooler temperatures and mountainside location make this a perfect escape from

the south. Built on a former coffee plantation, the bungalow-style rooms are furnished with modern amenities and there's a large swimming pool plus good restaurant with lovely views of the mountain and rice terraces. Tours, including one to the Blehmantung waterfall, can be organised. **$$**

KRAMBITAN

Puri Anyar Krambitan
Krambitan
Tel: 0361-812668
Southwest of Tabanan town is Krambitan. Puri Anyar (New Palace), where Tabanan royalty still live today, has simple guest rooms that recall a past grandeur – worth dropping by for a visit even if you're not staying. **$**

MARGA

Puri Taman Sari
Desa Umabian, Marga
Tel: 0361-28141
www.balitamansari.com
Located in Umabian village in Marga, this is the private residence of a relative of the Mengwi royal family. Within its grounds stands an annexe open to guests, providing an opportunity to experience life in an authentic Balinese village. There are only 14 rooms, and activities like village tours, trekking and cultural performances can be arranged for guests. A stay here

promises to be a truly unique experience. **$**

GUNUNG BATUKAU

Directly north of Tabanan is Gunung Batukau, the second highest mountain in Bali. On the mountain's eastern flank are the spectacular rice terraces of Jatiluwih.

Prana Dewi
Gunung Batukau
Tel: 0361-736654
www.baliprana resort.com
Found at the base of Gunung Batukau at Wongagede village and not far from Jatiluwih, this isolated resort is a welcome relief from the tourist hordes, and with tastefully furnished bungalows. Even if you don't stay here have lunch at the restaurant, which uses vegetables grown organically on site. **$**

Sarinbuana Eco-Lodge
Gunung Batukau
Tel: 0828-970 06079
www.baliecolodge.com
In a forest near Gunung Batukau, this is truly a nature lover's paradise. Cosy wooden bungalows offer views extending all the way to the south and the simple restaurant does healthy home-cooked food. Offers treks, workshops and retreats. 5 Bungalows. **$**

Activities: Bali

THE ARTS, NIGHTLIFE, SHOPPING, SPORT, SPAS, COOKERY SCHOOLS, CHILDREN'S ACTIVITIES AND TOURS

THE ARTS

Many people come to Bali to experience its rich arts and culture – ceremonies abound all over the island. You can pick up a schedule of events from the Denpasar Tourism Office or the Bina Wisata Ubud Tourist Office in Ubud *(see page 277)*. Many travel agencies also have information on rituals and ceremonies open to the public. Be wary of tour companies selling "tickets" to cremations and other rites – you are welcome at cremations, but other rites (baby ceremonies, weddings and tooth-filings) are by invitation only. At any of these events, you should dress and behave with decorum.

Performing Arts

The best way to see Balinese dance, drama and *wayang kulit* (shadow puppetry) performances is to attend an *odalan* (temple festival). There is one going on somewhere on the island almost every day. Public performances at various locations are mainly for tourists, but that doesn't mean they are inferior to genuine temple performances. Some of Bali's best

dancers and musicians regularly participate in tourist performances as it's a source of additional income. The shows last no longer than 90 minutes; photography is allowed, but flashes can be distracting.

Many of the large hotels in Sanur, Kuta and Nusa Dua have regular evening dinner shows, so call for information. It's also possible to "order" an entire performance. With a minimum of 10 people, guests will be met at a village with a torch-lit procession, feast on local food, and be entertained by dancers and musicians.

Denpasar's arts school STSI *(see page 102)* has student recitals that are open to visitors.

Hotel Dinner Shows

Listed here are some of the regular cultural performances held at hotels. These expensive affairs include dinner, either a buffet or a barbecue, with prices ranging from Rp 300,000 to Rp 600,000. **Oberoi Bali, Amphitheatre** (tel: 0361-730361). Performances of *Legong* and *Ramayana* (with buffet dinner) take place twice a week (usually on Thu and Sat) at 6.30pm. Call ahead to confirm. **Conrad, Suku Restaurant** (tel: 0361-778788). Fri 8.15pm, *Kecak* dance with Indonesian *rijsttafel*; Tue 8.15pm, *Gong*

dance (dinner from 7pm); Sun 8.15pm, *Jegog* dance. **Bali Intercontinental, Taman Gita Terrace** (tel: 0361-701888). Balinese buffet dinner and cultural show every Wed 6.30–11pm. Entertainment with Balinese procession and traditional dances. **Nusa Dua Beach Hotel, Budaya Cultural Theatre** (tel: 0361-771210). Tue 7pm, *Ramayana;* Sun 7pm, *Kecak* dance (both with buffet dinner).

Public Shows

Listed here are regular performances at various villages. The venues are simple, unlike hotels, but the performances are authentic and just as riveting. Admission fee is Rp 50,000 and includes only the cost of the show. **Barong Dance** – Sidan, Gianyar, daily 9pm. **Barong and Kris Dance** – Batubulan, daily 9.30am and 10.30am. Puri Saren, Ubud, Fri 6.30pm. Catur Eka Budi, Kesiman, Denpasar, daily 9.30am. **Calon Arang Dance** – Mawang, Ubud, Thu and Sat 7.30pm. **Children's Barong Dance** – Museum Puri Lukisan, Raya Ubud, Ubud, Jalan. 10.30am Sun. **Classical Mask and Legong Dance** – Br. Kalah, Peliatan, Ubud, Tue 7.30pm.

Gabor Dance – Puri Saren, Ubud, Thur 7.30pm.
Kecak Dance – Padang Tegal, Ubud, Sun 7pm. Puri Agung, Peliatan, Thu 7.30pm. Catur Eka Budi, daily 6.30pm. Werdi Budaya daily 6.30pm.
Kecak and Fire Dance – Bona Village, Sun, Mon, Wed and Fri 7pm. Batubulan Village, daily 6.30pm.
Legong Dance – Puri Saren, Ubud, Mon and Sat 7.30pm. Peliatan Village, Fri 7.30pm. Pura Dalem, Ubud, Sat 7.30pm.
Legong and Barong Dance – Br. Tengah, Peliatan, Wed 7.30pm.
Mahabarata Dance – Teges Village, Ubud, Thur 7.30pm.
Raja Pala Dance – Puri Saren, Ubud, Sun 7.30pm.
Ramayana Ballet – Pura Dalem, Ubud, Mon 8pm. Puri Saren, Ubud, Tue 8pm.
Sang Hyang Jaran – Benoa Village, Sun, Mon, Wed 7pm. Batubulan, daily 6.30pm.
Shadow Puppet Show (Wayang Kulit) – Oka Kartini's, Ubud, Sun and Wed 8pm.
Sunda Apasunda – Puri Saren, Ubud, Wed 7.30pm.
Topeng Dance – Br. Klalah, Peliatan, Tue 7.30pm.
Women's Gamelan with Childs Dancers – Peliatan Village, Sun 7.30pm.

NIGHTLIFE

There is no shortage of nightclubs, discos and bars with live music in South Bali's tourist hubs. **Kuta** tends to start throbbing earlier than Seminyak and closes at around 3 or 4am. The dance bars in **Seminyak** start getting busy at around 11pm; there are some clubs here where you can party until sunrise, but they don't start pumping until about 2am.

The bars in **Sanur** and **Ubud** close around midnight as do the ones in **Nusa Dua** and **Tanjung Benoa**, which are mostly found in the hotels.

Note: many of the nightspots

listed here function as a one-stop entertainment venue, with restaurant, café, bar and disco club all rolled into one.

Tuban, Kuta and Legian

Most of the nightlife in this area is centred on Jalan Legian and Jalan Pantai Kuta (the beach road).
Apache Reggae Bar
Jalan Legian 146
Tel: 0361-761213
The epitome of what every reggae club should be. Rasta motifs and dreadlocks abound, and pictures of the late Bob Marley and other famous reggae artists adorn the walls. Hosts live reggae music every night from 11pm. Popular with both Australian and Japanese tourists and locals. Food also served here.
Centerstage
Hard Rock Hotel
Jalan Pantai Kuta
Tel: 0361-761869
Hi-tech venue dominated by an enormous video screen and plenty of rock memorabilia. Live music and entertainment every night from 8.30pm until 11.30pm with slick local bands singing popular covers. Hosts parties, fashion shows and bar dancers; special guests include occasional big names. No cover charge but expect to pay up-market hotel prices for your drinks.
M-Bar-Go
Jalan Legian
Tel: 0361-756280
Gargantuan nightclub spread over two floors with an urban-chic industrial theme, minimal lighting and an underground vibe. Resident and guest DJs play booming house music. Attracts a mixed crowd of surfers, tourists and locals.
Pyramid
Jalan Dewi Sri 33
tel 0361-8500 300
www.pyramidclubbali.com
This strategically located pharoah-themed club comprises a lounge area where food can be ordered, a dance floor with a very extensive bar as well as a second

floor with a more relaxed environment, which can also be used for private parties. During the week it doubles as a casual dining venue serving a diverse selection of foods.
Sky Garden Lounge
Jalan Legian, Kuta
Tel: 0361-755423
One of the most pumping venues in Kuta and a hotspot for sophisticated cocktails. This multi-levelled restaurant and open-air rooftop lounge towers above the street. Chill out on comfy sofas and listen to some cool sounds.

Seminyak/Kerobokan

Late night entertainment here appeals to a more sophisticated but no less boisterous clientele. The most concentrated area of nightspots in Seminyak is Jalan Dhyana Pura, in addition to the beach front stretch of Jalan Double Six and a few scattered venues on Jalan Raya Seminyak.
Cocoon Beach Club
Jalan Double Six
Tel: 0361 731266
www.cocoon-beach.com
Offering fine dining, poolside lounging, and a relaxed ambience during the daytime and evenings, this multi-dimensional venue transforms into a sophisticated bar/lounge at night presenting good music and cocktails, enjoyed by a fashionably savvy crowd.
Maria Magdalena
Jalan Abimanyu (Dhyana Pura) 6, Seminyak
Tel: 0361-731622
Alfresco terrace bar and dance club on two levels with pool tables. Great entertainment with midnight extravaganza sexy show and excellent DJ music. Very popular venue on Friday and Saturday nights, doesn't get busy until after 11pm.
Mint
Jalan Raya Petitenget 919, Seminyak
Tel: 0361 4732 884
Chic dance club serving food and, cocktails. Features a club lounge,

a 25-metre central bar, and a booth with a bar-stage structure from which DJs play electronic house and pop energy sounds while punters get into the groove until late into the night.

Mozaic Beachclub
Jalan Pantai Batu Belig, Kerobokan
Tel: 0361-473 5796
www.mozaic-beachclub.com
With a pool, large deck, poolside bar and lounge, Mozaic Beachclub is perfectly located to enjoy stunning sunsets beside Batu Belig Beach. All-day poolside tapas, lunch and hearty afternoon delights are served in lounging areas. Day and night time mixologists' signature concoctions are perfectly paired with the surroundings and DJ music. Open daily until 1am, also hosts occasional dance parties and live music events.

Ku De Ta
Jalan Laksmana
Tel: 0361-736969
www.kudeta.net
Bali's most famous, sleekest and trendiest fine-dining restaurant, bar and nightlife venue right on Seminyak beach. Hosts dance parties, fashion shows and internationally renowned DJs. Wide choice of seating, both indoor and by the beach. Attracts a sophisticated and beautiful crowd.

Townhouse
Jalan Ayu Kaya 151
www.thetownhousebali.com
Covering five floors, this supersleek entertainment venue is part organic juice bar, part photo gallery, bistro, lounge and rooftop bar all rolled into one. A rotating roster of international DJs get the crowds up and moving at the lounge and nightclub on the third and fourth floors.

Charlie
Jalan Petitenget, 5
Tel: 0821-474 17332
www.charliebali.com
A hedonistic mansion where friends gather over a good meal, drop by for a cocktail or end up partying like rock stars. The ground floor is a bistro, while upstairs is a spacious bar lounge where it all happens at night, often to the accompaniment of excellent live acts and DJs.

Potato Head
Jalan Petitenget, Seminyak
Tel: 0361-737979
www.ptthead.com
This beach club is the place to see and be seen. It has access onto the sand, several restaurants a large swimming pool and utterly zany decor. Musical events are frequently held here too.

Sanur

A little bit more happening than Nusa Dua (where the nightlife is mainly confined to hotel bars), the after-dark scene in Sanur is relaxed and mellow with a few low-key dance clubs that attract a more mature crowd.

Jazz Bar and Grill
Komplek Sanur Raya
Jalan Bypass Ngurah Rai
Tel: 0361-285892
Regular live entertainment by well respected jazz bands from Bali and beyond. Warm atmosphere with plenty of cosy alcoves on two levels. Also has a restaurant dishing up a whole range of food, from sandwiches and pizzas to full meals.

Ubud

Ubud offers nightly Balinese dance shows that usually finish by 9pm. Most venues close before midnight.

Café Havana
Jalan Dewi Sri
Tel: 0361-972973
www.cafehavanabali.com
This is the place to come for salsa dancing in Ubud. There's music most nights, and salsa always on Saturdays (free classes from 5–6pm).

Jazz Café
Jalan Sukma
Tel: 0361-976594
www.jazzcafebali.com
Opened in 1996 by Balinese jazz musician Agung Wiryawan, this venue is popular with locals, expats and tourists. Friendly atmosphere, superb food, innovative cocktails and good live music performed by outstanding local musicians. Acoustic jazz and ethnic rhythm Tue–Fri nights, with some blues on Sat.

Napi Orti
Jalan Monkey Forest
Tel: 0361 970982
This is a good place to catch live music most nights of the week, as well as European football matches or arthouse movies on a big screen. Here, elegant Frenchstyle Regency furnishings mingle with garish neon signs, vintage movie posters and surrealist graffiti art. Offers an excellent menu of Western and Asian dishes including Thai food and pizzas. Open until late.

Gay Venues

The best-known gay bars in the Kuta/Seminyak area are on Jalan Abimanyu (Dhyana Pura). Outside of this area, there aren't many meeting places for gay people.

Bali Joe
Jalan Dhyana Pura No. 8,
Jalan Abimanyu, Seminyak
Tel: 0361-730931/0819 9910 0445
Gay-owned bar with comfortable sofas and lounge complemented by Eurasian Art Deco and old black and white celebrity photographs on the walls. Cute and friendly waiters, hot bartenders and upbeat jazzy music. The crowd includes local and Jakartan celebrities and models. Dancers on the bar and drag queen shows nightly.

Facebar
Jalan Dhyana Pura No.9,
Jalan Abimanyu, Seminyak
Tel: 081-79 70-1883
Facebar is a fun, lively place to hang out and drink cocktails. Entertainment includes male fashion shows, pole dancing and talent competitions.

Mixwell
Jalan Dhyana Pura No. 6,
Jalan Abimanyu, Seminyak
Tel: 0361-736864

Small lounge bar with open-air terrace. Resident DJ spins lounge music nightly and there are regular drag shows with lip-synching divas. This bar gets going around 9pm, which is considerably earlier than the other other bars in the street.

SHOPPING

Bali is a shopper's paradise; rare is the visitor who comes away without at least one bag of souvenirs. Thousands of artisans, craftspeople, tailors and painters are kept busy supplying the tourist demand. The variety is virtually endless and knowing where to shop and what to buy is probably the hardest part of all.

You could shop at one of Kuta's modern air-conditioned malls but more adventurous shoppers should seek out the stone-and woodcarving villages in the hinterland, browse the art galleries of Ubud and the silver workshops of Celuk, or visit Denpasar's colourful market, where fruit, vegetables, spices, baskets and handicrafts line its narrow alleyways.

Try and keep a sense of humour when vendors crowd around you at the beaches and tourist spots – offering everything from sarongs and pineapples to Rolex watches and silver toerings. A polite but firm "no" and a smile is the best way to handle the situation if you're not keen. Many shopkeepers have developed a hard-sell sales pitch and in Kuta they can be quite aggressive.

Antiques

As it's illegal to take items over 50 years old out of Indonesia, it is unlikely that you will find any really old antique pieces. Be careful, as many "new antiques" are actually reproductions, intentionally weathered and ravaged to look like the genuine things.

Antique shops in Klungkung sell old Chinese porcelains, Kamasan *wayang* puppet paintings, and antique jewellery and textiles. Singaraja has some of the best antique shops on the main streets of the city.

Arts of Asia
Jalan Thamrin, Block C 27–37, Denpasar
Tel: 0361-233350
Amazing gallery and shop with a huge collection of antiques, paintings, and ritual and folk artefacts from all over Asia. It represents the travels of owner, Verra Darwiko, and stocks old Javanese gold jewellery, Balinese ritual art including old *geringsing* weavings from Tenganan, Chinese blue and white ceramics, ritual masks, *wayang kulit* puppets, Samurai armour, Buddhist ritual objects, and some priceless *keris* with jewel-studded golden handles.

Hananto Lloyd
Jalan Raya Sayan, Ubud
Tel: 0361-7420748
An enchanting little treasure trove featuring antiques from Central Java and Sumatra. Features contemporary artefacts as well as stylish reproductions.

Mega Art Shop
Gajah Mada 36–38, Denpasar
Tel: 0361-224592
Comprehensive souvenir shop of Balinese handicrafts, and quality arts and crafts. Branches in Denpasar, Kuta, Bali Hyatt (Sanur) and Ayodya Resort (Nusa Dua).

Ceramics

Fragile terracotta ritual wares sold in most markets are made in Bedulu (Gianyar). Humorous figures and celadon-glazed porcelains come from Pejaten (Tabanan).

Jenggala
Jalan Uluwatu II, Jimbaran
Tel: 0361-703310
www.jenggala-bali.com
Internationally acclaimed (and pricey) range of ceramics and household accessories. Unique hand-finished pieces along with a full range of tableware, glassware and hand-crafted cutlery. Visit the ceramics gallery with exhibitions of work by local and international artists, relax in the café, or attend the hands-on sessions. Jenggala items also available at **Sari Bumi**, Jalan Danau Tamblingan 152, Sanur, tel: 0361-289363.

Children's Clothing

Indigo Kids
Jalan Pantai Kuta
Tel: 0361-755265
www.indigokidsglobal.com
Stylish and affordable export quality children's wear for boys and girls from babies up to 12 years of age.
Kiki's Closet
Jalan Raya Seminyak 57
Tel: 0361-7464892
Gorgeous collections of clothing for boys and girls aged 2–12. Presents a wide range of bold colours and prints. The styles are trendy, bright and bohemian.
Kuta Kidz
Jalan Pantai Kuta
Tel: 0361-755810
www.kutakidz88.com
Trendy and colourful clothing for babies and kids of all ages. High quality at affordable prices.

Adult Fashion

Body & Soul
Jalan Raya Seminyak
Tel: 0361-733011
www.bodyandsoulclothing.com
With numerous outlets in Bali, it offers high quality fashion for women, and children, and a constantly evolving stock that keeps up with trends. Key outlets at Jalan Legian, Jalan Raya Seminyak, Kuta Square and Bali Connection (Nusa Dua).
By The Sea
Jalan Legian 186, Kuta
Tel: 0361-757775; and Jalan Laksmana, Seminyak
Tel: 0361-732198
www.bytheseatropical.com
Aimed at families, with a striking collection of cool, loose-fitting and summery resort-wear for women, men and children, all in cotton.

Dinda Rella
Jalan Laksmana 45
Tel: 0361-736953; and
Jalan Raya Seminyak 44
Tel: 0361-734228
Chic cocktail dresses, flowing
frocks and glamorous gowns
fashioned in richly coloured satin
and crinkle silk, and finished with
decorative applications, including
Swarovski crystals, stones, dia-
mante jewels, beads, sequins
and embroidery.

Niluh Djelantik
Jalan Raya Kerobokan 144
Tel: 0361-733074
High-quality, handmade high-
heeled shoes, boots, sandals,
bags and belts designed by Indonesian home-grown talent Nilou.
Expensive but beautifully crafted
and made to last.

Paul Ropp
Kuta Galeria, tel: 0361-769359;
Sayan, Ubud, tel: 0361-974655;
Jalan Raya Seminyak, tel: 0361-
734208; and Jalan Penguben-
gan, Kerobokan, tel:
0361-730023
www.paulropp.com
Exotic silks and handwoven fabrics from India where they are
dyed and enhanced with intricate
embroidery and beading before
being shipped to Bali to be cut
and stitched into beautiful garments. Also has accessories like
bead-encrusted handbags,
leather belts and slippers.

Uluwatu
Jalan Danau Tamblingan, Sanur,
tel: 0361-755342; Jalan Pantai
Kuta, tel: 0361-755542; and
Jalan Monkey Forest, Ubud,
tel: 0361-977557
www.uluwatu.co.id
Famous for its handmade lace
resort-wear and nightwear for
women, and bed and table linens.

Surf Stores

Bali's surfwear stores stock
everything that you could possibly
want connected with surfing and
the lifestyle it encompasses. Most
of the following stores retail equipment, surfwear and eyewear by all
the usual big name brands.

BARGAINING TIPS

Bartering is essential and can
prove highly entertaining with
a lot of theatrical gestures, and
so-called "morning prices" and
"raining prices".
   In shops without "Fixed
Price" signs, bargaining is necessary. Start at one-third of the
asking price, and the vendor
will gradually lower the price as
you raise your offer. Stop at the
amount you really want to
spend – as a guide, half to
two-thirds of the original asking price would be fair. If the
seller refuses, just walk away;
you'll probably be called back
to close the deal at your last
bid. If accompanied by a guide
or driver, prices automatically
go up 30 percent to include his
commission.
   Most shops are open daily
from 9am to 9pm, but morning
hours are best for bargaining;
vendors believe that clinching
a deal in the morning will bring
them luck the rest of the day.

Bali Barrel: Jalan Legian, Kuta,
tel: 0361-767238/767240.
Jungle Surf: Jalan Legian Kuta,
tel: 0361-756644; Jalan Pantai
Kuta, tel: 0361-763581/755673.
Quiksilver: Jalan Legian, Kuta,
tel: 0361-752693.
Surfer Girl: Jalan Legian, Kuta,
tel: 0361-752693.
Genuine surfwear from well-
known brands together with
beach-, street- and leisure-wear
aimed at a young female clientele.
Ripcurl: Jalan Legian, Kuta,
tel: 0361-765889; also at Kuta
Square, Jalan Melasti.

Gold and Silver

Gold jewellery (22- and 24-carat)
is sold in shops along Jalan Hasa-
nudin in Denpasar and in major
town markets. As is the case
throughout Indonesia, gold jewellery is sold by weight.
   Silver jewellery is made in
Celuk (Gianyar), where numerous

shops line the roads. Here, silver
rings, bangles, necklaces, bracelets, pendants and accessories
are produced by master craftsmen whose skills and trade
secrets have been passed down
through generations of families.
Balinese work is nearly always
handmade and rarely produced
by casting. The jewellery is also
set with precious and semi-
precious gemstones. Styles are
distinctive, often highly ornate
with fine filigree work. The silver
workshops of Celuk are always
willing to fulfil special orders and
will work to any design. Despite
so-called "fixed prices", bargaining is essential.

Ketut Suardhana Silver
Jalan Raya Celuk, Sukawati
Tel: 0361-298241/298648
Traditional silversmith with a good
collection; pieces can be made to
order.

Mario Silver
Jalan Raya Seminyak 19, Legian
Tel: 0361-730977
www.mariosilverbali.com
Long-established retail and
wholesale store with a fine reputation for consistently good quality silver jewellery.

Prapen Gallery
Jalan Jagaraga, Celuk
Tel: 0361-291333
Visitors to Prapen Gallery can tour
the workshop where they will see
traditional Balinese silversmiths
at work. Also on site is a boutique
with a stunning collection of silver
jewellery for sale.

Suarti Collection
Jalan Raya Celuk, Sukawati
Tel: 0361-298914; and
Jalan Bypass Sanur
Tel: 0361-288739
www.suarti.com
Suarti's stunning designs marry
Western cutting-edge fashion and
contemporary design with Bal-
inese influences.

Suwo
Jalan Raya Legian, Legian
Tel: 0361-762330
Suwo's glamorous jewellery is
quite different from the usual Bali
style. Fashioned mainly in silver,
but occasionally embellished with

TRANSPORT
ACCOMMODATION
ACTIVITIES
A – Z
LANGUAGE

BEST SHOPPING MALLS

You probably don't want to be stuck in a shopping mall in Bali but if you insist, here are two of the best.

Architecturally inspired by the gentle contours of the rice terraces, the eco-friendly design of the open-air beach-side mall, **Beachwalk** at Kuta is characterised by traditional thatched roofs. Here, visitors are presented with a wide choice of sophisticated retail stores and eateries as well as the digital-format **Cinema XXI** with three studios.

Discovery Mall, located beside the beach in Tuban, is home to the **Centro** and **Sogo** department stores, together with branches of local and international fashion boutiques, shoe shops, jewellery outlets and interior and homeware stores. Restaurants and cafés include Starbucks, Black Canyon and Bali Colada.

gold and studded with uniquely cut gemstones.

Handicrafts

Many villages specialise in a single craft item. For instance, cattle bone and coconut shell carvings are made in Tampaksiring; and baskets are made in Pengosekan, south of Ubud. Coiled baskets made of ata (liana) vines are a home industry in Tenganan (Karangasem). *Lontar* (illustrated palm-leaf books) are also made here, but better ones come from Sidemen. Plaited leaf baskets and bamboo furniture are the speciality of Bona (Gianyar).

One of the best places to find a large variety of crafts at low prices is the huge **Pasar Seni** (Art Market) in Sukawati, Gianyar, where hundreds of stalls are jam-packed into a two-storey building and adjacent side-streets. Note, however, that most of the goods are cheap mass-produced stuff (for

better quality goods see Home Accessories *below*). Specialist shops include:

Matra'i Crafts
Jalan Sriwijaya, Kuta
Tel: 0361-764854
Specialists in Balinese and Lombok handicrafts, all made from natural materials such as bamboo and banana leaves.

Sanggraha Karya Hasta
Jalan Raya Tohpati, Denpasar
Tel: 0361-461942
Government-sponsored cooperative with a good collection of Indonesian and Balinese crafts.

Furniture and Home Accessories

Carlo Showroom
Jalan Danau Poso 22, Sanur
Tel: 0361-285211
www.carloshowroom.com
Natural and exotic materials, such as coconut shell, mother of pearl, woodskin, terrazzo and pebbles are combined in the creation of exquisite dining tables and chairs, beds, loungers, cabinets, trays, ice-buckets, picture frames, fruit bowls, dining placements, table lamps and much more.

Cempaka
Jalan Bypass Ngurah Rai 8, Kuta
Tel: 0361-766555
www.cempaka.biz
A stunning collection of innovative furniture, soft furnishings, fabrics, and accessories. Also has a collection of modern artwork, timeless tableware, funky lamps and authentic antiques. This is the perfect one-stop shop for doing up your home.

Disini
Jalan Basangkasa 6–8, Seminyak
Tel: 0361-731037 763715
Home interior store offering eye-catching and elegant collections of bed linen, quilted bedcovers, cushions and table linen, with matching accessories such as lamps, vases and other artefacts.

Haveli
15 and 18 Jalan Basangkasa, Seminyak
Tel: 0361-737160

www.equinoxtrading.com
A magnet for people looking for soft furnishings (cushions, bedspreads, table linen and curtains), fabrics and artefacts to enhance their homes. Gorgeously rich fabrics include taffeta, silks, satins, Indian sari silk and French linens.

Lio Collection
Jalan Raya Kerobokan 2
Tel: 0361-7800942; and
Jalan Raya Kerobokan 51X
Tel: 0361-730044
www.liocollection.com
Eclectic collection of outdoor furniture, pots, urns and statues, in addition to home accessories, both traditional Indonesian and contemporary in design.

Sunbebek
Jalan Raya Kerobokan 118
Tel: 0361-730596
www.sunbebek.com
A unique collection of soft furnishings and accessories created from handwoven ikat cloth. Products include tablecloths, runners, place mats, napkins, coasters, cushion covers, quilted bedspreads, bed linen and curtains. Products can be made to order.

Musical Instruments

If it's gongs, metallophones or drums you are looking for, the gamelan foundries in Tihingan (Klungkung), Sawan (Buleleng), and Blahbatuh (Gianyar) churn out instruments by hand for gamelan clubs in Bali and all over the world.

Paintings

For traditional paintings, go to Kamasan (wayang puppet-style), Pengosekan (flowers and birds), Penestanan (Young Artists style), Batuan, Peliatan and Ubud (village life and mythology). Tip: visit major galleries or museums, see which artist you like, and then seek them out at their homes.

A number of galleries are covered in the Ubud chapter (see page 121). For Kamasan-style paintings, head out east to Kamasan village (see page 159).

Stone Carvings

Mythological and modern figures are made from *paras* (compressed clay and ash), but due to their weight, packing and shipping is expensive. Numerous workshops line the roads along Batubulan in Gianyar.

Puppets

Flat figures with moveable arms are made from perforated and painted cattle hide. Many families in Sukawati create these.

Textiles

For Balinese hand-loomed *ikat* cloth known as *endek*, there are a number of factories in Gianyar, Sidemen (Karangasem), Gelgel (Klungkung) and Singaraja (Buleleng). The famous *geringsing* or double *ikat* is made only in Tenganan *(see pages 71 and 164)*, where threads in both directions are dyed and then woven.

Songket, brocade cloth with gold and silver threads, is woven in Sidemen, Singaraja, Gelgel, Blayu (Tabanan) and Negara (Jembrana). *Kain prada* or silk-screened gold cloths for dance costumes, fans and hangings are produced in Sukawati. Fine crochet tablecloths and bedspreads are made in Tampaksiring (Gianyar). Batik, from simple *cap batik* (stamped) to the glorious *tulis* (hand-drawn) ones, is everywhere. Some of what is sold by vendors is not real batik but printed cloth.

Jalan Sulawesi is Denpasar's textile street, devoted to cloth of all descriptions. You'll be spoilt for choice, but try and shake off the commission hunters who offer to be your guide.

Popiler
Jalan Gajah Mada, Denpasar
Tel: 0361-422498
Specialist in high-quality traditional batik, made in Bali at the company's factory in Tohpati.

Threads of Life
Jalan Kajeng, Ubud

Tel: 0361-972187
www.threads of life.com
See page 129 for a description of this interesting shop.

Woodcarving

Mas, Peliatan, Kemenuh, Bedulu and Buruan are major woodcarving villages in Gianyar.

Baris Gallery: Jalan Raya Mas, Ubud, tel: 0361-973201.

Citra Artshop: Jalan Raya Peliatan, Gianyar, tel: 0361-975187.

Njana Tilem Gallery: Jalan Raya Mas, Ubud, tel: 0361-974510.

SPORT

Participant Sports

Diving

Nearly all the dive operators are based in the south, especially Sanur. Most will arrange transport and others,such as Habitat-H2O, are mobile and without a base, and will take their customers to whichever dive sites they wish to visit.

AquaMarineDiving: Jalan Raya Seminyak 2, tel: 0361-730107, mobile tel: 081-2365 8829; www.aquamarinediving.com.

Habitat-H2O: mobile tel: 081-2363 8529; www.dive-bali.de.

Scuba Duba Doo Dive Center Bali: Jalan Legian Kelod 367, Kuta, tel: 0361-750703, mobile tel: 818-353060; www.divecentrebali.com.

Tauch Terminal: Tulamben, tel: 0363-22911; www.tauch-terminal.com.

World Diving Lembongan: Pondok Baruna Guesthouse, Jungutbatu, Nusa Lembongan, mobile tel: 081-2390 0686; www.world-diving.com.

Golf

Bali Handara Kosaido Golf and Country Club
Pancasari, Bedugul
Tel: 0368-288944
www.balihandarakosaido.com

An 18-hole championship course designed by Peter Thompson. The only course in the world set inside a volcano, it has been voted one of the world's top 50 most beautiful courses.

Nirwana Bali Golf Course
Tanah Lot, Tabanan
Tel: 0361-815960
www.nirwanabaligolf.com
Greg Norman's challenging course set amid rice terraces. Spectacular greens overlook the Pura Tanah Lot temple and the raging Indian Ocean.

New Kuta Golf Course
Tel: 0361-8481333
Jalan Raya Uluwatu, Kawasan, Pecatu Indah Resort
This 18-hole, championship course covers 85 hectares (210 acres) above Dreamland Beach, and was designed by Ronald Fream. Its signature hole, no. 15, commands splendid views.

Hash House Harriers

Bali Hash House Harriers
www.bali-hash.com
Bali Hash House Harriers' runs are open to everyone and take place every Monday and Thursday, starting at 4.30pm, and there's also the opportunity to join a hash run on Saturdays as well. At the end of every run, or walk if you want to take in the scenery, there's icy cold beer waiting for you at the Bintang Beer truck when you get back. The routes cover terraced rice fields and jungle ravines. Visitors' fees for the run are Rp 100,000 per head.

Horse Riding

Bali Equestrian Centre
Tel: 0361-8446541/8446533
Jl Karang Suwung, Berawa, Canggu
www.baliequestriancentre.com
Located in Berawa near Canggu, the stables offer everything from sunset beach rides and lessons to dressage tuition. Horses include thoroughbreds and ponies to suit adults and children of all ages. Also has restaurant and accommodation on site.

TRANSPORT

ACCOMMODATION

ACTIVITIES

A – Z

LANGUAGE

Paragliding

Bali Paragliders' Club
Tel: 0361-704769
www.baliparagliders.com
Fly over the Bukit Badung peninsula while harnessed to a set of
inflatable wings and using only
the wind as a source of power.
Tandem flights or full certification
courses can be arranged.

Surfing

Surfing is reasonably good
throughout the year, but the best
period is from June to August.
The best places for beginners are
Kuta, Legian and Seminyak.
Intermediate surfers should go to
Bingin to the south of the airport
or Canggu to the north of Legian.
Much further west are Soka
beach at Lalang Linggah in Tabanan and Medewi beach in
Jembrana. For expert surfers
there is Kuta Reef (accessible
only by boat), Suluban and
Padang-Padang. There is great
surfing at Nusa Lembongan
island as well. The following
places in Kuta sell and rent
equipment:
Quiksilver: Jalan Legian 318
Kuta, tel: 0361-752693.
Ripcurl: Jalan Legian, Kuta, tel:
0361-765889.

Surf Schools

Bali Learn to Surf Co.
Hard Rock Hotel, Kuta
Tel: 0361-761869, ext. 8116
www.balilearntosurf.com
Qualified surf instructors teach
you all the basics from beginner
to advance courses. Also runs a
5-day "surfari" for serious beginners.
Ripcurl School of Surf
Tel: 0361-735858
www.schoolofsurf.com
Comprehensive lessons ranging
from beginner (half-day) to intermediate (full-day) and advanced
(3 days) classes. Private lessons
available at higher rates.

Surf Tours

Partama Surfing Tours
Shop 6 Lebak Bena Street
Legian Kelod Kuta

Tel: 0361-754919
www.surfpartama.com
Tours from Bali to some of the
best surf spots in Indonesia,
such as Nusa Lembongan (Shipwreck, Laceration, Playground),
Sumbawa (Supersuck, Yoyos and
Scar Reef) and Lombok (including Desert Point, Gili Air and Gru-
puk, Ekas, Mawi, Arguli and
Belongas Bay).

Outdoor Activities

Multi-Activity Operators

The following two companies
operate a range of interesting outdoor activities; most are suitable
for teenagers and adults, but
younger children are catered for
as well. Enquire when you make
bookings.
Bali Adventure Tours
Jalan Bypass Ngurah Rai
Pesanggaran
Tel: 0361-721480
www.baliadventuretours.com
Bali's biggest adventure tour
company, an enterprise that was
founded in 1989 and has grown
extensively. Operates activities
such as white-water rafting,
mountain biking, paragliding,
rice field or jungle trekking, and
the Elephant Safari Park. Prices
of full- and half-day options
include transfers, insurance,
equip-ment and a meal.
Sobek
Jalan Tirta Ening 9, Sanur
Tel: 0361-287059
www.balisobek.com
Reputable operator offering a
wide range of activities, like sea
kayaking, birdwatching, jungle
trekking, white-water rafting and
mountain cycling. Both half- and
full-days tours with meals and
refreshments are offered.

Bali Bird Walks

Ubud
Tel: 0361-975009
email: su_birdwalk@yahoo.com
See some of the many species of
birds in Bali with experienced Balinese guides. Easy walks along
trails, across rice fields and rivers,

and through coconut groves. You
are likely to see around 30 different species. Fee includes binocu-
lars, lunch, refreshments and a
bird list.

Herb Walks

Bali Nature Herbal Walks
Ubud
Tel: 0361-975051
www.baliherbalwalk.com
Made Westi and his wife Wayan
Lilir take visitors on walks
through the rice fields around
Ubud, sharing their knowledge
about the native plants, their
medicinal properties, and the
practice of traditional Balinese
herbal healing. The walks start at
8.30am in front of the Museum
Puri Lukisan and will last about 3
to 4 hours with a stop at an
organic restaurant.

Fishing

Ena Fishing Discovery
Jalan Tirta Ening 01, Sanur
Tel: 0361-288829
www.enafishing.com
Based in Sanur, this outfit organises fishing trips in the waters
around South Bali and Nusa Penida island.

Land Tour

Waka Experience
Jalan Iman Bonjol, Denpasar
Tel: 0361-484085
www.wakaexperience.com
Experience the mystical heart and
soul of Bali, travelling by Land
Rover through terraced rice fields
and untouched rainforest.

Paintball

Paintball Bali
Jalan Karang Putih 1
Br. Jaba Pura, Kuta Selatan
Tel: 0361-770300
www.paintballbali.com
The exciting game of paintball
takes place at this sprawling site in
the Bukit Badung area. Features
all the latest equipment from the
US. Open daily 9am–9pm.

Trekking Tours

The two big multi-sport companies, **Bali Adventure Tours** and

JAVANESE MANDI LULUR

The *Mandi Lulur* treatment originated in the royal palaces of Central Java, Indonesia, and this exfoliation and body polishing treatment is now famous all over Bali. The traditional Lulur ritual begins with a massage using coconut oil infused with pandanus leaves and cempaka flowers. This is followed by exfoliation with a fragrant paste blended from sandalwood, turmeric, rice, herbs, jasmine flowers and other ingredients. It is spread over the body and then rubbed off to remove dead skin. A yogurt mix is then slathered over the body to restore balance to the skin. Finally, you soak in a bath laced with rose petals, frangipani blossoms and astringent leaves. The Lulur ritual usually lasts about 2½ hours.

Sobek *(see page 256)* operate fairly easy trekking tours through paddy fields and jungle terrain. For treks up **Gunung Batur**, contact licensed guide **I Wayan Sadu**, mobile tel: 081-3383 87232. A local cartel, the HPPGB discourages independent trekkers, and climbers are advised to take a licensed guide along. Also reliable is the **Jero Wijaya Tourist Service** (tel: 0366-51249) in Toya Bungkah.

Although it's much less hassle climbing up **Gunung Agung** on your own, you are strongly advised to use the services of a guide. Contact **Gung Bawa Trekking**, tel: 0366-24379, mobile: 081-2384 0752.

Sailing & Cruises

Bali Hai Cruises
Benoa Harbour
Tel: 0361-720331
www.balihaicruises.com
Operates day cruises to Nusa Lembongan island and sunset harbour/dinner cruises on board luxury catamarans. Particularly

thrilling is the ride in a custom-built raft that skims and bounces over the waves at speeds of up to 70 kph (45 mph).
Bounty Cruises
Benoa Harbour
Tel: 0361-726666
www.balibountycruises.com
Offers day cruises to Nusa Lembongan island (with a number of included activities like banana boat rides, snorkelling, glass-bottom boat rides and canoeing) and evening dinner cruises.
Sail Sensations
Benoa Harbour
Tel: 0361-725864
www.sailsensations.com
Offers day cruises to Nusa Lembongan with barbecue lunch on the beach or twilight dining with entertainment on board its 26-metre (87ft) yacht. Charters available.
Sea Trek Sailing Adventures
Tel: 0361-283358
www.seatrekbali.com
Offers scheduled cruises on board the *Ombak Putih* or the *Katharina* to the islands east of Bali. Both schooners have modern conveniences, with 12 air-conditioned cabins on board the *Ombak Putih* and six on the *Katharina*.
Traditional Schooners
A consortium of traditional wooden *pinisi* schooners based in Bali's Benoa Harbour sail regularly to the Gili Islands off Lombok, Komodo and Sulawesi. Divers are frequent passengers on these boats.

Adventure Park
Bali Treetop Adventure Park
Bedugul Botanical Gardens
Candikuning
Tel: 0361-8520680
www.balitreetop.com
Close-to-nature activity for families and groups. Venture from tree to tree using Suspended Bridges, Spider Nets, Tarzan Jumps and Flying Swings between 2 and 20 metres/yds high and Flying-Foxes up to 160 metres/yds long. You'll get a birds-eye view of nature. Open daily 8.30am until 6pm.

SPAS

Healing therapies, spiritual cleansing, massage and beauty rituals are an integral part of everyday life in Bali. Since the late 1990s, spas have proliferated and the island now hosts the highest concentration of spas in Southeast Asia.

The architecture and interior decor of Balinese spas range from Zen-inspired simplicity to over-the-top opulence. Others are romantic, rustic or traditional, with water always a key element. Open-air bathrooms and pavilions often house outdoor showers and oversized sunken bathtubs.

Herbal remedies utilise healing plants and spices, such as galangal, aloe vera, avocado, lemongrass, turmeric and papaya. Traditional beauty rituals, like the Javanese *Mandi Lulur (see box)*, which originated centuries ago in the palaces of central Java, are often included on spa menus.

An excellent resource for spas in Bali is www.balispaguide.com

Kuta

DaLa Spa
Jalan Legian 123b, Kuta
Tel: 0361-756276
www.dalaspa.com
Located in the heart of Kuta, its sensuous decor is reminiscent of a French boudoir. The award-winning spa has seven treatment rooms each named after an exotic flower, taking on a different interior theme.
Theta Spa by the Sea
Ramada Bintang Bali Hotel,
Jalan Kartika Plaza, Kuta
Tel: 0361-755726
www.thetaspa.com
A luxurious spa offering treatments derived from ancient Chinese, Indian and Indonesian traditions. Treatments include the aphrodisiac Chocolate Indulgence and the rather more brisk Marine Invigorator.

Seminyak

There is a large number of well run independant spas in the Seminyak area, which charge prices that are significantly lower than hotel spas.

Antique Spa
Jalan Lestari, Umalas, Kerobokan
Tel: 0361-739840
www.antiquebali.com
Modern and minimalist decor. Treatments include exfoliating body scrubs and aromatherapy massage; products are blended from natural ingredients.

Jari Menari
Jalan Raya Basangkasa, Seminyak
Tel: 0361-736740
www.jarimenari.com
Jari Menari means dancing fingers, and this place is devoted entirely to massage (regular customers claim that the massages here are the best in Bali). Expect long massage strokes together with a blend of stretching and rhythmic moves.

Prana Spa & Villas
Jalan Kunti 118X, Seminyak
Tel: 0361-730840
www.thevillas.net
A gorgeous Moghul-inspired spa complex, reminiscent of a sumptuous Indian palace. Complete range of face and body treatments and extensive spa facilities, plus a health food café.

Sicilia Spa
Jalan Arjuna, Seminyak
Tel: 0361-736292
www.siciliaspa.com
Pampering treatments and massages that won't break the bank. Choose from a menu of relaxing massages, body scrubs and steam face masks.

Jimbaran

Spa at Four Seasons Jimbaran
Jimbaran
Tel: 0361-701010
www.fourseasons.com/jimbaranbay
Located beside the Indian Ocean, this award-winning spa offers all-natural treatments using sea-based elements plus flowers and spices harvested from the gardens of the resort.

Thermes Marins Bali
Ayana Resort, Jimbaran
Tel: 0361-702222
www.ayanaresort.com
Indonesia's first thalasso spa features an Aquatonic pool and uses the curative benefits of seawater. Therapies use the filtered and heated mineral-rich seawater of the Indian Ocean.

Nusa Dua

Mulia Spa
Tel: 0361-3027777
www.themulia.com
In addition to 20 treatments rooms and a state-of-the-art Wellness Suite with hammam tables, Mulia Spa at Mulia Resort also features a Finnish wood sauna, the Aroma Steam Room and Asia Pacific's only ice fountain room with chromatherapy chakra cleansing colours, a hydro tonic pool with hot and cold water pools, and an outdoor meditation area.

Nusa Dua Spa
Tel: 0361-771210
www.nusaduahotel.com
Situated in the gardens of the Nusa Dua Beach Hotel, this was one of the first spas to be established in Bali. It offers a variety of beauty therapies, from massage to Balinese body polish.

Ubud

COMO Shambhala Spa
COMO Shambhala Estate at Begawan Giri
Tel: 0361-978888
cse.comoshambhala.bz
Exceptional spa facilities comprising outdoor hydrotherapy, swimming pools, yoga room, pilates studio, steam rooms, saunas and gym in a breathtakingly beautiful site. Wellness programmes are specially tailored and there is qualified medical staff on site. Its yoga retreats are led by international yoga masters.

Spa Alila
Alila Ubud,

Payangan
Tel: 0361-975963
www.alilahotels.com/ubud
Spa pavilions spill out onto lush gardens and ponds. Comprehensive spa menu with products using natural ingredients.

Spa at Maya Ubud
Maya Ubud, Perliatan
Tel: 0361-977888
www.mayaubud.com
The award-winning spa at Maya Ubud is a cluster of enchanting, double and single thatched treatment pavilions, dramatically suspended on the banks of the Petanu River. The body treatments are pure bliss.

Zen
Jalan Hanoman, Ubud
Tel: 0361-970976
www.zenbalispa.com
Cheap and cheerful spa with a good range of massages, scrubs and other body treatments. Male and female therapists.

COOKERY SCHOOLS

Alila Manggis
Buitan, Manggis, Karangasem
Tel: 0363-41011
www.alilahotels.com
Balinese cookery lessons take place in a grass-roofed pavilion, with much of the produce harvested from the resort's prolific organic gardens. Half-day, full-day, two-, three- and five-day courses available.

Bumbu Bali
Jalan Pratama, Tanjung Benoa, Nusa Dua
Tel: 0361-774502
www.balifoods.com
Ex-executive chef of Bali's Grand Hyatt, Heinz von Holzen runs a well known restaurant and cookery school with his Balinese wife. Classes start at 6am with a visit to the market followed by a hands-on cooking programme that ends with lunch at 2pm.

Casa Luna Cooking School
Jalan Raya Ubud, Ubud
Tel: 0361-977409
www.casalunabali.com

Set up by one of the pioneers of Balinese restaurants, Janet De Neefe, who moved to Bali from Melbourne in 1984. Married to a Balinese, she owns the Casa Luna and Indus restaurants. Five morning classes per week, two of which include tours of the market.

Sate Bali
Jalan Laksmana 22a
Tel: 0361-736734
e-mail: satebali@yahoo.com
In his morning cooking classes, Chef Nyoman Sudiyasa of Sate Bali restaurant teaches participants how to create delectable Balinese dishes.

The Secret Garden Cooking School
Penastenan, Ubud
Tel: 0361-979395
www.balisecretgarden.com
Offers hands-on, intensive, one or 2-day Balinese cooking courses. Conducted by Ni Luh Sudiani, a delightful Balinese cookery teacher, the classes have no more than six people, to ensure plenty of personal attention.

Waka di Ume
Jalan Suweta, Ubud
Tel: 0361-973178/973179
www.wakadiumeubud.com
Hands-on Balinese cookery classes, including an early morning visit to Ubud market. The open-air kitchen near the resort's vegetable and herb garden features a traditional wood burner fuelled by aromatic coffee wood.

CHILDREN'S ACTIVITIES

Bali is a paradise for children, with a myriad of activities to choose from that the entire family will enjoy. Some of the mountain biking trips offered by **Bali Adventure Tours** are ideal for those aged from 10 years upwards. The biking trip also includes a visit to the fun Elephant Safari Park. Anyone from 10 years of age upwards can raft along the Ayung River with Bali Adventure Tours or **Sobek Bali**. Another fun activity for older children is learning to

surf; some of the beaches in Bali are ideal for beginners (see pages 255 and 257 for details of the above).

A number of PADI dive schools offer cool programmes for children. PADI "Youth Scuba Diving" provides youngsters from 5 years upwards with the chance to enjoy a pool-only experience. The PADI "Bubblemakers" programme offers underwater adventure with lots of fun and games for kids from 8–12. Contact either **AquaMarine-Diving** or **Scuba Duba Doo Dive Center Bali** (see page 255).

Another family-friendly water activity is the **Odyssey Submarine Adventure** (tel: 0361-759777; www.submarine-bali.com). Participants will be submerged in the Odyssey II submarine (based near Candidasa) on a 45-minute journey under the sea to explore colourful coral reefs.

Most of the 5-star family oriented hotels offer supervised children's clubs so that harried parents can do their own thing safe in the knowledge that their children are in good hands. Painting and craft classes as well as Balinese dance are some of the things that will keep your young ones occupied.

The Places section highlights attractions that are ideal for families. These include **Bali Bird Park** (page 123), **Waterbom Park** (page 112), especially its Bombastic Aquatic Playground for chidren 12 years and under, **Bali Zoo Park** (page 123), **Elephant Safari Park** (page 141), **Rimba Reptil** (page 123) and **Bali Butterfly Park** (page 196). Also ideal for families is the **Bali Treetop Adventure Park** (page 257).

SIGHTSEEING TOURS

If you don't want the hassle of arranging tours and transport on your own, most hotels have a tour operator or tour desk located in the lobby which can take care of

such details. Alternatively, look for travel agencies along streets in the tourist areas; most will have signboards listing sightseeing trips from half-day to 3-day duration. You can also ask the agency to customise a tour for you. Trips can be arranged to see cremation ceremonies and temple festivals.

Standard Tours

These are some of the standard tours that tour agencies sell, but feel free to make up your own itineraries and discuss them with the travel agent.

Bedugul Tour: includes Sangeh Monkey Forest, Mengwi, Jatiluwih, Candikuning and the sunset at Tanah Lot.

Besakih Tour: includes Celuk, Mas, Batuan, Gianyar, Klungkung, Puri Besakih and lunch at Bukit Jambal.

Denpasar Tour: tour of the city including art centre, markets, museum and temples.

East Bali Tour: covers Celuk, Mas, Batuan, Gianyar, Klungkung, Kusamba, Goa Lawah, Candidasa and Tenganan.

Kintamani/Gunung Batur Tour: includes a dance performance at Batubulan, with stops at Tampaksiring and Kintamani, and lunch overlooking Gunung Batur and the lake. May also include craft shops at Celuk, Mas and Batuan, Goa Gajah and Pejeng.

Lovina–Singaraja Tour: takes in Mengwi, Bedugul, Gitgit waterfall, Singaraja, Lovina, Banjar and Pupuan.

Sunset Tour: goes to Mengwi, Marga, Alas Kedaton and takes in the sunset at Tanah Lot.

Travel Agencies

Bali Discovery Tours: Komplek Pertokoan, Sanur Raya No. 27, Jalan Bypass Ngurah Rai, Sanur, tel: 0361-286283; www.balidiscovery.com.
Smiling Tour: Jalan By Pass Ngurah Rai Sanur, tel: 0361-288224; www.mysmailing.com.

TRANSPORT: LOMBOK

GETTING THERE AND GETTING AROUND

By Air

Lombok International Airport, (Bandara Internasional Lombok, commonly abbreviated to BIL) opened in 2011, and is the only airport in Lombok, located at Tanak Awu, Praya; tel 0370 6157000. If you need a visa on arrival (and qualify for one), you can get it at the airport (see page 277). Other facilities include hotel reservations desks, cafés, moneychangers, ATMs and internet access.

The airport is mainly served by domestic flights from other parts

KEY AIRLINE OFFICES

International Carriers:
SilkAir: tel: 0370-628254; www.silkair.com
Indonesian Carriers:
Garuda Indonesia: tel: (call centre) 080 418 07807.
Airport: tel: 0370 649100; www.garuda-indonesia.com
Wings/Lion Air: tel: 0370-6627444/642180; www.lionair.co.id
TransNusa Air: tel: 0370-624555; www.transnusa.co.id
Batavia Air: tel: 0370-648998; www.batavia-air.co.id

of Indonesia. **Garuda Airlines** (www.garuda-indonesia.com) flies between Kuala Lumpur in Malaysia and Lombok every day, with a short stop-over in Jakarta, while other international airlines serving the airport include **Jetstar Airways**, which operates direct flights between Perth (West Australia) and Lombok four times per week (Tuesday, Thursday, Friday and Sunday). **Silk Air**, which flies direct between Lombok and Singapore, three times per week, and **Air Asia**, which operates direct flights every day between Lombok and Kuala Lumpur in Malaysia. All other international connections are available via Jakarta and Bali.

Garuda Indonesia has direct flights between Lombok, Bali, Surabaya, Makassar and Jakarta every day. **Lion Air** has daily flights between Lombok, Bali, Jakarta and Surabaya. **Trans Nusa Air** flies between Lombok, Sumbawa and Bima daily. **Batavia Air** has flights from Lombok to Surabaya and Jakarta (via Surabaya) every day. **Wings Air** (Lion Air) has daily flights from Lombok to Bali and Surabaya.

International departure tax is Rp 150,000, while **domestic departure tax is Rp 45,000**. There are desks at the airport where you can pay for the relevant tax.

By Sea

The picturesque sea crossing by ferry from Bali to Lombok is well worth the inconvenience of travelling to and from the ports. Public ferries depart every two hours for the trip between **Padangbai Harbour** (Bali) and **Lembar Harbour** (Lombok), about 20km (12 miles) south of Mataram; the crossing takes about four hours. A one-way ticket costs Rp 40,000. Padangbai Harbour is about two hours' drive from Kuta and South Bali, depending on whether you travel by car or public transport. Try to get an early start, or, better yet, stay at Candidasa in East Bali, which is just 20 minutes from Padangbai, the day before departure.

Lembar Harbour is about one hour south of Senggigi in Lombok. Arrange your own transport to the harbour and buy tickets direct from the desk, or use a reputable tour company who can provide a complete transfer package.

The most reliable tour agent is **Perama Tours**, which offers a complete transfer package that includes pick-up from destinations throughout Bali and Lombok, bus transfer to the local harbour, ferry ticket and transfer from the harbour to your destination on either island. Contact Perama in **Lombok**, tel: 0370-693007, 693008 or **Bali**, tel:

0361-751551, 751875; www.peramatour.com.

Fast Ferries

In addition, there are several daily fast boat services from Bali to Lombok: **Gili Cat** (www.gilicat.com) daily from Padangbai, Rp 600,000 one-way, and **Blue Water Express** (www.bwsbali.com), daily from Serangan Harbour, Rp 690,000 one-way. The fast boats from Bali make a stop first at Teluk Kode on mainland Lombok before continuing to Gili Trawangan.

GETTING AROUND

From the Airport

Lombok International Airport is 28km (17 miles) from Kuta and 50km (31 miles) from Senggigi.

Major hotels offer free pick-up, call from the airport or contact their representatives in the arrival hall. If you have not booked your transfers in advance with your hotel or travel agent, you can use one of the **airport taxis** that operate from the arrival hall. Be sure to purchase a prepaid voucher from the taxi desk; fixed prices to all locations on Lombok are displayed on a sign on the wall. Note: the airport taxis have a monopoly on the area, and their prices are generally higher than the metered rates that taxis elsewhere in Lombok charge.

Orientation

Lombok is an excellent escape from the tourist crowds of Bali, and many people combine a visit to both islands to make the most of their holidays. A week each on Bali and Lombok is a good introduction to both islands. Located about 35km (22 miles) east of Bali, Lombok is only slightly smaller in size than its neighbour. The main roads are generally in good condition and traffic is less congested than on Bali, making travel easier and safer for self-driving, motorbike riding and cycling tours.

The Indonesian word for road is "Jalan", abbreviated to "Jl" in street addresses. Names change without warning, but are essentially the same main roads, locally called "Jalan Raya" (big road). Many of the roads in Lombok are named Jalan Raya and then appended by the area that the main road passes through (e.g. Jalan Raya Senggigi).

The cities of **Ampenan**, **Mataram** and **Cakranegara** in West Lombok have merged into an urban sprawl, making it no longer obvious where one ends and the next begins. A main road links the cities, starting with Jalan Pabean in Ampenan, then becoming Jalan Yos Sudarso, then changing to Jalan Langko and Jalan Pejanggik in Mataram, before later becoming Jalan Selaparang at Cakranegara. Basically this is one major road that runs across the island from west to east, dividing into one-way streets heading west or east at the cities, and then reuniting to traverse across the island.

Another main road links Ampenan and **Senggigi** and continues north, eventually circumventing the island and ending in East Lombok, where it links to the main west–east road. Linked to this west–east road in the middle of the island is another major road that runs south to the airport and central Lombok hub of **Praya**, continuing on to the south coast and ending at **Kuta**.

Transport

Taxis

Light blue **Lombok Taxis** (owned by Bluebird Taxis) are easy to find and cheap. Drivers normally switch on their meters when you board and are not open to bartering. Metered taxis can be booked in advance directly from the hotel desks and taxi stands in Senggigi, or flagged down along the streets. Taxies can also be chartered for the day from:
Lombok Taxi
Jalan Koperasi 102, Ampenan
Tel: 0370-627000

Public Bemo and Bus

Bemo (minivans and buses) service all towns on the island but it's time consuming to rely on them. The central terminal is at the crossroads at Sweta, east of Cakranegara; there is another terminal near Kebon Roek, Ampenan. A signboard displays the official fares to all destinations. Bright yellow minibus *bemo* connect Ampenan, Mataram and Cakranegara, but you usually have to change buses at each terminal.

Small *bemo* ply the routes between Senggigi and Ampenan, and the main road up the west coast from Senggigi; use these for transport to Mangsit and areas north of Senggigi.

Both **Perama** (tel: 0370-693007) and **Lombok Mandiri** (tel: 0370-693477) operate tourist shuttle buses that connect to key places on the island.

Motorcycle Rental

It is easy to rent motorcycles in Ampenan, Mataram and Senggigi. Ask at your hotel or at any motorcycle shop on the main streets. You can bring a motorcycle from Bali on the public ferry, but rental cars cannot leave Bali.

Vehicle Rental

Privately operated cars and *bemo* are available for charter in the cities and Senggigi. You can charter a *bemo* to go anywhere on the island, but they are slow and uncomfortable. A better option is renting an air-conditioned car and driver by the day or hour. Prices start from Rp 400,000 a day without driver (or Rp 500,000–600,000 with driver). If your hotel can't arrange for a car and driver, contact one of the following:
Cinta Lombok Lestari (CLL)
Jalan Raya Senggigi, tel: 0370-693561.
Kotasi
Operates several tour counters in Senggigi, tel: 0370-693435
Trac Astra Rent-a-Car
Jalan Adi Sucipto, No. 5, Rembiga, Mataram, tel: 0370-626363, www.trac.astra.co.id

ACCOMMODATION: LOMBOK

SOME THINGS TO CONSIDER BEFORE YOU BOOK THE ROOM

Choosing a Hotel

Accommodation in Lombok is relatively cheap, even in the west where a tourism infrastructure is well established, especially when compared to Bali. Cheap *losmen* (guesthouses) can be found in all the cities as well as in the main tourist areas of Senggigi, on the west coast, Kuta, on the south coast, and the Gili Islands.

In recent years a good selection of mid-range hotels, as well as boutique hotels and luxurious resorts, have been built to cater to more well-heeled travellers. Small hotels will usually add a 10 percent tax to hotel bills while the larger hotels will impose a 21 percent tax.

ACCOMMODATION LISTINGS

WEST LOMBOK

MATARAM AND AMPENAN

There is no reason to stay in the inner cities as Senggigi is so close by, but here are two decent options in Mataram and Ampenan.

PRICE CATEGORIES

Price for a double room (subject to a 10–21 percent tax and service charge):

$$$$ = over US$200
$$$ = US$120–200
$$ = US$60–120
$ = below US$60

Lombok Raya Hotel
Jalan Panca Usaha 11
Mataram
www.lombokrayahotel.com
Tel: 0370-632305
Located close to the Mataram Mall, this is the best hotel in the city. Facilities include an outdoor pool, restaurant, bar, karaoke, business centre, meeting rooms, and laundry and room service. Rooms are large, come with a private balcony and air conditioning, and include a minibar, hot water and television. 135 rooms. **$$**
Nitour Inn
Jalan Yos Sudarso 4,
Ampenan

Tel: 0370-623780
This is a friendly place, and its air-conditioned rooms come with hot water, a minibar, a refrigerator, satellite television and a private balcony. 20 rooms. **$**

SENGGIGI AND SURROUNDS

Lombok's best international-standard hotels are located along Senggigi beach and points slightly north of it.

Bulan Baru Hotel
Jalan Raya Senggigi, Setangi
Tel: 0370-693785

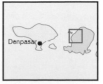

Email: bulanbaru@hotmail.com
This small, Australian-owned hotel is located 7km (4¼ miles) north of Senggigi and close to the beach. It has 12 rooms (with open-air garden bathrooms) set in tropical gardens surrounding a central swimming pool. Decent restaurant on site. **$**
Holiday Resort Lombok
Jalan Raya Mangsit

Tel: 0370-693444
www.holidayresort-lombok.com
Set in beautiful gardens right down to the beach front, with a large free-form pool, jacuzzi and swim-up bar. Facilities include a health club, tennis courts, kids' club, spa, dive centre and good restaurants. **$$**
Pool Villa Club
Jalan Raya Senggigi
Tel: 0370-693210
www.poolvillaclublombok.com
A private resort set within the grounds of the Senggigi Beach Hotel. There are 16 villas with luxurious furnishings, each with a private sundeck and jacuzzi. The canal-style swimming

pool flows around the villas, surrounded by lovely gardens. Each two-storey villa has satellite TV, IDD phone and internet, room service and more. There's a fine-dining restaurant and a Mandara Spa, plus access to all the main hotel's facilities. **$$$$**
Puri Mas Boutique Resort & Spa
Jalan Raya Senggigi, Mangsit
Tel: 0370-693831
www.purimas-lombok.com
Beach front villas and bungalows, located in pleasant surroundings, attract many repeat bookings and long-stay guests. Great restaurant on the beach, plus

swimming pool and library. 17 units. **$$**
Qunci Villas
Jalan Raya Senggigi, Mangsit
Tel: 0370-693800
www.quncivillas.com
A stylish boutique hotel on the beach front. There are 20 spacious units in minimalist, contemporary style, set in lovely gardens, with a small restaurant and swimming pool. More expensive 2- and 3-bedroom villas are also available. **$$$$**
Senggigi Beach Hotel
Jalan Raya Senggigi
Tel: 0370-693210
www.senggigibeachhotel.com
Set in beautiful grounds on a point with two

sweeping beaches. All rooms and villas are air-conditioned and have satellite TV, in-house movies and minibar. 149 rooms, 16 villas. **$$$**
Sheraton Senggigi Resort
Jalan Raya Senggigi
Tel: 0370-693333
www.sheraton.com/senggigi
International-standard hotel; rooms have satellite TV, room service and balcony. Features a stunning swimming pool with a swim-up bar, two restaurants, lounge bar, spa, tennis courts and a fabulous beach front location. 156 rooms. **$$$**

GILI ISLANDS

GILI AIR

There's a good range of accommodation on all three Gili Islands, but water shortages mean most hotels don't have lush gardens, the showers are salty, and many don't have hot water.

Coconut Cottages
Tel: 0370-635365
www.coconuts-giliair.com
Possibly the best place to stay on laid-back Gili Air, the cottages here sit back slightly from the beach in a shady coconut grove set within lovely gardens. 15 cottages. **$**
Hotel Gili Air
Tel: 0370-643580/6621448
www.hotelgiliair.com
Located on the north of the island, it's the only hotel on Gili Air with a swimming pool. All rooms have air conditioning or

fan, showers and hot water. Bar and restaurant on site. 30 rooms. **$**
Gili Air Santay
Tel: 081803758695 / 087878329914
www.giliair-santay.com
Simple bamboo bungalows, situated 50 metres/yards from a white sand beach. Built in traditional Indonesian-Sulawesi style surrounded by a tropical garden of coconut palms, each bungalow has a private bathroom, bedroom, fan and mosquito net, and a veranda with a hammock. No hot water and no air conditioning. 12 bungalows. **$**

GILI MENO

The Sunset Gecko
Tel: 081-576 6418
www.thesunsetgecko.com
Small Japanese-owned

eco-resort offering a beachfront two-bedroom traditional wooden house with a large balcony, and private open-air bathroom. Additionally, there are simple A-frame bungalows a short walk away from shared showers and toilets. All rooms are fan-cooled and there is a restaurant on site. **$**
Villa Nautilus
Tel: 0370-642143
www.villanautilus.com
Five bungalows in a peaceful location, with a restaurant on site. Spacious rooms have air con and hot water, plus large terraces with ocean views. **$$**

GILI TRAWANGAN

Big Bubble
Tel: 0370-6125020
www.bigbubblediving.com
Bungalows built from

natural materials, each with a hammock and day bed on a private terrace and facing a garden. Swimming pool on site. **$**
Desa Dunia Beda
Tel: 0370-6141575
www.desaduniabeda.com
Lovely resort on the north of the island, with traditional Javanese-style villas. Rooms tastefully furnished with natural materials, and all have garden bathrooms. Beach front restaurant and swimming pool. **$$**
H Rooms
Tel: 0370-639248
Five rooms at the chic Horizontal Lounge hangout. Each features a

jacuzzi, a glass-walled, air-conditioned bedroom, an open-air sunken communal lounge, and a private hatch through which room service may be received. **$$$**
Kelapa Luxury Villas
Tel: 0812 3756003
www.kelapavillas.com
1, 2, 3 and 4-bedroom villas hidden in a coconut plantation. Each villa has a private swimming pool and a fully equipped kitchen. Choice of self-catering or in-house menu. 10 villas. **$$$**
Ko Ko Mo
Tel: 0370-6134 920

www.kokomogilit.com
New villa resort with 1-, 2- and 4-bedroom villas, each with private swimming pool, freshwater plunge pool or a freshwater jacuzzi, as well as living and dining areas. Has the island's only fine-dining restaurant. **$$$$**
Marta's
Mobile Tel: 0812 3722777
Email: martas_trawangan@yahoo.com
Bungalows are comfortably furnished and have

air conditioning and hot water. Peaceful alternative to the beach front hotels. **$**
Hotel Vila Ombak
Tel: 0370-6142336
www.hotelombak.com
One of the best hotels on the island, the traditional-style Sasak huts and bungalows are air-conditioned, and have TV, IDD phones and mini bars. Swimming pool, beach front restaurant, spa and diving school. **$$$**

NORTH LOMBOK

MEDANA

The Oberoi Lombok
Tanjung Medana
Tel: 0370-6138444
www.oberoihotels.com/oberoi_lombok/
Lombok's most exclusive resort on secluded Medana beach in the northwest. All of the rooms are luxuriously outfitted and include

sunken baths, satellite TV and CD systems; some have ocean views. Most of the villas have garden showers and private pools. Facilities include restaurants, bar, pool, health club, beach club and spa. The only disadvantage is its relative seclusion, but this is exactly what some people crave. 30 rooms and 20 villas. **$$$$**

PANTAI SIRA

Hotel Tugu Lombok
Pantai Sira
Tel: 0370-6120111
www.tuguhotels.com/lombok/
Located on the pristine white sand Sira (or Sire) beach amongst palms, this hotel is a luxurious and romantic option. Like its sister hotel in Canggu, Bali, it is a

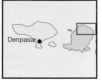

veritable museum, showcasing hundreds of Indonesian antiques and beautiful, original artworks. Indoor and outdoor spa. 18 rooms. **$$$$**

SOUTH LOMBOK

KUTA

Kuta Indah Hotel
Kuta
Tel: 0370-653782
There are beautiful beach views from the rooms here, which come with satellite TV, minibar and fan or air conditioning. The hotel has a swimming pool, spa, water sports facilities, restaurant and 24-hour room service. 43 rooms. **$**

Novotel Lombok Mandalika Resort
Pantai Putri Nyale, Kuta
Tel: 0370-6153333
www.novotel.com/gb/hotel-0571-novotel-lombok/index.shtml
This resort right on the beautiful beach front recreates a Sasak village, with standard rooms, as well as more expensive thatched bungalows, set around gardens with whimsical statuary. All rooms have air conditioning, satellite TV, IDD telephone and minibar. The resort fea-

tures three pools, two restaurants, a children's club, fitness centre and spa. The beaches and hills adjacent to the hotel are excellent for long walks. 100 rooms and 23 bungalows. **$$**
Sempiak Villas $$$
Selong Belanak
Tel: 0821 4430 3337
www.sempiakvillas.com
Four 1-bedroom boutique bungalows and one 2-bedroom pool villa, perched atop Sempiak Hill with breathtaking views of the

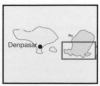

coastline and the beautiful, white-sand, Selong Belanak Beach below. Breakfast and dinner is served beside the main swimming pool, while lunch is available at Laut Biru Cafe and beach-club, just a short walk down the hill. **$$$**

A CTIVITIES: LOMBOK

THE ARTS, NIGHTLIFE, SHOPPING, OUTDOOR ACTIVITIES AND TOURS

THE ARTS

Unlike Bali, which has regular performances of dance and music at hotels and some villages on a regular basis, traditional Sasak dance and music are more difficult to come by. There are occasional performances at some of the larger hotels and certain villages famous for particular dance forms.

The most popular dance is the *cupak gerantang* based on the Javanese Panji tales. In the related *kayak sando*, also based on the Panji stories, the performers wear masks. The *gendang belek*, which gets its name from the traditional Sasak drum called *gendang*, is performed by men to accompany warriors going to the battlefield. Another traditional dance is *rudat*, performed by pairs of young men in black caps and jackets, and wearing black and white checked sarongs.

The **Senggigi Festival** in Lombok is the major annual festival of cultural and artistic performances, including traditional dance, music and theatre. Held in central Senggigi in July each year, this week-long event involves performers from villages all around Lombok and neighbouring Sumbawa.

Taman Budaya
Jalan Majapahit, Mataram
Tel: 0370-622428
This is the main venue for cultural performances on Lombok. There is no regular programme of events, so you have to call ahead to check. If no performance is scheduled, it's possible to attend rehearsals or to organise special performances for group bookings. Open Mon–Fri 8am–2pm.

NIGHTLIFE

Lombok isn't well known for its bars and clubs, but there is still some decent nightlife to be found in Senggigi and out on the Gili Islands, especially Gili Trawangan.

Senggigi

Bars
Happy Café
Jalan Raya Senggigi (on the corner of Senggigi Plaza)
Mobile tel: 081-2375 2233
Great live music every night. What may be lacking in the food department is made up for by a happy pub atmosphere. Friendly and fun staff.

The Office Bar & Restaurant
Jalan Raya Senggigi
Tel: 0370-693162

Laid-back bar right on the beach front, popular with the expatriate crowd, and great for a drink while watching the sunset over Bali. Reasonably priced drinks and food, pool table and a big screen TV for sports. Good CD collection.
Square
Blok B No. 10,
Jalan Raya Senggigi
Tel: 0370-6645999, 6644888, 693688
Senggigi's newest nightspot and a cool place to hang out. Very chic and contemporary with black stone floors accented by timber and glass. The chill-out lounge upstairs has subdued lighting, great music and a sophisticated ambience.

Nightclubs
Marina Pub
Jalan Raya Senggigi
Tel: 0370-693136
www.marinasenggigi.com
Probably the most popular nightclub in Senggigi, it is thronged with locals, expatriates and tourists. Great live bands, tasty wood-fired pizzas and snacks, and a feel-good atmosphere.
Sahara Club
Senggigi Plaza,
Jalan Raya Senggigi
Tel: 0370-692233
Stylish nightclub with regular guest bands from Jakarta and Surabaya. Popular at weekends and late at night.

TRANSPORT

ACCOMMODATION

ACTIVITIES

A – Z

LANGUAGE

Gili Trawangan

The Beach House
Gili Trawangan
Tel: 0370-642352
Always popular, this well-run bar and restaurant on the beach attracts a lively crowd every day. Good seafood barbecues at night. Great location, with friendly staff who make everyone feel at home.

The Blue Marlin
Gili Trawangan
Tel: 0370-6132424
This upper level venue has the largest dance floor on Gili Trawangan. Parties are held here on Monday nights (often themed) starting at 10pm.

Horizontal
Gili Trawangan
Tel: 0370-639248
Trendy Horizontal sets the tone with a fine-dining section, a slick bar and futuristic "escape pods". Regular guest DJs, exotic cocktails and a cool crowd make this bar a fun place to hang out.

Tir na Nóg
Gili Trawangan
Tel: 0370-6139463
Claims that Gili Trawangan is the smallest island in the world with an Irish pub on it. Popular hang-out that gets very busy, with party night on Wednesday.

Gili Meno

Tao Kombo Jungle Bar
Tel: 081-237 22174
This lively bar offers happy hour sunsets, late nights and cool music.

SHOPPING

If you want to go shopping in Lombok, don't look for modern malls and designer clothing because there is very little on offer. Instead seek out the local products – arts, handicrafts, basketry, pottery, Sasak sarongs, textiles and locally farmed pearls.

Antiques

There are some great examples of old Dutch and Chinese antiques, but most of what you will find is new and made to look antique. There are some good primitive carvings and reproductions of traditional pieces, while some of the furniture is made from old materials that have been recycled into stunning functional pieces.

Galeri Nao
Jalan Raya Senggigi, Meninting
Tel: 0370-626835
Contemporary furnishings made from local woods and recycled timbers. Unique pieces with stylish flair.

Parmour Antiques
Jalan Raya Senggigi 704
Features fine antiques and furniture collected by knowledgeable owner Agus Heri Gomanthy.

Baskets

Lombok's rattan and grass baskets, mostly produced in the eastern Lombok villages of Kotaraja and Loyok, are very fine and sturdy. They are also sold at the main market by the bus terminal in Sweta or at Pasar Cakranegara, west of Pura Meru.

Pottery

The villages of **Banyumulek**, **Masbagik** and **Penujak** produce distinctive and elegant pottery. Banyumulek probably has the largest selection. Be sure to go behind the shops to see pots being thrown and fired.

Lombok Pottery Centre
Jalan Sriwijaya IIIA, Banyumulek
Tel: 0370-640350
Offers high-grade products for sale, and exports Lombok pottery around the world. This place is sponsored by a New Zealand aid project that aims to improve the quality and crafting of the pottery.

Handicrafts

The craft village of **Sayang-Sayang** north of Cakranegara is filled with interesting and well-made handicrafts, especially wooden crafts. Traditional masks and statues, as well as more contemporary pieces, are displayed by the hundreds. The newer market on the main road has many stalls filled with inexpensive bargains. The following places are recommended for handicrafts:

Bayan Lombok
Jalan Raya Senggigi
Tel: 0370-693784
www.bayanlombok.com
Wonderful traditional and contemporary wooden products finished to a very high standard.

Kencana Gallery
Jalan Adi Sucipto 12
Tel: 0370-635727
More traditional wooden furniture and interesting home decor pieces.

Oleh-Oleh
Jalan Raya Senggigi
Good range of arts and crafts, home furnishings and gifts.

Senggigi Art Market (Pasar Seni)
Jalan Raya Sengiggi
An art market with many stalls and small shops selling souvenirs, clothing and artwork.

Textiles

For traditional textiles dyed and woven by hand, visit the villages of Sukarare, Pujung, Purbasari, Balimurti and Pringgasela. Sukarare has a large selection of woven fabrics from Lombok and Sumhawa, and daily weaving demonstrations by the women outside the shops. Also try the commercial fabric shops on the main street of Cakranegara.

C.V. Rinjani
Jalan Pejanggik, Cakranegara
Pak Abdullah's silk sarongs and matching *selendang* scarves are highly regarded by the fashion conscious in Bali and Jakarta.

Pearls

Lombok's pearl farms produce beautiful, high-quality South Sea pearls that are exported all over the world. The shops on Sultan Kaharudin Street in Sekarbela, near Mataram, stock a large selection of loose pearls and strands, as well as pearl-encrusted gold jewellery.

Shopping Mall

Mataram Mall
Jalan Pejanggik, Mataram
Lombok's only real mall, with four floors of shops and stalls. Good buys are shoes and fake designer bags and belts. There is also a department store, several electronics stores, and shops selling clothing, CDs and DVDs, as well as fast-food outlets.

OUTDOOR ACTIVITIES

Diving and Snorkelling

Some of the best diving in Indonesia is around the Gili Islands. Although much of the coral is dead in the shallower waters, there is still plenty to see, including magnificent coral shelves at deeper levels, thousands of varieties of tropical fish, reef sharks, moray eels, rays, and several turtle species.

There is good snorkelling at many of the beaches around Lombok, like Mangsit near the front of Windy Beach Resort, and at Nipah beach north of Senggigi. The Gili Islands are good for snorkelling as are the islands off the southwest coast, like Gili Nanggu, offshore from Sekotong.

Many dive centres operate from Senggigi and the Gili Islands. Dive trips to the Gilis start from about US$100 for two dives. Most of the dive operators also offer snorkelling tours and will organise day trips to the Gilis from Senggigi. **Perama Tours** has an escorted snorkelling day trip, including equipment, boat transfers and guide (minimum 2 people).

The following places operate dive and snorkel trips and conduct certification courses.
Bagus Divers: Jalan Raden Panji

Block C/09 Tangunkarang, tel: 0370-642892; www.bagusdivers.com
Big Bubble: Gili Trawangan, tel: 0370-625020; www.bigbubblediving.com.
Blue Marlin Dive: Jalan Raya Senggigi, tel: 0370-692003 or 693719; Gili Trawangan, tel: 0370-6132424, and Gili Air, tel: 0370-634387; www.diveindo.com.
Dream Divers: Jalan Raya Senggigi (near Bumbu Café), tel: 0370-692047; Gili Trawangan, tel: 0370-6134496, and Gili Air, tel: 0370-634547; www.dreamdivers.com.
Manta Dive: Gili Trawangan, tel: 0370-6143649; www.manta-dive.com.

Boating and Fishing

The waters around Lombok offer many opportunities for cruising and sailing. You can charter *jukung* or small outrigger boats from boat owners on Senggigi beach, to explore the coast or for day trips to the Gili Islands and surroundings, for around Rp 250,000 per day. Chartered outriggers for exploring the southwest islands can be organised from the car park (beside the main road) in Taun. Trips out to Gili Nanggu or Gili Gede cost around Rp 250,000 per day.

Fishing trips to the waters around Lombok are an excellent opportunity to catch huge marlin, tuna and other deep-water fish, all in plentiful supply.
Serigala
Blok A3/4 Senggigi Plaza Senggigi Mobile tel: 0817-573 0012
This is a locally owned, large and comfortable outrigger boat for charter to the Gilis and the islands to the south. Friendly, knowledgeable staff and reasonable prices.

Golf

Lombok Golf Kosaido Country Club
Jalan Raya Tanjung, Pantai Sira,Tanjung
Tel: 0370-640137
Email: sales@lombokgolfkosaido.com

A magnificent 18-hole course, overlooking the beach at Pantai Sira, with stunning views of the surrounding ocean and mountains. Designed by Peter Thompson, Michael Wolveridge and Perret, Kosaido (as it's locally known), is a world-class golf course in an outstanding location.
Rinjani Country Club
Golong, Narmada
Tel: 082897030270
www.lombok-golf.com
A Japanese joint venture, this simply landscaped par-72 course designed by Shunji Ohno is in a quiet setting under the shadow of Gunung Rinjani. A Japanese golf pro is in residence. Facilities include a clubhouse, tennis court, swimming pool and restaurant. Simple hotel rooms and villas are available at the course.

SIGHTSEEING TOURS

Travel/Tour Agents

Most hotels have a travel agent or a tour desk located in the lobby to take care of arrangements for tours and transport. Alternatively, the following travel agencies can organise tours and sightseeing trips:
Bidy Tour
Jalan Ragigenap 17, Ampenan
Tel: 0370-632127
www.bidytour-lombok.com
Perama Tours
Mataram Office: Jalan Pejanggik 66, tel: 0370-635928; and Senggigi Office: Jalan Raya Senggigi, tel: 0370-693007
www.peramatour.com
To arrange a climbing expedition up to the summit of Gunung Rinjani, including the provision of food, tents, sleeping bags, and porters and guides, contact:
Rinjani Trek Centre
Hotel Lombok Raya, Jalan Panca Usaha 11, Mataram
Tel: 0370-641124, 632305
www.lomboksumbawa.com

A–Z BALI AND LOMBOK

AN ALPHABETICAL SUMMARY OF PRACTICAL INFORMATION

A ddresses

Street names in Bali and Lombok are confusing because many have been renamed due to historical or political figures falling in and out of fashion. In many cases, streets are still referred to by their old names but the signposts will always show the new names.

Furthermore, in tourist areas it is not uncommon for a street to have a nickname (eg Double Six Street for Jalan Arjuna and Jalan Oberoi for Jalan Kayu Aya) taken from a long-established restaurant, nightclub or hotel that per-

haps dominates the street.

House numbers cause even greater confusion. Although in some areas buildings have been renumbered by the government, it is rare to find a street where the buildings display consecutive numbers. To make things worse, duplicated numbers within the same street are commonplace (some people just think of their lucky number and use it for their house address). It is not unusual to find private houses and businesses with numbers such as 100x, 100xx and 1000x. The Periplus Bali Street Atlas and Periplus Lombok

& Sumbawa map are useful sources of reference; taxi drivers are more likely to use local landmarks as a direction finder.

Admission Charges

Generally there is a small admission charge for entering government-run tourist sites. This is generally less than Rp 20,000 per adult and half-price for children. The ticket offices will issue tickets, but if you are travelling in a car, you will also be charged a car park fee. Some of the major temples charge entrance fees, but the majority will allow you to enter free of charge. In this case, you will be asked to give a donation towards the upkeep of the temple. Unless you have brought your own sarong and sash, you will be lent one, or expected to rent one for around Rp 3,000.

Age Restrictions

In Bali and Indonesia the age of consent for heterosexual sexual activity is 19 years for males and 16 years for females. The age of consent for homosexuals is 18. The legal age for drinking is 18. There is no enforced law against drinking and driving, but do NOT drink and drive, as the accident statistics in Bali are very high.

B udgeting for your Trip

Since the late 1990s Bali has become a lot more up-market with chic new bars and restaurants, exclusive villas, luxury hotels, designer boutiques and opulent spas. Lombok is generally cheaper for food and accommodation. However, what remains special about both islands is the availability of choice; there really is something for everyone. Backpackers and surfers (who, after all, started the influx of tourism to Bali in the 1970s and 1980s) have not been forgotten.

Accommodation in Bali and Lombok can cost anything between US$5 and US$5,000 per night. Likewise, when it comes to eating out, the islands cater for every taste, from street-food served out of boxes balanced on bicycles, to chic, fine-dining restaurants.

Anything imported is expensive; this is probably most noticeable in terms of food and alcoholic drinks. A bottle of local beer, for example, generally costs about half of its imported counterpart. Bar prices in the more up-market hotels are high, and watch out for that infuriating 21 percent tax and service.

While imported spirits and fine wines from around the world are available in Bali, the selection is often limited and prices are excessive due to the application of high customs and excise tax. This is causing great concern to Bali's business community, and has the potential to damage the island's tourism where the consumption of alcoholic beverages is an important part of the holiday experience.

Taxis are relatively cheap; the transport that the locals use is even cheaper but not particularly comfortable. If you live frugally you can survive on as little as US$25 per day for both meals and lodging, but if you intend to live it up by eating out at good restaurants then be prepared to spend $50 for a 3-course meal alone.

To help you with budgeting for your trip, the list below provides some average costs:
• A beer Rp 25,000, glass of house wine Rp 70,000 (local) or Rp 120,000 (imported)
• A main course at a budget restaurant Rp 25,000; at a moderate restaurant Rp 90,000; at an expensive restaurant Rp 150,000–250,000
• A cheap hotel US$10–50 per night; moderate hotel US$60–200; luxury hotel US$200–1,000
• A taxi journey to or from the main airport Rp 35,000–335,000
• A single bus ticket Rp 100,000.

Business Travellers

Most people come to Bali to relax. However, all of the large hotels, especially the 5-star resorts in the Nusa Dua area, have the expertise and facilities to coordinate professional meetings, seminars, receptions, private dinners and functions. Comprehensive business and conference facilities include fully equipped business centres, meeting rooms, boardrooms and auditoriums. Most villas and hotels provide internet facilities and, increasingly, broadband and wireless internet access.

C hildren

Children are universally loved in Bali and Lombok, welcomed every-

where and given a great deal of attention. Bali especially is a paradise for kids, offering a whole host of activities *(see page 259).* Babysitters are available at major hotels, and many hotels offer children's activities, child care facilities and children's clubs. The owners of even the smallest of homestays will be happy to look after your children for a few hours. Some of the large department stores and malls in Bali have amusement centres packed with video games.

Disposable nappies (diapers) are expensive in Bali and Lombok, and not always available, so bring your own. Baby food and soybean formula are available at the supermarkets, but at exorbitant prices. Remember to bring sunhats and sunscreen to protect delicate skin from the strong sun.

Climate

Temperatures in Bali vary between 21–32°C (70–90°F), with an average annual temperature of 27°C (80°F). Higher elevations can get cooler, especially during the dry season which, lasts from May to September (August is the coolest month). The hot rainy season, with accompanying high humidity levels, lasts from November to March;

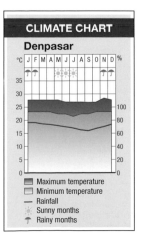

CLIMATE CHART
Denpasar

Maximum temperature
Minimum temperature
— Rainfall
☀ Sunny months
🌂 Rainy months

TRANSPORT

ACCOMMODATION

ACTIVITIES

A – Z

LANGUAGE

January is the wettest month with late afternoon thunderstorms. April and October are transitional months with intermittent rain and sun. Humidity is around 75 percent year-round.

Lombok has a similar weather pattern to Bali, but tends to be drier and less humid.

Clothing

Bring casual clothing of lightweight natural fabrics, which offer the best comfort in the heat and humidity. Bali has a thriving garment industry and clothes are readily available everywhere.

Sandals or footwear that can be slipped off easily are a good idea, especially if planning to visit homes – shoes are always removed before going into a house. Suits and ties are rarely worn. For formal occasions, men wear shirts made from local batik fabric. You'll need a light jacket or sweater if you're planning to visit mountain spots, where temperatures are considerably lower.

When visiting villages and temples (especially in more remote areas) as well as government offices, wear modest clothing and avoid showing too much skin: a T-shirt and mid-length shorts are fine (see also Temple Attire below).

Temple Attire

Anyone visiting a temple must tie a sash (umpal) around the waist. Many temples require exposed legs to be covered with a sarong, especially if a ceremony is taking place. Men may also be required to wear a head-cloth (udeng) and short overskirt (saput) at important temple festivals. Temple visitors (especially women) with bare shoulders or exposed midriffs may be denied entrance, so be sure to dress appropriately. Some large temples have sashes and sarongs that can be borrowed in return for a small donation (usually Rp 3,000), but if you intend to visit many holy places it makes more sense to purchase your own.

Consulates

Australia: Jalan Hayam Wuruk 88 B, Tanjung Bungkak, Denpasar, tel: 0361-241118; email: bali.congen@dfat.gov.au; www.dfat.gov.au/bali. Consular hours: Mon–Fri 8am–noon and 12.30–4pm. Visa hours: Mon–Fri 8.30am–noon.
Canada: Enquiries are handled by the Australian consulate.
New Zealand: Enquiries are handled by the Australian consulate (see above).
United Kingdom: Jalan Tirta Nadi 20, Sanur, Denpasar 80238, tel: 0361-270601; email: bcbali@dps.centrin.net.id. Consular hours: Mon–Fri 8.30am–12.30pm.
United States: Jalan Hayam Wuruk 310, Denpasar 80235, tel: 0361-233605; email: amcobali@indosat.net.id. Office hours: Mon–Fri 8am–noon and 1–4.30pm.

Crime & Security

While personal safety is not a general problem in Bali and Lombok, as with anywhere else in the world, be vigilant with your belongings and observe the following common-sense precautions.
• Be careful with bags, wallets and backpacks in crowded places. Don't count money in the open. Pickpockets, car break-ins and bag snatching seem to be the most common complaints.
• On public transport, you may be flanked by two friendly, usually English-speaking young men; one will engage you in conversation as a distraction while the other picks your pocket. Or they might ask you to change a large note to see how much money you're carrying before deciding if it's worth going any further. Don't fall asleep on public transport either, as you may wake up without your valuables.
• Don't walk alone along Kuta beach at night. Tourist Police who patrol the main road from Tuban to Seminyak speak some English and are helpful. Sanur and Nusa Dua beaches are fairly quiet, and its hotels are patrolled. In **Lombok** don't travel alone to the more isolated villages in the east.
• All narcotics are illegal in Indonesia. Their use, sale or purchase results in long prison terms – even death – and/or huge fines. Don't keep or carry packages for people you don't know.

Women Travellers

Bali is generally safer for women than some other parts of the world, but it is important to respect local customs. A female travelling alone in Bali will probably be hit on at least a few times a day, especially at Kuta beach, by local men. This may be annoying but it is not aggressive behaviour. For solo women it is advisable to avoid unlit alleys and the beach at night, and it's best to travel by taxi at night and sit in the back.

BELOW: prayers and an offering at Pura Ulun Danu Batur.

Women travelling alone on Lombok are generally no more at risk than in any other area, as long as they dress and behave modestly and take basic safety precautions.

Customs Regulations

In addition to your embarkation card, a customs declaration form must be completed before arrival in Bali and Lombok.

Indonesian regulations prohibit the entry of weapons, narcotics and pornography. Fresh fruits, plants, animal products, and exposed films and videos may be checked or even confiscated. Photographic equipment, laptop computers and other electronics can be brought in provided they are taken out on departure.

A maximum of 1 litre of alcohol, 200 cigarettes or 50 cigars or 100 grammes of tobacco, and a reasonable amount of perfume may be brought into the country.

There is no restriction on the amount of foreign currencies and traveller's cheques you can bring in or take out. However, anything exceeding Rp 10 million (in Indonesian currency) is prohibited.

Upon departure, limited quantities of duty-free purchases and souvenirs are exempt from taxes, but the export of antiques over 50 years old is not permitted. Ivory, tortoiseshell and crocodile skin products cannot be taken out.

D isabled Travellers

The Balinese believe that all physical and mental disabilities are punishments for improper behaviour in past lives. That said, people with physical disabilities are viewed with compassion.

Generally, there is very little consciousness in Indonesia about the special needs of disabled people. Due to rough pavements, high kerbs, an abundance of steps and a lack of ramps, it is difficult to move around Bali in a wheelchair. However, you will never have problems finding people who are more

than willing to help you. In addition, a number of luxury hotels in Bali are disabled-friendly.

E conomy

While agriculture, especially rice farming, is the main economic activity for most Balinese, tourism is the largest source of income per capita. This includes those employed in related industries, such as arts, crafts and souvenirs. Textiles and garments are also a major industry. Key agricultural products besides rice are tea, coffee, tobacco, cacao, copra, vanilla, soy beans, fruit and vegetables. Bali's fishing industry and seaweed farming provide other important export products.

Electricity

Indonesia (including Bali and Lombok) uses the 220-volt system, 50 cycles. The round, two-pronged plug is common; adapters are readily available but it's probably easier to bring one from home. Power failures are common, as are all-day scheduled power cuts, but most hotels and restaurants have back-up generators.

Emergency Numbers

Bali has an **Emergency Response Centre**: just dial 112 to be in touch with the modern communications centre that co-ordinates all emergency services on the island.
Ambulance: Tel: 118
Fire Brigade: Tel: 113
Immigration: Tel: 227828
Police: Tel: 110

Lombok

Ambulance: Tel: 623498 or 118
Fire Brigade: Tel: 672013 or 113
Regional Police Office: Tel: 110
Tourism Police: Tel: 672013
Immigration: Tel: 635333 or 635520

Etiquette

The people of Bali and Lombok are remarkably friendly and courteous.

They are also conservative as tradition is the backbone of their culture, Hindusim in the case of the Balinese, and Islam in the case of the Lombokians. Keep the following etiquette guidelines in mind:
• Don't venture beyond the beach or poolside area in a swimsuit. What appears to be a quaint beach side alley may lead to the courtyard of a house or temple. Nude bathing is not only considered improper, it is illegal.
• Using the left hand to give or to receive something is taboo (the left hand is for personal hygiene purposes and therefore considered unclean), as is pointing with the left hand. Never touch anyone, even a child, on the head; a person's head is considered to be the most sacred part of the body. Crooking a finger to call someone is impolite. Beckon to the person by waving the fingers together with the palm facing down instead. Aggressive gestures and postures, such as standing with your hands on your hips when talking, are considered to be insulting. Avoid pointing with the index finger as this gesture may be taken as a physical challenge.
• It is offensive to point with your toes (as when indicating an item displayed on the ground in the market) or sit with the soles of your feet pointing at other people – the feet are considered to be the lowliest part of the body. When passing in front of an older person or high-ranking person, especially if they are sitting down, bend your body slightly.
• Don't make an offer for something unless you intend to buy it. When bargaining *(see page 253)* remember that Rp 3,000 can make a great difference to the day's meal for local people, although to you it is nothing.
• Don't display large sums of money. In a place where the average annual income is under US$1500, all tourists are considered wealthy. The locals have a strong sense of pride.
• Unless there is a set admission fee, it is common to give a small

(see page 253)

TRANSPORT

ACCOMMODATION

ACTIVITIES

A – Z

LANGUAGE

donation (Rp5,000) when visiting a temple. This is used to help with maintenance.

• Apart from being properly attired when visiting temples *(see page 270)*, menstruating women and anyone with a bleeding wound must not enter temples. This is due to a sanction against blood on holy ground.

• At temple festivals, photography without flash is fine but never stand in front of a seated priest, as one's head should not be higher than that of a holy person. It is rude and even sacrilegious to climb on temple walls to get a better view. You should not remain standing when people are praying, so move to the back and wait quietly until the blessing is finished. If Balinese kneel in veneration as a procession goes by, do the same or move out of the way. These events are sacred rituals, not meant for the benefit of tourist cameras, and due respect should be observed.

G ay & Lesbian Travellers

Male homosexuality is tolerated to a certain degree in traditional Balinese society, but those involved are eventually expected to marry and have children. Flagrant displays of romance, both gay and straight, are considered distasteful in Bali and especially so in Muslim Lombok.

The tourist industry has helped to establish Bali as a gay-friendly destination; gay travellers will encounter few problems on the island, especially in the tourist areas of the south. Homosexual behaviour in Indonesia is not illegal, and gay and lesbian couples are unlikely to have any difficulties when booking a hotel room and will be welcomed at bars and restaurants.

A few bars and nightclubs in Seminyak *(see page 251)* cater to the gay community. For more information on Bali's gay scene, visit the following links:
www.balifriendlyhotels.com;
www.baligayguide.com.

The gay scene in **Lombok** is generally much less obtrusive. Part of the reason is the conservative Muslim culture.

H ealth & Medical Care

International health certificates of vaccination against cholera and yellow fever are required only from travellers coming from infected areas. Typhoid vaccinations are optional, as are Hepatitis A and B injections. Diphtheria and tetanus injections are recommended. Check the following websites for health updates:

World Health Organisation
www.who.int/ith/
MD Travel Health
www.mdtravelhealth.com

Malaria: Malaria is not a significant problem in Bali, but, dengue fever is. Dengue-carrying mosquitoes are distinguished by their black-and-white banded legs; they generally bite in the daytime. Protect yourself with long sleeves and trousers or use insect repellent. If you are sleeping in the open air or a non-air-conditioned room, use a mosquito net, ideally one impregnated with permethrin, which kills insects on your net.

Malaria can be a problem in some parts of Lombok, particularly during the rainy season, although tourist areas are not high risk.

Minor Ailments: Treat any cut or abrasion immediately with antiseptic or antibiotic cream as it can easily become infected in the humid climate. Antihistamine cream for relief of itches, antibiotic cream for cuts, ointment for fungal skin infections, insect repellent, and aspirin or other pain relievers are available at local *apotik* (pharmacies).

STDs: Sexually transmitted diseases are on the rise; Indonesia has one of the fastest growing HIV infection rates in the world, and Bali is one of the provinces with the highest increase in HIV prevalence. Prostitutes are not subject to health checks, and the "Kuta Cowboys" or local gigolos have multiple partners from all over the world. Condoms – Indonesian

and imported brands – are available at pharmacies and drugstores.

Stomach upsets: If you come down with a severe case of "Bali Belly", taking Lomotil and Imodium will stop the symptoms, not cure the infection. Drink strong, hot tea and avoid spicy food. Charcoal tablets will help alleviate the cramping. If you get a fever along with diarrhoea and cramps, see a doctor who will prescribe antibiotics. Mineral replacement salts for dehydration are available at local pharmacies.

General precautions: Bottled water is widely available. Brushing your teeth with untreated water is usually safe (but don't swallow the water).

Ice in eateries is generally safe as it is manufactured at licensed factories, but it is sometimes dumped right in front of the restaurant on the dirty pavement and not properly washed. If in doubt, drink only chilled drinks in cans or bottles.

Fruits should be peeled before eating, and avoid eating raw vegetables except at better restaurants geared towards tourists. Go easy on spicy food if you're not used to it. It is best not to take chances with street-food vendors, but if you are dead set on trying street food, stick to those that don't serve meat unless your system is already well adjusted.

Hospitals & Clinics

Bali and Lombok are getting better in terms of hygiene and medical facilities but they still have a way to go. You do *not* want to have a medical emergency here. Play safe and make sure you have medical insurance before you visit. Medical facilities and service are not up to Western standards and if you need treatment, particularly in case of a life-threatening emergency, get to Singapore or Bangkok if your insurance policy covers medical evacuations. If not, your consulate may be able to help.

For minor problems, most villages in Bali have a government

public health clinic called *puskesmas*, used by local people and very inexpensive. For major problems, go to the BIMC and SOS clinics which are geared towards the needs of tourists, or one of the big hospitals in Denpasar. All major hotels also have on-call doctors and well-stocked clinics.

Many hospitals and clinics charge different rates for Indonesians and foreigners. Be sure to check the list of fees for services so that you don't get a nasty shock when presented with the bill. If possible, stick with the places listed below.

Bali International Medical Centre (BIMC): Jalan Bypass Ngurah Rai 100X, Simpang Siur, Kuta, tel: 0361-761263 (24 hours); www.bimcbali.com.

International SOS Clinic Bali: Jalan Bypass Ngurah Rai 505X Kuta, tel: 0361-710505 (24 Hours Alarm Centre); tel: 0361-720100 (clinic); www.sos-bali.com.

BIMC Kawasan: BTDC Blok D, Nusa Dua, tel: 0361-3000911; www.bimcbali.com. Open 24 hours.

Rumah Sakit Dharma Usada (private hospital): Jalan Sudirman 50, Denpasar, tel: 0361-227560.

Rumah Sakit Umum Sanglah (public hospital): Jalan Diponegoro, Sanglah, Denpasar, tel: 0361-227911/2/3.

AEA International (Medical Evacuation): Jalan Hayam Wuruk 40, Denpasar, tel: 0361-228996.

Kuta Clinic: Jalan Raya Kuta 100X, Kuta, tel: 0361-753268.

Medical services in **Lombok** have improved considerably in recent years, but for serious problems, it's better to go to Bali or Singapore for treatment.

Rumah Sakit Umum: Jalan Pejanggik, No 6 Mataram, tel: 0370-622254. With a new emergency department, this is the best hospital on Lombok. It also has a tourist clinic with English-speaking doctors. Open Mon–Sat 8am–noon.

There is a tourist clinic at the **Senggigi Beach Hotel** in Senggigi. Contact hotel reception (tel: 693210) for the doctor on call.

Pharmacies (Apotik)

If you are using prescription drugs bring a sufficient supply. Pharmacies can often fill a prescription but the dosage may not be quite the same as your doctor has prescribed. Also, while travelling you should keep your vital medication with you or in your carry-on – in case your luggage is lost. Pharmacies, known as apotik, are widespread in the towns and tourist areas. They often sell medicines which you would need a prescription to buy back home.

Apotik Maha Sandhi: Jalan Raya Kuta 38, Kuta, tel: 0361-751830.

Bali Farma: Jalan Melati 9, Denpasar, tel: 0361-225152.

Farmasari: Jalan Danau Buyan 74, Sanur, tel: 0361-288062.

Internet

Internet cafés can be found all over the tourist areas of Bali; expect to pay Rp 100–300 per minute for access. Broadband access is now common. At the better internet centres, you can use a variety of computing services including burning CDs and downloading digital photos. Travellers with their own laptops and wireless cards can find wireless access at numerous cafés and hotels. Both **AT&T Globalnet** and **AOL** have local access numbers for Bali. AT&T is 0361-256737 and AOL is 0361-289652.

The local phone company, **Telkom**, allows anyone to access its network without having to establish a user account, making it easy to check your email on your laptop. (Telkom makes its money by adding a 50 percent surcharge to its normal per minute tariff). To access dial **0809-89999**; username: **telkomnet@instan**; password: **telkom**.

In **Lombok**, internet services in Senggigi can be found at **Millennium Internet** (opposite Papaya Restaurant) and **Star Internet Service**, located in Senggigi Plaza. Both have dedicated broadband services at reasonable rates.

Left Luggage

There is a 24-hour facility for storing luggage at the international terminal of Bali's Ngurah Rai Airport. The rate is Rp 20,000 per piece per day.

Lost Property

If your baggage goes astray, file a claim at the airline's office. In theory, they will bring your luggage to your hotel when it has arrived, but it may be quicker for you to go to the airport after the next scheduled flight has landed. If you have left behind items in one of the blue **Bali Taxi** vehicles, contact tel: 0361-701621.

Maps

Free maps of the island are available at many of the travel agencies. Most bookstores also stock maps of Bali. Useful map publications are **Insight Fleximap Bali**, **Periplus Bali** and **Periplus Lombok & Sumbawa**. The **Periplus Street Atlas Bali** is a more detailed A-Z type of map book.

Media

Newspapers

Newspaper boys frequently prowl the streets eager to sell you newspapers from Australia and the local English-language daily *The Jakarta Post*. Other newspapers like the *International Herald Tribune*, the weekly *Bali Times* and *Asian Wall Street Journal* are sold at major hotels, most bookstores and the magazine kiosks in Sanur, Kuta, Denpasar and Ubud.

The *Bali Advertiser*, filled with articles and advertisements, is available free at hotels and restaurants. In Lombok, you will find the *Lombok Times*, and the *Lombok Guide*, both of which are free tourism-oriented newspapers.

Magazines

In Bali, several free local tourism-oriented magazines with restaurant and nightlife reviews and articles on local culture and life-styles – like *Bali Now, Hello Bali* and *The Beat* – are available free at some hotels and shops. Others such as *The Yak, The Bud, KuBan, Exotic* and *FRV Travel* are available for sale in bookstores.

Bookshops

There really aren't any major international bookstores with a wide selection of books. Most large hotels and department stores have small bookstores, usually filled with the same tourist publications, coffee-table books, novels and English-language newspapers. These outlets are recommended in Bali:

Ganesha Bookshop
Jalan Raya Ubud
Tel: 0361-970320
www.ganeshabooksbali.com
Located near the main post office in Ubud, this is one of the best bookshops in Bali. It also has a music CD section and a corner devoted to second-hand books. They also stock bilingual (Indonesian/English) children's books.
Periplus: These bookstores are located in most of the malls in South Bali and also at Ngurah Rai Airport departure lounge. Good selection of books and magazines.

Radio & Television

The government station Radio Republik Indonesia or RRI (93.5 FM) has morning and evening programmes in English. Other FM stations play Western pop and rock music. For international news, tune in to the BBC World Service, Australia Broadcasting Corporation (ABC), and Voice of America shortwave broadcasts.

The government's television station TVRI has "Bali Vision", a locally produced English news broadcast daily at 6pm. Most of the better hotels and private villas in Bali and Lombok have satellite TV services with the usual mix of local and foreign channels (including Star TV HBO, CNN and the BBC).

Money

The Indonesian monetary unit is the rupiah, abbreviated to Rp. Coins are in Rp 100, 200, 500 and 1,000 denominations. Paper currency is printed in Rp 1,000, 2,000, 5,000, 10,000, 20,000, 50,000 and 100,000 notes. Be aware that there are several versions of the same denomination of note. At time of press US$1 was roughly equivalent to Rp 12,000 but this figure fluctuates from time to time.

Change for higher value notes (Rp 50,000 and above) is often unavailable in smaller shops, stalls or from taxis, so hang on to coins or paper currency of Rp 5,000 and below, especially when travelling in outlying areas.

Changing Money

Foreign currency, in banknotes and traveller's cheques, is best exchanged at major banks or authorised money changers (look out for signboards with the exchange rates posted). The best rates are in Kuta (**PT Central Kuta** is the biggest one); the rates in Ubud and elsewhere are slightly poorer. Ask if there is a "no commission" policy, otherwise you will get less than what is offered.

Be vigilant when dealing with money changers – they are renowned for their quick fingers and rigged calculators; the number of people being cheated is shameful. Beware of money-changers who offer a higher rate, as this is merely a ploy to attract your custom. Verify the exchange calculation (ask to use the calculator or even better, bring your own) and count your change before you leave the window. Be sure to ask for a printed or hand-written receipt as there are many unofficial (and illegal) money changers around.

Never exchange money in shops, the exception being Ubud where almost everyone gives the correct rate and there are few rip-offs. It is possible to change money in up-market hotels but you will

find that hotels (as well as airport exchange outlets) generally quote rates far below the official exchange rate.

Rupiah may be converted back into foreign currency at the airport when leaving the country, or you can spend your remaining notes at the shops there.

Bring only new and crisp paper currency (US dollar bills are the most widely accepted) as many places will not accept old and faded ones. Also, smaller US dollar denominations and traveller's cheques usually get a slightly poorer exchange rate.

Traveller's cheques are accepted at all major hotels and at some shops. Money changers are quicker than banks when it comes to changing traveller's cheques. Make sure to bring along your passport for identity and signature verification.

In Bali, **Wahana Khrisna Dana Money Changer** (tel: 0361-766811) is highly recommended. It offers a currency delivery service to your hotel and a complimentary pick-up service if you need transport to one of their offices.

In **Lombok**, the exchange rate is only slightly lower than in Bali. Money changers operate kiosks in all the main tourist areas, or better still, go to **PT Bali Maspintjinra** (Jalan Raya Sengiggi, tel: 692247, daily 9am–9pm). Money changers in Lombok are generally honest and don't operate the scams common in Bali.

BELOW: temple festival.

Credit Cards

Many large shops accept major credit cards, but an additional 3–5 percent will be added to your bill. Few places outside the major hotels and big restaurants generally accept American Express because of its higher commission charges.

Cash Advances

Cash advances can be obtained at Bali's major tourist areas – Denpasar, Kuta, Sanur, Ubud – and ATMs are common, especially at shopping centres and bank branches. The ones displaying the VISA/Cirrus logos dispense local currency at the prevailing exchange rate.

In **Lombok**, there are banks and ATMs in Mataram. Senggigi has one bank but numerous ATMs which operate 24 hours. There are no ATMs on the Gili Islands.

O pening Hours

Government offices in Bali are open Mon–Thu 8am–3pm, Fri 8am–noon, closed Sat and Sun. Indonesians like to get their work done in the morning before the heat of the day, so it's best to get there before noon. Banking hours are from Mon–Fri 9am–3pm. Retail shops, especially in tourist areas, are open daily from 9am–9pm, but many in the cities are closed on Sun.

In **Lombok**, business and government offices are open from Mon–Fri 9am–4pm. Being a Muslim island, most offices will close between 11.30am and 2pm on Friday for prayers at the mosque. Some banks and business offices are open on Saturday until noon. Otherwise, shops, restaurants and bars have similar operating hours to those on Bali.

P acking & Shipping

Packages less than 1 metre (3ft 3in) in length and under 10kg (22lbs) can be sent through the post. For larger items, find a reliable shipper who does packing,

and can handle export documentation and insurance. For fragile items, you may want to oversee the packing yourself. Shippers will even pick things up from the shop or come to your hotel. Be aware of restrictions or extra expenses (like customs duties) you may encounter in your home country.

Air cargo is charged by the kilo (minimum 10kg/22lbs) and can be expensive. Sea cargo is much cheaper because it is charged by volume, but takes two to three months to reach its destination. Some reliable shippers in Bali are: **Bali Smart Cargo**: Jalan Bypass Ngurah Rai 80X, Sanur, tel: 0361-270472; www.balismartcargo.co.id. **CAS Cargo**: Jalan Bypass Ngurah Rai 109X, Kuta, tel: 0361-720525; www.cascargobali.com. **DSR Cargo**: Jalan Raya Kuta 168, Kuta, tel: 0361-758264; www.diana.suryaratna.com.

Photography

Digital images can be professionally printed at a number of outlets, and several of Bali's internet cafés will be able to download your digital images onto a CD.

In **Lombok**, try **Diamond Photos**, Jalan Pejanggik 17, Mataram, tel: 0370-637273 for downloading and printing digital images.

Postal Services

In Bali, post offices (Kantor Pos) in every major town and city open from Mon–Thu 8am–2pm, Fri 8am–noon, Sat 8am–1pm, and in some places (such as Ubud) Sun 8am–noon. The **main post office** in Denpasar at Jalan Raya Niti Mandala, Renon, tel: 0361-223565, is open Mon–Fri from 8am–6pm.

Overseas letters to Western Europe and America take, on average, 10 days to arrive. In larger post offices, the **parcels** section is usually in a separate part of the building; sending one is expensive and time-consuming. Don't seal the parcel before

staff at the post office have checked what's inside it. In the larger towns there is usually a parcel-wrapping service near the post office.

In **Lombok**, the mail service is very slow and it's often better to post important items from Bali. Post offices are generally open Mon–Fri from 9am–5pm; Sat 9am–noon. The **main post office** is at Jalan Sriwijaya 37, Mataram, tel: 0370-632645. The **Senggigi post office** is located at Jalan Raya Senggigi (opposite Senggigi Abadi Supermarket), tel: 0370-693711.

Courier Services

DHL: Jalan Hayam Wuruk 146, Denpasar, tel: 0361-262713; Jalan Legian Kaja 451, Legian, tel: 0361-762138; Ary's Tourist Service (DHL agent), Jalan Raya Ubud, tel: 0361-976130.
Federal Express: Jalan Bypass Ngurah Rai 100X, Jimbaran, tel: 0361-701727; Jalan Raya Sanggingan 100X, Ubud, tel: 0361-977575.
TNT: Jalan Bypass Ngurah Rai 56, Jimbaran, tel: 0361-703519.

In **Lombok**, contact **DHL**: Jalan Pendidikan 28, Mataram, tel: 0370-627370, or **TNT**: Jalan Puring II, Mataram, tel: 0370-641055.

Public Holidays

People observe Muslim, Christian, Hindu and Buddhist holidays in Indonesia. The only fixed dates for public holidays are:
New Year's Day: 1 January
Independence Day: 17 August
Christmas: 25 December
All the following festivals are set by different lunar calendars, so dates vary each year.
Imlek or Chinese New Year occurs in late January or early February, with most celebrations happening in cities with large Chinese communities. Apart from Christmas, Christian holidays include **Good Friday** in March or April and **Ascension of Christ** in April or May.

TRANSPORT

ACCOMMODATION

ACTIVITIES

A–Z

LANGUAGE

Waisak, celebrating Buddha's birth, enlightenment and death, falls on the full moon in May. **Idul Fitri**, marking the end of the fasting month of Ramadan, is the most important Muslim celebration. It is a 5-day public holiday; in Bali it is celebrated only by Muslims but in Lombok it is a grand occasion for its majority Muslim population. Other Muslim holidays celebrated in Lombok are **Lebaran Topat** (seven days after Idul Fitri), **Hijriyah** (Islamic New Year), **Ma'ulud** (Mohammad's birthday), **Isra Mi'raj** (Ascension of Mohammad) and **Idul Adha** (Day of Sacrifice). **Nyepi** (Day of Silence) is only celebrated in Bali in March or April (see page 51). Other Balinese public holidays are **Siwalatri** (Night of Shiva), **Galungan**, **Kuningan** and **Saraswati**.

Public Toilets

There are few public toilets in Bali and Lombok, and those that exist are generally dirty and unpleasant. Better maintained public toilets can occasionally be found at the site of tourist attractions, where you will be expected to "donate" around Rp 1,000 per visit. Alternatively, if you're prepared to pay for a drink, you will be able to use the toilet in a restaurant or *warung* (café). Expect to find squat toilets in the simple *warungs*, and don't expect toilet paper or soap.

R eligious Services

In **Lombok**, the **Gereja Catholic Santo Antonius** (Jalan Majapahit 11, Mataram, tel: 0370-634397), has mass on Sun at 7.30am and 6pm. The **Gereja Protestant Indonesia** (Jalan Bungkarno, Mataram, tel: 0370-635504), has Sunday services at 7am and 10am.

In **Bali**, services are as follows:

Catholic

Catholic Church: Jalan Kepundung 2, Denpasar, tel: 0361-222729. Sun 7am, 9am, 5.30pm.

Church of St Francis Xavier: Jalan Kartika Plaza, Kuta. Sat 6pm.

Grand Bali Beach Hotel: Sanur, tel: 0361-288511. Sat 5.30pm.

Mary Mother of All Nations Church: Jimbaran. Sat 6pm, Sun 8.30am (in Indonesian) and 6pm (in English).

Protestant

Protestant Maranatha: Jalan Surapati. 9, Denpasar, tel: 0361-222591. Sun 6am, 9am and 6pm.

Protestant Bali: Jalan Legian Kelod, Gang Menuh. Sun 10am.

Pentecostal: Jalan Karna, tel: 0361-234352. Sun 8am and 6pm, Wed 7pm.

Evangelical: Jalan Melati, Denpasar, tel: 0361-227180. Sun 9am.

S moking

New smoking laws in Bali have now been implemented. You cannot smoke in any area which is declared a non-smoking zone. The Government is introducing a programme of "portable" courts to process violators of no smoking rules in public areas.

T axes & Tipping

Most hotels and restaurants in Bali and Lombok add a 10 percent government tax to your bill, with many high-end places charging a whopping 21 percent for tax and service. Tips for attentive service are appreciated in places without a service charge.

If you hired a car and liked the driver, then a tip of 10–15 percent is appreciated. Always carry small banknotes with you, as taxi drivers are often short of change, or so they claim. Rounding up the fare to the nearest Rp 5,000 is standard.

Airport or hotel porters expect at least Rp 1,000–3,000 per bag, depending on size and weight.

Telephones

There are two types of **telephone** office in Indonesia: the

government-run **Telkom** offices (open 24 hours), and privately owned **wartels** (*warung telekomunikasi*) usually open 7am–midnight; these tend to be slightly more expensive, but are generally very conveniently located along the streets of the main tourist centres. Both offer international and local call facilities, as well as fax services.

Bali's **main Telkom office** in Denpasar is on Jalan Teuku Umar 6 (tel: 0361-232112).

Public Phones

Public **payphones** are few and far between, and usually not in working order. Put the coins in only after someone picks up the phone and starts speaking. Many payphones now take telephone cards only (*kartu telefon*). Long-distance domestic calls (*panggilan interlokal*) are charged according to a zone system, each with different rates; it's cheaper between 9pm and 6am. These phone cards can be bought at post offices, *wartel* outlets, airports and supermarkets, and are a cheap way to make international calls, especially if you are staying in a large hotel which slaps hefty surcharges on phone calls made from your room.

Mobile Phones

These can be used in Bali and Lombok as long as your phone is operating on the GSM network. Alternatively you can purchase a prepaid phone card and get a local number for around Rp 50,000 from local mobile phone shops (like Simpati and ProXL in Bali). Reception quality is generally good as both islands are well served with transmission towers.

Local mobile phone numbers generally begin with the prefix 081.

Telephone Area Codes

Indonesia's **country code** is 62. When calling Bali from overseas, dial your local IDD code, followed by 62, the area code (without the zero) and the phone number. To make an international call from Bali, dial the IDD code (001, 008 or 017) followed by country and area codes and the phone number (in Lombok, the IDD code is 001 or 017).

When calling from within the same region in Bali from a land line, no area code is needed but if, for example, you are calling a hotel in Lovina (North Bali) from Kuta (South Bali), you have to dial the area code (with the zero) plus the phone number.

The following are Bali area codes:

Denpasar, Kuta, Sanur, Nusa Dua, Ubud, Gianyar, Tabanan: 0361

Singaraja, Lovina, Buleleng: 0362

Karangasem, Amlapura, Candidasa, Buitan, Amed: 0363

Negara, Jembrana: 0365

Bangli, Kintamani, Batur, Klungkung: 0366

Bedugul, Bratan: 0368

The area code for most places in **Lombok** is 0370; there are a few towns in east Lombok that use the area code 0376.

Useful Numbers (Bali)

International operator: 101, 102

Operator assisted calls within Indonesia: 100

Directory information Bali: 108

Directory information Indonesia: 100, 106

Time Zone

Bali and Lombok follow Central Indonesian Standard Time, eight hours ahead of Greenwich Mean Time. It is one hour ahead of Java, and in the same time zone as Singapore.

Tourist Offices

Don't expect the highest standards of efficiency from Bali's tourist offices. The quality of service varies enormously and may not be as efficient as one would expect. It really depends on the ability of the person answering the phone when you call. Only the ones worth contacting are listed here:

Denpasar Government Tourism Office: Jalan Surapati 7, Denpasar, tel: 0361-234569.

Bali Tourist Information Centre: Jalan Bunisari 7, Kuta, tel: 0361-754092.

Bina Wisata Ubud Tourist Office: Jalan Raya Ubud (opposite the palace), tel: 0361-973285.

Buleleng Tourist Office: Jalan Veteran 23, Singaraja, tel: 0362-25141.

In **Lombok**, there are two poorly managed tourism offices with a limited amount of printed information available. Better information is available at the tourist agencies in Senggigi and on the Gili Islands.

West Lombok Tourism Office: Jalan Suprato 20, Mataram, tel: 0370-621658.

West Nusa Tenggara Tourist Office: Jalan Singosari 2, Mataram, tel: 0370-634800.

V isas & Passports

The following information is accurate at time of press, but this being Indonesia, things may change at any time. Visitors from the UK, US, Australia New Zealand, Canada and most European countries are granted 30-day visas on arrival for US$25. Travellers from other countries should check with the Indonesian embassy before leaving home.

Those who overstay their 30-day visas by a few days (less than a week) are charged US$20 per day by immigration at the port of departure.

The only way to stay longer than your visa allows is to leave Indonesia and come back in again, the nearest place being Singapore. Alternatively, apply for a 60-day visa at an Indonesian embassy or consulate before arriving in Indonesia.

Extending business and social-cultural visas involves lots of paperwork at the **immigration** office in Bali, near Ngurah Rai Airport (tel: 0361-751038) and at Jalan Panjaitan in Denpasar (tel: 0370-0361-227828), both are open Mon–Thu 7am–1pm, Fri 7am–11pm, Sat 7am–midday. In **Lombok**, the immigration office is at Jalan Semmangi No. 10 (tel: 632520) in Mataram.

Other entry formalities: Your passport must be valid for six months from the date of entry into Indonesia. You must also have proof of onward passage (either return or through tickets). Be sure to complete a white, disembarkation-embarkation document, half of which must be retained and then presented upon departure. Do not lose this card or you will face a lot of problems when leaving.

W ebsites

The following websites provide useful information on Bali:

www.balieats.com – Bali's most comprehensive restaurant guide.

www.bali-paradise.com – Bali-based travel information service.

www.balitravelnews.com – Devoted to the promotion of hotels and travel news.

www.baliupdate.com – Informative weekly newsletter.

www.balidiscovery.com – Comprehensive site promoting hotels, tourist activities and Bali news.

www.balispaguide.com – Comprehensive directory of spas in Bali.

www.indo.com – Popular inbound portal of Bali and other Indonesian destinations.

www.strangerinparadise.com – Witty diary of landscape architect and writer, Made Wijaya.

The best **Lombok** websites are:

www.LombokNetwork.com – General information and news about Lombok.

www.LombokTimes.com – Lombok's only English-language newspaper.

Weights & Measures

Indonesia uses the metric system. Temperatures are measured in degrees Celsius.

L ANGUAGES: BALI AND LOMBOK

UNDERSTANDING THE PEOPLE

BAHASA INDONESIA

The English language is widely spoken in all tourist areas of Bali, and many local guides are trained in Japanese and the major European languages.

Although more than 350 languages and dialects are spoken in the archipelago, the Indonesian language and national tongue, known as Bahasa Indonesia, is spoken everywhere and easy to learn. Derived from Old Malay, which was for centuries the trading language of the Indies, it was first embraced in 1928 by the nationalist movement as the "language of national unity", a political tool to bring the diverse religious and ethnic groups of the archipelago together. Bahasa Indonesia is also the official language, used in commerce, schools and in the media.

Bahasa Indonesia is a non-tonal language and written in the Roman alphabet. It is among the easiest of all spoken languages to learn as there are no tenses, plurals or genders, and often just one word can convey the meaning of a whole sentence.

There are a few basic rules of grammar in Bahasa Indonesia. To indicate the past, prefix the verb with *sudah* (already) or *belum* (not yet); for the future, prefix the verb with *akan* (will). The word *pergi*, for example, is used to say that you are going, you went, and you have gone. The word *makan* is used to say that you are eating, you ate, and you have eaten. *Saya sudah makan* means "I already ate"; *saya belum makan* means "I've not yet eaten"; *saya akan pergi* means "I will go". To make a noun plural, the word is usually just repeated, e.g. *anak* (child), *anak anak* (children).

Spelling is phonetic with a few twists: The letter "c" is pronounced "ch" (eg *Candidasa*, Canggu); the letter "g" is always hard (eg *gamelan*, Garuda); "y" is pronounced "j" (eg Yogyakarta); the letter "c" is sometimes spelled "tj" (eg Tjampuhan instead of Campuhan); the letter "j" can also be spelled "dj" (eg Djakarta instead of Jakarta); and there is no letter "v": November, for example, is spelt Nopember.

Adjectives always follow the noun: *rumah* (house) with *besar* (big) means "big house". Word order is usually subject-verb-object: *saya* (I) *mau* (want) *minum* (to drink) *air* (water) *dingin* (cold), means "I want to drink cold water." The personal pronoun goes after the noun: *rumah saya* is "my house". The easiest way to make a question is to simply add a question mark and use a rising intonation, ie *Mau minum?* ("Want drink?").

Indonesians always show respect when addressing others, especially their elders. The custom is to address an older man as *bapak* or *pak* (father) and an older woman as *ibu* or *bu* (mother).

Both Bali and Lombok have their own indigenous languages, Bahasa Bali *(see page 40)* or in Lombok, Bahasa Sasak, which are more difficult to learn. However Bahasa Indonesia is widely used on both islands.

Useful phrases

thank you *terima kasih*
good morning *selamat pagi*
good day *selamat siang*
good afternoon *selamat sore*
good evening/night *selamat malam*
goodbye (to person going) *selamat jalan*
goodbye (to person staying) *selamat tinggal*
I'm sorry *ma'af*
welcome *selamat datang*
please come in *silahkan masuk*
please sit down *silahkan duduk*
what is your name? *siapa nama saudara?*
my name is... *nama saya...*

TRANSPORT

where do you come from? *dari mana?*
I come from... *saya datang dari...*
how are you? *apa kabar?*
I am fine *kabar baik*
nice to meet you *senang berkenalan dengan anda*
see you later *sampai jumpa lagi*
please (requesting) *tolong*
please (offering) *silakan*
you're welcome *kembali* or *sama-sama*
I do not understand *saya tidak mengerti*
I do not speak Indonesian *saya tidak mengerti bahasa*
what is this? *apa ini?*
excuse me *permisi/ma'af*
please help me *tolonglah saya*

Forms of Address

I *saya*
you (singular) *saudara* (formal); *anda/kamu* (informal)
he, she *dia*
we *kami* (excluding the listener)
we *kita* (including the listener)
you (plural) *saudara-saudara*
Mr *Bapak, Pak*
Mrs *Ibu, Bu*
Miss *Nona*

Directions & Transport

left *kiri*
right *kanan*
straight *terus*
near *dekat*
far *jauh*
from *dari*
to *ke*
inside *didalam*
outside of *diluar*
here *disini*
there *disana*
in front of *didepan, dimuka*
at the back *dibelakang*
next to *disebelah*
car *mobil, motor*
bus *bis*
train *keretapi*
bicycle *sepeda*
motorcycle *sepeda motor*
where do you want to go? *mau kemana?*
where is? *di mana?*

I want to go to... *saya mau ke...*
stop here *berhenti disini, stop disini*
railway station *stasiun keretapi*
petrol station *pomp bensin*
bank *bank*
post office *kantor pos*
immigration office *kantor immigrasi*
tourist office *kantor pariwisata*
embassy *kedutaan besar*

Food & Drink

restaurant *restoran*
food *makanan*
drink *minuman*
breakfast *makan pagi*
lunch *makan siang*
dinner *makan malam*
boiled water *air putih, air matang*
iced water *air es*
tea *teh*
coffee *kopi*
milk *susu*
rice *nasi*
noodles *mie, bihun, bakmie*
fish *ikan*
prawns *udang*
chicken *ayam*
beef *daging sapi*
pork *babi*
vegetables *sayur*
fruit *buah*
egg *telur*
sugar *gula*
salt *garam*
black pepper *merica, lada*
chilli pepper *cabe, lombok*
cup *cangkir*
plate *piring*
glass *gelas*
spoon *sendok*
knife *pisau*
fork *garpu*

Shopping

shop *toko*
money *uang*
change (of money) *uang kembali*
money changer *penukar uang*
to buy *membeli*
price *harga*
expensive *mahal*
cheap *murah*
fixed price *harga pas*
how much? *berapa?*

Signs

open *buka, dibuka*
closed *tutup, ditutup*
entrance *masuk*
exit *keluar*
don't touch *jangan pegang*
no smoking *jangan merokok*
push *dorong*
pull *tarik*
gate *pintu*
ticket window *loket*
ticket *karcis*
information *keterangan*
city *kota*
market *pasar*

Days of the week

Monday *Hari Senin*
Tuesday *Hari Selasa*
Wednesday *Hari Rabu*
Thursday *Hari Kamis*
Friday *Hari Juma'at*
Saturday *Hari Sabtu*
Sunday *Hari Minggu*

Numbers

Zero *nol*
Half *setengah*
Approximately *kira-kira*
1 *satu*
2 *dua*
3 *tiga*
4 *empat*
5 *lima*
6 *enam*
7 *tujuh*
8 *delapan*
9 *sembilan*
10 *sepuluh*
11 *sebelas*
12 *dua belas*
13 *tiga belas*
21 *dua puluh satu*
30 *tiga puluh*
100 *seratus*
150 *seratus limapuluh*
200 *dua ratus*
1000 *seribu*
2000 *dua ribu*
10,000 *sepuluh ribu*
100,000 *seratus ribu*
1,000,000 *sejuta*
Note: the teens are *"belas"*, the tens are *"puluh"*, the hundreds are *"ratus"*, thousands are *"ribu"*, and the millions are *"juta"*.

TRANSPORT
ACCOMMODATION
ACTIVITIES
A – Z
LANGUAGE

GLOSSARY

A

adat customary law
alang-alang (or *lalang*) tall grass used for thatching in roofs
aling-aling a short wall designed to deflect troublesome spirits
Anak Agung title given to someone of the princely caste
arak strong spirit from sugar palm

B

babi guling spit-roast suckling pig
bale open-air pavilion with roof
bale banjar village meeting place
balian traditional faith healer
banjar small hamlet that is part of a larger village; the basic social and political unit
banten religious offerings
Bali Aga aboriginal pre-Hindu inhabitants of Bali
Barong mythical beast representing good; danced by two men inside an ornate costume
bebek betutu duck cooked in banana leaves
bemo public minibus
Brahmana the priestly caste; highest of the four castes
brem a sweet rice wine
bukit a hill or hilly area

C

candi bentar split entrance gateway to a temple
Cokorda title of prince or king

D

dalang puppet master
danau lake
desa village
dewa generic name for god
dewi generic name for goddess
Dewi Sri Goddess of Rice
dokar two-wheeled pony cart

E – G

endek Balinese *ikat* cloth
gado gado steamed vegetables served with peanut sauce

Galungan key Balinese festival celebrated every 210 days
gamelan percussion orchestra
gang small lane or alley
garuda mythological bird, the vehicle of the god Wisnu
geringsing rare double *ikat* cloth woven in Tenganan
gunung mountain
Gusti title given to members of the *wesia* caste

H – I

homestay small family-run guesthouse; also called *losmen*
Ida Ayu/Ida Bagus title used by the male/female members of the Brahmana caste
ikat traditional handwoven textile

J

jalan street, road; to walk
jukung outrigger sailing boat

K

kain cloth; also sarong
kantor office
keris dagger with a wavy blade
ksatria princely class, second in ranking to *brahmana*
kulkul hollow wooden drum to summon villagers

L

legong Balinese dance; also the name given to the dancer
leyak a witch or sorcerer
lingga a Hindu phallic symbol
lombok chilli
lontar a species of palm; also refers to a palm-leaf manuscript
losmen see *homestay*
lumbug a traditional rice barn

M

Mahabharata Hindu epic
Melasti purification ceremony
meru holy Hindu mountain; also a temple's pagoda-style roof

N

naga dragon, water serpent
nusa island (also called *pulau*)

Nyepi Balinese New Year, usually occurring in March or April

O

odalan temple anniversary festival
ogoh-ogoh huge papier-maché monsters
ojek motorcycle taxi

P

padi rice in the husk, when growing in the field
pantai beach
paras sandstone used in building temples and for stone carving
pasar market
pedanda Brahmana high priest
pemangku temple lay priest
puputan Balinese fight to death or ritual suicide
pura temple
pura dalem temple of the dead
purnama full moon
puri palace

R

Ramayana Hindu epic
Rangda the widow-witch representing evil
rumah sakit hospital

S

satria see *ksatria*
sawah rice field
subak irrigation society
sudra lowest of the four Balinese castes; also called *jaba*

T

taman garden
tirta holy water
topeng mask
tuak palm wine

U & W

udeng men's head-covering
wantilan open pavilion used as a hall in a village or temple
wartel telecoms office
warung simple café where food and drinks are served
wesia the third and lowest of the aristocratic class

Further Reading

History & Culture

A Short History of Bali, by Robert Pringle. The history of Bali from before the Bronze Age to the presidency of Megawati Sukarnoputri and the tragedy of the Kuta bombings in 2002.

Bali: A Paradise Created, by Adrian Vickers. Bali, the "last Paradise", seen through Western eyes. Fresh insights on the history and culture of a traditional island faced with a massive invasion of paradise-seekers.

Bali: Sekala & Niskala Volume I – Essays on Religion, Ritual, and Art, by Fred B. Eiseman. An exploration of Balinese religion, ritual and performing arts.

Bali Sekala and Niskala Volume II – Essays on Society, Tradition and Craft, by Fred B. Eiseman. Covers the geography, social organisation, language, folklore and material culture of Bali.

Fiction

A Little Bit One O'clock, by William Ingram. A beautifully written novel exploring the web of relationships within a Balinese family.

Midnight Shadows, by Garrett Kam. Historical novel with the Communist coup of 1965 as the setting. It looks at the reasons behind the terrible violence that engulfed the island by interweaving actual events and history with mythology, dreams and rituals.

A Tale from Bali, by Vicki Baum. First published in 1937, this wonderful and classic tale of love and death in Bali is set against the backdrop of turmoil faced by the Balinese in their struggle against the Dutch colonialists.

Under the Volcano, by Cameron Forbes. Written in a compelling style and traversing a vast array of subjects relevant to Bali today, this book will open your eyes to Bali's history and the current challenges communities here face.

Art/Music/Dance

A House in Bali, by Colin McPhee. First published in 1947 and one of the most enchanting books ever written about Bali, this book tells the story of how, in 1929, a young Canadian-born musician chanced upon rare gramophone recordings of Balinese *gamelan* music that were to change his life forever.

Offerings, the Ritual Art of Bali, by Francine Brinkgreve and David Stuart-Fox. This beautifully illustrated book provides a rare glimpse into the pageantry, ritual and devotion that accompany the creation of offerings in Bali.

Dance and Drama in Bali, by Beryl de Zoete and Walter Spies. This important ethnographical book documents the history of Balinese dance and drama. Spies lived in Bali for 12 years from 1927 and was an accomplished painter, musician and dance expert. De Zoete was trained in European dance.

Balinese Paintings (second edition), by A.A.M. Djelantik. A concise but well-documented guide to traditional Balinese paintings, including that of Ubud's Pitamaha painters and the Young Artists of Batuan and Penestanan.

Bali Sacred and Secret, by Gill Marais. A remarkable revelation of a rarely-witnessed, mystical world of Balinese ritual and magic.

General

Fragrant Rice: My Continuing Love Affair with Bali, by Janet de Neefe. The memoir of an Australian restaurateur who married a Balinese man and raised four children here, this is another easy-read introduction to the culture of the island — with recipes.

The Island of Bali, by Miguel Covarrubias. First published in 1937, this book is still regarded by many as the most authoritative text on Bali and its culture and people.

Our Hotel in Bali, by Louise G. Koke. A re-issue of the 1987 publication that documents how a young American couple, Bob Koke and Louise Garret, came to build Bali's first hotel in 1936, the Kuta Beach Hotel.

Bali Today – Real Balinese Stories, by Jean Couteau. Couteau is well known for his humorous stories in the Indonesian press about Bali and the Balinese way of life. His observations are witty, ingenious and hilariously funny.

Eat, Pray, Love, by Elizabeth Gilbert. Traces the author's journey through Italy, India and Bali on a quest to discover worldly pleasure, spiritual devotion, and what she really wants out of life. The story was made into a Hollywood movie starring Julia Roberts and partly filmed on location in Bali.

Bali Daze – Freefall off the Tourist Trail, by Cat Wheeler. A Canadian writer moves to the country town of Ubud in Bali and learns to deal with randy ducks, rampant vegetation, roasted spiders, a haunted river bank and all the quirks and delights of living in a Balinese community.

Secrets of Bali, by Jonathan Copeland with Ni Wayan Murni. From Balinese gods to Balinese *gamelan*, difficult subjects are simply explained in this beautifully written and illustrated work.

2

Art and Photo Credits

123RF 81, 158, 167, 217, 220
32Elite Havens 235B
Alamy 8TL, 9TR, 60, 186R
Alila Hotels & Resorts 86
John Anderson/Apa Publications 45
Archives of the Royal Tropical Institute, Amsterdam 34, 35, 36, 37
AWL Images 76
Begin Ende Voortgargh Vande Oost-Indische Compagnie 33L&R
Bigstock 225T
Corbis 206
Francis Dorai/Apa Publications 31, 41, 125T, 150T, 165T, 171TR&BR, 174T, 176T, 177T, 180T, 191, 193T, 226T
Dreamstime 7CR&BL, 12/13, 49, 62L, 172, 188, 219
Getty Images 39, 61, 80
Jack Hollingsworth/Apa Publications 3B, 5B, 10B, 29, 40L, 52B, 75BR, 105T, 119TR&BR, 126BL, 140&T, 141T, 157T, 187T, 207&T, 208&T, 209
iStock 7TR, 9BR, 51, 53TR, 65, 79, 201, 202, 210T, 219T, 265
Leonardo 235T
Photoshot 11L

Prana Spa 11TR
Private Archives 72
Robert Harding 216
Bart Speelman 184
Starwood Hotels & Resorts 214T, 262
University of Leiden, Amsterdam 30
Watergarden Hotel & Spa 87
Martin Westlake/Apa Publications 1, 8B, 32, 40R, 52TL&CR, 53B, 74TL&B, 75CL&TR, 109L, 118BR, 119C, 125BR, 126T&BR, 131T, 135L, 136(all), 138, 139, 149T, 151, 164T, 174, 175, 194&T, 196T, 218, 220T
Corrie Wingate/Apa Publications 2B, 2/3, 4B, 4/5, 6C&BR, 6/7, 7TC&CL, 8CR, 9CL, 10TL&TR, 14/15, 16, 17, 18, 19, 20&B, 21L&R, 22, 23, 24, 25, 26L&R, 27, 42/43, 44, 46L&R, 47, 49B, 50, 52/53, 54, 55, 56, 57, 58, 59, 62R, 63, 64, 66, 67, 68, 69, 70, 71, 73, 74/75T, 77, 78, 82, 83, 84, 85, 88/89, 90/91, 92, 93, 96, 97, 99&T, 100&T, 101, 102&T, 103, 104, 105, 106, 107&T, 108&T, 109R, 111(all), 112&T,

113, 118TL&BC, 118/119, 119CL, 120, 121, 123&T, 124, 125L, 127, 128, 129&T, 130, 131, 132&T, 133, 134, 135T&BR, 137, 139T, 142(all), 143&T, 144(all), 148, 149, 150, 152, 153, 155, 156, 157L&BR, 159&T, 160&T, 161, 162, 163&T, 164, 165, 166&T, 167T, 170TL, BC&CR, 170/171, 171CL&BL, 173, 176, 177, 178&T, 179&T, 180, 182, 183, 184, 186L, 187, 188T, 189, 190, 193, 195, 196BL&R, 198/199, 200, 203, 204, 210, 212, 213, 214, 222, 223, 224&T, 225, 226, 228, 230, 245, 249, 260, 268, 270, 274, 278
Zuma/Rex Features 48
Public domain 28

Map Production: original cartography Berndtson & Berndtson, maps updated by Stephen Ramsay and APA Cartography Department.

© 2014 Apa Publications UK Ltd

Production: Rebeka Davies

Cover Credits:
Front Cover: Sekumpul Waterfall *AWL Images*
Spine: puppet *iStock*
Back Cover:
(top) The Lotus Garden Temple of

Saraswati, *Corrie Wingate/Apa Publications*; (middle): Barong and Kris Dance at Solo, *Dreamstime*
Front Flap: (from top) villages celebrating their 'Odilan', Temple festival, Seseh,

Sunset from Karma Kayak, Gili Twanangan,
Tegalalang rice terraces, Ubud & surroundings,
View of Kuta Beach, Lombok,
All Corrie Wingate/Apa Publications

GENERAL INDEX – BALI

GENERAL INDEX – LOMBOK

See Bali index for practical information listings